HAROLD MACMILLAN: ASPECTS OF A POLITICAL LIFE

Also edited by Richard Aldous and Sabine Lee

HAROLD MACMILLAN AND BRITAIN'S WORLD ROLE

Also by Sabine Lee

AN UNEASY PARTNERSHIP: British–German Relations between 1955 and 1961

Harold Macmillan
Aspects of a Political Life

Edited by

Richard Aldous
Lecturer in Modern History
University College, Dublin

and

Sabine Lee
Lecturer in German History
University of Birmingham

Foreword by Alistair Horne

First published in Great Britain 1999 by
MACMILLAN PRESS LTD
Houndmills, Basingstoke, Hampshire RG21 6XS and London
Companies and representatives throughout the world

A catalogue record for this book is available from the British Library.

ISBN 0–333–71373–7

 First published in the United States of America 1999 by
ST. MARTIN'S PRESS, INC.,
Scholarly and Reference Division,
175 Fifth Avenue, New York, N.Y. 10010

ISBN 0–312–21906–7

Library of Congress Cataloging-in-Publication Data
Harold Macmillan : aspects of a political life / edited by Richard
Aldous, Sabine Lee.
p.   cm.
Includes bibliographical references and index.
ISBN 0–312–21906–7
1. Macmillan, Harold, 1894–   . 2. Great Britain—Politics and
government—1945–1964.   3. Prime ministers—Great Britain–
–Biography.   I. Aldous, Richard.   II. Lee, Sabine.
DA566.9.M33H373   1998
941.085'5'092—dc21
[B]   98–38450
                                                              CIP

This book is printed on paper suitable for recycling and made from fully managed and
sustained forest sources.

10   9   8   7   6   5   4   3   2   1
08   07   06   05   04   03   02   01   00   99

Printed and bound in Great Britain by
Antony Rowe Ltd, Chippenham, Wiltshire

Contents

Foreword
Alistair Horne

In July 1996 I had the greatest good fortune to be invited to attend the oration to the joint Houses of Parliament by Nelson Mandela in St Stephen's Hall. During it I reflected how, as a young journalist, I had had the equal good fortune to listen to President de Gaulle, in the same place and on the last such auspicious occasion, when he had been invited by Harold Macmillan in 1960. Looking round the great hall, I reckoned that I was probably one of a very small handful privileged to have been at both. In his remarkable speech, Mandela singled out Macmillan and 'The wind of change' as one of the few British statesmen deserving of any praise. De Gaulle, in his speech, duly lauded Macmillan and British institutions; then returned home to slam the door on Macmillan's application to join the EEC less than three years later!

The bracketing of those two red-letter events reminded me last summer of the remarkable range covered by Harold Macmillan's seven years in office. From the turmoil which accompanied Eden's resignation in 1956, from Suez to the Cuban Missile Crisis, to the frenzy that surrounded Macmillan's resignation in 1963, these years covered some of the most dramatic events in recent British history.

His first four years were triumphant – he established closest relations with both Presidents Eisenhower and Kennedy; as first peacetime PM to visit Moscow, in 1959, with Khrushchev he began to break the log-jam of the Cold War; and, that same year, he returned the Tories to power with a hundred majority. From then on, events conspired against him; the economy turned sour; he recognized the 'wind of change' in Africa, but failed to resolve the crisis in Rhodesia; and, in 1963, de Gaulle vetoed his application to join the EEC. That same year the Profumo scandal came close to destroying him. But his premiership was redeemed by his pioneering the Nuclear Test Ban with the Soviets, which presaged the Gorbachev–Reagan accords of the 1980s. In October 1963, a sudden prostatectomy forced his retirement – in all probability, unnecessarily.

December 1996 marked the tenth anniversary of Macmillan's death, and therefore it seems to me most timely and apposite that this conference should have been set up in Christ's College, Cambridge, in September of that year to re-examine his career.

Political reputations have a curious way of advancing and receding with almost indecent speed. Who can now recall how once the British popular press trumpeted Nigel Lawson, following his famous tax-slash budget, as the 'greatest Chancellor since . . .'; since *who* . . .? Indeed, perhaps, there may be British schoolchildren in a decade's time unable to recall who, and wherefore, was the 'Iron Lady'?

When he died, in the middle of the Thatcher epoch, Harold Macmillan was covered in laurels. Perhaps it was because he was regarded, romantically, as some kind of king-over-the-water antithesis to Thatcherdom. Now, derided once again as the 'old actor-manager', his reputation seems to lie at the other end of the scale.

In the 1980s, the years of his extreme old age, Harold Macmillan emerged into a kind of new golden age. Though the Enoch Powells and the Tebbits may have growled, his maiden speech in the Lords, with its highly emotive appeal about the miners and the dangers of a divided society received widest acclaim. So did his less well-judged, rather mischievous subsequent sally about 'selling off the family silver'. In December 1986 he died venerated as the grand old man of British politics, in affection and respect.

Yet, had he died in 1996 one feels he might almost have shuffled off the scene the forgotten Prime Minister, if not actively misprized (especially by the 'young fogeys' of Tory journalism) as the progenitor of all our current woes. Why this sudden reversal in his fortunes? Could it be that at the peak of Monetarism, people yearned for those halcyon days of 'You've never had it so good'? That we reached towards 'Supermac' as a kind of antidote to Maggie? That in contrast, perhaps, the less confrontational, more 'middle-road', world of John Major's resembled a little too closely Macmillan's own?

There are some rather tendentious parallels. If Macmillan had come back to earth around the time of the sacking of Norman Lamont, he might well have thought that – with all the talk about soaring unemployment, high interest rates, inflation, and a sluggish economy – Selwyn Lloyd was still at the Treasury, and long overdue for a 'night of the long knives'. (Except, of course, that Selwyn would have gone without such a frightful, undignified howl as Norman! Times change.)

Selfishly, this official biographer comes out of this swing in reputations as an extremely lucky man. Had my two volumes appeared in the 1990s instead of the 1980s, I have little doubt that they would have almost disappeared without trace, relegated to the dustier shelves of Hatchards!

Often one is asked – now that the 30-year rule has released most of the papers for the Macmillan years, and other material has emerged – would you have changed much? My answer: some details, some fine-tuning possibly, but otherwise not a great deal; tactics versus strategy. Since the *Aldington v. Tolstoy* case, I would now be a good deal *less* harsh in apportioning blame to Macmillan for the repatriation of the Cossacks in 1945; in fact I would absolve him almost entirely. I would be harsher on him for the cover-up over Calder Hall in 1957 – which I certainly missed in writing my biography; and I think I would be harsher over his whole handling of the EEC business. *Pace* the reproofs of the young fogeys, I do not think I would be any more severe with Macmillan over his handling of the economy, or the trades unions, than I have been already. Perusal of the Public Record Office documents for 1963 showed little to change one's recounting of the Profumo Affair. Nevertheless, doubtless time will show that there are still nuggets to be found – missed by an idle and incompetent official biographer!

But what does change, has changed, is the *point of view*.

When writing an 'update' on Macmillan back in 1993 (to mark the thirtieth anniversary of his resignation), I interviewed a number of survivors from his entourage – including the late Lord Thorneycroft (who, however, remained unforgiving, and critical, of the 'little local difficulties' of 1958 and the reasons behind his own resignation). Most agreed on four scores: with the one aberration of the 'Night of the Long Knives' (when he sacked a third of his Cabinet in July 1962), he was superb in his appointments, and particularly in the 'team' which ran his inner office. Secondly, his reputation as a thinker survives intact. (Part of the duties of his 'team' was to protect the space he created for himself in which to think – and read.) None of his successors can challenge his claim to have been Britain's best-read PM. Thirdly, and not least, 'Supermac' did have that elusive, indefinable quality of style; nobody can take this away from him, and with him it vanished from Westminster forever.

And, fourthly, he and the Tory Party of his times could reckon on – what seems today – an amazing degree of traditional loyalty, in both directions. Sacked ministers did not immediately sit down and pen whingeing, *sua culpa* (and generally unreadable) memoirs. Even Rab Butler – disloyal and indiscreet as he could be on occasions – would never have become a Norman Lamont!

The Macmillan diaries reveal, underneath the often flippant exterior, a most penetrating mind which asked all the key questions of our times. The tragedy was – in common with some of his successors – the answers all too often just eluded him. 'Events, events', as he once sighed.

Frequently in his conversations with me in the 1970s and 1980s, Macmillan would reckon that his greatest success had been the Nuclear Test Ban he had signed with Kennedy and Khrushchev in 1963; 'partial' only, but it led to the 'SALT' [Strategic Arms Limitation Talks] agreements of the 1980s. Perhaps, today, he would rate his highest achievement as that of keeping the Tory Party together in face of the EEC challenge. But maybe, also, Macmillan's Tory government of 1963 can be viewed as sharing one thing with John Major's: did it in fact 'overstay its leave', to become – in the words of that octogenarian party loyalist Bill Deedes – 'like a horse carrying more lead than it can manage?'

As I remarked earlier, facts don't change; what does change, has changed, is the *point of view*. By way of an example, last year I was invited by BBC2 to act as 'adviser' on a programme dealing with Macmillan's career, under a series entitled 'Reputations'. I said I would only do it if there would be no 'trivialization' – i.e. the prevailing mode. I was assured it would be an in-depth, serious representation. The researchers seemed respectable and highly diligent. Yet, just before screening, I was told that the producer had decided it needed 'livening up'. Instantly my heart sank! In the event it hit the small screen entitled *The Macmillans*. Approximately three-quarters dealt with Lady Dorothy and her affair with Bob Boothby; only seventeen minutes out of sixty related to the Macmillan premiership; and the whole programme managed to get by without once mentioning Khrushchev, the Cuban Missile Crisis, or the Nuclear Test Ban of 1963 (which, after all, Macmillan did consider to be his greatest contribution – and indeed history may well prove him to have been right).

In sum, the BBC's performance was much more revealing of our times, our attitudes and points of view, than Harold Macmillan's. If nothing else, it proved – once again – the paramount importance of rewriting history and biography regularly, by trained historians and biographers, and not leaving it to the media whizz-kids and associated Paxmanism.

For this reason alone, I am particularly delighted that this conference should be taking place, and most flattered to start the ball rolling.

The above were, approximately, the remarks I made from the Chair when introducing the Macmillan Conference on 5 September 1996, reconstituted from my scribbled notes. Not being possessed of clairvoyance, however, I could not then anticipate the excellent standard of most of the ensuing contributions. Given alt the distortions of the media over past years, what was particularly gratifying to me was the objectivity of the younger participants, who would not have been around in Macmillan's day. They were not led astray by the beguiling images of the grouse-moor, dukeries or Old Etonians, which gave *Private Eye* so much fun in those days (in fact, its first *raison d'être*) but were able to get – most critically – at the *real* Macmillan within, his mistakes and his achievements. I personally came away strongly impressed, and encouraged, and look forward to publication of this book as a serious contribution to the historical record.

Acknowledgements

This volume is based on a conference held at Christ's College, Cambridge, in September 1996. The editors would like to thank the Centre of International Studies, Cambridge, the Department of Modern History, University College, Dublin, and the School of History, University of Birmingham for their financial support, and the Masters and Fellows of Christ's College, Cambridge, for their splendid hosting of the conference. The editors would like to express their gratitude to Professor Corelli Barnett, Dr Peter Caterrell, Dr Alan Clark MP, Dr Ian Clark, Professor Ronan Fanning, Dr Anthony Howard, Dr Philip Towle, Professor D. C. Watt and Dr Nevil Wylie for their advice and invaluable contribution to the conference. Finally, they would like to thank Annabelle Buckley of Macmillan Press, who has been helpful as ever in seeing the publication of the volume through all its critical stages.

Notes on the Contributors

Richard Aldous is College Lecturer in Modern History at University College, Dublin. He co-edited, with Sabine Lee, *Harold Macmillan and Britain's World Role* (1996) and is currently writing a biography of Sir Malcolm Sargent.

Nigel Ashton is Lecturer in International History at the London School of Economics. Previously he held posts at the University of Liverpool and the University of Salford. He is the author of *Eisenhower, Macmillan and the Problem of Nasser: Anglo-American Relations and Arab Nationalism, 1955-59* (1996), and is currently working on a book looking at Anglo-American relations in the early 1960s, to be published under the title *Kennedy and Macmillan: A Very Special Relationship?*

S. J. Ball is Lecturer in Modern History at the University of Glasgow. Educated at Brasenose College, Oxford, and Christ's College, Cambridge, he is the author of *The Bomber in British Strategy* (Oxford, 1995) and *The Cold War* (London, 1997).

N. J. Crowson undertook his doctoral research at Southampton University. He became Fellow of the Department of Politics, Queen's University, Belfast, before joining the Institute of Contemporary British History as Director of Research. Currently he is Lecturer in Modern and Contemporary British History at the University of Birmingham. He is author of *Facing Fascism: The Conservative Party and the European Dictators, 1935–1940*.

Alistair Horne was educated in Switzerland, the United States and Jesus College, Cambridge. Over the last four decades he has published widely on a wide variety of historical subjects. His publications include the prize-winning titles *The Prize of Glory: Verdun, 1916* (1992), *A Savage War of Peace: Algeria, 1954–62* (1977), *The French Army and Politics, 1870–1970* (1984), *How Far from Austerlitz: Napoleon, 1805–1815* (1996), and the widely acclaimed official biography of Harold Macmillan (1988/9).

Lewis Johnman is Quintin Hogg Research Fellow in History at the University of Westminster. He is author, with Anthony Gorst, of *The Suez Crisis* (1996).

Sir Curtis Keeble joined the Diplomatic Service in 1947 and held several overseas appointments including Berlin and Washington before taking charge of the Foreign Office Department responsible for the first round of EEC entry negotiations. In 1974 he was appointed first British Ambassador to the German Democratic Republic, in 1976 Deputy Under Secretary of State in the Foreign and Commonwealth Office and in 1978 Ambassador to the Soviet Union. His publications include *Britain and the Soviet Union* (1990).

Richard Lamb was educated at Downside and Merton College, Oxford. He is author of several books on contemporary history including *The Macmillan Years,* which was the first publication to use the official documents on Macmillan's premiership. He has recently published *Mussolini and the British* and is currently editing for the Public Record Office the CD ROM on the Macmillan documents covering 1957–63.

Sabine Lee was educated at the Universities of Düsseldorf and Cambridge. She completed her PhD with a thesis on British–German relations. She worked as Lecturer in Modern European History at the University of Hull and is currently Lecturer in German History at the University of Birmingham. Her publications include *An Uneasy Relationship: British–German Relations between 1955 and 1961* (1995) and, co-edited with Richard Aldous, *Harold Macmillan and Britain's World Role* (1996).

W. Scott Lucas is Head of American and Canadian Studies at the University of Birmingham. He is the author of numerous books and articles on British and US foreign policy after 1945. His next book, *Freedom's War: The US Crusade against the Soviet Union, 1945–1956,* will be published in early 1999.

N. Piers Ludlow was educated in Italy and Belgium before reading modern history at Trinity College, Oxford. His doctorate from St Antony's College, Oxford, examined European reactions to Britain's first EEC application. He is the author of *Dealing with Britain: The Six and the First UK Application to the EEC.* He is currently Lecturer in International History at the London School of Economics.

Charles Lysaght studied politics and economics at University College, Dublin, before proceeding to Christ's College, Cambridge. In 1964 he succeeded Kenneth Clarke and Norman Lamont as President of the Cambridge Union. He was subsequently called to the Bar and has worked as barrister, lecturer and legal adviser in Dublin. He is author of a biography of Brendan Bracken.

Donette Murray studied modern and contemporary history at the University of Ulster and has recently completed her PhD with a thesis on Anglo-American defence relations during the Kennedy Presidency. She is currently Lecturer at the Queen's University of Belfast.

John Subritzky is a graduate of the Universities of Auckland and Cambridge. He is currently completing a book on the Malaysian–Indonesian confrontation. He currently works as policy officer in New Zealand's Ministry of Foreign Affairs.

Sir Oliver Wright was educated at Solihull School and Christ's College, Cambridge. After four years in the Royal Navy, he joined the Diplomatic Service in 1945. He has held numerous overseas appointments including New York, Bucharest, Singapore, Berlin, and South Africa. Between 1960 and 1963 he was Private Secretary to the Foreign Secretary, from 1964 to 1966 to the Prime Minister. He served as Ambassador to Copenhagen, Bonn and Washington between 1966 and 1986.

1 Introduction
Richard Aldous and Sabine Lee

Shirley Williams, the former Labour Cabinet Minister, once remarked that the most important quality required for political success is stamina. This was a trait Harold Macmillan possessed in
abundance. Behind the panache and elegant wit lay a dogged re-
lentlessness in the face of disappointment. Like a heavyweight boxer
who will not fall down, Macmillan absorbed punch after punch
throughout his career but always kept going. In the end it was not
scandal or political embarrassment for failed policies that saw him
off. Harold Macmillan only relinquished his grip on power because
he thought he was dying. Only days after offering his resignation
to the Queen he knew it was a mistake and regretted it until his
death twenty-three years later.

For almost fifty years it seemed unlikely that Harold Macmillan
would succeed at the highest level. Macmillan was not one of the
stars of his generation. Of his Etonian contemporaries, Macmillan
lacked the good looks and intellectual arrogance of Eden or the
blue-blooded sense of purpose of 'Bobberty' Cecil. Between 1894
and 1939, despite opportunities and privilege, Macmillan exuded
failure and mediocrity. He was a sickly child at Eton and displayed
little academic or sporting accomplishment. At Oxford, he arrived
(after private tuition) as a promising Exhibitioner, yet gained only
a second-class degree. Real achievements seemed to pass unno-
ticed. He fought courageously and was wounded in the First World
War but was not decorated. Success in entering the House of Commons at a relatively young age was dissipated by becoming a mav-
erick within his own party. Many considered his beliefs on welfare
and poverty to be more akin to Socialism than Toryism. His vocal
opposition to appeasement confirmed his image as a disaffected
'crank'. When he burnt an effigy of the Prime Minister, Neville
Chamberlain, at Birch Grove on Bonfire Night it symbolized not
only the dissatisfaction with his own party but also his impotence
within it.

Macmillan's professional failure was not helped by the appalling
circumstances of his private life. He did not have the dashing good
looks or sparkling wit to make him a ladies' man. Some historians

1

have even tried, without much conviction, to imply that Macmillan was homosexual. Closer to the truth is that Macmillan as a young man was extremely shy with women and showed little inclination to woo. Working for the Duke of Devonshire after the First World War brought him into contact with the duke's teenage daughter, Lady Dorothy, who made all the running for him. A horsy girl with little in the way of looks or brains, she had spent most of her childhood in rural Ireland. She knew very little of men and less of sex. They married in 1920 but Dorothy quickly bored of him. Matters were not helped by her family. Her sisters found Macmillan dull and middle-class. Before dinner at Chatsworth they would draw lots to see who had to suffer his company. Slights of this kind might have been endured if his wife had remained true. In fact, the marriage was a disaster. After years of promiscuity during the early part of their marriage, Dorothy took a regular lover in 1929 and kept him until her death in 1966. Her choice could hardly have been more vicious. Bob Boothby, Conservative MP, was one of Macmillan's closest friends and political allies. This was a cuckolding of the most spectacular and humiliating kind.

Politically and privately, therefore, Macmillan's life until the outbreak of the Second World War was not happy. We might speculate that had Lord Halifax kept his nerve against Churchill in May 1940 and replaced Chamberlain as Prime Minister, Harold Macmillan might well have disappeared into political obscurity. It was the Second World War that made Macmillan. He gained preferment from Churchill and demonstrated that he had the capability to be a government minister. More importantly he came to believe that politics was a game in which he could win. The transformation was dramatic, not least on the outside. The badly cut tweed suits were replaced by something altogether sharper. Snagged teeth were capped and straightened. The glasses were removed for the cameras and a bushy moustache trimmed. Even the personality seemed changed. Earnest, bookish, dull-dog Macmillan was replaced by a witty raconteur whose dry humour made him amusing company and apparently unflappable in a crisis.

The set-backs continued to come. Macmillan forfeited his seat in 1945 and lost ground to Rab Butler in setting the agenda for post-war Conservatism. Back in the Commons in 1951, he was disappointed only to be offered the Ministry of Housing by Churchill who, anyway, did not have the paternal affection for him that Macmillan desired. Nevertheless, he later acknowledged that it was his public relations triumph at Housing and not his record in higher offices that eventually made him prime minister. Success at Housing was followed by a disastrous spell at the Ministry of Defence and a frustratingly short time at the Foreign Office. As Chancellor of the Exchequer, Macmillan badly misjudged American attitudes to British action at the Suez canal and, having been a leading hawk before the campaign, abruptly became first of the 'bolters' on the eve of victory. And yet from the political carnage of the Suez crisis, it was to the barnstorming, media-friendly Harold Macmillan that the Conservative party turned for salvation. A lifetime of withstanding embarrassment and disappointment had finally resulted in Harold Macmillan reaching the top of the 'greasy pole'.

Macmillan's transformation from shambolic wreck to elegant statesman has done little to help his historical reputation. The sense that he was 'all style and no substance' was already established in 1963 and remains to this day. Papers from his Premiership now available under the Thirty-Year Rule enable essays in this collection to attempt a more considered judgement of Macmillan's political legacy.

It is immediately clear that, as Prime Minister, foreign affairs dominated Macmillan's thinking, a fact he acknowledged in his memoirs. The late 1950s and early 1960s were times of international tension and danger. Macmillan, like other world statesmen, assumed he was the best man to deal with the difficulties of the Cold War. He had a measure of success in re-establishing a special relationship with American presidents if not the US foreign policy-making establishment itself. Personal diplomacy was Macmillan's favoured approach although it was also one in which he frequently failed, particularly in European affairs. An over-estimation of his own personal standing as well as misjudgement of Britain's bargaining power with the Six led to a souring of relations with his most significant European partners. In particular Britain's policy hampered a good understanding with France and damaged that with the other key European player, Germany. Strain in the relationship between Adenauer and Macmillan was exacerbated by the latter's attempts at personal diplomacy with the Soviet leader, Nikita Khrushchev. Macmillan's visit to Moscow in 1959 shortly after Khrushchev's Berlin ultimatum did much to undermine the cohesion of the Western camp and was even more detrimental for Anglo-German relations.

There is no doubt about Macmillan's enthusiasm for European co-operation and Britain's role in a wider economic grouping.

Whether his attempt at getting Britain into the European club was a symbol of his own political success is more debatable. Macmillan did not succeed in securing entry to the EEC for Britain during his premiership. He only alienated de Gaulle and frustrated negotiators at Brussels with the 'conditional application' in 1961. Nevertheless, he initiated a major reversal in British thinking about the virtues of European integration and Britain's place in Europe. Perhaps without this radical reappraisal of policy Britain would not have joined after de Gaulle's downfall.

Macmillan's shift in European policy necessitated a corresponding re-evaluation of colonial commitments. Despite the enthusiastic, even radical, rhetoric of the 'Wind of Change' speech, Macmillan's attitude towards Empire was of pragmatism in the face of a wider problem in redesigning Britain's world role (as the case of Malaysia demonstrates only too clearly). Macmillan was too preoccupied with summiteering, joining the Common Market and guaranteeing Britain's status as a nuclear power to deal with colonial affairs. Despite this fundamental lack of interest, Macmillan did knowingly initiate a process which would bring about an end to British rule in Africa that was dignified and relatively peaceful.

Despite Macmillan's obsession with foreign affairs, some of his most important successes lay in the hard reality of electoral politics and the management of his party's affairs. He succeeded in rebuilding the government and his party after the humiliation of the Suez Crisis. Few would have predicted in January 1957 that the Conservatives would win the next general election. The lion's share of the credit for the 1959 victory went to Harold Macmillan, not least because he had displayed such ruthlessness and singlemindedness in achieving a hundred seat majority. He convinced the electorate that they had 'never had it so good' at home and lived in a country once again taken seriously on the world stage. In the process SUPERMAC was born. Could he have won again in 1964? By the time of his resignation in 1963, the Profumo crisis had been seen through and the deadwood of a party in power since 1951 had been cut back in the 'Night of the Long Knives'. In reality, the Conservatives in 1964 came within four seats of victory when led by a man easily ridiculed for his matchstick economics and eighteenth-century demeanour. Whether the more populist and flamboyant Macmillan would have found one more electoral rabbit to pull out of the hat must remain an unanswered question. It would not have been his first such trick.

In the end, perhaps Macmillan's most important legacy is not so much what he achieved but what was put in train. He took the important first step towards redefining Britain's relations with western Europe and initiated a dignified process of decolonization in Africa. In *The Middle Way* and as Chancellor and Prime Minister, he showed a willingness to reform, even revolutionize, Britain's spending priorities, most notably in the defence budget. And he always gave himself time to think – perhaps unusual for a politician – about long-term policy. The Future Policy Committee and the Grand Design are indicative of Macmillan's determination that government should not simply be a question of management but also of vision and strategy. Perhaps it is this belief in the intellectual nature of politics (notwithstanding an eye for the main chance) that distinguishes him from those who followed. From his days as a young man in the trenches fulminating against Irish nationalists to his speeches as Lord Stockton about selling off the 'family silver', Macmillan adored thinking about politics in its historical and philosophical context. In his maiden speech in the House of Lords he acknowledged that his time in politics had not always been successful and that he had often been regarded with 'dislike by the leaders of my party' (although, he continued, 'I was, fortunately, able to deal with the matter fairly soon by becoming the leader of the party myself'). The battle for Macmillan's historical reputation continues and this volume makes a contribution to the debate. But whatever judgements await Harold Macmillan, there can be no doubting that his was a magnificent political life.

2 Macmillan: a View from the Foreign Office

Sir Oliver Wright

One of the many pleasures of taking part in the Macmillan Conference was to go back to Alistair Horne's splendid two-volume biography of him who was known affectionately to his staff as Uncle Harold, to refresh memory and sort out fact from accrued fiction. Indeed, one judges a book about someone who, like Harold Macmillan, played a central role in one's professional life, by whether the author gets right, in fact and judgement, the events of which one has first-hand experience. By this test Horne gets a Triple A rating. His accounts – for example of the Cuban missile crisis, of Nassau and Polaris, of de Gaulle's first veto – strike me as being bang on target. One has confidence that if he is right about things one knows about, he is not likely to be wrong on matters which one doesn't.

I first came in contact with Mr Macmillan at the 4-Power Foreign Ministers' Conference in Geneva in October 1955 on 'The Reunification of Germany'. He was somewhat less than half-way through his short stint as Foreign Secretary. I was a very junior diplomat in Berlin, handling the affairs of what we still called the Soviet Zone of Germany, in the days before the Wall. They needed someone in Geneva to fill the British slot in the International Secretariat which was to produce the minutes of the Conference. It was a measure of the low expectations of the Conference that they should send to it someone as junior as myself.

Macmillan had in July accompanied Eden to an earlier 'Summit' on the same question. The summiteers – Khrushchev and Bulganin, Dulles, Faure and Eden – had in two days agreed on nothing except to refer the problem to their foreign ministers. What the Heads of Government had been unable to resolve in two days, the foreign ministers were unable to resolve in two weeks. There were two sessions daily, morning and afternoon, Monday to Friday; we listened to Mr Molotov say 'no' to German reunification in ten not very different ways. The only agreement that the International Secretariat had to record each evening was that the four foreign ministers would meet again the next day.

Macmillan had his own technique for surviving these bum-numbing sessions. When it was his turn to speak, Pat Hancock or Fred Warner, two accompanying officials from the Foreign Office, would pass up notes of 'points to make' and Macmillan would gracefuly improvise on these themes for 15 minutes or so. When it was not his turn to speak, he would encourage the time to pass more agreeably and more quickly by reading a book placed on his knees out of sight under the conference table. I remember being very shocked at first, thinking that our Foreign Secretary should be taking his work more seriously; but after a time, I realized how wise he was and only wished I could do the same.

Most evenings were passed in official entertainment, each Head of Delegation entertaining and being entertained by other Heads of Delegation, together with their entourages. The negotiating indigestion of the day was succeeded by the gastronomic indigestion of the evening. It is not often appreciated by the general public how much diplomats are obliged to ruin their digestions in the service of their country. One evening, when Macmillan had a night off, I was invited to have dinner with him and a few other members of his delegation. That was a bit of a shock too. I had rather expected to participate in, or at any rate listen to, a wise and witty survey of the Conference to date. Not a bit of it. Macmillan had switched off completely. The conversation was purely social from beginning to end; from soup to coffee not a word of shop. Afterwards I asked John Wyndham, who was Macmillan's sort of private secretary–boon companion and author of a delightful slim volume of memoirs, 'Wyndham and Children First', why I had been invited. 'No reason at all, dear chap; the PM just likes to have a new face or two around.' Alistair Horne gives less than a page to the two weeks of the 1955 Geneva Foreign Ministers' Conference. About right.

Macmillan's brief spell at the Foreign Office followed by his lengthy tenure of No. 10 Downing Street was a pretty fraught time in international affairs. The 1950s under Eden were, I suppose, the most disastrous period in British foreign policy since the Second World War; which is odd when you think that Eden's main strengths were held to lie in his knowledge of international affairs and his experience in diplomacy. The Suez adventure and the failure to realize the seriousness of purpose of the negotiations at Messina which led to the Treaty of Rome were unmitigated disasters.

At the time of Suez I was still stationed in Berlin. I and all my colleagues were particularly sickened that this barmy escapade at the end of the Mediterranean was distracting international attention from something far more heinous happening in our own back yard: the Soviet invasion of Hungary. In London the Chief Clerk of the Foreign Office, the person in charge of personnel, was deluged by letters of resignation from members of the Service who wanted nothing to do with this act of piracy. Eventually tempers calmed; Eden withdrew from Suez and colleagues withdrew their letters of resignation. Just as well, really; otherwise the nation would not have had enough diplomats to carry on the nation's diplomacy. Consciences were soothed when it was pointed out that the unwritten contract between public servants and their political masters states that civil servants advise, ministers decide and civil servants carry out ministers' decisions. After all, politicians are the elect of the people and are answerable to Parliament; civil servants are neither.

Suez marked a parting of the ways for Britain and France. Both were partners in the Suez débâcle. Both felt let down by the Americans. Each reacted in a totally different way. Macmillan's first priority when he became Prime Minister was to re-establish our relations with Washington. The French priority was to distance itself from the United States by giving full attention to the Treaty of Rome, creating a Common Market of the Six which France could and would lead, and setting the seal on the post-war reconciliation between France and Germany. Both were conspicuously successful. Both had enduring consequences. Unfortunately both successes and consequences proved to be mutually incompatible. Since Suez, France has enjoyed a difficult relationship with America and Britain has been unable to develop a satisfactory relationship with Europe.

That Macmillan was successful in restoring relations with the Americans and particularly where it mattered, the White House, is beyond dispute. And that the successful pursuit of this objective has been of great and long-lasting benefit to Britain is equally not in dispute. He was able to re-establish fairly quickly the friendship with Eisenhower which he had formed during the war years when he had been our man in North Africa and Ike had been Supreme Allied Commander in Europe. Ike was no doubt equally glad to be on good terms with his old friend again. The first fruits of this policy was the repeal in 1958 of the McMahon Act, which restored nuclear collaboration between Britain and the United States.

When Kennedy succeeded Eisenhower at the White House,

Macmillan was himself doubtful whether he would be able to establish the same relations of trust with this younger, charismatic figure as he had with his much older predecessor. He did so at first with a message of congratulations, which was also a message of ideas; a masterly survey of the world and a vision of what needed to be done. The draft underwent many revisions and crossed and re-crossed Downing Street many times. It struck a chord in Kennedy's mind and from their first meeting the two men found that they enjoyed each other's company and thought much along the same lines.

It was the Cuban Missile Crisis of late 1962 which cemented Macmillan's quasi-avuncular relationship with Kennedy. I well remember the morning that Hugh Stevenson, chairman of the Joint Intelligence Committee, came into the Private Office and asked to see the Secretary of State. He had brought with him a portfolio of photographs to show Lord Home aerial proof of the presence of Soviet missiles in Cuba. Gromyko had lied in his teeth when Home had pressed him on the subject at the UN, denying that any were there.

In the Private Office we were well aware of the nightly telephone calls between the White House and No. 10. Horne rightly describes them as something less than consultation, something more than information. Kennedy, not Macmillan, always placed the calls; he would not have done so if he had not wanted to; he would not have continued to do so if he had not felt them useful, even necessary. It is lonely at the top, any top; loneliest of all at a time of crisis when one false step might have meant war, nuclear war. And even presidents need someone outside the immediate circle, whose experience they acknowledge, whose sympathy they can rely on, whose judgement they value and whose discretion they can trust, to talk through the events of the day with and to help harness their thoughts for the morrow. Macmillan supplied this need; and of enormous benefit to Britain it was. I have heard this unique exchange described as 'international samaritanism', a remark which suggests a gift for phrasemaking unsupported by insight or judgement.

Macmillan got his reward and Britain its benefit perhaps sooner than expected, at Nassau in December 1962: the Polaris missile, when Kennedy overruled all his staff to give his friend what he needed. The benefit was of immediate and lasting value. Twenty years later, when I was in Washington, during the Reagan–Thatcher political love affair, the successor missile to Polaris, Trident, went through 'on the nod'.

The third important consequence of the Macmillan–Kennedy relationship was the Partial Nuclear Test Ban Treaty, signed for Britain by Lord Home in Moscow in August 1963. Macmillan, while convinced of the necessity of nuclear deterrence and of Britain's possessing its own deterrent, saw the complementary need for bringing these weapons of mass destruction under some sort of control. And he had from the start of his premiership been working on both Eisenhower and Kennedy, who, he realized, had to be the prime movers on the Western side. It was the Cuban missile crisis which made Kennedy finally receptive to his ideas. And so the first step was taken. The Nuclear Treaty was to be the last major foreign policy act of the Macmillan administration. It was also to be the fore-runner of a whole series of later arms limitation treaties – SALT 1 and SALT 2 – and, in Reagan's day, of the abolition of a whole nuclear weapons system by the INF Treaty. Actions have consequences and they can be both beneficial and durable: Macmillan's transatlantic policy was both. The Campaign for Nuclear Disarmament (CND) ceased to be a serious political embarrassment thereafter.

It is a favourite pastime of sceptics to call the 'special relationship' into question. No practitioner would do so since it provides the background to the Embassy's daily work in Washington, DC. Indeed, it is perhaps the phrase itself which has become the main impediment to public acceptance of its reality. Of course, it is not exclusive; there are quite a number of special relationships among the nations of the world: the United States with Israel, for example; France with Germany; Britain with Ireland. The continuing intelligence and naval nuclear co-operation are but two of the on-going practical manifestations of this unique way of conducting business between our two nations. And, of course, it does not exclude flaming rows on occasion – Grenada, for example – which furnish the sceptics with proof that the special relationship is a thing of the past. None the less, it persists in persisting. America gave Britain the sort of help over the Falklands that it would have given to no other nation. Naturally, it works best when the personal chemistry of the people in charge and their national interests coincidence: Churchill and Roosevelt, Macmillan and both Eisenhower and Kennedy, Thatcher and Reagan. And as I know from personal experience, if the empathy is right at the top, it is right all the way down. Doors open, minds become receptive, deals are cut.

There is, not surprisingly, a downside to all this. It is Europe. After Suez, while Britain gave priority to the restoration of transatlantic relations, France deliberately turned her back on the Atlantic. For de Gaulle, America and Britain became indiscriminately 'les anglo-saxons' and virtually beyond the pale. France instead set about creating a continental Europe of the Six in her own image, using Europe to harness and control the re-emerging power of Germany and actively promoting Franco-German reconciliation, all of which Germany financed, a role in which Germany, burdened with history, acquiesced. Neither Eden nor Macmillan expected the negotiations at Messina to succeed or the Treaty of Rome to work. It was a catastrophic misjudgement. It fell to Macmillan to try to rectify the mistake. Negotiations for Britain to join in 1961 and 1962 went well, if laboriously, up to Edward Heath's level. They failed at the top. They came up against the insuperable rancour of de Gaulle, who had never recovered from the humiliation of France in 1940 and had always resented the fact that he had had to seek sanctuary in Britain and that Britain had given it. Churchill's 'Cross of Lorraine' pronounced his first veto in January 1963.

Macmillan also came up against the mutual dislike which had developed between himself and Adenauer. Adenauer, a Rhinelander, did not much care for Britain; indeed he did not have much reason to, having been dismissed at the end of the war from his position as Lord Mayor of Cologne by the British Town Major of the day. A summit in Bonn between Macmillan and Adenauer in 1962, which I attended, was a complete waste of time. Macmillan must have thought so too, for he took a nap during the after-lunch session and Alec Home had to keep the talks going. Adenauer soon got his revenge. Only days after de Gaulle's veto, he went to Paris and signed with de Gaulle the Franco-German Treaty of Friendship and Collaboration. The Treaty set the seal on Franco-German reconciliation. It also effectively put paid to any likelihood of Britain's being able to be 'at the heart of Europe'.

This legacy of Harold Macmillan's is also with us still. By taking his eye off the ball at Messina, Britain lost the chance of helping to build a Europe tailored to our tastes and taking account of our interests. We have been playing 'catch up' ever since and show no sign of winning, whichever party is in power.

The last time I was in Uncle Harold's company was in Sweden in August 1963, when for some reason best known to himself the PM had decided to accept the return hospitality of the Swedish Prime Minister, Tage Erlander. I had accompanied my own greatly revered boss, Lord Home, to Moscow for the signature of the Nuclear

Test Ban Treaty and we caught up with the Macmillans in Stockholm. We spent the weekend at the Swedish Chequers, Harpsund. It was crayfish time. We started the evening in a pavilion in the grounds of the main house eating crayfish and drinking akvavit. Very soon our Swedish hosts, led by their foreign minister, were merrily singing Swedish drinking songs, of which there are many. The British were acutely embarrassed. Then the deep diapason of a contralto voice could be heard above the hubbub: Aunt Dorothy had come to the rescue of British honour with the opening bars of 'Annie Laurie' and we all joined in. Next time it was our turn, Aunt Dorothy launched us into 'The Minstrel Boy'. And so it went on, Swedish drinking songs in antiphon with Scottish minstrel lays, with generous refills of akvavit the while.

The evening was not, however, at an end. We repaired to the main house, some of us unsteadily, for dinner. There, toasting the Macmillans, Erlander delivered, in faultless English, one of the wittiest after-dinner speeches I have ever heard and tears of laughter ran down our cheeks. When Uncle Harold got up to respond, he knew instinctively that it would be wrong to try to top that and that he had to come up with something quite different. So he pulled out the vox humana and plunged at once into variations, andante e maestoso, on the 'ties that bind'. Soon the tears of laughter changed to tears of deep felt emotion and the PM sat down to a satisfactory round of applause.

Afterwards, in the drawing room, I went up to him and in the sycophantic manner of which only Private Secretaries are masters, said: 'Prime Minister, you were in very good form tonight.' He looked at me from beneath those hooded eyelids and replied: 'Did you think so, my boy? I gave them my mood voice.' An actor indeed. But then, all successful politicians, indeed, all successful leaders – archbishops, field marshals, even in a modest way, ambassadors – have to be able to play their part when on stage. It goes with the leadership thing: 'be yourself – plus'.

The successful conduct of foreign policy depends to a certain extent on the personal chemistry between the Prime Minister of the day and the person he or she has appointed to the Foreign Office. It also depends on the degree of the PM's personal interest in 'the foreign'. Eden and Macmillan did not have a very satisfactory partnership, perhaps because both were strong personalities and both regarded themselves as experts in this field. Macmillan and Selwyn Lloyd were an uninspiring combination: there are horses for courses and Selwyn really found his metier as Speaker of the House of Commons.

Macmillan and Home were in many ways an ideal team. Both had been to Eton and Oxford. Macmillan had married the daughter of a duke and so was at ease with having an earl at the FO. Moreover, for the first four years of Macmillan's premiership, Home had been at the Commonwealth Office; the two men had come to trust each other's judgement and got on well together. Macmillan had suffered under Eden, learned from the experience and so handled the Foreign Office with a light touch. Home for his part always made certain that the PM knew what he was doing and was happy with it: five or ten minutes occasionally before or after Cabinet, fixed by the two Private Offices, was all that was necessary to keep the two men on the same wavelength and for Home to carry great weight in Cabinet, since he could always carry the PM with him.

Macmillan naturally kept '*haute politique*' for himself; Alec saw the value of his doing so and did not for a moment resent it. In any case there was plenty of other interesting work for him to cope with. There was a great deal of travelling in his programme – too much in Home's view – to keep the alliances in repair: NATO, SEATO and CENTO were all active, and if not all of them were particularly useful, they took up a good deal of time. The UN was very time-consuming as was the Laos problem. Moreover, Alec was never one to seek the limelight. He was happy to answer for the FO in the House of Lords and Their Lordships were delighted to have him in their midst. Down the corridor, Ted Heath handled the accession negotiations for Europe and answered in the House of Commons. So for three years all was sweetness and light between No. 10 and the FO. When Home retired, he always used to look back on his time at the Foreign Office as his 'golden years'. I, his Private Secretary, thought them just that too.

So I have always thought it strange that Macmillan, with all his gifts and his many and varied contributions to the safety of our nation and to our standing in the world, does not enjoy a reputation consistent with his merits. Perhaps it is a case of a prophet not being without honour save in his own country. Perhaps his character and personality do not appeal to later generations when the sound bite has superseded rational argument in politics. The delightful cartoon by Terry Jeffrey on the front of the programme of the Cambridge Conference encapsulates a good deal of the problem: Macmillan presents an old-fashioned appearance and is carrying an old-fashioned book.

Yet that languid face hid a complex personality and an acute political brain; the old-fashioned appearance belied a man with a forward-looking, even visionary concept of what he would like the world to be. The book correctly indicated a well-furnished mind, widely read in history and literature. He had a perspective in which to place the problems he had to deal with. He was an astute judge of human nature, particularly of political human nature: hence his addiction to Trollope. He saw things in depth.

When I followed Home to No. 10, a quotation from *The Gondoliers* written in Macmillan's own straggly hand, framed, stood on the broad window ledge to the left of the Principal Private Secretary's desk:

Quiet, calm deliberation untangles every knot.

If only that were so. Just because there is a problem does not mean that there is a solution to it. People, and nations, often need their problems more than they need solutions to them, for it is the problems that give them a sense of identity, a meaning to their lives. As de Toqueville correctly observed 150 years ago: 'Nations are like men; they prefer what flatters their passions to what serves their interests.'

It would seem that the world demands spectacular success before it is prepared to recognize greatness; and not always then. And one failure can undo many successes. It is interesting to speculate that had Macmillan been able to negotiate British entry into the European Community in 1963 he would have been buoyant enough in spirit to ride the scandals of that unhappy summer and would have taken his place among the great Prime Ministers of our country. As it was, de Gaulle's veto was a blow, political, psychological and physical, from which he never really recovered. And it showed. His illness was proof. For all that, he was a man who understood how the world we live in works, who knew what he wanted to do about it and achieved much of what he set out to do. For a practitioner, he was a statesman to admire, a politician to respect, a marvellous man to work for.

As a young diplomat I was grateful for my worm's eye view of the great man at work. Thirty-four years on, recollecting in tranquillity, my admiration grows for a unique person, unique in the number and magnitude of the problems he had to face and unique in the quiet, calm deliberation with which he brought his manifold gifts to bear upon them. In comparison, today's international scene, whilst abounding in insoluble problems and human misery, presents what are essentially second-order problems: the great issues of war and peace are thankfully not at stake as they were in Macmillan's day. So perhaps it does not matter that we seem only to have second-order personages to deal with them.

As for Macmillan, we shall not see his like again, nor, with a bit of luck, the magnitude of the problems he had to face. Life has moved on.

3 The Cost of Myth: Macmillan and the Illusion of the 'Special Relationship'[1]

W. Scott Lucas

In February 1993, British Prime Minister John Major travelled to Washington for talks with the new US President, Bill Clinton. The visit came at a particularly tense time for Anglo-American relations. There were divisions over policy in Bosnia, a US initiative to send an envoy to Northern Ireland, the development of trading relations through the North American Free Trade Area (NAFTA), and even the European development of the Airbus. Major's Conservative Party had not helped matters by indiscreetly advising Clinton's Republican opponents in the 1992 Presidential election. All of this paled, however, before the faith of the British press in the Anglo-American alliance. In the words of *The Times*, 'The special relationship between America and Britain, rarely evoked on the other side of the Atlantic and mentioned by British diplomats only in private whispers, remains a benchmark of London's influence on the international stage.'[2]

Very little was resolved during Major's visit, which lasted less than two days. The *Financial Times* struck a sceptical tone with the snide comment, 'The truth is that relationship is special above all in its lopsidedness.'[3] For the majority of the British press, however, the illusion remained:

> One meeting may say little about the future of the special relationship, but it has helped to confirm a common language.... There is still something to be said for a common language.[4]

The US journalist R. W. Apple joined the chorus: 'The special relationship between Britain and the US, whose obituary has been written so often, is alive and well.... It is language, shared experience and common political culture that make the bonds between Britain and the US so strong.'[5]

Even more striking is the perpetuation of these images by British historians. Alan Dobson, in a recent survey of Anglo-American relations in the twentieth century, ignores his own chronicle of divisions between London and Washington to assert blithely, 'In crisis after crisis . . . Britain and the USA have approached things similarly and in a partnership that is suggestive of there being further life in the relationship.'[6] Nicholas Cull, writing about Britain and the US during the Second World War, goes even further by stressing the permanent 'essence of the Anglo-American relationship, which is not purely a pragmatic creation of the elite but a confluence of culture and historical necessity'.[7]

In one sense, this rose-tinted vision was fostered by the image of a 'Grand Alliance', albeit one belatedly joined by the US, against the Axis in the Second World War. Yet Churchill's invocation of the 'special relationship of the English-speaking peoples' in the Iron Curtain speech of 1946 was buffeted throughout the early Cold War by tensions between British and American interests and policies, culminating in the traumatic division over the Suez War. It was Harold Macmillan, fighting for his new Government and his political reputation as well as any Anglo-American alliance, who enshrined the concept of an 'interdependence' across the North Atlantic.

No judgement need be made of Macmillan's manipulation of history and his persistent repackaging of the 'special relationship', both in his memoirs and in his recollections to biographers, to bolster his reputation. There was a great cost, however, in Macmillan's strategy of reliance, in rhetoric and in deed, on a London–Washington axis. In doing so, the Prime Minister added to the growing estrangement of Britain from 'Europe'. Six years later, when Macmillan belatedly tried to get Britain into the European Economic Community, the legacy of Atlantic 'interdependence' would help provoke a French veto.

Macmillan's account of his premiership, in his public statements, his memoirs and his testimony to his biographers, moves from tales of camaraderie with Dwight Eisenhower, his old buddy from the Second World War, to his extraordinary bond with John F. Kennedy.

Macmillan always harked back to his comment of 1943 that Britain played the Greeks to the Romans of the US, providing the brains to complement American brawn in the international contest with Soviet Communism.

The portrayal served both Prime Minister and country. His government would be marked by the ongoing contraction – military, economic and diplomatic – of Britain's global position, but Macmillan was loathe to shun the mantle of greatness. The illusion of the 'special relationship' offered a personal and national solution. Through the claim to partnership with Washington, Macmillan and Britain would still be players in superpower contests.

Any rigorous examination dispels the myth. Macmillan's account of a confederation of equals, on the personal or political level, is not corroborated by US evidence. After he left the presidency in 1961, Eisenhower only corresponded once with his 'old friend' Macmillan. His administration may have been concerned with the public portrayal of British support for the US at certain critical points, such as the aftermath of the Soviet launch of *Sputnik* in October 1957, but general strategy was not based on an Anglo-American partnership. To the contrary, in key areas such as the Middle East, Africa and Asia, the US was more concerned with establishing a policy 'independent' of British influence. What is striking about the records of Eisenhower's National Security Council is not how often Britain is mentioned but how rarely attention is paid to London's position.

Nor does Macmillan's 'special relationship' correspond with the logic of 'alliance'. Co-operation between London and Washington was not an unconditional emanation of a shared heritage. It was dependence upon organizational links and a convergence of interests. Where British support was unnecessary for the achievement of American goals, for example in Latin America, there was no special relationship. Where interests conflicted, as in the issue of relations with Communist China, there was perpetual tension in Anglo-American consultations, a tension resolved only when Macmillan abandoned Britain's freedom of action on the issue in 1957. The Foreign Office captured the nature of 'alliance' in February 1957, 'We should pursue a policy in step with that of the US. We have no alternative.'[8]

These simple but essential realities are obscured by the ability of Macmillan to manipulate the illusions of 'alliance' throughout his career. The son of Indiana's Nellie Belles, he later celebrated his own Anglo-American heritage for publicity's sake; in fact, his early life showed few signs of involvement with affairs across the Atlantic. Bonds forged in North Africa and Italy in the Second World War may have had a limited influence – Macmillan worked closely with Robert Murphy, who would eventually become the third-highest official in the State Department – but their long-term impact was mythological. Macmillan may have trumpeted his involvement with the Supreme Allied Commander, Dwight Eisenhower, for political advantage in the 1950s; however, there was little reciprocation. The future US President never elevated the wartime contacts beyond an acquaintance with Macmillan and his work.

Indeed, Macmillan's attentions in the decade after the Second World War would be devoted to domestic politics. Losing his seat in the 1945 election, he had to secure a sanctuary through a by-election in Bromley four months later. Entry into the Cabinet in 1951 in the relatively minor position of Minister of Housing had to be parlayed into the triumph of building 300,000 council houses in a year and his stay at the Ministry of Defence was abbreviated by Winston Churchill's departure.

When the Eden government finally yielded the prize of Foreign Secretary, Macmillan was far too pragmatic in his approach for a personal celebration of Anglo-American partnership. He sensibly allowed Eden to seek the plaudits from the Geneva Summit in July 1955, assuming the burdens of the subsequent Conference of Foreign Ministers. His relationship with US Secretary of State John Foster Dulles was a warm one, particularly given the undeclared state of war between Eden and Foster Dulles; however, its benefits came through the details of sustaining Britain's position on the Cyprus question, securing West Germany's entry into NATO, or negotiating Britain's export of copper wire to Communist countries. On occasion, the Foreign Secretary would even test the notion of 'alliance' while leaving himself a route for retreat if his plans went awry. He pressed for British occupation of the Buraimi oasis, an area disputed between British-backed sheikhdoms and Saudi Arabia, in defiance of US wishes. Far less successful was his venture to bring Jordan into the Baghdad Pact, an initiative which almost led to the overthrow of King Hussein and prompted Eisenhower to write, 'The British never had any sense in the Middle East.'[9] Macmillan was shrewd enough to distance himself from the débâcle and suffered no ill will from Washington. After Eden moved Macmillan to the Treasury weeks later, Foster Dulles wrote that he was 'terribly disappointed'. He added, 'I have come to have great trust and reliance in you and because of this I have looked toward the future with greater confidence.'[10]

It was the Suez Crisis, the watershed for so much of post-war British foreign policy, that ultimately shaped Macmillan's conception of the Anglo-American 'alliance'. Macmillan's priority during the affair was the assertion of British power in the Middle East, with or without US assent. He pressed the War Cabinet to co-operate with Israel in an attack upon Egypt. To reassure colleagues that Britain could afford a war, he misled them about the state of the foreign reserves. Most importantly, he lied to Prime Minister Eden about the US position. Macmillan, told directly by Foster Dulles that Washington was opposed to military action and given no indication of support by President Eisenhower, still informed Eden that the US 'quite realised that we might have to act by force. . . . Our threat of force was vital, whether we used it or not, to keep Nasser worried.'[11]

Yet, when the British collusion with France and Israel failed to topple Nasser quickly, when the foreign reserves drained away as the US exerted economic and diplomatic pressure for a cease-fire, Macmillan suddenly distanced himself from the operation and personally sought reconciliation with Washington. First he appealed for American loans and provision of oil supplies. Then, to negotiate behind the Prime Minister's back, he assured US contacts that Eden would soon resign. At the same time, political manoeuvring within the Conservative Party ensured that Macmillan would move into Number 10 if Eden stepped down.

Thus, when Macmillan's intrigues yielded him the premiership on 10 January 1957, he entered not with an inherent belief in a 'special relationship', but with a recognition of his dependence upon US power. His position as Prime Minister, as well as Britain's military and economic strength, rested upon transatlantic co-operation. Of course, it would be politically inexpedient to admit London's subservience to Washington, so Macmillan instead proclaimed a global partnership of equals. Speaking on television a week after his accession, he asserted:

> The life of the free world depends upon the partnership between us. . . . We don't intend to part from the Americans, and we don't intend to be satellites.[12]

Macmillan was assisted by the assessment of US leaders, made even before the end of the Eden government, that 'alliance' must be sustained despite the traumas of Suez. Eisenhower, confronting advisers hostile to London, finally announced, 'We must face the question, what must we do in Europe and then the question, how do we square this with the Arabs?'[13] He also claimed, 'Nothing would please this country more nor, in fact, could help us more, than to see British prestige and strength renewed and rejuvenated in the Middle East.'[14]

These conclusions were reached not because of an a priori belief in 'alliance' but because of a pragmatic assessment of US interests. This was best captured by the British Ambassador to Washington, Harold Caccia:

> The new era is one of more strictly business relationships, with much sentiment cut out and our special position temporarily, at least, impaired, but not totally dissipated.
>
> The Americans will remain convinced that Communism is their principal enemy and challenge. They will need Allies and on the whole they like doing business with us, provided that we talk in plain and blunt business terms. We should avoid at all costs appealing to emotion and old associations when doing business.[15]

In Whitehall, the Official Committee on the Middle East added, 'One of the underlying objectives of US policy would ... be the continuance of oil supplies to NATO countries, and for this reason her policy was likely, in general, to coincide with our interests.'[16]

The litmus test for Macmillan was an arrangement on atomic weapons. A reduction in expenditure on conventional forces, a priority for Macmillan's economic plans, could only be achieved if Britain developed its bomber and missile capabilities.[17] This in turn rested upon access to US technology, access which had been restricted since the 1946 McMahon Act. In his memoirs, Macmillan spelled out the linkage between 'alliance' and nuclear co-operation:

> The most urgent, and at the same time most delicate, task which confronted me on becoming Prime Minister was to repair and eventually to restore our old relationships with Washington. With this was closely linked the new defence organisation and strategy for the United Kingdom, which must now take full account of the impact of nuclear weapons.[18]

Visiting Washington at the end of January, Minister of Defence Duncan Sandys tried to prepare the ground in discussions with his US counterpart, Charles Wilson. When Wilson assessed that US legislation 'could not be changed at the moment', Sandys did not challenge the statement but reminded Wilson that, if active forces were decreased, then the amount of firepower per soldier had to be increased. He also conceded that atomic bombs could remain in US custody if they were placed on British airfields, a point Wilson eagerly endorsed.[19]

On the eve of Macmillan's first summit with Eisenhower in Bermuda, *The Times* reiterated the link between the personal and strategic alliances:

> To complete the work of repair is, far and away, the most urgent task before the new Bermuda. Fortunately Mr Eisenhower and Mr Macmillan have known, liked and trusted each other in the past, and they can pick up the partnership without formalities. . . .
>
> [The task is] to ensure closer cooperation at all levels. A fuller exchange of atomic information could be the first welcome result: assurances in the past have not always led to action lower down.[20]

The summit at Bermuda and the subsequent meeting with Eisenhower in Washington in October appeared to be unmitigated vindication for Macmillan. The first summit was presented as a personal victory, with Macmillan writing to Cabinet colleagues:

> We have not been in the dock. On the contrary, the Americans have been rather apologetic about their position. . . . The personal relations between myself and the President have been established upon a level of confidence which is most gratifying.[21]

Australian Prime Minister Robert Menzies was assured that there was 'no doubt that, as far, as the President is concerned, things are back on old footing', although Foster Dulles 'lags a little behind his Head of State'.[22]

The Washington summit, held after the shock of the Soviet launch of *Sputnik*, was a purported triumph for the strategic relationship, as the Eisenhower Administration pledged to repeal the McMahon Act and provide technical information and material for nuclear warheads to Britain. The Americans also agreed to a Declaration of Common Purpose (although they rejected Macmillan's preferred label of a Declaration of Interdependence):

> The concept of self-sufficiency is now out of date. The countries of the free world are interdependent and only in genuine part- nership, by combining their resources and sharing tasks in many fields, can progress and safety be founded. For our part, we have agreed that our two countries will henceforth act in accordance with this principle.[23]

Macmillan's skill at self-promotion, both at the time and subse- quently, ensured that the nuclear deal achieved legendary status, but closer examination raises doubts about the British achievement. The preliminary agreement at Bermuda to station sixty US Thor intermediate-range ballistic missiles on British soil, ostensibly under a dual-key system, provided a secure base for American strategists. After the summit, Eisenhower thanked Macmillan profusely, 'We are pleased that you found your way clear to allow United King- dom bases to be used for AQUATONE if it should at some time become necessary.'[24] The benefits of US nuclear technology soon paled in the face of mounting costs for a British deterrent; in the end, London would be dependent on the provision of US weaponry.

In 1955 Macmillan had foreseen the danger of relying on a US deterrent:

> I think this is a very dangerous doctrine. . . . Politically it surren- ders our power to influence American policy and then, strategi- cally and tactically, it equally deprives us of any influence over the selection of targets and the use of our vital striking forces. The one, therefore, weakens our prestige and our influence in the world, and the other might imperil our safety.[25]

Yet, in the end, Macmillan's 'success' was British dependence on the US. In January 1957 he admitted to the Defence Commit- tee that Britain would not use strategic or tactical nuclear weap- ons 'except in wars in which the US were engaged as our Allies or were otherwise giving us their full support' although he held on to the fig leaf that 'we should . . . have within our control sufficient weapons to provide a deterrent influence independent of the United States'.[26] The British Chiefs of Staff were blunter in their assess- ment on the eve of the Washington agreement nine months later:

We must either accept that we were a junior partner of the US (in which case we should have an unbalanced programme ourselves) or we must stick to our balanced programme (which, it was clear, we had not the capacity to support). It was difficult to compromise between two alternatives and the Prime Minister was in favour of the first, although if we once accepted that position it would be extremely difficult ever to return to a balanced programme.[27]

Macmillan had achieved no more than 'a quid pro quo for . . . the provision of "real estate" in the United Kingdom for such things as intermediate-range ballistic missile sites'.[28] As Geoffrey Crowther, the managing director of *The Economist*, had predicted in *Foreign Affairs* at the start of 1957, 'alliance' would be based on the US as the 'only member that has any substantial freedom to choose its course of action for itself'.[29]

Diplomatic concessions made by Macmillan to the Americans were even more significant. Ever since it had recognized Communist China in 1949, Britain had held out against giving up its 'independent' line on Peking, quarrelling with Washington over 'strategic' exports and China's admission to the United Nations. Macmillan agreed that Britain would now defer to US wishes. In the Middle East, Britain stood aside as the US took over the Western strategy of dealing with Gamal Abdel Nasser; Macmillan's wish to cut the Egyptian President down immediately was replaced by unilateral US activity, such as the initiative to overthrow the Syrian government. US freedom of action in Latin America and Southeast Asia was implicitly, if not explicitly, confirmed.

The most telling effect of Macmillan's quest for the Special Relationship was never mentioned at Bermuda. The Prime Minister, in effect, had chosen between an Anglo-American 'alliance' and a British relationship with the emerging EEC. Whitehall had remained aloof from talks about the EEC since 1955 – Macmillan, as Foreign Secretary, had overseen the policy of detachment – but in the aftermath of Suez, some British Ministers, supported by officials, sought a review of Britain's Atlanticist position.

On 9 January 1957, as the Six were negotiating the Treaty of Rome, Foreign Secretary Selwyn Lloyd put a memorandum before the Cabinet. He argued that Britain, diplomatically and militarily, should work through the Western European Union rather than NATO:

Such an association would not be a 'Third Force' between America and Russia. Its object would rather be to develop into one powerful group within the North Atlantic Treaty Organisation almost as powerful as America and perhaps in friendly rivalry with her.

Then Lloyd took a stance on the nuclear issue which would differ radically from Macmillan's later policy. Because Britain was ahead of other European powers in the nuclear field, the Foreign Secretary claimed, 'We should be in a strong position to see that the arrangements were made on our terms.' While present links with the US and Canada should be maintained 'in substantially their present form', Lloyd foresaw that Britain would 'enlist not only the resources and skill of our European neighbours, particularly the Germans, but also their finance'. He put the question to the Cabinet, 'Might it not be better... to pool our resources with our European allies so that Western Europe as a whole might become a third nuclear power comparable with the US and the Soviet Union?... A policy on these lines need not imply antagonism towards the US; it might well be developed in cooperation with them.'[30]

Lloyd's proposals were sharply challenged by senior Ministers. The Lord President, Lord Salisbury, asserted, 'Our main aim at the present time should be to repair the breach which had been made in Anglo-American relations by the Suez dispute.' He was supported by the Commonwealth Secretary, Lord Home, and Minister of Defence Antony Head, and there was general agreement that European co-operation should not be based on nuclear strategy.

Yet the Cabinet was far from dismissive of Lloyd's initiative, as 'strong support was expressed for the general concept of a closer association between the United Kingdom and Western Europe'. Some Ministers emphasised 'that there must be some change in the basis of Anglo-American relations' since 'it was doubtful whether the US would now be willing to accord to [Britain] alone the special position which we had held as their principal ally in the war'.

In the end, the Cabinet tried to have it every possible way, calling for political leadership in Europe, Commonwealth cohesion, and maintenance of the Anglo-American 'alliance'. Ministers agreed to resume consideration of Lloyd's memorandum. They also instructed the Foreign Secretary to communicate their views to Eden. It was an empty injunction, of course, since the Prime Minister was already preparing his resignation.

Unfortunately, Macmillan's position is not recorded in the Cabinet minutes. Nor is it clear whether Macmillan, anticipating Eden's departure, recognized that Lloyd's proposal would have to be taken up by a new government, possibly under his leadership. What is clear is that Macmillan, once in Number 10, moved quickly along the line proposed by Salisbury. Preparing for a summit in Paris which would feature discussion of the European common market, Macmillan stressed that the visit would be packaged 'primarily in an European context' as it was 'important that we should not give the impression that we are forming an Anglo-French front vis-à-vis the US before the Bermuda meeting'.[31] The British delegation would threaten 'that, unless greater consideration could be shown for our point of view in the future, it might well be that we should find it impossible to enter an European Free Trade Association'.[32]

By the time Macmillan returned from Bermuda, the die was cast. A Cabinet committee concluded, 'There is another feature of Britain's present position in the world which we must not allow ourselves to forget, we have accepted partnership and alliance with the United States as a basic fact of life. In the strategic sphere indeed we have accepted America as the major partner.'[33]

The Treasury foresaw the dangers of British isolation with the Six's completion of the Treaty of Rome, signed within days of Bermuda, noting:

> This exposes the United Kingdom to a most dangerous situation. If the Customs Union comes into existence and there is no Free Trade Area, this will represent a very grave economic threat to the United Kingdom. Yet, once the Customs Union Treaty has come into effect, it will become increasingly difficult for us to be sure of attaining the Industrial Free Trade Area which we need to safeguard our interests.[34]

Macmillan claimed in his memoirs that he warned the Cabinet of the seriousness of the situation, saying he intended to speak frankly to West German Chancellor Konrad Adenauer, but he offered no concessions in his policy towards the US nor did he pick up Lloyd's renewed suggestion for the Grand Design of European nations.[35] Instead, the Cabinet maintained the curious illusion that, through the European Free Trade Area, it could sustain both the Atlantic alliance and association with the European Community. Discussing the Treasury memorandum, Ministers agreed:

We must ... expect resistance to any action on our part which could be interpreted as an attempt to diminish the impetus of this movement or, by linking the new European grouping too closely with the Atlantic community, to make it less independent of the United States. Nevertheless, if this effort to establish a European 'Third Force' succeeded in its present form without our being associated in some positive fashion with the new alignment of power in Europe, the consequences would be grave. Our existing European policy would be undermined and our special relationship with the United States would be endangered if the United States believed that our influence was less than that of the European Community.[36]

Macmillan, throughout his wooing of Eisenhower, clung to this fantasy, even as the story wore thin. The official records of his meeting with Felix Gaillard, the French President du Conseil, in November 1957 cannot obscure the tension exacerbated by the Washington summit of the previous month. Macmillan insisted:

[I have] been most disappointed to find that Anglo-American intentions had been misinterpreted and that [I] and the President were suspected of a conspiracy in Washington to advance an Anglo-American hegemony. The statements in the Declaration of Interdependence were quite to the contrary. The United States and United Kingdom had not worked out anything. There were no cut-and-dried plans for presentation to NATO or anyone else.

Gaillard's reply was acidic:

The NATO Alliance consisted, on the one hand, of people residing outside the Continent of Europe who were brought into the war and, on the other hand, of people who had been invaded and humiliated. The latter had a complex. They considered themselves to be a most advanced people and would not accept to be cast in the role of infantry of footsloggers in the next war.

It was no use saying: 'Let us share the task of making a car,' and then asking France and Germany to make the windscreen and the wipers, while the United States and the United Kingdom did the technical work of making the engine, chassis, and coachwork.

When Gaillard suggested closer Anglo-French co-operation on nuclear issues, Macmillan had to face the consequences of his decision. The American commitment to repeal the McMahon Act on exchange of nuclear information extended only to Britain; there was no hope of getting the Eisenhower Administration, let alone Congress to extend the offer to France. The Prime Minister finally told Gaillard that he did 'not want to run any risk of jeopardising the amendment' of the McMahon Act. Even Gaillard's suggestion of co-operation on civil nuclear matters was turned away by Macmillan.[37]

The British government was committed to its gamble on the Special Relationship. Dependence on the United States would be paraded as interdependence, economic and military limitations would be transformed into strengths, and the tricky question of Europe would be set aside. Macmillan told a television audience in February 1958:

> The independent contribution ... gives us a better position in the world, it gives us a better position with respect to the United States. It puts us where we ought to be, in the position of a great power. The fact that we have it makes the United States pay a greater regard to our point of view, and that is of great importance.[38]

About the same time, Paul Gore-Booth, the Deputy Under-secretary for Economic Affairs in the Foreign Office, warned, 'In order to ward off the danger of our becoming a satellite we must balance our relationship with America by a closer relationship with our other friends, particularly in Europe.... In general we want the United States to remain involved as firmly as possible all round the world, but at the same time there are United Kingdom interests in defence of which we still need to retain the right and ability to act for ourselves.'[39] Such counsel would go unheard until it was far too late.

Of course Macmillan's emphasis on the Special Relationship in 1957 was not solely responsible for Britain's exclusion from Europe in the 1960s. The policy of limited co-operation with the Messina Conference had already damaged London's position before Macmillan's accession to power. Still, the new Prime Minister's deci-

sion to put his future and that of his government in the hands of
the Anglo-American 'alliance' confirmed the divergence between
Britain and Europe. Even Macmillan's reverent biographer Alistair
Horne notes this, although without considering the implications:

> Macmillan's diary ... reveals a fundamental parting of the ways
> in Franco-British relations. Britain henceforth would pursue the
> road of the Special Relationship; France would go separately and
> – implicitly – on a lower level, to Washington. Macmillan clearly
> and consciously gave the London–Washington entente priority
> over relations with Europe.[40]

Even after Macmillan belatedly tried and failed to bring Britain
into Europe, his vain equation of a personal relationship with the
President with an immutable Anglo-American alliance would be
the overriding priority. As he wrote to John F. Kennedy after their
last meeting in July 1963:

> I felt that it was a wonderful example of the way in which coun-
> tries, and perhaps even more individuals, who trust each other
> can work rapidly and effectively together. ... It has been a great
> pride to me to feel that in that at least we have been in part
> equal to the Churchill–Roosevelt relationship at the most criti-
> cal moment of history.[41]

Alistair Horne blithely accepts this contention and effuses, 'One
is entitled to speculate what [Macmillan and Kennedy] might have
gone on jointly to achieve, had not both been removed prema-
turely.'[42] To the contrary, advance in Britain's relations with Europe
could only be achieved after the impediment of Macmillan's 'Special Relationship' had been removed. It was in 1973, when a later
Conservative government would bring Britain into the EEC, that
Macmillan could give the Europe-first strategy the fullest support
in the concluding page of his memoirs:

> It is in the new unity of Europe that we may, with full loyalty to
> our Commonwealth responsibilities, play our part to meet what-
> ever unknown dangers and to exploit whatever new possibilities
> the next 50 years may bring.[43]

NOTES

1. I am grateful to Nick Gray, a postgraduate student at the University of Birmingham, for access to his research on the Macmillan government and to Alistair Morey, a PhD candidate at the University of Birmingham, for his comments on the draft.
2. 'Common Interest', *The Times*, 26 February 1993, p. 15.
3. 'Not So Special', *Financial Times*, 26 February 1993, p. 14.
4. 'Common Interest', *The Times*, p. 15.
5. R. W. Apple, 'Just Good Friends, Nothing Special', *The Times*, 26 February 1993, p. 14.
6. Alan Dobson, *Anglo-American Relations in the Twentieth Century* (London: Routledge, 1995), p. 177.
7. Nicholas J. Cull, 'Churchill, and the Myth of a Special Relationship', *Parliamentary Brief*, October 1995, p. 88.
8. Draft to UK delegation to Southeast Asian Treaty Organization, 14 February 1957, Public Record Office (hereafter cited as PRO), FO371/127748/V1051/40.
9. Eisenhower minute, 16 December 1955, DDE, Ann Whitman Series, Ann Whitman Diary, Box 7.
10. Foster Dulles to Macmillan, 20 December 1955, DDE, John Foster Dulles Papers, Subject, Alphabetical, Box 11, Eden–Macmillan–Lloyd Correspondence (2).
11. Macmillan to Eden, 26 September 1956, PRO, PREM11/1102.
12. Harold Macmillan, *Riding the Storm* (London: Macmillan, 1971), p. 196.
13. Eisenhower to Humphrey, 21 November 1956, DDE, Ann Whitman Series, DDE Diaries, Box 19, November 1956 Telephone Calls.
14. Eisenhower to Churchill, 27 November 1956, DDE, Ann Whitman Series, International, Box 18, Winston Churchill.
15. Washington to Foreign Office, Despatch 411, 28 December 1956, PRO, PREM11/2189.
16. OME (57)3, 2 February 1957, PRO, CAB134/2338.
17. D (57)2, 18 January 1957, PRO, CAB131/18.
18. Macmillan, *Riding the Storm*, p. 240.
19. Record of Sandys–Wilson meeting, 28 January 1957, PRO, FO371/129306.
20. *The Times*, 21 March 1957, 11.
21. Quoted in Horne, p. 26.
22. Macmillan to Menzies, 25 March 1957, PRO, PREM11/1789.
23. Macmillan, *Riding the Storm*, p. 757.
24. Eisenhower to Macmillan, 23 March 1957, PRO, PREM11/1763.
25. Quoted in Andrew Pierre, *Nuclear Politics: The British Experience with an Independent Strategic Force* (London: Oxford University Press, 1972), p. 93.
26. D (57) 2nd meeting, 27 January 1957, PRO, CAB131/18.
27. COS (57) 81st meeting, 21 October 1957, PRO, DEFE4/101.
28. Joint Planning Staff, JP (57) Note 12, 'Common Defence Policy for UK/US', 21 October 1957, PRO, DEFE6/45.

29. Geoffrey Crowther, 'Rebuilding the Alliance', *Foreign Affairs*, January 1957, p. 173.
30. CP (57) 6, 'The Grand Design', 5 January 1957, PRO, CAB129/84; CM 3 (57), 9 January 1957, PRO, CAB128/30.
31. Foreign Office to Paris, Cable 473, 27 February 1957, PRO, FO371/130646.
32. GEN580/1, 'The Common Market and the Free Trade Association', 8 March 1957, PRO, CAB13/123.
33. OI (57) 23, 26 March 1957, PRO, CAB134/2319.
34. Thorneycroft memorandum, CP (57)106, 30 April 1957, PRO, CAB129/84.
35. Macmillan, *Riding the Storm*, p. 435; Lloyd to Macmillan, 28 May 1957, PRO, PREM11/1841.
36. CC (57) 37, 2 May 1957, PRO, CAB128/31.
37. Record of Macmillan–Gaillard meeting, 25 November 1957, PRO, FO371/130646.
38. Quoted in Pierre, *Nuclear Politics*, p. 178.
39. Gore-Booth memorandum, 12 February 1958, PRO, FO371/132330.
40. Horne, p. 22.
41. Quoted in Horne, p. 518.
42. Horne, p. 526.
43. Harold Macmillan, *At the End of the Day* (London: Macmillan, 1973), p. 523.

4 Opportunity Knocks: Macmillan at the Treasury, 1955–7

Lewis Johnman

The fundamental dilemma of providing any assessment of the tenure of Harold Macmillan at the Treasury lies in his short-term occupation of the office of Chancellor of the Exchequer, and in the difficulty of separating any discernible economic policy that bore Macmillan's own stamp from the use of the office itself as a springboard to the Premiership. It is worth remembering just how minor a position Macmillan held in the Churchill Cabinet of 1951; not figuring at all in the initial list and eventually appearing as the third most junior member in a Cabinet of sixteen.[1] As his official biographer has noted, 'the road upwards looked effectively blocked... to an ambitious politician'.[2] It was to be a remarkable rise from Minister of Housing in 1952 via the Ministry of Defence, Foreign Secretaryship and Chancellorship, to be Prime Minister by January 1957. Given that his Premiership has recently been described by one commentator as 'by far the best of Britain's Post-war Prime Ministers, and that his administration performed considerably better than any of their successors', his 'attitude to the economy' being such that it 'would have prevented the galloping inflation of the late 1960s and 1970s', it is perhaps time that some analysis was given to Macmillan's occupation of the Treasury in both economic and political terms.[3] It was, however, to be a Chancellorship neatly divided between the inherited economic policy of the previous administration and the developing Suez Crisis; the latter providing what John Turner has perceptively referred to as 'the opportunity'.[4]

Macmillan inherited the post of Chancellor of the Exchequer from R. A. Butler, who had held the office for four years, in December 1955. Although there exists a range of accounts of the Cabinet re-shuffle of late 1955 – not least by the protagonists themselves – many are at odds and the one insight that can be made with any certainty is that the process was very poorly handled and left plenty of room for the development of strong political resent-ments, envies and ambitions.[5] This position had, in its turn, been strongly overshadowed by the prolonged clinging to office of Churchill, which had provoked in his successor, Eden, the desire to stamp his own authority by means of a general election, but paradoxically failure to carry this through by a major reconstruction of the govern-ment either before or after the May 1955 election. When such a major re-shuffle was not undertaken, the result, as Eden's official biographer remarked, was one of 'discontent, concern and criti-cism', with one Cabinet colleague remarking that 'Anthony never built a Cabinet in his own mould. He inherited one, and then tink-ered with it.'[6] What is clear is that Eden's desire to replace Butler at the Treasury was provoked more by his desire to get Macmillan out of the Foreign Office and replace him with a Foreign Secre-tary who was more inclined to do the Prime Minister's bidding than was Macmillan. Despite the fact that the Chancellor of the Duchy of Lancaster, Lord Woolton, had told Eden to 'get rid of Butler' and had received the reply 'You are so wise', it was more Eden's distrust of Macmillan's independence of mind, than the fact that the election had had to be followed by packages of deflation-ary measures and an Autumn Budget, that prompted the move.[7]

Indeed, Eden and Macmillan had clashed most notably over the issue of Europe – where Macmillan had urged a far more positive approach to the Messina Conference than Eden was prepared to make – and, intriguingly, over the situation developing in Egypt, when Eden floated the idea of an international military force to protect the Suez Canal in the event of war between Egypt and Israel, only to be told that Macmillan did 'not propose to pursue' the idea.[8] Certainly, Butler did not demure from Eden's request in the summer of 1955 that he leave the Treasury, asking only that the Prime Minister delay the move, although this made something of a mockery of Eden's declaration in November 1955 in the House of Commons that 'In all his work my Right Hon. Friend, the Chan-cellor of the Exchequer, will continue to have my full support.'[9] In contrast to Butler's acceptance of the change, Macmillan was furious at Eden's proposal, seeing poisoned chalices all around. Concerning the move from the Foreign Office, Lord Woolton noted that 'Macmillan wondered whether his departure from the Foreign Office at a time when things were not going very well – he described them as "Eden's chickens coming home to roost" – would not give the appearance of failure', whereas on arrival at the Treasury,

Macmillan himself was to note that 'The position is much worse than I had expected. Butler had let things drift, and the reserves are steadily falling. If and when they are all expended, we have total collapse, under Harold Macmillan!'[10] Eden had, however, confided in, of all people Butler, as to how awkward he found Macmillan to deal with as Foreign Secretary. As Butler himself somewhat waspishly noted, 'The PM is an artist far more able and resolute than the newspapers give him credit for. He had, he said sedulously attempted to avoid interference with the Foreign Office. Having been there so long he found it difficult to work with so strong a character as Harold Macmillan.'[11] Whilst Butler went with relative quiescence, although not without some considerable admonishment from his friends, the irate Macmillan was to drive a very hard bargain with Eden. In Macmillan's view there was 'no point in my leaving the Foreign office to be an orthodox Chancellor of the Exchequer. I must be, if not a revolutionary, something of a reformer.' But more sinisterly, at least for Butler, if not at this stage, Eden, he insisted that he must be the 'undisputed head of the Home Front', occupying a position that was 'not inferior' to Butler, and that the latter should not be termed the 'Deputy Prime Minister'. This was a strident posture, but Eden was determined enough to affect the change that he agreed a form of words with Macmillan in that Butler 'in the absence of the Prime Minister... will continue as hitherto to preside over meetings of the Cabinet'.[12] The rise from third junior spot in the 1951 Cabinet had been meteoric indeed, and lest Eden felt that the manoeuvring had helped his own position, there was always Macmillan's statement to Woolton that 'he saw no reason why if he was going to take over all the troubles of the Treasury, he should be ruled out of the succession for the Premiership in order to ease in Butler', to disabuse him.[13] The opportunity to ditch Eden and elbow Butler aside was not to be long in arriving, but firstly Macmillan had to contend with the peculiar frailty of the British economy.

The policy which Macmillan inherited from Butler was familiar; the maintenance of full employment, stable prices, economic growth, balance of payments equilibrium and moving the pound towards convertibility. The problem lay in squaring the aims of strong economic growth and full employment – it was Butler, after all, who had predicted the doubling of the British standard of living in the next twenty-five years at the 1954 Tory party conference – with stable prices, low inflation and a steady currency.[14] Butler's April

Budget of 1955 has been termed 'a serious blunder... handing out £135 million of tax reliefs in the middle of a raging boom'.[15] Certainly Butler's sentiments in February 1955 would not have indicated a 'give away' budget. In minutes to Eden, prior to the February Statement on the economy, Butler was commenting on a deteriorating balance of payments position, largely caused by excessive demand sucking in imports, and he suggested 'a tighter monetary policy and some restraint on the proliferation of hire purchase' to check the position.[16] Accordingly, Butler decided to tighten monetary and credit policies, raising the Bank Rate, which had been at 3 per cent since May 1954, in two stages to 4.5 per cent and reintroducing hire-purchase restrictions which had been abolished the previous July.[17] With the government having allowed the Bank of England to support the rate for transferable sterling in February 1955 – widely viewed by the markets as a significant step towards convertibility – there was a general view that convertibility of sterling would be at a floating, rather than a fixed, rate. This tended towards a situation wherein a weak balance of payments position encouraged speculation against the pound, with a strong position tending to strengthen sterling. With the budget slack and the election won, the economy roared away; demand remained stubbornly unchecked, the balance of payments position, the reserves and sterling all deteriorated under various pressures.[18] By July, Butler had introduced restrictions on bank advances, cut the investment programmes of local authorities and nationalized industries and imposed new credit and hire-purchase restrictions.[19]

By September, however, the July measures were showing few signs of having had any impact and Sir Robert Hall was commenting that the economy was 'in a vicious circle which can only be broken by real deflationary action'.[20] With Butler having to reiterate at the Istanbul meeting of the International Monetary Fund (IMF) that convertibility of the pound would only be at a fixed rate, in an attempt to stem speculation against sterling, it became abundantly clear that an autumn budget could not be avoided. With senior officials, Butler worked out a series of measures designed to further dampen demand in the economy and relieve the strain on the balance of payments.[21] The Budget measures raised purchase tax by 20 per cent at all levels and extended the range of the measure, increased profits tax by 5 per cent, and sharply reduced local authority building programmes. By this stage, however, Butler knew that he was to leave the Treasury and the internal debates on the economy over the summer, where Eden had canvassed the views of various Cabinet colleagues, had been marked by the tabling of a paper by Harold Macmillan, which Eden suggested should be circulated as a Cabinet paper. Entitled 'Dizzy with Success', Macmillan sought in two pages to deal with the problems which the Treasury machine had been grappling with for years. The solution was simple; 'to use a variety of methods (recognising that growth is healthy in itself) calculated to prevent rank and excessive expansion. All that is wrong today is that the pace is a bit too hot.' The methods, according to the Foreign Secretary, involved reducing the basis of credit and raising the Bank Rate; abolishing all subsidies on consumption and reducing all government financed or supported schemes of capital development; achieving a 'real economy of effort' in defence; reducing tax on incomes and purchases and considering 'all schemes for making savings more attractive'. Assuming that his prescription was followed, Macmillan concluded on convertibility that:

> we might as well take the plunge. At present, we are in the absurd position that no foreigner will buy sterling against his future commitments until he needs it, because of the fixed rate. Since he doubts whether we can maintain the $2.80 rate, he holds off. He can't lose by doing so, and he may gain. But do not devalue to a fixed rate. You won't be able to hold it. Get some flexibility.[22]

In common with much of Macmillan's political *oeuvre* this was a bravura performance, mixing as it did hard analysis with seemingly incontrovertible solutions, in a tone that suggested that things were nowhere near as bad as they seemed. Certainly the upbeat tone of the paper was in marked contrast to other contributions and to a somewhat crisis-ridden air surrounding the government. How far it played on Eden's mind in the re-shuffle is difficult to ascertain, it probably ranked below his desire to get Macmillan out of the Foreign Office, although moving both Butler and Macmillan at the same time doubtless had its appeal. It was not long before Macmillan would have the opportunity to put his economic ideas into practice.

The confidence of August, however, was not to carry over into the New Year. In his first statement to the Cabinet, Macmillan's mood was drear. Reviewing the course of events and policy since February 1955, his view was that the trade figures for November and December failed to indicate that the pressure was being relieved. Rather than the required surplus of £250–300 million, the forecast was for a deficit in 1955 of £100 million: figures which, in Macmillan's mind, supported 'the view that our position is getting worse'. With the gold and dollar reserves standing at $2,120 million, just above the critical level of $1,500–2,000 million, they were 'in danger of falling so low that confidence in our ability to maintain the value of sterling will be lost'. The new Chancellor's conclusion was that the government was 'faced with the necessity of taking immediate action over a wide field of a more drastic character than has hitherto seemed necessary. Time is running out.'[23] Throughout January, Macmillan kept up the pressure, commenting that the country had reached 'the same vulnerable position as a private business which persisted in trading beyond its means', calling in minister after minister and pressing for cuts in expenditure, and telling the Economic Policy Committee that failure of the policy would mean a siege economy and 'the final end of the attempt to run our economic affairs on more or less freely organised lines'.[24] By the end of the month, Macmillan was seeking Cabinet sanction for a wide ranging package of measures well in advance of the budget on the grounds that what was needed was 'to take a substantial block from the load now pressing on our resources'. The blend was much as Macmillan had previously outlined but with greater detail and vastly increased scope. The suggestions were *inter alia*: a severe curtailment in the investment programmes of the nationalized industries and local authorities; cuts in all programmes financed by central government, with the abolition of the bread and milk subsidies and a sustained brake on investment in the private sector.[25] The scale of this, however, gave Eden pause for thought. Commenting that there had been several economic statements and two budgets, the Prime Minister's view was that 'the more I feel that if it can possibly be avoided it would be a real advantage to hold over any further statement or action until the Budget'. The budget, Eden thought, should be 'a great occasion, and the only one'.[26]

Macmillan's view was that 'it would be nice if we could do everything in a single operation', but that this was impossible. Citing both the parliamentary timetable and that for setting the local authority expenditure programmes, Macmillan asked for a package of measures in mid-February, including the abolition of the bread and milk subsidies and an increase in the Bank Rate to 5.5 per cent and that the budget should 'give some stimulus to savings and to incentives for the middle classes'.[27] Despite the fact that this argument between Eden and Macmillan continued to rumble on, Macmillan conceded to his officials 'that a startling or revolutionary Budget is off'.

The failure to bring forward a Capital Gains Tax denied Macmillan his budget theme of 'Slash the Speculator' and, accordingly, Macmillan asked his officials to work on the theme of savings and incentives. However, the disagreement between Macmillan and Eden continued to dog efforts to prepare an economic package. In February, Macmillan returned to the attack, stating that a rise in Bank Rate alone would be interpreted as a sign of weakness, whereas a package of measures plus a rise in Bank Rate would be taken as a sign of strength. As Eden temporized on the issue of subsidies, Macmillan's reply was that in being asked 'to abandon the most significant item' he was being expected to 'take a responsibility which, with all my desire to help you, I cannot accept'.[28] Eden was finding that he had swapped a resolute and independent minded Foreign Secretary for a similar Chancellor. When the issue went to Cabinet on 13 February, the divide was clear, with Eden arguing that ending the subsidies would make any appeals on wage restraint impossible, whereas Macmillan continued to argue that the proposed action was necessary 'in order to check on the inflationary movement' with 'the national accounts . . . tending towards insolvency'.[29] Eden's suggestion was that he could accept the package, including raising the Bank Rate but without the removal of the subsidies, which should go into the budget.[30] Over the next two days the Cabinet continued to debate the issue, with Macmillan arguing that he would agree to a policy of phasing the subsidies out if his colleagues would agree to the suspension of tax allowances on investment. Not surprisingly, this infuriated the man who had introduced them, Butler, who commented that it was a 'retrograde step' and that he 'deplored the necessity for adopting this course'. But it was to be of no avail and the Cabinet accepted the new package with its announcement due on 17 February.[31]

By the end of March, however, although the Treasury was conceding that the measures were showing signs of working, Macmillan resumed his assault on the Prime Minister in the run up to the budget, by stating that the only way in which the economy could be restored 'is by really getting down to the defence problem'. Commenting that 'we get no defence from the defence expendi-

ture', Macmillan alleged that 'we know that it is defence expenditure which has broken our backs'. Accordingly, the Chancellor pressed
the Prime Minister for 'a new approach to the whole defence
problem', otherwise, he would have to 'abandon all ideas of giving
some reliefs in the Budget and content myself with a swingeing
increase of taxation'.[32] This approach now crystallized into a debate
on the shape and content of the budget with Eden's private secretary,
Frederick Bishop, commenting that whilst a budget which cut government expenditure would please government supporters, he did not
think that they 'would particularly like the cut to be on defence'.
Bishop's advice to Eden was that the budget should be 'temporis-
ing' with 'some little encouragement and incentive to the middle
classes'.[33] The Treasury, by contrast, as the Permanent Secretary,
Sir Edward Bridges minuted to Macmillan, believed that 'the safe
side of this Budget is the stiff side'.[34] Prodigiously armed with the
Treasury's latest statistics, Macmillan confided in the Prime Minister that in the view of his advisers there would be an economic
crisis between August and November. (In view of later events they
could not have known how correct they would be.) 'On present
form', as Macmillan put it, 'the betting is pretty heavy odds on
compulsory devaluation', with the only solution being increased
taxation or reductions in government expenditure to raise between
£100 and £150 million. Declaring that everybody was looking to
the budget to 'decide the issue', the Chancellor proposed a package which would raise £144 million, whilst handing out £41 million
on the savings package and allowances.[35] Eden finally had to acquiesce
and the result was a deflationary budget dressed in the language
of growth; as one commentator has noted, 'the combination of an
expansionist speech and a restrictant Budget . . . [was] . . . symptomatic
of Macmillan's whole conduct of economic policy'.[36] But in the budget
which had introduced Premium Bonds, Macmillan had not been
able to do anything about defence, although he was to return to
this issue only a few weeks later.

In the immediate wake of the budget, Macmillan had Eden agree
to a saving of £100 million in the Estimates for 1956–7. By early
May, Macmillan was chiding the Minister of Defence, Walter
Monckton, that his department was £20 million short of the £45
million which he was expected to contribute to the overall total.[37]
When the issue went to a small group of ministers later in the
month, Macmillan pressed the case that without major reductions
in defence expenditure, cuts would have to fall on the social side,

including increasing charges for school meals, milk and prescriptions, a proposal which the Lord Privy Seal, Butler, termed 'of doubtful social wisdom'. With Eden agreeing that it was 'highly desirable' to avoid further reductions in social expenditure, the hapless Monckton was told to press for what cuts he could and report to the full Cabinet in June.[38] By the time of the June meeting, Macmillan had only been able to secure £72 million of his £100 million package and as the Chief Whip, Ted Heath, commented, 'Government supporters would be disappointed that better results had not been achieved', and that 'a difficult political situation might therefore arise in the House of Commons'. The Prime Minister, this time with no prompting from Macmillan, took the view that 'the right course was to look again at the possibility of some effective cut in defence production', and accordingly, Monckton was sent off to try again.[39]

With the Suez Crisis about to intervene and come increasingly to dominate all other issues, Macmillan could have drawn some comfort from the Report of the Committee on Balance of Payments Prospects, which predicted a current surplus of £135 million for the first six months of 1956, during which period the reserves had risen by £95 million. On the basis that current deflationary policies were not relaxed, the Committee felt able to forecast an overall surplus for 1956, although it concluded that

> Even if we secure the better outrun for which we hope this year, we still have a long way to go before we have re-established our economy to the point at which exports are expanding fast enough to meet the demand for imports and provide a margin for building up the reserves.[40]

There could be no let up in the deflationary pressure and despite the increasing strain caused by Suez, Macmillan returned to the issue of defence savings. As he reported to Monckton, he was still £24 million short of his £100 million target and that whilst there was 'no intention ... of trying to find the £24 million and enough to cover the extra Defence expenditure on the Suez affair', he was still expecting defence to yield the £24 million.[41] By October, Macmillan had managed to close the gap to £5 million, with defence, health, agriculture and education all realizing further savings.[42] Thus, on the eve of the major strains of Suez falling on the economy, Macmillan with considerable insouciance, returned to the issue of defence with the new Minister of Defence, Anthony Head.

As Macmillan put it at the end of November, 'we face the most difficult economic situation in our history'. The Chancellor forecast drains on the gold and dollar reserves and an oil shortage, with 'the impact of these events' being 'felt in our economy for a long time to come'. Commenting that the circumstances made the need for economies more pressing than ever, Macmillan's view was that it was 'inevitable' that he 'should look to the Defence Budget for substantial savings'. Macmillan argued that he now needed greater savings than had been contemplated in August, and he suggested that the order of priorities which had been established in defence policy in October 1955 now needed to be radically overhauled. Macmillan's view was that the V-bomber force should be limited 'in more conservative terms' and a sustained attempt should be made to convince the Americans to contribute a greater share to the development of ground to ground ballistic missiles. Furthermore, the Suez experience had convinced Macmillan that there was now no point in even considering fighting 'local wars'. Accordingly, there should be 'major reductions in our forces in the Middle East and Far East', as the 'budgetary saving should . . . be very large – to say nothing of the effect on our balance of payments'. On the issue of global warfare, Macmillan's view was that even while this was at the bottom on defence priorities, the country could not afford to 'carry too many insurance policies'. As the Chancellor put it, the country could not 'hope to emerge from a global war except in ruins' and, accordingly, Macmillan suggested that this programme should be cut to an extent that did not diminish Britain's ability to influence world affairs and did not alienate essential allies. As Macmillan concluded: 'there is an urgent need to make real economies and to show that the Government are making them. I hope therefore that I shall very soon be able too to discuss with you the "ceiling" for the 1957–58 Defence Budget.'[43] It was an intriguing position. To be fair to Macmillan he had had the scale of defence budget in his sights for some time; but the Chancellor had been the leading cheerleader of the Suez operation and despite his protestations about the need for economies, he as much as anyone had taken the lead in imperilling the economy in the Suez Crisis.

On the eve of the Suez crisis, therefore, the condition of the economy could hardly be described as robust. Action by the Treasury followed immediately upon the nationalization of the Suez Canal on 26 July 1956. Two days later the Suez Canal Company's assets in the UK and France were frozen, Egyptian sterling balances were blocked and Egypt was expelled from the transferable account area. Only one week later, however, the Treasury was arguing that economic sanctions would take a long time to have any impact and that the key to their success was American support and action. The Treasury had not, as yet, given its full consideration to the likely economic impact of any protracted crisis, but the Chancellor's position was already fixed as the American diplomat, Robert Murphy, reported:

> I have had private separate and lengthy talks with Eden and Macmillan. . . . They said British Government has decided to drive Nasser out of Egypt. The decision they declared is firm. They expressed simple conviction military action is necessary and inevitable. . . . Macmillan indulged in much graphic discussion on British past history and stressed that if they had to go down now the Government and he believed British people would rather do so on this issue and become perhaps another Netherlands. To do another Munich leading to progressive deterioration of ME position and in end the inevitable disaster is he said something he Eden and his colleagues in Government are simply not prepared to do.

This telegram from Murphy to the American Secretary of State, Dulles, somewhat belies the accounts which have stressed the supposed confusions over US support for British military action. Indeed, despite the fact that Murphy had 'advanced all of the considerations' which Dulles and President Eisenhower had 'raised':

> Eden, Macmillan and Lloyd showed throughout unexpected calm and no hysteria. They act as though they really have taken a decision after profound reflection. They are flexible on procedures leading up to showdown but insist over and over again that whatever conferences, arrangements, public postures and manoeuvres might be necessary, at the end they are determined to use force.[44]

This message from Murphy to Dulles, drew from Eisenhower to Eden, the President's 'personal conviction' of the 'unwisdom even of contemplating the use of military force', believing 'that the American reaction would be severe and that great areas of the world would share that reaction'.[45] Thus, as early as the last day of July, positions had been struck which would remain pretty consistent throughout the crisis; certainly Macmillan's position would remain relatively unaffected by the impact of the crisis on the economy.

By 8 August, the Joint Permanent Secretary at the Treasury, Sir Edward Bridges, warned Macmillan that the Suez situation was already putting the balance of payments and gold and dollar reserves under considerable strain, and he warned that even if the London Conference were successful this was likely to remain the case. The more protracted the crisis became the more the proportionate strain on the economy was likely to be. To Bridges:

> The action to be taken is almost totally different according to the situation which we are faced with – a limited war, or a not so limited war – a war in which we go it alone, or a war in which we have the Americans with us from the onset. Frankly, I doubt whether anything much can be done under this head until we can know more clearly the assumptions which should be made . . . it may be that there are one or two essential matters that should be looked at to avoid our being caught short.[46]

It was a prescient view: Macmillan knew the assumptions but did not inform his officials, and he knew the Treasury advice but did not inform the Cabinet. Macmillan did ask the Treasury to work on a package of contingency measures, which included a 6*d.* rise in the rate of income tax, an increase of between 6*d.* and 1*s.* in petrol duty, increases in tobacco duty and perhaps on purchase and profit taxes. Given that any military venture would be bound to raise government expenditure, the Treasury was gloomy as to the efficacy of monetary policy and they also considered raw material import and exchange controls, along with the possible recourse to a fully floating exchange rate and 'a really big step backwards from convertibility'. The Treasury concluded that 'we are not in at all a happy position to bear any great degree of extra strain on our resources. Our resources are still dangerously low, and are certain to fall pretty sharply this month'.[47] This was a dire portent, representing as it did the utter ruin of the economic policy which the government had followed since 1951. Given the centrality of trying to edge sterling towards convertibility, its strength or otherwise was widely taken as a crude measure of the country's economic strength; therefore, anything which tended to actively encourage speculation against sterling had been anathema to previous Chancellors. There is little doubt that had the Treasury's view gone to Cabinet then there may well have been rather more reluctance to support military action against Egypt.

By early September, the Treasury had become thoroughly alarmed at the prospect of unilateral British action. Bridges outlined two alternative scenarios: the first envisaged Britain acting in accordance with United Nations wishes and overt support from the USA, Commonwealth and other countries; the second, rather prophetically, foresaw Britain, France and one or two other countries acting in opposition to the UN, USA, Commonwealth and other countries. As Bridges saw the situation:

> It seems to us that unless we can secure at least US support and a fairly unified Commonwealth then it is not possible to predict either the exact timing or the magnitude of the strains that are likely to come on our currency. At the worst, however, the strains might be so great that, whatever precautionary measures were taken we should be unable to maintain the value of the currency.... What this points to therefore is the vital necessity from the point of view of the currency and our economy of ensuring that we do not go it alone, and that we have the maximum US support.

This memorandum, with its trenchant warnings, is annotated by Macmillan with a laconic 'Yes: this is just the trouble the US are being very difficult.'[48] Remarkably enough, having had copious advice from the Treasury over the last six weeks and armed with this latest gloomy prediction, Macmillan went to Cabinet on 11 September, four days after receiving the Treasury's memo and one day after annotating it, and urged the Cabinet towards a military solution. Macmillan argued that:

> This was of great importance from the point of view of the national economy. If we could achieve a quick and satisfactory settlement of this issue, confidence in sterling would be restored; but if a settlement was long delayed the cost and the uncertainty would undermine our financial position.

This was an intriguing reformulation of the advice tendered by Bridges, which omitted the *sine qua non* of the Treasury mandarin's memorandum, the absolute necessity of having American support.

By the end of September, the Treasury was contemplating what action it could take if the drain on reserves continued. Among the possible options which they and the Bank of England considered were: the breaking up of the transferable account area and a reversion to a bilateral system of payments; the depreciation of sterling, either through devaluation or letting the rate float; and the possibility of approaching the International Monetary Fund for a fund drawing and claiming the Waiver on interest payments under the US Loan Agreement. Most of these options were considered to be as problematic as the problem they were attempting to solve. Contributing to this discussion the Chief Economic Advisor, Sir Robert Hall, remarked that 'sterling could hardly remain a currency in which people would hold substantial balances if we had another devaluation so soon after 1949' and there was general agreement that parity should be held as long as it was possible.[49] Throughout October, as the military situation developed, the Treasury continued to report somewhat bleakly to Macmillan that at least tacit American sympathy was essential if Britain's position were not to become catastrophic. Sir Leslie Rowan, the Second Secretary at the Treasury, estimated a loss of $80 million for October, and calculated that the reserves would fall below $2,000 million by the end of the year, what he termed 'a rather crucial dividing line'. The Treasury and the Bank of England were split over whether an approach should be made to the IMF, with the Treasury favouring an early approach on the grounds that it would not appear as if the country had been forced into such action, whereas the Governor of the Bank argued that an approach would, in and of itself, be construed as a sign of weakness. Both, however, were united in the view that without reasonable Anglo-American relations, either an approach to the IMF or a potential claim on the Waiver, would be more difficult than otherwise.[50] On 30 October, the day after Israel had attacked Egypt, and the day on which the Anglo-French ultimatums had been issued, Macmillan chaired a meeting of senior Treasury and Bank of England officials and declared that the policy was 'to remain firm and see the issue through'.[51]

Before the British and French landings on 5 November, it was becoming very difficult to remain firm and see the issue through.

By 2 November, the Treasury estimated that $50 million had been lost in two days, and reasoned that if the Canal were closed and the pipelines cut, the country would face a shortage of oil amounting to 25 per cent of total supplies, with the likely cost of obtaining alternative supplies costing between $500 and $700 million per year. Contemplating 'emergency action', the Treasury again rehearsed a familiar set of options, including approaching the IMF, imposition of a range of physical controls and exchange rate policy. Despite intensive analysis, the officials believed that they had reached 'a somewhat negative set of conclusions', in that the only way in which the capital outflow could be stemmed was by going to the IMF, whilst addressing the balance of payments problem through fiscal and monetary measures. The first intimation that the Cabinet had of how precarious the economic situation had become, occurred in the midst of a discussion of the ultimatums to be issued to Israel and Egypt, and the likelihood of this causing 'offence to American public opinion'. Macmillan had observed, with the absolute minimum of detail that 'Our reserves of gold and dollars were still falling at a dangerously rapid rate; and, in view of the extent to which we might have to rely on American economic assistance, we could not afford to alienate the US Government more than was absolutely necessary.'[52] Given the view of his officials and his own knowledge, Macmillan's use of the word 'might' is coy in the extreme. By the night of 5 November, however, Macmillan was telephoning the US, in advance of a Cabinet meeting in London on the morning of 6 November, in an attempt to arrange support for sterling, only to be told that no such support would be forthcoming without a cease-fire. With $85 million having been lost from the reserves in the first week of November, Macmillan was facing what his officials had been predicting for months. One commentator has remarked on the absence of 'stark' memoranda from Treasury officials for the days 5–6 November, but given that the officials had been telling their political master exactly what was likely to happen, with increasing force since 8 August, the absence seems of little note.[53] Before entering Cabinet on 6 November, Macmillan told the Foreign Secretary, Selwyn Lloyd, that 'in view of the financial and economic pressures, we must stop'.[54] According to Butler, Macmillan had 'switched overnight from being the foremost protagonist of intervention to being the leading influence for disengagement'.[55]

With a cease-fire arranged for midnight GMT on 6 November, worse was to come for the Chancellor, in that he was shortly to learn that a cease-fire, of itself, would not be enough to satisfy the Americans, but that the price of economic assistance would be withdrawal from Egypt. The Treasury, via the British Ambassador in the US, Sir Harold Caccia, sought the likely American response to a request for standby arrangements with the IMF of $236 million on the gold tranche, $325 million on the first credit tranche and an approach to the Export–Import Bank in New York. Caccia's reply was that 'there is at present no possibility of aid, which in any event would not be available until after further Congressional action and I think we must take it that there is at present no possibility of an EXIM bank loan'.[56] The stumbling block for the British Cabinet was that in an effort to retain some dignity and some control over the situation, they insisted on British troops being allowed to take part in the United Nations Emergency Force, then being assembled to oversee the Israeli–Egyptian cease-fire. Try as they might, however, with Selwyn Lloyd dispatched to New York to argue the case, British participation would not be countenanced by the UN or the USA. The situation in London, moreover, was continuing to deteriorate with the new Permanent Secretary at the Treasury, Sir Roger Makins, informing Macmillan, that in the view of the Governor of the Bank of England, sterling was 'a major casualty of recent events and that radical treatment ... [would] ... be required to save it', with the most important ameliorative measure 'an improvement in our relations with the Americans'.[57] Treasury and Bank officials were gloomy as to the prospects, noting that:

> We cannot continue to lose reserves at the present rate, and continue at the same time to hold sterling at its present value ... the cohesion of the Commonwealth would be severely tested and there might be dangerous consequences to the structure of NATO arising from our inability to meet its commitments.

The officials, moreover, were in no doubt, as they had consistently been, as to the necessary steps: 'the most important and adequate measure which might be taken involves an approach to the United States and would require a friendly and compliant attitude on their part'.[58] A view that was reinforced the following day, when Rowan informed Makins that 'we should take every practicable step in other spheres of policy, eg withdrawal of troops from Egypt, to ensure the opening at the earliest possible date of general conversations with the United States and preferably at the highest level'.[59] Still the Cabinet tried to cling to participation in the UNEF as a face-saving device.

Macmillan now began to act in a manner which suggests that if he had not engineered 'the opportunity' he certainly perceived it. He and the Tory grandee Lord Salisbury called on the American Ambassador, Winthrop Aldrich, at his official residence in London. With Eden having announced that he was to go to Jamaica to 'rest', Lloyd in New York and Butler acting as Prime Minister, Macmillan now acted sedulously to cultivate American opinion. In the course of a long conversation with Aldrich, much of which was political window dressing, Macmillan revealed the economic figures to the ambassador, in advance of telling the Cabinet and indicated that a change of policy was imminent. Aldrich drew the conclusion 'that the British Cabinet is prepared to withdraw from Egypt now and leave to the UN the settlement of the problems involved in the relations between Israel and the Arab world and the problems relating to the operation of the Canal'.[60] This was remarkable in that it was not the policy which was being followed, and indeed, foretold a change in that policy. But, the same evening, 18 November, Macmillan was back in Ambassador's residence, although this time alone. If the earlier conversation had left Aldrich 'wondering whether . . . some sort of movement is on foot in the Cabinet to replace Eden', the second could have left him in no doubt. As he telegraphed to Washington:

> Macmillan came to residence tonight at his request. . . . Eden has had physical breakdown and will have to go on vacation immediately, first for one week and then for another, and this will lead to his retirement. Government will be run by triumvirate of Butler, Macmillan and Salisbury. While Macmillan did not say so specifically, I gather that eventual set up will be Butler Prime Minister, Macmillan Foreign Secretary, Lloyd Chancellor of the Exchequer, with Salisbury remaining Lord President of Council. Possibly Macmillan might be Prime Minister. First action after Eden's departure for reasons of health will be on withdrawal of British troops from Egypt. Macmillan said, 'if you can give us a fig leaf to cover our nakedness I believe we can get a majority of the Cabinet to vote for such withdrawal without requiring conditions in connection with location of United Nations forces and methods of re-opening and operating Canal although younger members of the Cabinet will be strongly opposed'.[61]

As yet, however, there was no Cabinet agreement on unconditional withdrawal.

It was not to be long, however, before there was, and a Cabinet which had seen nothing from the Treasury for months, began to have papers tabled with each one prophesying ever more dire consequences as a result of continued American alienation. On 20 November, Macmillan revealed to the Cabinet, for the first time, the enormity of the situation which confronted them:

> The Chancellor of the Exchequer said that the Cabinet might shortly face the grave choice of deciding whether to mobilise all our financial resources in order to maintain the sterling/dollar rate at its present level, or to let the rate find its own level with the possible consequences that sterling might cease to be an international currency.

The Cabinet was doubtless shocked to learn of the grave choice confronting them and may well have felt inclined to question what the Chancellor had been doing for months had they known the substance of earlier Treasury advice. As it was, Macmillan began the process of softening the Cabinet up to change the policy, as he had already intimated to Aldrich, stating that 'we could not look for any assistance from the US in this course until the situation in the Middle East had been sufficiently clarified to enable us to re-establish our normal political relations with the US government'.[62] Memoranda from officials, which had previously been met by profound apathy, were now assiduously produced to keep up the pressure on the Cabinet. Accordingly, a very sharp memo from Rowan to Makins and Macmillan, which declared that:

> if we are to have any real chance of succeeding in our crash action, or better still of avoiding the necessity for it the first essential is the re-establishment of relations with the United States. It is quite clear that there is a conflict between economic and political considerations, and that the longer political considerations are allowed to prevail the greater danger there is to the whole fabric of our currency[63]

served to bring the Cabinet, meeting the same day, to a position of authorizing a 'token' withdrawal of British forces. However, the Cabinet remained convinced that full withdrawal should remain contingent upon clearance of the Canal and negotiations on the future status and operation of the Canal.

But this was not enough to convince the sceptics within the State Department and the Treasury; Hoover, the Secretary of State, and Humphrey, the Economic Secretary, continually informed Caccia and Lloyd that a resumption of relations along with the provision of financial aid was contingent upon 'full compliance with UN resolutions', and that the 'introduction of UN force and phased withdrawal of UK–French force should take place without delay and . . . once this is well under way we can enter into consultation with the British on basic issues'.[64] Humphrey, however, was somewhat disingenuous in stating that he was 'profoundly shocked' by the losses in Britain and that the Americans were prepared to act as soon as 'HMG has shown in a way which the world could accept that we were conforming to rather than defying the UN'.[65] Once the political situation allowed, the US would support drawing on the gold and first credit tranches, and a loan from the EXIM bank.[66] Although an increasingly cordial relationship between Macmillan and the US administration was being built up, through the channel of Aldrich, a frosty atmosphere continued to mar Anglo-American contacts in New York and Washington. As Selwyn Lloyd reported to R. A. Butler, acting in Eden's stead,

> the hard core of policy-makers some of whom have been strongly pro-British in the past are now against us . . . if we are going to have difficulty with the Party over announcing withdrawal I think we may have to tell certain selected individuals that the Americans have no intention of lifting a finger to help preserve us from financial disaster until they are certain that we are removing ourselves from Port Said quickly.[67]

This brought to an end a week of Cabinet meetings which had fruitlessly sought some face-saving compromise allowing as dignified a withdrawal as possible. The economic pressures had, in the end, however, proved to be too strong. As Macmillan informed the Cabinet on 28 November, the situation was so bad that an approach would have to be made to the IMF, but:

> For this purpose the goodwill of the United States Government was necessary; and it was evident that this goodwill could not be obtained without an immediate and unconditional undertaking to withdraw the Anglo-French force from Port Said.[68]

Having led the *volte face*, Macmillan was now speeding it along. At the Cabinet the following day he reiterated the point, claiming that the likely loss for November would be around $270 million, with $100 million lost in the third week of the month alone.[69] Two days later, the Chancellor, by now thoroughly warmed to his theme, told the Cabinet that the reserves had fallen below the benchmark figure of $2,000 million, and that by the year end, would not be far from the lowest post-war level of $1,340 million in September 1949, the outcome of which had been devaluation. In Macmillan's view 'no fundamental improvement in the situation could be expected unless we succeeded in re-establishing normal political relations with the United States'.[70] The Cabinet acquiesced and the formal announcement was made in the House of Commons on 3 December.

There was to be further political and economic fall-out before the end of the affair. With Eden not returning to London until 14 December, Macmillan in the United States for meetings with Treasury officials could only have been delighted to learn that his cultivation of Aldrich had paid off. As Macmillan informed R. A. Butler:

> In the course of a most private conversation with Mr Humphrey, he undertook to give us all possible assistance.
>
> He said it was like a business deal. They were putting a lot of money into the re-organisation of Britain and they would hope very much that the business would be successful. But, of course, when you were reconstructing a business that was in difficulties, the personal problems could not be ruled out.
>
> I said: 'Don't you trust the board?' and he said: 'Well, since you ask me, I think it would be as well if we could deal as much as possible with the directors.' This rather cryptic observation he enlarged on to say that he would like to feel that he could always be on terms of private, and, where necessary, telephonic, communication with you and me.[71]

Explicit evidence that the American administration had at least tacitly approved of the replacement of Eden. But the ultimate prize was still some weeks away and Macmillan had to shepherd the economy through the economic crisis. By 8 December, Washington was reporting to London that 'we now look certain of getting $1,300 million from the International Monetary Fund', and commented that 'another $700 million would give us the formidable total of $2 billion'.[72] But it was to be 21 December before Macmillan was able to report, to the recently returned Eden, that the EXIM Bank had

authorized a line of credit of $500 million to Britain.[73] The Gover-
nor of the Bank of England, however, drew very firm conclusions
from the Suez affair, claiming that it had exposed to public view
weaknesses in the economy of which the Bank and Treasury had
been long aware. The economy had been moved to uneasy equilibrium, but the basic problems had been left unsolved and confidence in sterling had been maintained by only a slender margin.
To Cobbold, it was time to mount 'a radical attack on some of the
fundamentals' and he argued that 'the fundamental trouble is that
the economy and the public purse have been over-extended for
many years'. He concluded that, 'dramatic far-reaching and convincing measures were needed and that there was no point in trying to "keep up with the Jones"' in relation to political and military
affairs which would destroy the country's economic strength.[74] Eden's
view was that 'Mr Governor rather likes making our blood run
cold', and although he did concede that one of the main lessons of
Suez was that economically Britain was no longer strong enough
to 'go it alone', given that Cobbold's suggestions could only be
met by checking public expenditure, he saw this as raising 'acute
political difficulties'.[75] Eden then asked his Chancellor if there were
any way of easing the burden on sterling, to which Macmillan replied that:

> There is no way of avoiding the dangers which come from our
> being bankers to the sterling area. We have inherited an old family
> business which used to be very profitable and sound. The trouble
> is that the liabilities are four times the assets. In the old days a
> business of this kind, like Coutt's or Cox's bank would have been
> sold to one of the big five. The trouble is I do not know who is
> to buy the sterling area banking system. I tried it out on Humphrey
> but he was not taking it. So we must either carry on the business
> with all its risks, or wind it up and pay 5s in the £.[76]

Stated with typical insouciance, Macmillan was arguing that the
issues of confidence and the strain on sterling would simply have
to be borne.

This was to be almost the last exchange between Eden as Prime
Minister and the man who was to supplant him, but not quite. Only
two days before his resignation as Prime Minister, Eden could not
resist annotating a memorandum by Macmillan on the 'State of
the Economy' with his view that 'I do not think that the events of

Suez can be reckoned as a tactical defeat'.[77] But for some time, the state of the economy had been taking second place to a bigger prize, that of replacing Eden as Prime Minister. The manoeuvring had began even before Eden had left for his 'rest' in Jamaica, and it had continued thereafter, and it was to rebound to Butler's disadvantage. To the casual, and indeed, to the informed observer, if the press reports following Eden's resignation are anything to go by, it appeared that Butler was the natural successor to Eden in the same way that the latter had been to Churchill. The end of his spell at the Treasury, however, had been marked by firstly overheating the economy and then having to take strong deflationary measures to correct it and this undoubtedly tarnished his reputation. Still, as the man who had 'acted' as Prime Minister in the absence of both Churchill and Eden, and then of Eden alone, it was widely assumed that Butler would inherit. This view, however, took no account of views in the Conservative Party on Butler's performance in the absence of Eden. He had, at best, been a lukewarm supporter of the Suez operation, although loyal to Eden, and it had fallen to Butler to chair a Cabinet and defend a policy in the House of Commons, unconditional withdrawal, which was deeply unpopular in the wider party.[78] Following an announcement in the Commons on 22 November, which began softening the Party up for full withdrawal, Butler and Macmillan were due to address the backbench 1922 Committee the same evening. It was to be, according to Butler's biographer, 'a highly expensive mistake', with Butler speaking 'briefly, sombrely and somewhat flatly', whereas Macmillan produced 'a veritable political organ voluntary lasting thirty-five minutes – pulling out every stop and striking every majestic chord', and it certainly had its impact. In the view of the then backbench MP Enoch Powell:

> One of the most horrible things that I remember in politics was seeing the two of them at that 1922 Committee Meeting – seeing the way in which Harold Macmillan, with all the skill of the old actor manager, succeeded in false-footing Rab. The sheer devilry of it verged upon the disgusting.[79]

It may not have been exactly a defining moment, but Macmillan had taken another step towards the Premiership. Unlike Butler, no taint of ambivalence over Suez attached to Macmillan, he had been amongst the strongest advocates of force. His apostasy could be disguised as a simple recognition of the facts and, even so, it was Butler, not Macmillan, who had been acting head of the administration when unconditional withdrawal was announced.

The denouement, when it came, was brusque. As Eden's biographer has commented on the Prime Minster's first appearance in the House of Commons: 'at that moment one knew it was all over'.[80] The Christmas recess then intervened and although the Chief Whip and the Chairman of the Party both thought that Eden could get through to the summer recess, Macmillan had told Butler that younger members of the Cabinet 'did not think Eden could or would go on'. A fact which in Butler's mind became linked with 'frequent talks and reunions . . . in the study at No 11' and 'a secret meeting of four Cabinet Ministers . . . on the very day the public drama of Eden's resignation began to unfold'.[81] Ostensibly, Eden had been told, on the basis of a number of medical opinions, that if he did not resign then he would die. Eden told his last Cabinet that he was to resign that evening, 9 January, and left the Cabinet Room with Butler and Macmillan. The rest of the Cabinet was then asked by Lord Salisbury, in the presence of the Lord Chancellor, Lord Kilmuir, as to their preference for the succession. The result produced an eleven to three majority for Macmillan. He saw the Queen the next day, 10 January, and the deed was done; Macmillan was Prime Minister.

It is impossible to separate Macmillan's tenure at the Treasury from his own breathtaking rise through the Cabinet ranks; rising from junior minister in 1951 to be the incumbent of two of the highest offices of state by 1955–6. Furthermore, assessing Macmillan's record as Chancellor, just over a year in office and with only one budget, is rendered all the more problematic in that it is inextricably linked with the political dynamics of both his rise and the opportunity represented by Suez. It is certain that Macmillan could do very little else than continue the policies inherited from Butler, but there are strong indications that he wanted to stamp his own authority on the office and, as the Sandy's Defence Review of 1957 betokens, the defence budget would have been early in the firing line. Additionally, a more pro-active line on Europe may have been forthcoming, although the later pursuit of this and Macmillan's involvement in Suez and cultivation of the US, probably doomed him and the pursuit of the policy, in General de Gaulle's eyes. The early indications of how a Macmillan Chancellorship would develop are, however, obscured by Suez. It should be noted, nevertheless, that Macmillan, on taking the job, had wrung a range of concessions and already perceived himself as being in a position to mount a challenge to Butler. It is perhaps too much to see Suez as a concerted effort by Macmillan to unseat Eden, but then it is also very difficult to account for the absence of any Treasury memoranda on the likely outcome, until almost the very end of the affair when they came thick and fast. There is also the testimony of Sir Guy Millard, Eden's Downing Street private secretary, who handled the paperwork concerning Suez, that: 'I'm not sure Eden saw the Treasury warnings. I didn't see them. Macmillan saw them, but he was a hawk.'[82]

There can, however, be no doubt that by 18 November, when Macmillan opened lines of communication to the US administration through Aldrich, that the Chancellor had the clear ambition of gaining the Prime Ministership and little else subsequently gives cause for much doubt. Once presented with 'the opportunity', Macmillan seized it with, depending on one's point of view, either an élan or ruthlessness, which, in either case, was quite breathtaking. His own biographer has noted that during the Suez Crisis one of the books which Macmillan read was Villari's biography of Machiavelli.[83] It is fair to conclude that Macmillan was well acquainted with the works of the subject.

NOTES

1. A. Howard, *RAB: The Life of R. A. Butler* (London: Jonathan Cape, 1987), p. 180.
2. A. Horne, *Macmillan, 1894–1956* (London: Macmillan, 1988), p. 332.
3. R. Lamb, *Macmillan: The Emerging Truth* (London: John Murray, 1995), p. 15.
4. J. Turner, *Macmillan* (London: Longman, 1994), pp. 95–126.
5. See, for example, H. Macmillan, *Riding the Storm, 1956–1959* (London: Macmillan, 1971), pp. 692–3; R. A. Butler, *The Art of the Possible* (London, 1971), pp. 178–82.
6. R. Rhodes James, *Anthony Eden* (London: Weidenfeld & Nicolson, 1987 edn) pp. 404–5.
7. A. Howard, op. cit., p. 15. See also J. Turner, op. cit., p. 106.
8. R. Rhodes James, op. cit., p. 410. Given the amount of material relating to the establishment of both the Common Market and the European Free Trade Association, no attempt has been made to discuss these

issues here. For the most recent analysis, cf. J. R. V. Ellison, 'Perfidious Albion? Britain, Plan G and European Integration, 1955–1956', *Contemporary British History*, vol. 10, no. 4 (1996), pp. 1–34. The relevant Treasury papers are at PRO T234/181 to 236.

9. Howard, op. cit., pp. 215–20.
10. Quoted, Turner, op. cit., p. 106.
11. Butler, op. cit., pp. 180–1.
12. Turner, op. cit., p. 106; Howard, op. cit., p. 217 and H. Macmillan, *Tides of Fortune 1945–1955* (London, 1969), pp. 692–3.
13. Quoted in Howard, op. cit., p. 221.
14. On the general performance of the economy in the 1950s cf. S. Brittan, *The Treasury under the Tories, 1951–1964* (Harmondsworth: Penguin, 1964); J. C. R. Dow, *The Management of the British Economy, 1945–1960* (Cambridge: Cambridge University Press, 1964); A. Shonfield, *British Economic Policy since the War* (Harmondsworth, 1959) and G. D. N. Worsnick and P. Ady (eds), *The British Economy in the 1950s* (Oxford: Oxford University Press, 1962).
15. Brittan, op. cit., p. 177.
16. PRO T172/2126, Chancellor's Personal Secret and Top Secret Carbons. Minute from R. A. Butler to Sir Anthony Eden, 17 February 1955.
17. For the debate on the issue cf. ibid., 'Economic Situation', Memorandum by Sir Robert Hall, 6 April 1955.
18. See PRO T171/450 to 468, 1955 Budget.
19. PRO T172/2126, op. cit., The Economic Situation and Government Expenditure. Letter from the Chancellor of the Exchequer to Ministers in Charge of Civil Spending Departments, 3 August 1955.
20. PRO PREM 11/887, memorandum from Sir Robert Hall to the Chancellor of the Exchequer, 1 September 1955.
21. PRO T234/266, Balance of Payments Prospects. Report of Committee on Balance of Payments Prospects, 14 October 1955 and 10th Meeting of Economic Policy Committee, 19 October 1955.
22. PRO CAB 129/77 CP (55) 111, The Economic Situation. Memorandum by the Secretary of State for Foreign Affairs, 30 August 1955.
23. PRO CAB 129/77 CP(56) 7, The Economic Situation. Memorandum by the Chancellor of the Exchequer, 5 January 1956.
24. PRO PREM 11/1324, UK Economic Situation, 1956.
25. PRO CAB 129/70 CP(56) 17, The Economic Situation. Memorandum by the Chancellor of the Exchequer, 21 January 1956.
26. PRO PREM 11/1324, UK Economic Situation, 1956. Letter from the Prime Minister to the Chancellor of the Exchequer, 29 January 1956.
27. PRO T172/2127, Chancellor's Personal Secret and Top Secret Carbons. Letter from the Chancellor of the Exchequer to the Prime Minister, 3 February 1956.
28. Ibid. Letters from the Chancellor of the Exchequer to the Prime Minister, 11 and 13 February 1956.
29. PRO PREM11/1324, op. cit., Cabinet, Confidential Annex CM(56)12 Minute 2, 13 February 1956.
30. Ibid. Note for the Record, 13 February 1956.

31. Ibid. Cabinet, Confidential Annex CM(56) 14 Conclusions, 15 February 1956.
32. PRO PREM 11/1326, Budget 1956. Letter from the Chancellor of the Exchequer to the Prime Minister, 23 March 1956.
33. Ibid. Memorandum from F. A. Bishop to the Prime Minister, 26 March 1956.
34. PRO T171/473, 1956 Budget. Minute from Sir Edward Bridges to the Chancellor of the Exchequer, 26 March 1956.
35. PRO PREM 11/1326, op. cit. Budget. Memorandum from the Chancellor of the Exchequer to the Prime Minister, 5 April 1956.
36. Brittan, op. cit., p. 183.
37. PRO T172/2127, op. cit. Letter from the Chancellor of the Exchequer to the Minister of Defence, 9 May 1956.
38. PRO PREM11/1327, Government Expenditure, Estimates for 1956. Government Expenditure: Economies. Cabinet Gen 527/1st Meeting, 16 May 1956.
39. Ibid. Cabinet CP(56) 43rd Conclusions, 14 June 1956.
40. PRO T234/266, Balance of Payments Prospects, 1955–1958. Committee on Balance of Payments Prospects, Report on Balance of Payments Prospects for 1956, 4 July 1956.
41. PRO T172/2127, op. cit. Letter from the Chancellor of the Exchequer to the Minister of Defence, 20 September 1956.
42. PRO PREM 11/1327, Government Expenditure. Estimates for 1956. Cabinet CM(56) 71st Conclusions. Minute 1, 18 October 1956.
43. PRO T172/2127, op. cit. Letter from the Chancellor of the Exchequer to the Minister of Defence, 14 November 1956.
44. Quoted in A. Gorst and L. Johnman, *The Suez Crisis* (London: Routledge, 1996), p. 63.
45. Quoted, ibid., p. 66.
46. Quoted, ibid., p. 128.
47. Quoted, ibid., p. 129.
48. Quoted, ibid., p. 129.
49. PRO T236/4188, Measures to Protect Sterling. Memorandum by Sir R. Hall, 2 October 1956.
50. Ibid., The Reserves. Memorandum from Sir L. Rowan to Sir R. Makins, 26 October 1956.
51. Ibid., Note for the Record by Sir L. Rowan, 31 October 1956.
52. Quoted in K. Kyle, *Suez* (London: Weidenfeld & Nicolson, 1991), p. 357.
53. See Kyle, ibid., p. 464.
54. Selwyn Lloyd, *Suez 1956* (London, 1978), p. 209.
55. Quoted in Turner, op. cit., p. 118.
56. PRO T236/4189, Measures to Protect Sterling. Telegram, Washington to the Foreign Office, 9 November 1956.
57. Ibid., Memorandum from Sir R. Makins to the Chancellor of the Exchequer 9 November 1956.
58. Ibid., Note of a Meeting held in Sir Leslie Rowan's room, 12 November 1956.
59. Ibid., Memorandum from Sir L. Rowan to Sir R. Makins, 13 November 1956.

60. Quoted in Gorst and Johnman, op. cit., p. 139.
61. Quoted, ibid., pp. 147–8.
62. Quoted, ibid., pp. 139–40.
63. Quoted, ibid., p. 141.
64. Quoted, ibid., p. 141.
65. PRO FO371/120816, UK Financial Situation Resulting from the Suez Crisis, Telegram from Washington to the Foreign Office, 26 November 1956.
66. Ibid., Telegram from Washington to the Foreign Office, 27 November 1956.
67. PRO PREM 11/1106, Memorandum from Selwyn Lloyd to R. A. Butler, 27 November 1956.
68. PRO CAB 128/30 Pt ll, CM(56)90, 28 November 1956.
69. PRO CAB 128/30 Pt ll, CM(56)91, 29 November 1956.
70. Quoted, Gorst and Johnman, op. cit., p. 144.
71. PRO T172/2127, Chancellor's Personal, Secret and Top Secret Carbons. Macmillan to Butler, 13 December 1956.
72. PRO PREM 11/1826, Washington to Foreign Office, 8 December 1956.
73. PRO PREM 11/1818, Financial Policy. Letter from the Chancellor of the Exchequer to the Prime Minister, 21 December 1956.
74. PRO PREM 11/1826, Letter from the Governor of the Bank of England to the Chancellor of the Exchequer, 20 December 1956.
75. Ibid., Letter from the Prime Minister to the Chancellor of the Exchequer, 28 December 1956.
76. Ibid., Letter from the Chancellor of the Exchequer to the Prime Minister, 31 December 1956.
77. Ibid., Note by the Prime Minister, circulated to Cabinet, 7 January 1957.
78. See, for example, Howard op. cit., pp. 229–48.
79. Ibid., p. 241.
80. Rhodes James, op. cit., p. 592.
81. Turner, op. cit., p. 123 and Howard, op. cit., p. 245.
82. Quoted, *Contemporary Record*, vol. no. 1 (Spring 1987), p. 5.
83. Horne, op. cit., p. 402.

5 Much Ado about Nothing: Macmillan and Appeasement

N. J. Crowson

I

During an interview in November 1958 Harold Macmillan told his interlocutor that in his opinion it did not matter if a Conservative MP rebelled against the party line provided the individual concerned had justified the behaviour with the local constituency party chairman.[1] Such a statement suggesting that the national party structure is powerless to discipline a rebel is not unique, but it is surprising that it should be so publicly stated by a Conservative Prime Minister. However, it was an observation based upon personal experience from the 1930s. During this time Macmillan was drawn into conflict with the leaderships of Stanley Baldwin and Neville Chamberlain over the conduct of British foreign policy towards the European dictators. The purpose of this study is to examine the attitude to appeasement adopted by Macmillan and to evaluate the implications of his behaviour in relation to the Conservative party.

Macmillan had entered Parliament in 1924 as MP for the northern industrial seat of Stockton. He continued to represent the constituency (with the exception of the years 1929–31) until defeat in the general election of 1945. During this time he established a reputation amongst the parliamentary party for being something of an eccentric.[2] As the decade of the 1930s drew to a close he appeared isolated and on the periphery. The Macmillan of the interwar years was seen as a radical, to the left of the party, who by his own admission in 1939 was close to ending his association with it.[3] Only the resignation of Chamberlain in May 1940 revived his political fortunes when his former political mentor, Winston Churchill, secured the premiership.

II

Little has been written explicitly about Macmillan's attitude to the national government's foreign policy. His official biographer devotes only a few pages, as does the most recently published biography; whilst for the most part the historian has been reliant upon Macmillan's own testimony as outlined in his memoirs.[4] Of course, these are recognized for what they are – Macmillan's projection and justification of his actions. The sole scholarly work has been Adrian Smith's review of Macmillan and Munich, which although based upon only published primary sources, highlighted the role the young MP played in facilitating contacts between the Conservative 'rebels' and Labour foreign policy specialists during the summer/autumn of 1938.[5] The analysis of Conservative foreign policy critics has a tendency to be skewed towards the events of 1938–9. Further it has been focused towards the activities of the Edenites and Churchill Group (something of which this author has also been guilty). With the gradual opening up of the Macmillan archives at the Bodleian Library, one is left wondering whether perhaps the emphasis has been wrong? There is increased evidence that the period 1935–6 was more significant for the evolution of foreign policy criticism than has been previously supposed. With the emphasis upon those around Eden and Churchill (to the mutual exclusion of all others), historians have been missing the point that the era was a time of turmoil, when backbenchers played an influential role in defining the parameters in which Britain's foreign policy was conducted. It was in these environs that Macmillan operated.

III

The outright opposition of the Stockton MP to foreign policy first became apparent in the immediate aftermath of the 1935 general election. The foreign secretary, Samuel Hoare, had secretly sought to reach a diplomatic compromise to the Italo-Abyssinian war. When news of the Hoare–Laval plan leaked in Britain a political outcry from the Conservative backbenches obliged Baldwin to insist upon Hoare's resignation.[6] Macmillan had been vocal in his demands for the removal of Hoare. Having been a passionate supporter of the League of Nations and collective security, Macmillan believed the

Hoare–Laval plan signed the death warrant for the League. Writing to *The Times* he welcomed the prospect of Hoare's removal and noted the irony that the Prime Minister was being supported in his foreign policy by those right-wing Conservatives who had been agitating for his removal since the beginning of the decade:

> It must indeed be galling for the Prime Minister to reflect on the character of the limited support which his new foreign policy is receiving. In the House of Commons many members on the government side are in open revolt; many more anxious and distressed.

Concluding, he drew an analogy with a funeral for a murdered man believing 'that at such a ceremony some distinction is made between the mourners and the assassins'.[7] The appointment of Anthony Eden to the Foreign Office as Hoare's successor was welcomed by Macmillan based upon an assumption that the new foreign secretary would continue to strive for collective security and ensure that British policy would thereafter 'be characterised by consistent support for the League Covenant'.[8] To Macmillan's mind support for the League was 'the cardinal and basic element' necessary to successfully maintain peace.[9]

The Hoare–Laval fiasco was the impetus for a number of Conservatives, encouraged by Edward Spears (Carlisle's MP), to form a dining club. The original conception was that the Club would convene on alternate months 'for the purposes of meeting distinguished British and foreign statesmen whose views it might be of interest . . . to hear'. But furthermore it was conceived that 'it might also be called together at any time the political situation warranted it . . . and could, if deemed desirable, place its views before the government'. Macmillan was one of those national government supporters initially approached; the criteria for selection being based upon the ability of the individual concerned to be

> perfectly prepared in a real emergency to take independent action of the Whips . . . and who . . . realise the enormous interest taken by the country in the League of Nations and in foreign affairs.[10]

Macmillan's response was positive, although once the December Club began meeting his attendance was somewhat erratic.[11] His limited involvement most likely explains why the dining club receives no mention in Macmillan's memoirs. The lack of active participation may have stemmed from Macmillan's belief in his own superiority which led to an inability to accept the role of subordinate and team player. This had already been highlighted with regard to his involvement in the Next Five Years Group and the Northern Group of MPs.[12] At the same time, ill health and personal tragedy did beset the Macmillan family during 1936, providing ample distraction from political affairs.

Within a few months of Hoare–Laval, with British attentions still distracted to the Mediterranean and Africa, Hitler remilitarized the Rhineland zone in March 1936. It was an event that destroyed the 1925 Locarno treaty and broke another clause of the 1919 Versailles peace treaty. The episode raised questions about the viability of sanctions and the League, and also placed the new British defence programme into perspective. Whereas Macmillan had found himself expressing the views of the majority of the parliamentary party over Hoare–Laval, with the Rhineland crisis he was very much out of line with the prevailing assumptions. With the backbench foreign affairs committee providing the forum for the party's debate it was quickly evident that the crisis was obliging many Conservatives to begin a rapid re-evaluation of their expectations. Although many condemned Hitler's behaviour, it was generally accepted that there was a legitimacy to the event. Furthermore, a sizeable number were concerned that French intransigence might drag Britain unwillingly into a conflict with Germany. The conclusion reached by the committee shortly before the Parliamentary debate on the incident was that energies should be directed to diplomatically resisting Germany. This could be achieved by detaching Italy from Germany. This would only happen if the government admitted sanctions had failed and recognized the conquest of Abyssinia. Italy would then be able to return to the negotiating table. This was a position Macmillan could not accept. For him, Britain had possessed two options: either resist Mussolini; or ignore Abyssinia with the aim of keeping Italy out of the Nazi camp. Baldwin's attempt to steer a middle path meant Britain had lost on both accounts.[13]

From the beginning of the Abyssinian crisis a major debate had been occurring amongst the backbenchers about the suitability of imposing economic sanctions upon the Italians. It was a debate that closely involved Macmillan and one which ultimately brought him into direct conflict with his leaders. Once the Baldwin administration had decided to resist Mussolini by economic sanctions Macmillan favoured their rigid imposition. He feared that

> unless the League can effectively prevent her [Italy] from 'getting away with it' (to use a common phrase), I think it will be the end of the League. Moreover, from the English point of view, I think it immensely increases the danger of German aggression.[14]

When Hitler re-took the Rhineland, Macmillan's doomsday scenario appeared prophetic. It intensified the need to continue the sanctions and for bolstering the League of Nations.[15] Yet Macmillan found himself increasingly isolated amongst Conservatives; only Vyvyan Adams, Conservative MP for Leeds West, appeared to earnestly favour their maintenance. From March 1936 the imperialist right wing of the party, who had argued that continued British action increased the risks of war and inevitably threatened universal peace, began winning the argument. Amongst the wider party a consensus began to emerge recognizing that to continue sanctions effectively drew Germany and Italy closer together – the very effect British foreign policy had been trying to prevent. Conversely Macmillan, although having no wish to see this scenario, felt that having adopted sanctions they had to be fulfilled with resolution. To drop them now would show weakness to the dictators and encourage further aggression. He felt that since Hoare–Laval, British foreign policy

> had fallen between two stools so that our prestige had been lowered in every part of the world, and the international situation rendered more dangerous by the failure of the League to preserve the peace even between two of its own members.[16]

Keen to add resolve to the Cabinet's deliberations on the maintenance of sanctions, Macmillan added his name to a Early Day Motion tabled on 11 May stating approval for the policy. It drew support from only 27 Conservatives.[17] However, Neville Chamberlain, the Chancellor of the Exchequer, sealed the fate of sanctions when during a speech in early June 1936 he condemned their retention as 'the very midsummer of madness'. When the matter was debated in the Commons, Macmillan joined Vyvyan Adams in condemning the government's behaviour. At the calling of the division both men voted against the government. From some of the material being released amongst the Macmillan archive it is evident that the Stockton MP's actions were being encouraged by others from outside the party. Filed amongst his papers is literature from the Friends of Abyssinia organization, highlighting the plight of the Abyssinian nation since the Italian invasion. Included was a picture postcard showing an aeroplane bombing/gassing a village with a native woman and child in the foreground weeping.[18] In addition, Macmillan was invited by Norman Angell, Walter Layton, Wickham Steed and Eleanor Rathbone to attend an 'informal and strictly private' conference on Abyssinia that included representatives from the League of Nations Union, the trades unions, Press, academia, women's organizations and opposition parties. The conference's agenda was to decide:

> What action should be taken in respect of:
>   (i) any remaining means of [putting] pressure on Italy, e.g. through refusal of financial aid;
> (ii) protection of native rights and welfare in Abyssinia;
> (iii) protection of European and British interests;
> (iv) the future of the Stresa front;
>   (v) the future of the coercive provisions of the covenant?[19]

Such a gathering was very much in keeping with Macmillan's ideal of a new central political coalition. No doubt it encouraged his decision to go a stage further and resign the National government whip – a deed which 'received a frigid note from Mr Baldwin'.[20]

To Macmillan's mind, the options before the British government with the ending of sanctions were clear. Strong leadership was required in order to prevent any further misunderstanding of Britain's position. Furthermore, the opportunity should be seized to take the initiative in reconstructing the League. In addition, Germany should be invited to participate in a conference

> in which this country should announce its readiness to give a fair deal in an effort to negotiate a completely new world peace settlement. If Germany refused to do so or the conference broke down, the only course open to us would be protective alliances with our neighbours in western Europe, it being made clear to Germany that she could always come into this circle whenever she desired.[21]

The lineage for this support of the League and collective security can be traced back at least as far as Macmillan signing the 1934 Liberty and Democratic Leadership manifesto which evolved into the Next Five Years Group.[22]

When Neville Chamberlain succeeded Baldwin in May 1937, Macmillan, in common with many Conservatives, welcomed the new leader believing that he would provide the necessary lead in foreign affairs. To show his approval he reapplied for the national whip. On a different level it was an admission that 'independents' could achieve little influence without the necessary party coupon. The concession was eased by the virtue of Eden remaining as foreign secretary, and to Macmillan's mind Eden was still committed to the League of Nations. As a consequence, Macmillan was quickly drawn into conflict with the leadership when Eden resigned in February 1938. Macmillan's name was added, along with other members of the December Club, to a parliamentary motion which deplored the circumstances obliging the foreign secretary's resignation.[23] He followed this 'rebellion' by abstaining in the censure vote on Eden's departure. However, the impact of his abstention is less clear. Macmillan admitted in his memoirs that 'to "abstain" is not perhaps a very courageous Parliamentary gesture'.[24] Furthermore it appears that he was soon expressing remorse to his Stockton Association. Whilst he 'regretted' Eden's resignation, 'he felt that the difference of opinion was merely one of method rather than objective'. He then sought to score party political points by noting the irony that the opposition were now championing Eden whereas six months before he had been an object of vilification.[25]

For Macmillan the March 1938 *Anschluss* was further evidence of the dangers presented by the dictators. Certainly, many Conservatives were left feeling uncomfortable with the yields of Chamberlain's foreign policy. Nevertheless, in public the Stockton Member maintained a conciliatory tone. He felt able to tell the ladies of his local Conservative Association that the German breaches of Versailles thus far 'were not, in principle, of a kind to which real objections could be made'. Indeed, he felt 'there was a good deal of reason' behind the reoccupation of the Rhineland, rearmament and the *Anschluss*. He did qualify this by adding that in Austria's case 'it was not the actual union which provoked resentment, but the brutality and persecution which would inevitably follow'.[26] Furthermore, contrary to the impression Macmillan gave in his memoirs, he felt sufficiently reassured by the Prime Minister's response to the crisis with his 24 March statement to the House of Commons to be able to support the government in the division lobbies against a Labour vote of censure.[27] It was an action accorded by a number of the other normally sceptical backbenchers.[28]

As the Czech crisis deteriorated during the summer and autumn of 1938, Macmillan continued to be disturbed by the direction of Chamberlain's foreign policy. When the Prime Minister began his shuttle diplomacy to Germany in September, Macmillan became involved in the discussions amongst a small band of backbenchers centred around Anthony Eden. He also discussed the diplomatic and international situation with the small number of acolytes who courted Churchill. The significance of Macmillan's involvement in these two groupings of foreign policy sceptics was that he acted, along with Edward Spears, as a intermediary between Churchill and Eden.[29] This culminated in both factions meeting on the morning of the Munich parliamentary divisions and agreeing to co-ordinate their voting strategies and abstain *en bloc*.[30] However, Macmillan was seeking to do more than unify the various Conservative opponents to Chamberlain. He was also in close contact with senior Labour figures, particularly the Shadow Foreign Secretary, Hugh Dalton, seeking to draw together the various strands of parliamentary opposition into a centre/popular front grouping. Ultimately nothing came of these approaches, but it illustrated Macmillan's continued flirtation with the idea of creating a new centre party, between the best elements (to his mind) of the Labour and Conservative parties.[31] It also suggested an ugly duckling syndrome offering an indication of his isolation from his fellow Conservatives, his having not been admitted to the very inner sanctums of the foreign policy sceptics. This desire to support a new third party, combined with his opposition to appeasement, meant that Macmillan felt able to publicly support the Master of Balliol, A. R. Lindsay, when he stood as an independent against the official Conservative candidate, Quintin Hogg, in the October 1938 Oxford by-election. This by-election was taken as a referendum on the Munich agreement. As it stood, Macmillan felt, the Munich agreement represented 'a complete capitulation to the racial principles of Nazi philosophy'.[32] The young undergraduate Edward Heath, later to be Macmillan's chief whip, also supported the Lindsay campaign.[33] However, the Lindsay campaign failed to attract support from other leading Conservative sceptics and Hogg managed to retain the seat for the Conservatives, whilst Macmillan was faced with expulsion from the Carlton Club and the possibility of party disciplinary action.[34]

In common with a number of other foreign policy sceptics during this period Macmillan had begun championing rearmament. Given Macmillan's interest in both foreign affairs and economics this was not surprising. His book *The Middle Way* linked his views on foreign policy with the need for planned capitalism – a half-way house between the free market and socialism that allowed a mixed economy in which there was both central co-ordination and ample scope for free enterprise. In the aftermath of Munich he privately published a short pamphlet in which he argued that economic planning was necessary to ensure that rearmament did not disrupt the civilian economy,[25] arguments that were articulated further in his 1939 publication *Economic Aspects of Defence*.[36] As a result of his favour for planning, Macmillan was an advocate for the creation of a Ministry of Supply, a cause espoused also by Churchill. Unsurprisingly, the idea for such a ministry found little favour with the Chamberlain administration and it was only in mid-1939 that one was created, albeit with limited powers. Furthermore, the idea of a Ministry of Supply had only restricted support amongst Conservatives. This Macmillan discovered in November 1938 when he defied a three-line whip and supported a Liberal call for such a ministry. He found only Churchill and Brendan Bracken from the Conservative side in the 'Aye' lobby. His support for the cause most likely explains Churchill appointing Macmillan as parliamentary secretary at the Ministry of Supply in May 1940.[37] With the belief that a strongly defended Britain would deter the dictators from further acts of aggression, Macmillan also became a convert to the cause of national service. By April 1939 with the international situation continuing to deteriorate and it being evident that the government's voluntary scheme of national service was failing to attract enough recruits, Macmillan sought to put pressure on the government by writing to *The Times* announcing his conversion to conscription.[38] On a more practical level, Macmillan's support for rearmament was influenced by the nature of his Stockton constituency. Its experiences with the Depression and the likelihood that any expanded rearmament programme would lead to economic benefits for distressed areas such as the North East of England made rearmament an attractive cause to espouse.[39]

IV

This study began with Macmillan's observation that to be a successful rebel in the Conservative party required keeping the local
association on side. He was speaking with the wisdom of action.
Whilst representing Stockton between 1924 and 1945 he was never
once subject to a motion of censure from the Association, despite
regularly failing to support his government and in 1936 resigning
the whip in protest at the abandonment of sanctions. This level of
flexibility granted to Macmillan by his Association made his role
as a foreign policy critic considerably easier. This was something
that was unusual for the era. From reading the Association's minute
books it is apparent that Macmillan heeded his own advice, always
taking consummate care to ensure that the local executive was briefed
on his actions. For example, in September 1935 he specifically re-
quested a meeting to explain his economic policies as outlined in
The Next Five Years. Likewise, the following year on resigning the
whip he sought to explain his opposition to the Baldwin government's Abyssinian policy and in return received a vote of confidence.[40] It should be observed that other local Associations during
this period were not so tolerant of 'rebel' Members, as the Duchess
of Atholl in Kinross and Vyvyan Adams in Leeds West discovered
to their cost.[41] As with these other foreign policy dissidents, Macmillan
sought to justify his action upon the grounds that he had

> made it abundantly clear that he reserved to himself a consider-
> able degree of latitude as to how he should exercise his vote on
> any particular question, and asked for a free hand from the
> electors.[42]

Yet Macmillan was faced with only limited grumbling from sections of his Association – why? A number of factors can be identified to explain this phenomenon. These illustrate Macmillan's skills
as a politician, but also the extent to which he was not a 'natural'
Conservative, and maybe if he had been representing any seat other
than a marginal one he would have felt obliged to leave the party.
The first point is that Macmillan always adopted a conciliatory tone
when addressing the Association. Although from his memoirs the
impression is given that when speaking to his activists he clearly

laid out his criticisms, the reader is actually being treated to selective quotation, as the speech to the Stockton women after the *Anschluss* referred to earlier illustrates.[43] Second, to a considerable extent his 'independence' was bought. The survival of the Association throughout the inter-war years relied upon Macmillan's financial generosity. Financial assistance in itself was not an unusual feature, but the extent of Macmillan's was. For example, in 1928 he found £2,000 to help buy new premises, the following month he gave £67 to clear the Association's overdraft. In 1935 he arranged and paid for the re-decoration of the Association's meeting hall. The following year he, alongside the Association's chairman, Leonard Ropner, paid off the Association's £332 overdraft. By 1938 he was paying the salaries of the Agent and the Women's Organizer. As the new chairman remarked the following year, 'if it were not for the generosity of Mr Macmillan, it would be impossible for the Organisation to carry on'.[44] The third factor links in with the financial position of the Association, namely, the marginal nature of the Stockton constituency located in the industrial north. It granted Macmillan that extra degree of independence. This was borne out when, having lost in Stockton in 1929, Macmillan considered contesting the safe seat of Hitchin in the Home Counties in a by-election. Despite having the support of Lord Beaverbrook, the Press magnate, it is apparent that the Hitchin Association began to have second thoughts about Macmillan's suitability. They were aware of his radical views, but had initially seen these as still compatible with mainstream Conservatism. However, Macmillan had written a letter to *The Times* in May 1930 commending Oswald Mosley for his unemployment pledges and for having resigned from MacDonald's government. An article in the right-wing journal *Patriot* later that year attacked Macmillan for being a free-trader and for threatening to vote against Baldwin. This caused Macmillan to inform the local chairman that he had no intention of yielding his radical beliefs to right-wing threats. In due course his nomination floundered when the sitting member was persuaded to reconsidered his decision to step down.[45] The marginal nature of Stockton had a further benefit for Macmillan. The level of activism was minor and characterized by abominable laziness and indifference, which meant that in occasions of strife he had fewer people to convince of the legitimacy of his actions.[46]

V

In the post-war years as Macmillan steadily rose through the political ranks, it became apparent to many observers that he was both a very ambitious individual and a very calculating politician. His actions, especially once Prime Minister, were conceived and acted out for maximum political effect, as with his 'little local difficulties' aside prior to his departure on the Commonwealth tour in 1958. The fact remains that the same was true of the Macmillan of the inter-war years. His bursting into a discordant rendition of *Rule Britannia* on hearing the results of the Norway division in May 1940 being one of the few occasion when genuine spontaneity took over.[47] His decision to become a Conservative was driven by opportunism rather than political conviction. As a young man he had been influenced by three very distinct political traditions: the old radicalism of the Christian Socialist Movement; orthodox Liberalism (pre-Home Rule split); and Unionism.[48] During his days at Oxford he had been inspired by Lloyd George and even into the 1930s the 'Welsh Wizard' continued to influence the Conservative backbencher. His marriage to Dorothy in 1920 meant him marrying into a Whig family and there is evidence that serious consideration was given to standing as a Liberal MP. However, the Macmillans were ambitious and from 1922 with the Carlton Club revolt and the continued divisions amongst the Liberal party it was evident that the Conservatives offered the best political career opportunities. Joining Labour was not a consideration. He had 'to remember that I am a very rich man'.[49] Once a Conservative, a persistent theme for Macmillan became the need for the Party to occupy the centre ground of British politics. In 1924 he had stated that the Party stood for 'a temperate and moderate policy of progress'.[50] It was a theme he returned to in his speech accepting adoption as party leader in 1957, when he drew the analogy that the Conservative Party was a 'broad stream' which 'was fed by many tributaries which we must not allow to dissolve into a shapeless delta'.[51] When, during the 1930s, he became disillusioned with what he perceived as the Conservative's self-interest, he gave consideration to the formation of a British popular front, or 'Centre Party', comprising the left of the Conservatives and the right of the Labour under the possible leadership of Herbert Morrison. Not untypically, the matter is underplayed in his memoirs, but the episode was symptomatic of his desire to take the 'Middle Way' and continue along the route trodden by Disraeli and other Tory Democrats. At the same time, Macmillan sought to manipulate the system to his advantage. His resignation of the whip in 1936 happened to be purely for the 'national' and not the 'Conservative' whip. As a consequence he had not gone beyond the pale. It guaranteed him national attention and added to his notoriety amongst colleagues, but, as the executive committee of the National Union of Conservative Associations decided, because he retained the party whip he could still be treated as a Conservative MP.[52] Furthermore, his ability to both charm and bankroll the local constituency Association was politically shrewd. The autonomy of local associations meant that they held the ultimate decision over selection and deselection. So long as a rebel retained the sanction of the local party, Central Office would have found it next to impossible to run an 'official' candidate against them.[53] Overall, Macmillan's experiences in the inter-war years were important lessons for the ambitious career politician and were a solid apprenticeship for the future leader. It is questionable whether Macmillan's alternative vision of 1930s foreign policy would have been viable. The League of Nations as it was constituted lacked the necessary international clout to effectively intervene, either diplomatically or militarily. Most Conservatives recognized that with many of the leading nations either absent from Geneva or having never joined, there was little point in giving it new duties which it had no hope of carrying out. It would be highly speculative to suggest that any revision of the League's Covenant would have secured the necessary international unanimity. As with much of Macmillan's political thinking in the 1930s, his response to appeasement placed too great an emphasis upon an idealism that accorded little reality to the situation. It is likely that behind the need to challenge the orthodoxies of party policy lay an element of political frustration which stemmed from his own failure to secure political advancement. Overall, Macmillan's views on appeasement made him an isolated figure on the Conservative backbenches. Equally, as this study has shown, Macmillan's own carefully crafted version of the 1930s bears only a limited resemblance to the actualities and the heroism of his stance against party and constituency pressure is fatally weakened.

NOTES

1. R. Jackson, *Rebels and Whips* (London: Macmillan, 1968), p. 254n.
2. R. R. James (ed.), *Chips: The Diaries of Sir Henry Channon* (London: Weidenfeld & Nicolson, 1968), 8 July 1936, 16 November 1939, pp. 69, 225; S. Ball (ed.), *Parliament and Politics in the Age of Baldwin and MacDonald: The Diaries of Sir Cuthbert Headlam Diaries, 1924–35* (London: The Historian's Press, 1992), 13 October 1934, 13 December 1934, pp. 311–12, 317.
3. Headlam Mss: unpublished diaries, 10 June 1939, D/He/34, Durham Record Office.
4. A. Horne, *Macmillan, 1894–1956*, vol. I (London: Macmillan, 1986), pp. 112–21; J. Turner, *Macmillan* (London: Longman, 1994), pp. 44–6; H. Macmillan *Winds of Change, 1914–1939* (London: Macmillan, 1956).
5. A. Smith, 'Macmillan and Munich: The Open Conspirator', *Dalhousie Review*, vol. 68, no. 3 (1988), pp. 235–47.
6. N. J. Crowson, *Facing Fascism: The Conservative Party and the European Dictators, 1935–40* (London: Routledge, 1997), pp. 58–65.
7. *The Times*, 18 December 1935.
8. Macmillan Mss: Macmillan to Raymond Buell, 26 December 1935, MS. Macmillan dep. c. 99 f. 34, Bodleian Library.
9. Stockton C[onservative] A[ssociation], special general meeting 23 July 1936, DX332/5, Durham Record Office.
10. Macmillan Mss: Edward Spears to Macmillan, n.d., MS. Macmillan dep. c. 99 ff. 358–9. The following national government supporters had agreed to attend: W. H. Carver; R. Bower; H. Nicolson; Marquess of Hartington; V. Cazalet; A. Crossley; R. Boothby; J. Mellor; H. Macmillan; A. Herbert; B. Cruddas; J. W. Hills; G. Bower; E. Makins, R. Tree; E. Spears; H. P. Latham. See Macmillan Mss: E. Spears to Macmillan, 12 February 1936, MS. Macmillan dep. c. 100 ff. 307–8.
11. Macmillan Mss: Macmillan to Edward Spears, 2 January 1936, MS. Macmillan dep. c. 99 f. 357. I am grateful to Paul Short (an MA student at LSE, who was working on aspects of the December Club) for our discussions on the December Club and for the information about Macmillan's attendance.
12. Ball (ed.), *Headlam Diaries*, 24 July 1935, p. 338.
13. Horne, *Macmillan*, vol. I, pp. 112–3.
14. Macmillan Mss: Macmillan to Ernest Imeson, 15 January 1936, MS. Macmillan dep. c. 99 f. 174.
15. Macmillan Mss: 'draft' letter to *The Times* from the executive committee of the Next Five Years Group, 28 March 1936, MS. Macmillan dep. c. 101 f. 36.
16. Stockton CA, special general meeting 23 July 1936, D/X332/5.
17. *Notice of Motions*, 11 May 1936.
18. Macmillan Mss: MS. Macmillan dep c. 104 f. 104.
19. Macmillan Mss: 'The Question of Continued Sanctions against Italy', 12 June 1936; 'The Abyssinian situation and its results', agenda, MS. Macmillan dep. c. 104 ff. 1–2, 314.

20. Macmillan, *Winds of Change*, pp. 458–9; James (ed.), *Chips*, 8 July 1936, p. 69.
21. Stockton CA, special general meeting, 23 July 1936, D/X332/5.
22. Turner, *Macmillan*, p. 45.
23. *The Times*, 23 February 1938. Compare these names with those listed in Macmillan Mss: MS. Macmillan dep. c. 99 ff. 358–9.
24. Macmillan, *Winds of Change*, pp. 538–9.
25. Stockton CA: men's branch AGM 10 March 1938, D/X322/8.
26. Stockton CA, women's AGM 19 March 1938, D/X322/11.
27. *Hansard* vote of confidence 4 April 1938.
28. See N. J. Crowson, 'Conservative Parliamentary Dissent over Foreign Policy during the Premiership of Neville Chamberlain: Myth or Reality?', *Parliamentary History*, vol. 14, no. 3 (1995) p. 325.
29. Smith, 'Macmillan', pp. 240–5.
30. See editorial in J. Barnes and D. Nicholson (eds), *The Empire at Bay: The Diaries of Leo Amery* (London: Hutchinson, 1988), pp. 483–90.
31. Macmillan, *Winds of Change*, pp. 568–9, 589.
32. H. Macmillan, *The Price of Peace: Notes on the World Crisis* (London: Heron, 1938), p. 9.
33. J. Campbell, *Edward Heath: A Biography* (London: Pimlico, 1993), pp. 33–4.
34. Macmillan, *Winds of Change*, p. 584.
35. Macmillan, *Price of Peace*, pp. 17–19.
36. Macmillan, *Winds of Change*, pp. 645–51.
37. Although this was only a very junior position, Macmillan threw himself into his job to the amusement of Westminster observers. James (ed.), *Chips*, 29 May 1940, p. 255.
38. *The Times*, 23 March 1939.
39. Horne, *Macmillan*, vol. I, p. 113.
40. Stockton CA, special executive 26 September 1935 and special general meeting 23 July 1936 D/X322/5.
41. For further examination see Crowson, *Facing Fascism*, pp. 85–7.
42. Stockton CA, special general meeting 23 July 1936, DX332/5
43. Compare this with the part of the speech quoted in Macmillan, *Winds of Change*, p. 542, which puts an entirely different gloss on affairs.
44. Stockton CA: finance committee 27 April 1928, 22 May 1928, 7 October 1935, 23 November 1938, executive 27 February 1939, D/X322/4, D/X 322/5; Macmillan MSS: Leonard Ropner to Macmillan, 17 January 1936, MS Macmillan dep. c. 99 ff. 322–3.
45. Horne, *Macmillan*, vol. I, pp. 90–2.
46. Macmillan MSS: Leonard Ropner to Macmillan, 17 January 1936, MS Macmillan dep. c. 99 f. 323.
47. James (ed.), *Chips*, 8 May 1940, p. 247.
48. H. Macmillan, *Past Masters: Politics and Politicans, 1906–1939* (London: Macmillan, 1975), p. 20.
49. Horne, *Macmillan*, vol. I, p. 127.
50. Stockton CA, newsclipping *Darlington and Stockton Times*, 26 January 1924, D/X322/4.

51. N. Nicolson (ed.), *Harold Nicolson: Diaries and Letters, 1945–62* (London: Collins, 1968), Nigel Nicolson to Harold and Vita Sackville-West, 22 January 1957, p. 330.
52. Conservative Party Archive: Micro Fiche Archive, National Union Executive 16 July 1936, card 54.
53. As acknowledged by party chairman, Douglas Hacking, Collin Brooks MSS: journals 5 October 1938.

6 Macmillan and Europe[1]
Richard Lamb

Alistair Horne has written that in 1949 Harold Macmillan had boundless, almost excessive, enthusiasm for Europe. This is correct, but between 1949 and 1961 he was not consistent and at one period did his best to sabotage the EEC in order to preserve the interests of the Commonwealth.[2]

Winston Churchill as leader of the Conservative Party in the immediate post-war years displayed great enthusiasm for the Council of Europe, which he envisaged as a European parliamentary authority, and at the first Congress of Europe at The Hague in 1948 he had launched the European Movement which brought together the various groups in Britain and Western Europe working for European unity. Then he called for unity in high-faluting although imprecise terms, playing down his reservation that Britain while working closely with Europe would never became integrated.

The first positive move towards the Common Market came in May 1950 when Robert Schuman, the French Foreign Secretary, unexpectedly launched dramatic proposals for pooling the coal, iron and steel resources of France and Germany and of any other European country willing to join them under the control of an independent high authority. This was followed in October by a proposal to place each of Nato's armed forces under a supranational authority to create an European army. The Attlee government spurned both proposals, with the Prime Minister telling the French Ambassador that they could not hand over the key coal and steel industries 'to irresponsible persons' while the Foreign Secretary, Ernest Bevin, commented 'We cannot buy a pig in a poke.'[3]

In a Commons debate at the end of June 1950, during what amounted to a vote of censure on the Government for refusing to negotiate over the Schuman Plan, Churchill said 'We are prepared to consider and if convinced to accept the abrogation of sovereignty provided we are satisfied with the conditions and safeguards... national sovereignty is not inviolable.' Eden in the same debate said he would be prepared to enter discussions to set up a high authority whose decisions would be binding upon the nations who were parties to the agreement.

Macmillan agreed enthusiastically with Churchill and Eden. However, the high hopes aroused with pro-Europeans in Britain were soon dashed. Once in office in 1951 the Conservative government under Churchill, like their Labour predecessor, refused to consider yielding power to the supranational institutions proposed, and they ate the words they had uttered in opposition.

On 28 November Eden, now Foreign Secretary, announced in Rome that Britain would not participate in an European army, and a fortnight later Eden and Churchill in Paris told Schuman that they could not join in the Schuman Plan.[4]

Macmillan, like other Europhile Conservatives, was dismayed and wrote to Eden in January 1952 that Britain should give a lead to Europe in the creation of a confederation organized on the same lines as the Commonwealth, with a common currency and a European customs preferential area interlocking with Imperial Preference. Eden was negative when Macmillan raised the issue in Cabinet, replying that Macmillan ignored that 'much of Europe wants to federate'. This was true. Unhappy with the Cabinet discussion Macmillan wrote to Churchill stating that the government's continued opposition to the movement for European unity was inconsistent with the pronouncements, while in opposition, by Churchill and Eden on the Schuman Plan and the European army, and with the conduct of the Conservative delegates to the Council of Europe at Strasbourg.

At this stage, Churchill was enjoying being Prime Minister. Eden, who was adamantly opposed to Britain being part of Europe, was his popular heir-apparent and Churchill was not going to make life difficult for himself by having a brush with his Foreign Secretary. He snubbed Macmillan saying nothing more than what Eden was doing was practical.[5] Churchill had become ambivalent and had probably created his plan for an united Europe with a view to establishing political ascendancy over Attlee by re-evoking his role as the great wartime saviour of Europe. Perhaps Churchill was guilty of muddled thinking, but as leader of the opposition he was definitely inspired by both the vision of a European parliamentary authority and of a European army. Out of touch with civil servants, he probably became carried away by his own oratory. Yet as Prime Minister, in deference to Eden from 1951 to 1955 he consistently rejected any suggestions of European union which involved supranational institutions.

Without Britain, the high authority of the European Coal and

Steel Community assumed office in August 1952, and Jean Monnet, their first President, became the driving force behind an ever-strengthening move towards a united Europe which was to become the Common Market of the Six (EEC). Monnet extended European co-operation to atomic energy (Euratom) and prepared plans for a customs union. Britain was ready to join a free trade area but not a customs union, because the government was determined not to erode or abolish Commonwealth preference which would be inescapable in a customs union. When the Faure government, which included several convinced federalists, took office in France in February 1955, the drive for a European customs union gathered pace.

When Eden succeeded Churchill as Prime Minister in April 1955, Macmillan became Foreign Secretary. The enthusiasm for a united Europe he had displayed a few years before had disappeared. When the Foreign Ministers of the Six (France, Germany, Italy, Belgium, the Netherlands and Luxemburg) met at Messina at the beginning of June 1955 and laid down realistic plans for a Common Market Treaty, Eden and Macmillan made the fatal mistake of not even sending a representative. Churchill would never have made this mistake.[6]

At Messina the Six wanted Britain to participate from the start, and a great opportunity to join with the EEC tailor-made for British requirements was thrown away. Eden as Prime Minister dominated foreign policy, but both he and Macmillan had the gut feeling that there were three great powers – Britain, the USA and the Soviet Union – and they would not contemplate Britain abandoning Imperial Preference and accepting equal status within the Six by pooling national sovereignty and entering a customs union. Macmillan has made it clear in his memoirs that in 1955 he did not want a Six-power Europe with a customs union.

At Messina Paul-Henri Spaak, the Belgian Foreign Minister, was made Chairman of a Committee of the Six in Brussels to prepare a formal treaty, and he drove ahead at great speed. Although Britain had no intention of joining the Six, the Cabinet appointed a senior civil servant, Russell Bretherton, to joint the committee mainly to find out what was happening. Bretherton, who favoured the EEC ideal, told the author that he found himself in great difficulties because he could not guide the propositions into shape without giving the impression that Britain would be committed to the result, while on the other hand if he sat back and said nothing, unpleasant things would get into the report from the UK point of view whether we took part in the Common Market or not.[7] Bretherton hoped the British government would change their minds and join the EEC, but the Cabinet Economic Policy Committee firmly rejected the idea. After Bretherton had reported that it was certain the Six would succeed in finalizing a treaty, the Cabinet tried to divert the discussion into the Organization for European Economic Cooperation (OEEC) in Paris. This was abortive and led Macmillan as Foreign Secretary into making a hostile statement in Paris in December 1955 which enraged the Ministers of the Six. Impervious to British objections, at Venice at the end of May 1956 the Six agreed their terms for the Treaty.[8]

Overtures to Britain were made by the Six; these were rejected, but as it became clear the Six were about to sign a treaty to establish economic integration, the Cabinet decided an alternative must be found. Macmillan, now Chancellor of the Exchequer, much concerned at British exports being disadvantaged by high tariffs in the Common Market, pushed the civil servants, and on 27 July, the day on which the Suez crisis erupted, he circulated a note prepared by the Foreign Office, Treasury and Board of Trade, with help from the Ministries of Agriculture, the Colonial Office, the Board of Customs and Excise and the Bank of England. This became the report entitled *UK Initiatives in Europe: Plan G.*

Plan G was a milestone because it envisaged Britain changing from having her industry protected by high tariffs to being part of a free trade area. This meant abolishing the high level of protection for British industries which had been cushioned against competition from imports by the 1932 Import Duties Act together with other out-of-date tariffs such as the 33 per cent Key Industries Duties dating back to the First World War. However, Plan G envisaged allowing into Britain duty free Commonwealth food imports and low tariffs on Commonwealth industrial goods. This was anathema to the Six, and they correctly recognized the plan as a tactic designed to wreck the Common Market with its customs union and supranational institutions. A free trade area as a substitute had no attractions for them. However, Macmillan held high but unwarranted hopes for the success of Plan G and wrote to Spaak on 3 October entreating him:

to keep things as fluid as possible at the meeting of the Foreign Ministers of the Six on 20 October so as to permit us and other countries to associate with the Customs Union in a wider Free Trade if you can do so. Binding decisions at this stage might be difficult.[9]

At the end of September Macmillan discussed Plan G in general terms with the Commonwealth Finance Ministers at their meeting in Washington. According to Macmillan, 'the younger Ministers seemed favourable; some of the older ones doubtful or hostile'. On his return to London Macmillan told the Cabinet:

We must be satisfied before we would contemplate entering a Free Trade Area in Europe that agricultural products were excluded and we preserved both the interests of Commonwealth agriculture in the United European market and of the system of Commonwealth preferences.[10]

This meant Plan G was doomed because the Six had now decided to include agriculture in their treaty.

An important ministerial meeting of the Six Messina powers in October went badly. Both the Germans and the French made reservations and it was the first real setback Spaak had experienced. For a short time British hopes were raised that the EEC Treaty might not come off and instead the French and Germans might be tempted by Plan G. However, just as it seemed French intransigence might provide a successful opening for Free Trade Area negotiations on the lines of Plan G, Spaak gave France all the concessions she wanted and the fleeting opportunity disappeared.[11]

Faced with a *fait accompli* by the Six, the Cabinet at their meeting on 13 November during the Suez crisis decided to announce in Parliament that Britain would negotiate with the Six for a Free Trade Area.[12]

In the Commons on 16 November Macmillan argued strongly for Plan G, and the Labour Party, influenced by Harold Wilson, concurred. The government spokesmen emphasized that agriculture would be completely excluded. This led Roy Jenkins to say the Six would not 'swallow' this. Indeed Plan G was so ill-received by the Six that it led them to press on even faster with their treaty.

On 7 January 1957, two days after Eden resigned and Macmillan became Prime Minister, Spaak came to London. Macmillan told Spaak that agriculture must be excluded from any agreement and that was 'non-negotiable'. Alas, it was also the sticking point for

Spaak, and the visit was a failure with Spaak insisting if there was agreement on a Free Trade Area all British food imports must pay the EEC common external tariff; he objected strongly to Britain continuing to keep the price of food low by deficiency payments to farmers because this cheap food gave Britain considerable economic advantages.[13]

The European Economic Community came into being despite the Macmillan government doing everything in their power to thwart the Messina powers by importuning with them for a Free Trade Area. The European Press was full of reports that Britain was trying to sabotage the EEC and, spurred on by fears of British proposals bringing negotiations to a halt, the Six signed the Treaty of Rome on 27 March 1957 with internal tariff reductions beginning on 1 January 1958, much to Britain's disadvantage.

After the signing of the Treaty of Rome the Macmillan government strove hard to create an EFTA of Seventeen which would include the Six and Britain and the other ten OEEC countries with tariffs harmonized from 1 January 1959. Two years of negotiations ending in success had given the Six a sense of cohesion; they feared that a larger Free Trade Area would prejudice the evolution of the Common Market.

In October 1957 important OEEC meetings in Paris boded well for Britain. The Council declared its determination 'to secure the establishment of a European Free Trade Area (of Seventeen) which would associate on a multilateral basis with the EEC and other member countries'. An intergovernmental Committee of Ministers was set up, and Reginald Maudling, President of the Board of Trade, was elected Chairman. (Macmillan had put him in charge of European negotiations.) Significantly, at the first meeting of the Maudling Committee the French delegate Edgar Faure declared baldly that unless the Treaty of Association of EFTA was roughly similar to the Treaty of Rome the French would not accept it. This was the writing on the wall.[14] Gladwyn Jebb, the British Ambassador in Paris, reported growing French opposition to Commonwealth food being imported duty free by Britain; this, as should have been foreseen, became the main stumbling block. On 17 March Maudling had a long conversation with Macmillan which made it clear a breakdown was probable. However a ray of light appeared when Guido Carli, the Italian Foreign Minister, put forward proposals by which the goods of the Eleven, who had widely varying external tariffs, should circulate freely throughout EFTA except when the country's import tariffs were above a 'norm'. If the country's import tariffs were above the norm compensatory tariffs would be levied upon them.[15] Here was the germ of a solution, but the snag was that producing certificates of origin by customs authorities was too complicated, and least of all were Carli's own Italian customs capable of operating such a system. The Carli Plan was examined exhaustively by OEEC committees and there was more optimism about the successful outcome of the negotiations for the Seventeen than at any other point. It was eventually rejected because of the mammoth customs complications.

While the Carli Plan was under debate the French produced their own Faure Plan. This stipulated that British Commonwealth countries must accept at preferential rates a quota of European goods which would pay only the standing Imperial Preference duty. Faure complained that the British would not open their markets to the Six's farm produce, and because of this there must be substantial compensation in other fields. However, the rest of the Six would not accept the Faure Plan and when the French government fell in April 1958 it was abandoned.[16]

With France without a government, the visit to London of Adenauer, the German Chancellor, was important. Maudling briefed the Prime Minister that the French had been working hard on him recently and had told Adenauer:

(1) That the British never liked the Common Market, and the Free Trade Area is merely a plan to sabotage it.
(2) That the British were trying to put pressure on France to fall in with a scheme designed to meet British interests.
(3) That the British are trying hard to have it both ways particularly in maintaining Commonwealth Preference while claiming access to the Common Market.

At this stage both the French and Germans hoped they might obtain advantages out of Commonwealth Preference. Christopher Steel, Ambassador to Germany, reported 'The Germans have an idea of using the Free Trade Area as a means of getting a cut out of imperial preference.' Maudling's reaction was that 'We should firmly resist the suggestion that we owe the Six some form of compensation for Commonwealth entry.'[17]

The Macmillan–Adenauer talk in which Maudling and Ludwig Erhard, the pro-British German Finance Minister, also took part went well, with the Germans promising to pressurize the French towards a satisfactory settlement.

On 1 June 1958 de Gaulle became Prime Minister of France and Britain faced a tougher struggle. Faure while Prime Minister had genuinely tried for an agreement between the Six and the Eleven, but now he was outside the government. The Maudling Committee made no progress in the autumn of 1958. Macmillan became frustrated and on 24 June even sent a memorandum to the Foreign Secretary toying with withdrawing British troops from NATO if de Gaullist France stayed intransigent. He was out to wreck the EEC if the Six would not give way.[18]

On 10 October de Gaulle announced that France would not consider any arrangements which excluded agriculture and because of France's many concessions it was up to the United Kingdom to make some. On 6 November the French Foreign Minister, Couve de Murville, came to London and finally dashed Britain's hopes by saying the Free Trade Area was 'unacceptable' to the French, and the Six must have a special position between themselves. Macmillan told Couve that it depressed him that 'Sparta and Athens must quarrel; the Russians were getting stronger and stronger all the time and here was the free world voluntarily weakening and dividing itself. History will regard this as a tragic decision and the crowning folly of the twentieth century in Europe.' In a letter he begged de Gaulle to do something to prevent the erection of barriers 'between two halves of Europe'.

De Gaulle paid no attention, and a week later (13 November) on de Gaulle's orders the French Minister of Information, Jacques Soustelle, announced 'It was not possible to form a Free Trade Area as had been wished by the British to result in free trade between the Six and the Eleven other OEEC countries unless there was a common external tariff and harmonisation in the economic and social spheres.' With the Soustelle veto the Free Trade Area of Seventeen was dead.[19]

After the Soustelle veto, Macmillan more than any other member of the Cabinet strove for an agreement with the Six and still hoped for a *modus vivendi* until February 1959 when Walter Hallstein, President of the EEC Commission, met Maudling in London and stated categorically that it would be 'useless' to bring the Seventeen together again. Macmillan then gave up hope of negotiating a *modus vivendi* with the Six and in retaliation decided to try for a Free Trade Area of Seven to bargain with the Six.[20] The countries were to be Britain, Norway, Sweden, Denmark, Austria, Portugal and Switzerland, and the project was christened Uniscan.[21]

The first important Foreign Office minute about it stated: 'A Uniscan FTA has many drawbacks. It will serve to divide Europe even more deeply and our initiative in producing it will provoke US displeasure.' This was correct. America was keen on France drawing Germany out of Soviet influence and disliked the Uniscan initiative. At first Macmillan saw Uniscan as a strong bargaining counter from which to make a bridge with the Six. Later he blew cold on the Seven, and sought a British settlement with the Six regardless of the rest of the Seven.

The member countries of the Seven at Stockholm on 21 July 1959 signed an agreement to remove all import tariffs between them. Macmillan's hopes that this might improve the chances of an agreement with the Six came to nothing, and in fact EFTA of Seven became an added complication in Britain's tortuous relations with the EEC; it also angered America. So vehement was Douglas Dillon, US Under Secretary of State, when he came to London that Macmillan sent a minute to the Foreign Secretary querying whether the Special Relationship still existed.[22]

Initially there had been enthusiasm in Britain for the Uniscan Plan as a reaction to the humiliation suffered at the hands of France by their veto on the proposed linking of the Six with the Eleven. By the time the Stockholm convention was ratified on 20 November 1959 this had largely vanished mainly because trade figures showed that despite the tariff barrier British exports to the Six were increasing far faster than to the Seven.

At the end of November 1959 the Six accelerated their internal tariff reductions, and despite Macmillan appealing to de Gaulle to halt the acceleration these came into operation on 1 July 1960. This convinced Macmillan that he was backing the wrong horse, and he persuaded the Cabinet to appoint Sir Frank Lee, Joint Head of the Treasury, to examine all possible solutions to the European problem and to report on how the Six could join the Seven as a unit and how Britain could be part of a Customs Union while retaining the advantages of Imperial Preference and excluding agriculture completely.

This shows Macmillan as accepting the inevitability of Britain joining the EEC, although he was unrealistic in believing that farming could be excluded because by now the Six had embarked on their agricultural policy and wanted uniform food prices throughout the

Community, which was incompatible with Britain enjoying cheap Commonwealth food.

Sir Frank Lee's report became the watershed; and after digesting it Macmillan started in earnest to try and convince his colleagues that Britain's future definitely lay with the Six. In his report Lee wrote 'our exports becoming increasingly disadvantaged in the growing markets of the EEC would be a serious matter for Britain' and the creation of a 'bridge between the Six and Seven was improbable'. His conclusion was:

> We must maintain our broad objective of having the UK form part of a single European market . . . we shall not get the solution we want on the cheap . . . we shall have to be prepared for the sort of settlement we want – in political terms of inconvenience for or damage to some of our cherished interests – the Commonwealth domestic agriculture, our tariff policy, perhaps indeed our political pride and sense of self reliance.

The Lee Report was discussed at an important Cabinet meeting on 13 July 1960. Heathcoat Amory, Chancellor of the Exchequer, was ready to join the EEC 'provided it did not impair our relations with the Commonwealth'; Maudling disagreed, saying to join would be 'disastrous', while Duncan Sandys, Minister of Aviation, a strong European, disagreed strongly with Maudling and wanted Britain to join 'where she might hope eventually to achieve leadership'. Although a majority of the Cabinet were against joining, Macmillan had broken the ice, although in the Commons on 25 July the government attitude was that there were 'insuperable difficulties' in the way of joining. After a Cabinet reshuffle Macmillan made the European enthusiast Edward Heath Lord Privy Seal and entrusted him with exploring the possibility of Britain applying to join.[23]

Heath, with Macmillan's backing, got the upper hand over the Eurosceptic Maudling in Cabinet, and began to make informal approaches through the Ambassadors to the Six. These were followed by a visit by Macmillan to de Gaulle at Rambouillet in January 1961. Particularly discouraging was de Gaulle's remark to Macmillan that he did not see how it was 'possible for the Commonwealth and the Six to make an economic community without destroying one or the other'. The official account of the talks shows that de Gaulle was off-putting, but Macmillan recorded 'Broadly speaking

I think we made good progress.' Sir Pierson Dixon, the newly appointed Ambassador in Paris, who was present was doubtful of a successful outcome to any negotiations. Dixon's view was confirmed when Frank Lee met Oliver Wormser, the chief French negotiator. Wormser stated abruptly that if Britain decided to join the EEC she must abandon her cheap food policy, although he assured Lee that if Britain did decide to join then the response would be one 'of unreserved welcome'. As Wormser had just told Lee that if Britain joined she would have to apply the common external tariff to all Commonwealth imports including food, it was unpromising.[24]

In meetings held on 20 and 21 April 1961 Macmillan pressed his Cabinet to agree to apply to join. Macmillan said that for some time after the war Europe had been dependent on American aid and content to accept Anglo-Saxon leadership, but she had now regained her strength and there was now a new situation in which the economic state of Britain might be 'undermined'. Therefore it was in our interest to join the Six if we could gain admission on terms which would be tolerable. De Gaulle did not want us in since he wanted to hold the reins in Europe, but his attitude might change if he saw that the West 'could not prevail against the Communists unless its leading countries worked together'. The Cabinet conclusion was that there was no reason of principle why the United Kingdom should not accede to the Treaty of Rome subject to the interests of the Commonwealth and the other EFTA countries.

Macmillan had cleverly swung his colleagues round. However, he had not dared to suggest that Commonwealth Preference and cheap food must be abandoned.[25]

Talks in Paris on 22 and 23 June between Sir Roderick Barclay of the Foreign Office and Sir Eric Roll of the Ministry of Agriculture with Wormser were the red light. They should have made it clear to Macmillan and Heath that only minor concessions over the Commonwealth would be wrung out of the French, and in effect Britain had to accept the Rome Treaty hook, line and sinker or stay out. Maudling saw it that way and wrote to Macmillan that the French had rejected in advance 'any proposals on the points of vital interest to us'.[26]

Macmillan, although he had a high regard for Maudling, ignored Maudling's letter, and at a weekend conference at Chequers on the weekend of 17–18 June 1961 a majority of ministers were in favour of making a formal application to join the EEC provided that special terms were given for the Commonwealth. The Cabinet approved the Chequers decision and after ministers had been sent on a fruitless round of visits to soften up Commonwealth Prime Ministers, the Cabinet decided that Macmillan should announce in the Commons on 31 July 1961 that Britain was applying to join the EEC.[27] In the debate there were only twenty-two Conservative abstentions and the Conservative Party Conference also gave overwhelming support. This near consensus in favour of Europe by a former generation of Conservatives is a marked contrast with the way in which Eurosceptics wreck the Conservative Party today.

Macmillan's main problem was to persuade the Six to allow preferential treatment for the Commonwealth and to prevail upon the Conservative pro-Empire lobby to accept some watering down of Commonwealth preference. Also he had to convince the Six that Britain would co-operate with the ideals and principles of the Six as expressed in the Treaty of Rome despite there being few signs of British enthusiasm for federalism or supranational institutions.

The Cabinet hoped that the Six would make slashing concessions over Commonwealth food, but to do so ran counter to the whole thrust of the EEC common agricultural policy which was already outlined in the Mansholt report. A thorn in Macmillan's flesh was Lord Beaverbrook. Passionately devoted to the Empire, his influential newspapers backed to the hilt British opponents of EEC entry.

Heath put his finger on the main problem in his 'introductory statement' to the EEC Council of Ministers in October 1961, saying that Britain could not join the EEC under conditions in which the Commonwealth trade connection was cut with grave loss and 'even ruin for some of the Commonwealth countries'. Heath also pointed out that under the Treaty of Rome generous treatment had been given to the former French African colonies and Tunisia.[28] Unfortunately Britain was too late. The Six were not prepared at this stage of their evolution to water down their common agricultural policy by agreeing to the continuing entry to Britain of cheap Commonwealth food, nor would they accept tariff free competition for industrial goods from the Commonwealth. In December, without consulting Britain, the Six as part of their agricultural policy agreed to put levies on all imports of food and to use these levies both to subsidize farm food production and dump surplus food production abroad. This made Heath's negotiating position difficult.

As 1962 opened, the British tried to speed up negotiations in the hope of becoming a full member by January 1963. There was a reluctance on both sides for tough negotiations over the Commonwealth problem for fear of a breakdown. Five out of the Six wanted Britain in, but de Gaulle was rigidly opposed, although he did not want France to be seen as the obstructionist.

From his post at Geneva as Secretary General of EFTA Sir Frank Figures of the Treasury had a ringside view. He was pessimistic on 28 February, writing:

> he doubted whether our present tactics would solve the Six/Seven problem and were causing real distress not only to our friends amongst the Six but also to some countries within the Seven . . . the only hope was the acceptance of the Treaty of Rome subject not only to special arrangements for the Commonwealth and adoption of their agricultural policy would be necessary. We should not underestimate the feeling of hatred against the UK being put out at all levels by both the European Commission and the French administration.

Figures was correct in diagnosing 'the feeling of hatred' towards Britain in France. However, this was due not to the attempt to adjust the Treaty of Rome to accommodate the Commonwealth but to the refusal of Britain to help France to become a nuclear power on which aim de Gaulle had set his heart. Dixon from Paris told Heath in March that the reaction of the French to the British application 'would depend to a great extent on whether France is now considered to be a nuclear power'.[29]

A minute from Heath shows that he saw this nuclear policy as the key factor in securing French agreement to British entry into the EEC. Heath minuted:

> What alarms me more than anything else is that, at the same time as we are trying to negotiate our entry into the EEC – in which we have all too few cards to play – we are giving every indication of wishing to carry out political policies which are anathema to the two most important members of the Community. . . . What they see here is our apparent determination with the United States to prevent the French from developing their atomic and nuclear defence.[30]

At the time the Americans insisted on strict interpretation of the rule that there should be no dissemination of nuclear secrets to the French. In Cabinet it was never questioned whether Britain should, in order to placate de Gaulle, try to break this US ruling. Dixon and Heath were correct; if Britain had aided de Gaulle in his efforts to make France an independent nuclear power he might have yielded over EEC entry.

Dixon, who was both Ambassador in Paris and head of the British negotiating team in Brussels, continued to send gloomy reports from Paris pointing out that de Gaulle did not want the negotiations to succeed and was hoping that we would abandon our attempt to join. Within the Paris Embassy there was a cold sense of realism, but in London unjustifiable optimism existed, and a disregard that Dixon was better placed than anyone else to gauge the chances of success.[31]

Heath and his team of civil servants ponderously negotiated in Brussels; Commonwealth imports and British farm policy were tough problems, but solutions to them were in sight when in July there came increasing indications that France would say 'No'; these were heavily signposted from the British Embassy in Paris. In May the British had insisted that part or all of the levies (financial contributions) collected on imported food should be returned to the country collecting them and would not be part of the community's budget income. Then in August the French demanded that no monies from levies should be returned to the collecting country. As the biggest food-importing country this would hit Britain hard.

Feeling against the financial contribution was strong both in Britain and the Commonwealth. John McEwan, the Australian Deputy Prime Minister, had made a devastating statement in London on 16 July:

> A price basis as you suggested would mean that Britain would be paying for Australian wheat substantially less than would be paid from a supplier in the community. She would be collecting on Australian wheat levies at least part of which could very well be used to subsidize community wheat to our disadvantage in other markets. This is a situation to which we would have strong objections.[32]

In his memoirs Macmillan wrote that 'we' were encouraged by Mr McEwan's general attitude to the Common Market. This cannot be true.

At a marathon session on the night of 5/6 August the French prepared a trap for the British on de Gaulle's orders, undoubtedly with a view to causing a breakdown. At 3 a.m. in the morning of 6 August Couve de Murville for the French produced a paper which meant that no levies would be returned so that the levies on Commonwealth food could be used to subsidize EEC food exports and the British liability would be sky high with no refunds allowed.

Heath, taken unawares, refused to discuss the French paper. Pierson Dixon wrote in his diary that the night of 5/6 August was 'the end of the Brussels negotiations'.[33] He was correct; he did not mean that the levy problem was insoluble but that de Gaulle was determined to find some pretext to keep Britain out.[34]

The Deputy Prime Minister of New Zealand, John Marshall, said hopefully 'The death sentence has been pronounced.' Arnold France, a Treasury representative at the British Brussels delegation, wrote that the French had tried to bounce Heath by highly discreditable means into a formal agreement that the levies on food imports from the Commonwealth could be used for the community budget, and France with a high proportion of their own food would pay only small levies while Britain would pay large levies.[35]

Neither Heath nor Macmillan accepted that all was lost. De Gaulle was hoping that the Commonwealth Prime Ministers at their London Conference starting on 10 September would be so opposed that Britain would be forced to abandon the application. He was disappointed.

Adroitly, Macmillan prevailed on the Commonwealth Prime Ministers to agree to an anodyne press statement:

> The Prime Ministers took note that the negotiations in Brussels were still incomplete, and that a number of important questions have still to be negotiated. Only when the full terms were known would it be possible to form a final judgement.

Macmillan's next hurdle was the Conservative Party Conference in October. Here all went swimmingly. An anti-Common Market amendment moved by the Conservative former ministers Robin Turton and Derek Walker Smith was defeated with only fifty out of 4,000 voting for it. So enthusiastic were the delegates after Macmillan's winding up speech that Heath feared it would give the Six the impression that Britain would join at any price and thus weaken his bargaining position at Brussels.

Meanwhile, France had a political crisis. On 5 October the Pompidou government was unexpectedly defeated; Parliament was dissolved, with 25 November scheduled for a General Election; simultaneously de Gaulle called for a referendum on his presidency. It is possible that while the outcome of the French elections was uncertain British pressure for urgent agreement to accession might have succeeded. The fleeting moment, if it existed, was lost in unrewarding discussions on how long it should take to align British farm policy with the Community's, the financial regulations, and what preferences should be given to the Commonwealth. The Gaullist parties convincingly won the General Election, and de Gaulle triumphed in the referendum so that his political authority was absolute.

At this period Macmillan had doubts about whether de Gaulle would allow British entry. In his speech to the Conservative Party Conference he insisted that arrangements must be made to safeguard the Commonwealth, home agriculture and fellow members of EFTA – a repetition of his message to the Commons in the July 1961 debate. Iain Macleod, Chairman of the Conservative Party, said Britain must not pay too high a price for entry, while Fred Erroll, President of the Board of Trade, declared 'it would be no disaster' if Britain stayed outside. These statements, obviously co-ordinated, may have been a ploy to convince the Six that Britain would not join unless the terms were satisfactory; more probably they were to prepare the British public for failure.

A revealing circular was sent to all British Ambassadors on 26 November stating that it was out of the question for us, as the Six have suggested, to abandon our whole (farm) deficiency payments 'immediately upon entry'; it was essential to 'secure reasonable arrangements to safeguard Commonwealth interests and the successful outcome of the Commonwealth Conference should not be allowed to obscure the very serious misgivings which exist and which we must strive to meet'.[36]

On 12 December in a Commons debate Harold Wilson (Leader of the Opposition) said that an enormous revenue would go to the European Fund partly to subsidize European agriculture and partly to subsidize exports of high-costing European produce to the Third World countries, and it would 'have the effect of penalizing further Commonwealth producers who have already been pushed off our market'. 'We cannot', he declared, 'accept the agricultural programme if it is based on this penal levy.'

At the same time, a Gallup Poll showed that the percentage in favour of joining 'on the facts as you know them at present' had declined from 40 per cent in October to 29 per cent, while the figure for those who opposed had risen from 28 to 37 per cent.

Thus there were dark clouds over the negotiations when de Gaulle and Macmillan met at Rambouillet on 15 and 16 December 1962. Long discussions according to Macmillan's memoirs became a 'wrangle'. De Gaulle told the British Prime Minister bluntly that 'it was not possible for Britain to enter tomorrow', and the arrangements inside the Six 'might be too rigid for Britain'. Macmillan replied that he was 'astonished and deeply wounded'. De Gaulle's last point was that France at the moment could say 'No' to any policies of the Six with which she disagreed, but once Great Britain and Scandinavia joined then it would be different. Macmillan's final words to him were 'If this was really the French views it should have been put forward at the very start.'

Macmillan had run up against a brick wall. Sir Michael Butler told me the Prime Minister was very distressed, and in the library at the Paris Embassy was almost in tears when he related to the Embassy staff that de Gaulle intended to block Britain's entry, and thus all the negotiations had been in vain.[37]

False hopes then sprang up in Macmillan's breast. On the first day of talks at Rambouillet, de Gaulle indicated that he had no real interest in nuclear weapons, which he knew France could not manufacture, but for the prestige of France he wanted a token *force de frappe*. Macmillan misunderstood and believed that if he could persuade President Kennedy to allow France nuclear weapons de Gaulle might soften his attitude to British entry. At Nassau on 19 December 1962, Macmillan, with considerable difficulty, prevailed upon Kennedy to supply both France and Britain with launchers for Polaris atomic missiles.[38] He hoped this would be the quid pro quo which would induce de Gaulle to change his mind about British entry. He could not have been more wrong. It only strengthened de Gaulle's resolve to veto British entry.[39]

De Gaulle looked on the offer of Polaris by America as evidence that Britain rejected all co-operation between France and Britain over atomic weapons. Heath told me his firm view is that de Gaulle was intensely annoyed at the patronizing way in which Kennedy and Macmillan at Nassau offered France a share in a NATO nuclear deterrent subject to American strings, and that without this provocation he might still have been able to overcome the difficulties and successfully negotiated entry at marathon meetings in January 1963.[40]

Heath's view that the Nassau offer was the deciding factor in de Gaulle denying British membership is not shared by survivors of his negotiating team or the Paris Embassy. The truth must be that unless Britain pooled her nuclear secrets with France de Gaulle would not allow us in, and the Americans rigidly refused to allow the British to disseminate nuclear knowledge. De Gaulle was intent on a nuclear weapon independent of America.[41]

Despite the gloom shed by Rambouillet, the Cabinet still hoped that agreement on entry would be reached at the meetings of Ministers in mid-January 1963. On 20 December 1962 Heath told the Cabinet:

> My expectation is, and certainly my hope is, that we shall be able to achieve satisfactory arrangements. Beginning on 14 January there will be a series of Ministerial meetings in Brussels as a result of which I hope to bring the negotiations to a successful conclusion.

On the controversial financial levy, Heath explained that he had reason to hope that Britain's share would be agreed 'as equal to that of France and Germany' at about 22 per cent. The Cabinet gave him a mandate to settle the outstanding issues on the basis of a Cabinet paper which he had submitted to the meeting.[42]

No more negotiations took place. Instead, de Gaulle imposed a veto. At a press conference on 14 January he declared Britain 'unfit for membership'. With his hopes for co-operation in nuclear know-how shattered by Nassau, the French President was not prepared to share leadership of the Common Market with Britain.

Although Macmillan had throughout been reluctant to face up to the implications of full membership, he was convinced there was no other acceptable course. His comment was 'All our policies at home and abroad are in ruins.'[43] The negotiations had caused friction with the Commonwealth; in return there was nothing to show except that Britain might never have become a member after de Gaulle's downfall if it had not been for this first try.

NOTES

Richard Lamb's *The Macmillan Years: The Emerging Truth* (London: John Murray, 1995) pp. 102–203 covers the negotiations for EFTA of Seventeen, EFTA of Seven and the application for entry to the EEC with numerous quotations from official documents.

Jacqueline Tratt's *The Macmillan Government and Europe* (Basingstoke: Macmillan, 1996) is an in-depth survey of relations with Europe from 1956 to 1961.

Miriam Camps' *Britain and the European Community* (Princeton, N.J.: Princeton University Press, 1964) covers the whole period, but was written before the official documents were available in the Public Record Office.

1. Based on a paper given to the Centre of International Studies at Christ's College, Cambridge, on 5 September 1996.
2. Alistair Horne, *Macmillan: 1957–1986*, vol. 1 (London: Macmillan, 1989), p. 314.
3. Richard Lamb, *The Failure of the Eden Government* (London: Sidgwick and Jackson, 1987), p. 61.
4. FO 953/1207.
5. Cab 129/50; Prem 11/153; Cab 128/24.
6. A myth has arisen that a Board of Trade official attended. This is incorrect.
7. Conversation with Russell Bretherton, 1986.
8. Ibid.; BT 11/5402; FO 371/122023; FO 371/122024; T 234183; Lamb, op. cit., pp. 60–92.
9. FO 371/122035.
10. Lamb, op. cit., p. 97; Cab 129/82.
11. FO 371/134520; Prem 11/2826.
12. Cab 129/82; FO 371/122046.
13. FO 371/122035; FO 371/134488; FO 371/134886; Prem 11/2133; Lamb, *The Macmillan Years*, pp. 109–10.
14. Prem 11/2531.
15. Maudling in his memoirs described Carli as 'one of the most able men I have had the good fortune to encounter'. Maudling, *Memoirs* (London: Sidgwick and Jackson, 1968), p. 70.
16. FO 371/134450; FO 371/134498.
17. FO 371/134450; FO 371/134504.
18. Prem 11/2532.
19. FO 371/134510; FO 371/134511; FO 371/134513.
20. The original suggestion for this had come from Bretherton who from his observation post in Brussels had realized no agreement would be reached between the Six and the Seven. FO 371/134450.
21. Prem 11/2827; Prem 11/2826; FO 371/134450.
22. FO 371/134514; FO 371/142504; Prem 11/3132.
23. Cab 128/34; Prem 11/3133.
24. FO 371/158264; FO 371/158171; Macmillan, *Pointing the Way* (London: Macmillan, 1972) p. 327.
25. Cab 128/35.

26. FO 371/157178; FO 371/158177.
27. Prem 11/3557; Prem 11/3558; Cab 128/35.
28. Lamb, op. cit., pp. 158–61.
29. FO 371/164778; FO 371/171149.
30. FO 371/171149.
31. FO 371/164835; FO 371/164780; FO 371/164781.
32. Cab 134/1537.
33. FO 371/837; FO 371/164802; Piers Dixon, *Double Diploma* (London: Hamish Hamilton, 1968), p. 292.
34. Letters to author from Sir Patrick Reilly and Lord Roll.
35. Cab 134/1536.
36. Cab 134/1539.
37. Prem 11/4230; interview with Sir Michael Butler.
38. De Gaulle would have to rely on US nuclear warheads.
39. Ian Clark, *Nuclear Diplomacy and the British Relationship* (Oxford: Oxford University Press, 1994). p. 481, quoting from papers in the Kennedy Centre.
40. FO 371/173308; interview with Sir Edward Heath.
41. Interviews with Sir Patrick Reilly and Sir Michael Butler. Reilly who was in charge at the Foreign Office much admires Heath for the way in which he conducted the negotiations. Butler, who worked with Dixon in Paris is highly critical believing Heath should have signed on the dotted line and renegotiated afterwards.
42. Cab 128/36.
43. Horne, op. cit., vol. 2, p. 447.

7 'Ne pleurez pas, Milord':[1] Macmillan and France from Algiers to Rambouillet

N. Piers Ludlow[2]

France was much less central to Macmillan's thought than the United States. There are long tracts of his memoirs, and lengthy sections of his two most recent biographies, in which no reference to the French can be found.[3] Yet dealings with France contributed significantly to the start and the end of Harold Macmillan's ministerial career. His war-time success in handling the Free French in Algiers represented Macmillan's first, significant achievement as a minister; his failure to manage the French during Britain's unsuccessful bid to enter the European Community in 1961–3 was, by contrast, his last great failure. An examination of Macmillan's handling and mishandling of France thus forms an important part of any audit of his career. This article will look briefly at Macmillan's North African interlude, before assessing in rather more detail the disappointments of the 1950s and 1960s. Particular attention will be given to the 1961–3 membership application and to the vision of Anglo-French leadership in Europe with which Macmillan hoped to win over President de Gaulle.

Macmillan's activities in North Africa in 1943 were important for two reasons.[4] First, Macmillan's success in handling the French in general, and Charles de Gaulle in particular, was a major feather in his cap. He had arrived, as Roosevelt's envoy in North Africa put it, without 'any exceptional knowledge of French or African affairs'.[5] He left having played an important role in managing the tense internal politics of the Free French and, in particular, having contributed to General de Gaulle's triumph over his American-sponsored rival General Giraud. Both his reputation and his self-confidence grew significantly as a result. Second, Macmillan had acquired in the process a wide range of contacts with what was to become the post-war French élite. While in Algiers he had the opportunity to encounter three future French Prime Ministers, Henri Queuille, Pierre Mendès-France and Maurice Couve de Murville; two subsequent IVième République cabinet ministers, Daniel Mayer and Jacques Soustelle; René Massigli, Henri Bonnet and Hervé Alphand, three of the most influential post-war French diplomats; and Jean Monnet, the architect of both French post-war economic recovery and of the early stages of European integration. And, of course, he had had extensive dealings with de Gaulle himself. These had not been easy. Nevertheless, both men appear to have developed a wary respect for each other and an awareness of each other's strengths. Furthermore, Macmillan had been able to develop an insight into the difficulties of dealing with the future French leader that few of his British counterparts could have matched. His war-time assessment of de Gaulle was uncannily prescient:

> General de Gaulle is one of those horses which either refuses to come to the starting-gate at all, or insists on careering down the course before the signal is given, or suddenly elects to run on a race-course different from the one appointed by the Stewards of the Jockey Club.[6]

Given this early opportunity to gain experience of de Gaulle, it is all the more remarkable that of all post-war British politicians it should have been Macmillan who suffered most at the General's hands.

It was over European integration that Macmillan's next serious dealings with the French occurred. Throughout the 1950s, Macmillan distinguished himself as one of the few senior British politicians who took at all seriously the process of integration underway between France, Germany, Italy and the Benelux nations. This did not always mean that he was supportive of their efforts. Indeed, in 1950 a joint plan by Macmillan and David Eccles to create a non-supranational body to control the European coal industry was angrily dismissed by Jean Monnet as an attempt to sabotage the much more ambitious European Coal and Steel Community, while in 1955 Macmillan as Foreign Secretary bore at least partial responsibility for a British *démarche* which was seen by many on the continent as an effort to nip in the bud the negotiations that eventually led to the EEC's formation.[7] But even unsuccessful policy ventures such as these highlighted the extent to which Macmillan felt that Britain could not stand idly by as its continental neighbours strove to de-

velop both economic and political unity. They are therefore consistent with Macmillan's more positive moves, such as his 1952 memo
to Anthony Eden in which he called for a new British policy
towards Europe or his 1955 insistence that Britain send a high-level
representative to the Spaak committee discussions about a possible European common market.[8] In total contrast to his long-standing
rivals 'Rab' Butler and Eden, Macmillan was never bored by European integration.[9]

Equally distinctive was Macmillan's awareness that the process
underway among the Six was about more than simple economic
co-operation. In a period when responsibility for following developments in the integration process tended to be left to the economic sections of the Whitehall machinery, and when, tellingly,
Britain's representative on the Spaak committee had been a relatively junior Board of Trade official rather than the senior foreign
ministry delegates sent by the Six, Macmillan was already conscious
that a successful outcome of the Messina process might pose a
serious political danger to Britain. In February 1956, for instance,
he had written in alarmist fashion about the possibility of Germany
becoming the dominant power in Europe through the integration
process, and he concluded: 'I do not like the prospect of a world
divided into the Russian sphere, the American sphere and a united
Europe of which we are not a member.'[10]

Despite this anxiety about the prospect of German dominance
in the long term, Macmillan was convinced that in the immediate
future the key player among the Six was France. It was the French
who had made the original decision in 1950 to press ahead without
Britain, it was the French who were the principal determinants of
the pace of the Treaty of Rome negotiations and it was the French
who would need most persuading if Britain was to be allowed either
to join or in some way to associate itself with the EEC project. In
the late 1950s, just as was to be the case during the 1961–3 application, Paris, not Bonn or Brussels, was the focal point for
Macmillan's attention. At times, indeed, Macmillan's reflections about
how to redefine Britain's position *vis-à-vis* the Continent convey
the impression that Germany, Italy and the Benelux countries
mattered only in so far as they could coax, cajole or pressurize
France into agreement with the UK. But for all his interest in what
was happening on the Continent, for all his sensitivity to the political
as well as economic dimension of integration, and for all his awareness
of the centrality of France to the whole process, Macmillan, first

as Foreign Secretary, then as Chancellor of the Exchequer and finally as Prime Minister, endorsed and promoted a policy response to the Messina process which was hamstrung from the outset by its failure to take into account the needs, hopes and anxieties of the French.[11]

Plan G was an ingenious policy. In essence it was a proposal to create a free trade area for industrial goods encompassing all eighteen members of the Organization for European Economic Cooperation (OEEC).[12] It represented a major development in UK commercial policy, but one which, because of the exclusion of agriculture and the absence of any requirement to harmonize tariff levels towards the rest of the world, would leave Britain's trade links with the Commonwealth largely unaffected. Furthermore, it could be seen as compatible with the parallel arrangements being devised among the Six. If the Six succeeded in their attempt to create a closely knit economic community, complete with a common external tariff, strong institutions and a common agricultural policy, they would constitute the inner kernel of a wider European free trade zone, but their co-operation would not harm economically those Western European countries which chose to remain outside of the EEC. If, by contrast, the Six failed, a scenario which the Foreign Office deemed likely until 1957 at least, an OEEC free trade area would ensure that their set-back did not undermine the wider process of trade liberalization within Europe. The plan thus seemed to reconcile both Britain's European and Commonwealth ties and to cater for either completion or collapse in the Treaty of Rome negotiations.

The proposal, moreover, appeared likely to reconcile a number of apparently incompatible interests. Thus the advocacy of Macmillan and Peter Thorneycroft, the President of the Board of Trade, was sufficient to win the backing of the British Cabinet in September 1956, while at a specially convened conference of Commonwealth representatives in July 1957, the acquiescence, albeit grudging, of Britain's former empire was obtained.[13] Several European governments also seemed enthusiastic. In West Germany and in the Benelux countries there were many who had expressed anxiety that the Six constituted too narrow and too restrictive an outlet for trade. The prospect of tariffs being removed throughout Western Europe was therefore warmly welcomed. In Germany, the Minister for Economics, Ludwig Erhard, tried in October 1956 to persuade the Cabinet to abandon the deadlocked negotiations about the EEC in favour of the British plan.[14] He was defeated, but his personal support for the British scheme survived and was shared by much of the German political and industrial élite. Others, such as the Belgian Christian Democrat Baron Snoy, saw the scheme as a useful supplement to, rather than replacement of, the EEC.[15]

Unfortunately for Macmillan, however, there was little such support for the scheme in France. This was not due to Anglophobia. On the contrary, many amongst the French élites had regretted the 1950 decision to start building European institutions without Britain, had welcomed the brief flurry of Anglo-French co-operation which had culminated in the joint operation in Suez, and were keen to see close cross-channel co-operation reestablished.[16] But the free trade area was ill-designed to bring about such a *rapprochement*. Indeed, the whole scheme constituted a major threat to the French government's plans to win public and parliamentary approval for the EEC. It was therefore essential for France that the project be postponed for as long as possible, if not abandoned altogether.

The French government's approach to the Treaty of Rome negotiations had been extremely cautious. The Prime Minister, Guy Mollet, and his closest collaborators were acutely aware that the proposed common market would provoke strong opposition both from those such as the Gaullists who were politically hostile to supranational integration and from the economic interests who had successfully thwarted several planned customs unions in the late 1940s. Public and parliamentary opinion was thus encouraged to concentrate on the proposals for European co-operation in the field of nuclear energy – a project which enjoyed widespread support in France – while French negotiators in Brussels were instructed to win a wide variety of concessions designed to make the common market scheme more palatable. Foremost amongst these was a pledge that the EEC would incorporate a common agricultural policy, thereby opening up the prospect of lucrative foreign trade for French farmers, and special provisions for the soon-to-be-independent French territories in Africa. Equally important to France were a series of measures designed to ensure that the liberalization brought about by the EEC would not give too severe a shock to the fragile French economy. Paris had thus insisted that the level of the common external tariff be set at a point substantially above the average German or Benelux tariffs and that internal tariff disarmament be accompanied by steps to harmonize social security costs across the Community. A further goal dear to the French was the inclusion

of safeguard clauses, intended to allow the French to delay imple-
mentation of certain aspects of the Treaty of Rome should the French
economy encounter difficulties. The French government thus hoped
that the EEC would bring about a controlled and partial abandonment of traditional French protectionism, inside a Community which
would also enable the French to obtain certain long-cherished aims.[17]

The free trade area plan offered no such guarantees. It specifically excluded both agricultural trade and commerce between European states and their imperial or former imperial territories. It
provided for no common external tariff barrier nor any timetable
for the harmonization of social security provisions across all eighteen participating countries. It made no mention of safeguard clauses.
And of course it would confront the French economy with unhin-
dered competition from all seventeen other members of the OEEC
rather than just her five European Coal and Steel Community (ECSC)
partners. It also lacked the long-term political aim of the EEC:
the yearning for a stronger Europe, less dependent on the US,
which had reached new heights in France in the aftermath of the
Suez crisis, would not be satisfied by a mere free trade arrangement.[18] None of the features of the European Community that were
central to the French government's plans to win parliamentary support
were thus shared by the free trade area. Furthermore, the French
saw a real danger that the British proposal might undermine all
that they were trying to achieve in the Treaty of Rome negotiations.
Germany, they feared, would be much less likely to acquiesce in
an expensive agricultural policy, a set of measures designed to assist
Francophone Africa, and provisions for the harmonization of social
costs – all aspects of the Treaty of Rome that had been highly
controversial within the Federal Republic – if the British were offering
the prospect of industrial free trade without any of the associated
costs. The free trade area was thus not only unappealing *per se*,
but it also threatened to destroy all that the French hoped to obtain
from their involvement in the Treaty of Rome process.[19]

The French thus mounted a determined effort to delay and obstruct
the British plan. It could not be rejected outright – it enjoyed too
much support elsewhere in the Community, and Britain was too
close an ally to be summarily rejected.[20] But it could both be delayed
– an objective which was attained in the spring of 1957 when the
French received a promise from London not to press ahead with
the free trade area scheme until the ratification of the Treaty of
Rome was complete – and, through careful diplomacy, transformed

into something much more akin to the Treaty of Rome. The OEEC committee which was to examine the proposal was inundated with French requests designed to transform the British project into something more substantial than a simple free trade area. With the Six divided and the British unwilling to allow their scheme to be totally altered, deadlock was the inevitable result.

Macmillan's response was ineffective. He had placed too much faith in the French fear of Germany, calculating wrongly that France would be ready to pay a high economic price in order to secure close British involvement in European cooperation.[21] When France proved to prefer more economically advantageous co-operation with Germany and without Britain, he had little to fall back upon. He did try briefly to put together a series of limited British concessions on agriculture. He also successfully persuaded the cabinet to endorse the idea that the free trade area should have strong common institutions.[22] But neither of these steps proved enough to satisfy the French; indeed, the token nature of such concessions only underlined the extent to which Macmillan had allowed his policy proposal to become so hemmed about with promises to the Commonwealth or pledges to British interest groups that substantial movement away from the UK's starting position proved impossible. Nor did Macmillan, by now Prime Minister, use his increased personal clout to launch a bilateral diplomatic offensive in support of his scheme. He did travel once to Paris for talks with Felix Gaillard. He also went to Bonn and urged Adenauer to intervene on Britain's behalf with the French. But on neither occasion did the Prime Minister have much to offer and little was accomplished as a result.[23] Furthermore, both Continental visits were totally overshadowed by Macmillan's much more evident diplomatic effort to mend fences with the Americans after the strains of the Suez affair. As James Ellison has argued, there was little in the overall thrust of British diplomacy at this time to convince either the French or their allies amongst the other five that Britain was serious in its intent to transform its relationship with Europe.[24]

De Gaulle's return to power in June 1958 briefly seemed to renew the prospects of the free trade area. An outspoken critic of supranational integration, the General would not necessarily abide by the Treaty of Rome and might, some predicted, opt instead for looser and wider co-operation within a free trade area without supranational powers. Macmillan indulged briefly in such speculation.[25] But as quickly became apparent, de Gaulle was also a pragmatist, well aware that his hopes of modernizing the French economy and of forging close ties with the Germans in particular – both essential prerequisites of his longer-term plans – would not be furthered by reneging on his predecessors' promises. France thus implemented the Treaty of Rome on time and in full.[26] The free trade area by contrast was brushed aside. On 11 November 1958, de Gaulle's spokesman announced that France was no longer ready to consider the British scheme. A week later the President travelled to Germany and persuaded Adenauer to accept that the free trade area plan was dead.[27] Taken together, these two events publicly underlined the impossibility of Macmillan's hopes. In reality, the failure to address French needs had ensured that the prospects of the free trade area plan had never been good, and by mid-1958 the scheme was clearly moribund. What has sometimes been described as de Gaulle's first veto was, in fact, an act of euthanasia.

Macmillan was angered and shaken by the French rejection of the free trade area. In bilateral discussions with the Americans he is widely reported to have compared the formation of the EEC without an accompanying free trade area to Napoleon's planned economic integration of Europe, and suggested that Britain's response should as vigorous in the twentieth century as it had been in the nineteenth.[28] But to his credit, the Prime Minister soon channelled this anger and frustration into the search for a new constructive approach to the Six. Thus, little more than a year after the collapse of the free trade area scheme, Macmillan seems to have privately decided that Britain's future lay inside the newly formed European Community. It would not be easy, however, either to win round his cabinet and party colleagues or to persuade public opinion that so significant a policy change was required.

The story of Macmillan's efforts to coax his government to a point where a membership application became possible has been well told elsewhere.[29] What is relevant to this essay is that by mid-1961 the Prime Minister had secured the consent of his cabinet, the Conservative Party and the Commonwealth to a new approach to Europe, this time based upon a conditional membership bid. Furthermore, Britain's new policy had been enthusiastically received by five of the six Community member states. The exception, repeating the pattern of 1957–8, was France.[30]

French qualms about British membership had a wide variety of explanations. At an economic level, the French government feared that the UK, both during the membership negotiations themselves and once inside the Community, would damage or destroy the fledgling CAP, lower the level of Community tariffs on a range of sensitive products, and alter the advantageous system of EEC support for former French colonies in Africa and the Caribbean. Politically, moreover, British membership threatened to disrupt Franco-German *rapprochement*, lessen the ability of the French to assume the political leadership of the grouping, and bolster American influence within the EEC. With Britain inside the Community, de Gaulle's hopes of transforming the EEC into a unified political grouping, able, under French leadership, to play a role on the world stage which was increasingly autonomous from the United States would be seriously compromised. That de Gaulle's response to the British diplomat who delivered the news that the UK had decided to apply was stiffly polite and totally lacking in the enthusiasm so noticeable in other European capitals was not at all surprising.[31]

In 1961, however, Macmillan had anticipated French opposition. Over the preceding years the Premier had toyed with a variety of ideas designed to give France a political incentive to resolve the division of Western Europe between the EEC and EFTA. These had included the suggestion that Britain might intervene in Washington in favour of de Gaulle's quest for greater tripartite consultation and, more radically, the possibility that the UK might in some way assist the French in their lengthy and time-consuming struggle to develop an independent nuclear deterrent.[32] By December 1960 these varied strands had come together in a document which Macmillan was to describe as his Grand Design.

The Grand Design quite deliberately set out to place British membership of the EEC in the wider context of Western unity. The Free World, it argued, risked losing ground to the Soviet bloc unless it could come to terms with the reappearance of a dynamic and strong Western Europe. Britain and America's priority aims should therefore be the resolution of the Six/Seven divide – an economic split which, according to Macmillan, risked hardening into a harmful political fracture – reform of the Atlantic Alliance, and the incorporation of French efforts to develop a nuclear deterrent of its own into a safe Alliance framework. De Gaulle and France were central to all three projects. As a result Britain and America would have to make an effort to satisfy de Gaulle's aspirations in the latter two fields in exchange for French acquiescence to the entry of Britain into the European Community. The Grand Design was thus in essence the sketch of a complex transatlantic bargain between Britain, America and France.[33]

Unfortunately for Macmillan, the American consent so central to his plans did not prove forthcoming. Neither a series of letters setting out his vision to Kennedy, nor Macmillan's April 1961 visit to Washington, were sufficient to convince the new US administration that so much had to be done to win over de Gaulle. Kennedy was loud in his praise of the British decision to apply for EEC membership, and Dean Rusk, his Secretary of State, declared his country's willingness to help British accession, but neither were prepared to promise nuclear assistance to France so as to bribe de Gaulle into allowing Britain in. To do so, Kennedy made clear, would violate the US stance on non-proliferation, invite demands from the Federal Republic for similar assistance, and incur the wrath of the US Congress.[34]

Macmillan was deeply disappointed by this American reply. In May he wrote in his diary that the European problem was 'obviously insoluble'; a month later he confessed that 'my great plan has failed'.[35] But despite his momentary depression, Macmillan did not abandon all hope. Neither the American veto of spring 1961, nor a second American prohibition on nuclear deals with the French that was delivered almost exactly a year later, destroyed the Prime Minister's belief that an arrangement could be reached with de Gaulle. Instead he pressed on, using the three summit meetings with de Gaulle that took place between Britain's application to the EEC and the collapse of the negotiations in January 1963, to set out a far-reaching vision of European co-operation centred on an Anglo-French core.[36] So radical was some of the rhetoric about Anglo-French co-operation employed by Macmillan in his encounters with the French leader that it deserves to be looked at in detail.[37]

The Prime Minister deliberately tailored his vision to fit in with de Gaulle's plans for political union among the Six. Indeed, one of the most remarkable tactics used by Macmillan in his attempts to win over the French leader was the repeated affirmation of Britain's belief in, and support for, an intergovernmental political grouping organized along the lines set out by the French President. At Birch Grove in November 1961 Macmillan declared himself to be in favour of a 'union des patries' – a label for European political union normally associated with de Gaulle; in May 1962 the Prime Minister informed de Gaulle that he was fully in agreement with the views on political union which the General had set out in his May 15 press conference; at Champs, the British statesman ridiculed the obstinacy which Belgium and the Netherlands were showing towards de Gaulle's plans; and at Rambouillet in December 1962 the premier predicted that political union would actually be agreed more easily once Britain was inside the Community than while she remained without.[38] The French President was thus left in no doubt as to the harmony that existed between British views of political union among the EEC member states and his own attitudes.

Macmillan also went out of his way to emphasize the importance of European political unity in general and Anglo-French co-operation in particular. At the Birch Grove meeting in November 1961 Macmillan, as so often, used an historical analogy to underline the dangers of a persistent split between the Six and the Seven and the necessity of political union, warning 'that if the solution [to the question of British membership] was not found in 1962 the idea of the restoration of Europe would fail. History would regard it as a repetition of the story of the city states of Greece which could not unite or could only unite occasionally as at Marathon. The dream of French and British leadership of Europe would be gone for ever as would all hope of giving Europe a strong and individual personality which would enable it to survive as an independent force in the world.'[39] Six months later at Champs the Prime Minister made use of rather more recent history. This time he emphasized the importance of cross-channel co-operation by suggesting that both World Wars might have been averted had harmony existed between Paris and London. Russia had now replaced Germany as the principal threat, but the need for a strong Anglo-French entente remained as pressing as ever.[40]

Even more striking were the Prime Minister's references to the need for Anglo-French co-operation in the field of defence. These could be traced back as far as the January 1961 summit at Rambouillet, in the course of which Macmillan had first floated the idea of the United States, Britain and France together acting as 'trustees of nuclear weapons' for all of the Free World, but they became more radical as Macmillan's determination to succeed in the membership application grew.[41] In the wake of Kennedy's refusal to sanction Anglo-French nuclear co-operation, Macmillan's comments also began to contain pointed references to the need for a European defence mechanism which was not totally dependent on the United States. In November 1961, the premier suggested that

'Europe could be organised in concentric circles. There could be a political and military core around which there would be an economic organisation' – the implication clearly being that Britain and France would constitute this inner core.[42] Then, in the run-up to the Champs summit Macmillan had two very confidential meetings with Jean Chauvel, the outgoing French Ambassador in London, and Geoffroy de Courcel, his replacement. The Prime Minister explained to both men his belief that, in the light of Russia's newly acquired parity with the US in the nuclear field, Europe could no longer rely on the American nuclear guarantee. Britain and France should thus take the lead in transforming Europe into a credible nuclear power in its own right. To this end, technical co-operation between the two countries was desirable. No specific details were provided on either occasion, but in the meeting with de Courcel Macmillan again spoke of Britain and France holding their nuclear weapons as 'trustees for Europe'.[43]

At the Champs meeting itself, Macmillan was somewhat more circumspect. Contrary to press speculation at the time, and much academic discussion since, no nuclear deal was struck between the two leaders. Nevertheless, the way in which the British Prime Minister claimed to envisage the future of the Western Alliance and of Franco-British co-operation continued to be extremely radical. NATO, he argued, should become 'a double-headed alliance' – in fifty years time, he explained, it would be much better for Europe as a whole to be putting its views to the Americans, rather than individual states doing so. Indeed, as he explained the next day, the inclusion of Britain in the evolving Europe would open up a wide range of possibilities: 'There might be a European organisation allied to the United States. There would be a plan for the defence of Europe. The nuclear power of European countries would be held as part of this European defence.' Once again, the premier remained vague both about the details of any such European defence co-operation, and about the time-frame within which such an arrangement could emerge. But for a British leader to talk to his French counterpart in such terms, albeit without specifying when and how any European defence co-operation would occur, was all but unprecedented.[44]

Taken together, Macmillan's comments to de Gaulle and to the two French Ambassadors constituted a remarkable declaration of Britain's newly found European credentials. The UK, the Prime Minister appeared to suggest, was not only ready to contemplate European co-operation in the political as well as economic field, but was also ready to see transatlantic relations alter accordingly. The special relationship would not necessarily disappear, but it would be complemented by an equally close rapport between Paris and London. Macmillan, in other words, seemed to be ready to accept both de Gaulle's 1958 call for tripartite consultation between France, Britain and America and the General's subsequent schemes for European political union. Furthermore, as part of its joint effort with France to develop a credible European defence policy, Britain, it seemed, would be willing to co-operate in the technical development of atomic weapons. The nuclear assistance for EEC membership deal, about which so much speculation has raged, was not mentioned overtly, but Macmillan did imply that nuclear co-operation was a likely component of any new, closer, London–Paris axis.

Unfortunately for Macmillan, however, the vision he described was ill-suited to persuade de Gaulle. From a French point of view there were three major flaws. The first was simply that Macmillan's suggestions lacked credibility. Talk of extensive Anglo-French co-operation in the defence field, or of a British commitment to a European defence scheme, was far removed from Britain's traditional policies, from the discourse of other British politicians during the 1961–3 period, and from the disappointing realities of ongoing Anglo-French co-operative projects.[45] It was therefore difficult to treat Macmillan's ideas as anything more than airy mirages, designed to lure the French from their intended course. Furthermore, the British proposals were highly dependent on American consent. As a result, even if Macmillan was in earnest, and even if the Premier succeeded in converting the British Cabinet and Parliament to his radical new approach, there was still a strong probability that the US would quash any talk of Anglo-French co-operation in the nuclear field. The gift offered by Macmillan was not entirely in his control.

Second, the Prime Minister's vision remained too Atlanticist for de Gaulle. For all his talk of close Anglo-French co-operation, Macmillan had not promised to abandon either the special relationship or the Atlantic Alliance. Indeed in both of his conversations with the French Ambassadors, Macmillan had specifically acknowledged that Britain could only proceed in the direction outlined with US consent. Somewhat implausibly, he had suggested to Chauvel that this might not prove particularly difficult to obtain. The US, after all, was keen to share the tremendous burden of Western leadership with responsible partners. But, as de Gaulle was well aware, no partnership that the US would agree to was likely to provide Europe with the degree of independence to which he aspired. A *Europe européenne* was unlikely to be sanctioned by Washington.

Third, Macmillan's vision, although described as an Anglo-French partnership, would have given Britain too many advantages, and France too few. The UK would have represented the central player in the new Atlantic arrangements, the most established voice on the world stage, and the senior partner in any Anglo-French nuclear co-operation; France, by contrast, would be weakened economically by the likely effects of Community enlargement, and overshadowed by Britain in all international fora. These disadvantages were particularly striking if the arrangements suggested by Macmillan were contrasted with de Gaulle's own plans for European unity centred on a Franco-German core. Within a Franco-German pairing, the General was confident that France would assume and retain the leadership role. Of the two powers, France alone would be a nuclear power, France alone would be a permanent member of the United Nations security council, France alone would retain strong world-wide links with its former colonies. Germany, moreover, had strong reasons to avoid being assertive on the international stage, and had shown in Community negotiations a recurrent tendency to sacrifice much in order to preserve French goodwill. Paired with Britain, by contrast, France would see most of its assets matched and would, moreover, have to deal with a country accustomed to making its views known internationally and unlikely to give much away in negotiation. It was not in de Gaulle's interest to give up so much in return for so questionable a gain. Macmillan's political strategy for overcoming the French was thus deeply flawed.

Macmillan's greatest mistake *vis-à-vis* France, however, lay not in the shape of the political offer with which he tried to woo de Gaulle, but in his belief that France needed to be wooed at all. Had the Premier examined the French position more carefully, he might have realized that de Gaulle's sullen response to the news of the impending British application concealed serious weaknesses on the part of the French. France and de Gaulle needed the Community. Without it French economic modernization would be seriously disrupted. Furthermore, they needed Franco-German *rapprochement*, since without harnessing West Germany's economic muscle French ambitions of becoming a major international player once more were unlikely to be fulfilled. Both the Community and Franco-German understanding would, however, have been severely shaken, if not destroyed, had de Gaulle tried summarily to reject a British membership application which all five of France's partners were eager to accept. And the international repercussions of an early move against Britain would have been mirrored by the consequences within France. Any rejection of British membership before the Parliamentary elections of November 1962, when the Gaullist Union pour la Nouvelle République (UNR) unexpectedly gained an absolute majority, would have prompted a rebellion by the Mouvement Républicain Populaire (MRP) and centrist deputies upon whom the coalition governments of Michel Debré and Georges Pompidou depended. The result would almost certainly have been an early general election, fought on the unfavourable terrain of European issues. As de Gaulle was told forcefully by his cabinet colleagues in July 1962, France could not bar Britain's road overtly. Its only hope was to use the technical discussions in Brussels to place as many obstacles as possible in Macmillan's route.[46]

Britain could thus have defied de Gaulle. His goodwill was not necessary for Community enlargement to go ahead, since he was in no position to veto British accession until late 1962. An early agreement in Brussels – bought at the price of British concessions on Commonwealth trade and British agriculture – would have thwarted the French. Unfortunately, Macmillan overestimated the power of the French leader and shied away from the sacrifices in Brussels which would have been necessary if the General were to be frustrated. He opted to speculate about a distant future of Anglo-French nuclear and security co-operation rather than to deliver immediate economic concessions which would have outflanked the French in the Brussels negotiations and clearly demonstrated Britain's new European credentials. A readiness to buy French wheat in place of Australian, or to oblige British farmers to accept CAP protection in place of the deficiency payments to which they had become accustomed, was the route to success in 1961–3. Instead, Macmillan tried to talk his way into the Community, over-confident of his ability to win the General round to his side and unaware that his vision of a Franco-British partnership was neither credible nor desirable for France. In 1943 much of Macmillan's success in Algiers had been attributable to his deft handling of de Gaulle. Two decades later, the greatest foreign policy failure of his years as Prime Minister, ironically, sprang precisely from his erroneous belief that personal intervention with de Gaulle would once again prove the most effective and painless route to success.

NOTES

1. The comment de Gaulle was supposedly tempted to make to Macmillan after he had made clear in the course of their December 1962 Rambouillet meeting that he would not allow Britain to join the European Community. See Alain Peyrefitte, *C'était de Gaulle* (Paris: Fayard, 1994), p. 333.

2. The author would like to thank James Ellison, Martin Schaad, Liz Kane and Constantine Pagedas for their help in preparing this piece – and Richard Aldous and Sabine Lee for persuading him to attend the Macmillan conference in the first place.

3. Alistair Horne, *Macmillan*, 2 vols (London: Macmillan, 1990, 1991); John Turner, *Macmillan* (London: Longman, 1994).

4. See Horne, *Macmillan*, vol. 1, pp. 153–90.

5. Robert Murphy, *Diplomat among Warriors* (London: Collins, 1964), p. 206.

6. Macmillan to Churchill, May 1943; cited in Horne, *Macmillan*, vol. 1, p. 181.

7. John W. Young, 'Churchill's "No" to Europe: the "Rejection" of European Union by Churchill's Postwar Government, 1951–2', *Historical Journal*, vol. 28, no. 4, p. 927; Young and Michael Dockrill (eds), *British Foreign Policy, 1945–56* (London: Macmillan, 1989), pp. 210–15; Paul-Henri Spaak, *Combats inachevés* (Paris: Fayard, 1969), vol. 2, p. 77.

8. Young, 'Churchill's "No" to Europe', p. 932; Simon Burgess and Geoffrey Edwards, 'The Six plus One: British Policy-making and the Question of European Economic Integration, 1955', *International Affairs*, no. 64 (1988), p. 399.

9. See Michael Charlton, *The Price of Victory* (London: BBC, 1983), p. 195.

10. Referred to in James Ellison, 'British Policy towards European Integration: The Proposal for a European Free Trade Area, June 1955–December 1958', PhD thesis, Christ Church College, Canterbury (1997).

11. The following section draws heavily upon Elizabeth Kane, 'Tilting to Europe? British Responses to Developments in European Integration 1955–1958', DPhil thesis, Oxford (1996) and James Ellison, 'British Policy towards European Integration'.

12. The Plan is reproduced as an appendix to Harold Macmillan, *Riding the Storm* (London: Macmillan, 1971), pp. 753–4.

13. Kane, 'Tilting to Europe?', pp. 106–11.

14. Hanns Jürgen Küsters, *Fondaments de la Communauté Economique Européenne* (Brussels: Editions Labor, 1990), p. 197.

15. Jean-Charles Snoy et d'Oppuers, *Rebâtir l'Europe* (Paris: Duculot, 1989), pp. 116–33.

16. For one outspoken critique of the 1950 break with Britain see René Massigli, *Une comédie des erreurs 1943–1956: Souvenirs et réflexions sur une étape de la construction européenne* (Paris: Plon, 1978), pp. 199ff.

17. Christian Pineau and Christiane Rimbaud, *Le Grand Pari: L'aventure du traité de Rome* (Paris: Fayard, 1991), pp. 151–218; Pierre Guillen, 'Europe a Cure for French Impotence? The Guy Mollet Government and the

Negotiation of the Treaties of Rome', in Ennio di Nolfo (ed.), *Power in Europe? Great Britain, France, Germany and Italy and the Origins of the EEC, 1952–1957* (Berlin: Walter de Gruyter, 1992), pp. 505–16.

18. Pineau and Rimbaud, *Le Grand Pari*, pp. 219–39.
19. Bernard Picot, 'La France et l'entrée de la Grande-Bretagne dans le Marché commun', PhD thesis, Lyon (1965) pp. 91–5.
20. For good examples of French equivocation see 'La Zone de Libre Echange devant l'Opinion Française', *Revue du Marché Commun*, vol. 1, no. 1 (1958), pp. 30–2.
21. Ellison, 'British Policy towards European Integration'.
22. Ibid.
23. Ibid.
24. James Ellison, 'Harold Macmillan's Fear of "Little Europe": Britain, the Six and the European Free Trade Area' (University of Leicester Discussion Papers on Britain and Europe, BE95/5), pp. 12–20.
25. Martin Schaad, 'Anglo-German Relations during the Formative Years of the European Community, 1955–1961', DPhil thesis, Oxford (1995) pp. 181–2.
26. Jean-Marc Boegner, '1958, le général de Gaulle et l'acceptation du traité de Rome', *Espoir*, no. 87 (1992), pp. 28–30.
27. Gérard Bossuat, 'The Choice of "La Petite Europe" by France, 1957–1963: An Ambition for France and for Europe', in Richard Griffiths and Stuart Ward (eds), *Courting the Common Market: The First Attempt to Enlarge the EEC, 1960–3* (London: Lothian Foundation Press, 1996), pp. 59–82.
28. PRO FO371 150269; Steel to FO, 31 March 1960.
29. Wolfram Kaiser, *Using Europe, Abusing the Europeans: Britain and European Integration, 1945–63* (London: Macmillan, 1996), pp. 120–67; Richard Lamb, *The Macmillan Years: The Emerging Truth* (London: John Murray, 1995), pp. 126–57; Miriam Camps, *Britain and the European Community, 1955–1963* (Oxford: Oxford University Press, 1964), pp. 274–376.
30. For more detail on this and most of the following points see N. Piers Ludlow, *Dealing with Britain: The Six and the First UK Application to the EEC* (Cambridge: Cambridge University Press, 1997).
31. PRO FO371 158179; M615/195; Sir A. Rumbold to FO, 28 July 1961.
32. See Kaiser, *Using Europe*, pp. 157–66; Constantine Pagedas, 'Troubled Partners: Anglo-American Diplomacy and the French Problem, 1960–3', PhD, King's College, London (1996), pp. 73–164.
33. Ibid.
34. PRO PREM 11 3311 contains details of both the visit and the correspondence.
35. Cited in Kaiser, *Using Europe, Abusing the Europeans*, p. 165 and p. 166.
36. For the second American refusal see PRO PREM 11 3712l, Ormsby-Gore to Macmillan, 17 May 962.
37. Many of the points that follow are discussed at greater length in N. Piers Ludlow, 'Le Paradoxe Anglais, Great Britain and Political Union', *Revue d'Allemagne*, vol. 29, no. 2 (April–June 1997), pp. 259–72.

38. The records of the three encounters are in PRO PREM 11 3561, 24–5 November 1961; PREM 11 3775, 2–3 June 1962; PREM 11 4230, 15–16 December 1962.
39. PRO PREM 11 3561, 25 November 1961.
40. PRO PREM 11 3775, 2 June 1962.
41. Pagedas, 'Troubled Partners', p. 160.
42. PRO PREM 11 3561, 25 November 1961.
43. The meeting with Chauvel is in PRO PREM 11 3792, 19 April 1962. That with de Courcel is in PREM 11 3775, 9 May 1962.
44. PRO PREM 11 3775, 2–3 June 1962.
45. For the halting reality of Anglo-French scientific co-operation, see the description of the ELDO project in Pagedas, 'Troubled Partners', pp. 119–45.
46. This argument is developed in more detail in Ludlow, *Dealing with Britain*, pp. 239–40.

8 Pragmatism versus Principle? Macmillan and Germany[1]

Sabine Lee

Anglo-German relations have never had the special quality that has been attributed at times to Anglo-American or Franco-German relations. The period of Harold Macmillan's premiership was no exception. He never saw in Germany a partner of similar significance to the United States, the Soviet Union or, indeed, France. However, his view of Germany changed over time and, partly as a function of this, the development of relations between Britain and Germany took a decisive turn for the worse while he held office in 10 Downing Street.

As with many of Macmillan's attitudes and policies, the key to his perception of Germany lies in his formative years and especially in his experiences during the two World Wars. Although his first-hand experience of fighting in the Great War was brief, he suffered two injuries which resulted in years of physical pain. Far worse and longer lasting were the mental pains of being one of a few survivors of a large group of university acquaintances and friends, a feeling of guilt which affected him for the rest of his life.[2] It is not surprising, therefore, that he should have had ambivalent feelings about the country with greatest responsibility for the outbreak of both World Wars. Germany was associated with militarism, manifested across Europe especially in its Prussian image. The strength of Macmillan's feelings about war and his recollections of the First World War in particular, made a certain reserve *vis-à-vis* Germany almost inevitable. He remained sensitive to anything resembling his recollections of Prussian militarism. This apprehension survived in Macmillan despite his experiences of decades of Germany as a democratic and explicitly non-militaristic state as part of the Western world after 1945.

As Harold Macmillan pointed out in a conversation with Alistair Horne, his impression on attending Konrad Adenauer's funeral in 1967 pointed in this direction: 'The guard of honour, all those coal-scuttle helmets ... they haven't changed.'[3]

But this resentment was only one side of the coin. As a power politician with clear sight of political necessities, he was one of the first to advocate the integration of West Germany into the Western bloc. In this he followed Winston Churchill's policy of bringing the Germans into Europe. Against calls for harsh denazification, he demanded in the House of Commons to accommodate the Germans in order to avoid them becoming a menace to world peace again. He entirely agreed with Churchill's assessment that the immediate threat to peace had moved from Germany to the Soviet Union. Consequently Germany had to become an ally, the country had to enter the West 'as a free and equal member',[4] if it was to be won for the West. But the integration of the Federal Republic into Western Europe was at the same time part of Macmillan's grander concept for Europe, and it corresponded with the role he envisaged for the United Kingdom, first at the fringe and later at the heart of Europe.[5]

In these few examples we find traces of what at first sight appears to be an inconsistent attitude to the country across the Channel. But his views, rather than being inconsistent, reflected a multifaceted approach to a country which throughout Macmillan's political career could be found in the roles of enemy, alliance partner, economic rival, Cold War player and object, occupied and sovereign, dictatorship and democracy alike. Therefore, it is less surprising that we find a multitude of different and discrepant views about and a variety of policies *vis-à-vis* Germany. Anglo-German relations in the post-war period reflected these altering policies just as they were influenced by them.

Anglo-German relations never really took off after the war. They lacked the warm quality of the Franco-German axis that formed between Adenauer and de Gaulle, and certainly never reached a level of understanding as existed between the United Kingdom and the United States, however 'special' these relations may have been.[6] The reasons for this are manifold. The atrocities committed by the Germans during the war are only one, and probably not the primary, factor. Although the British associated (and probably still associate) Germany with aggression, militarism and nationalism, the nature of the bilateral relationship is less crude and the underlying reasons for the problems of both countries are more subtle. When the *News of the World*, in 1969, proclaimed: 'It is the simple truth that the British never liked the Germans and will never like them', many British people would have agreed. There was a strong sense of bitterness, because whereas Germany had by now experienced an economic miracle, Britain had failed to recover from the war in the same way. On the contrary, the British had lost their position as the centre of the Empire, and even the position as No. 1 partner of the United States in Europe was under threat not least from the increasingly strong Germany.[7] If the early post-war years had been characterized by a sense of responsibility for the defeated Germany which was in desperate need of food and fuel, attitudes changed with the changing fortunes or rather degrees of economic recovery.[8] On the other hand, the Germans were equally prejudiced against the British, seeing them as a nation of shopkeepers whose main characteristics were jealousy and scepticism. Hence, intellect and ability as well as commitment were often underestimated. Chancellor Adenauer spoke for many when he quoted an English friend of his saying: 'If the English worked six days a week, they would be a lot better off. But they finish work Friday lunch time and don't start again until Monday morning. They should not complain when they don't succeed.'[9]

But it was not prejudice alone which accounted for a difficulty in overcoming the effects of the war on the mutual relationship. There were differences in outlook which were the effect of what could be described as 'national character'. One former Federal President juxtaposed British pragmatism and German principle[10] – a comparison which sums up the difference in outlook well. It was felt in politics and international affairs: in particular it became a stumbling bloc for British–German relations in the field of East–West relations, where the German legalistic approach came face to face with British pragmatism.[11]

During the height of Macmillan's political power, the man firmly in charge of affairs in Germany was Chancellor Konrad Adenauer. Just as Macmillan had certain reservations about Germany, Adenauer had ambivalent feelings about Great Britain. These grew stronger as his commitment to Franco-German reconciliation became more pronounced. When he developed strong links with de Gaulle's France after late 1958 his appreciation of Britain's role in Europe and the world decreased.[12]

The relationship between the leaders of the two countries is a complex one, and the image of it always having been tainted by their respective prejudices is too simplistic. Even though their personal understanding never reached the level of cordiality of de Gaulle or Dulles and Adenauer, or Kennedy and Macmillan, in the early years of Macmillan's premiership the relationship between them was good.

It appears that until 1957/8, when relations between the United Kingdom and Germany were improving (especially after Eden's activities in the aftermath of the failure of the EDC), these neither prevented nor promoted mutual understanding on a private level. Conversely, it was hoped that private friendship between the two statesmen could influence inter-state relations and politics. When in 1958/9 more important conflicts arose, the inability to solve them hampered the personal relationship between Macmillan and Adenauer. At this point, it became clear that 'personal chemistry' did not transmit the positive influence that was being felt in the relations between, for example, France and Germany.

There is plenty of evidence for this assertion. Looking at the letters and messages between Chancellor and Prime Minister, one detects a clear change of atmosphere throughout Macmillan's Premiership. The early correspondence developed from a respectful to a friendly tone in the mid-1950s, and there appears to have been a distinct wish on both parts to come to a satisfactory working relationship. Macmillan, for instance, wrote to Adenauer before his first state visit to Bonn, in May 1957, in very forthcoming terms, keeping him informed about his recent communications with the Soviet leader, Bulganin: 'I look forward to discussing this with you at the end of next week. You can be sure that in any case I should not act on it without the closest consultation with my friends.'[13] During the visit itself, the impression of a generally friendly atmosphere was confirmed.[14] Macmillan himself was pleased with his own performance in Bonn and was convinced that his carefully pitched speeches left the Chancellor impressed.[15] In the regular exchange of notes and letters that followed the visit, Macmillan did not tire of stressing the importance which he personally attached to their relationship and he expressed particular interest in a return visit of the Chancellor.

In those early years, there is no indication that there were any serious difficulties in the mutual relationship, but here, already, another trait of Macmillan's policy *vis-à-vis* the Chancellor is obvious. He continually overstated his own influence on Adenauer, the Chancellor's fondness of him and his own ability of impress the German. Macmillan was aware, from their first encounter in 1954 onwards, but even more so after becoming Prime Minister, that the only way to achieve anything with regards to German foreign policy was to get Adenauer on his side.[16] Therefore, he rightly concentrated his efforts on the 'old man'. Harold Macmillan had been impressed by Adenauer in previous encounters. He had not yet experienced the repetitions of Adenauer's elaboration of the dangers of Soviet expansionism and communism and the history of Germany, which caused considerable boredom during many of their later encounters. Macmillan's generally positive impression of Chancellor Adenauer in the mid-1950s, however, gave rise to the assumption that it would be an achievable task to influence him. In particular, the Prime Minister expected that he would succeed in gaining Adenauer's support in the policy area closest to his interest, the negotiations of a free trade area with the nascent EEC.[17] An additional factor that came into play at that time was the political disarray in France which seemed to present a good chance of steering the Germans away from too close a political alliance with France and 'bending him [Adenauer] in the right direction'.[18]

The first half of the year 1958 saw a continuation of a friendly atmosphere between Bonn and London with a return visit of the German Chancellor to London, which again took place in a good and amicable climate.[19] In the latter half of the year, however, a new dimension to the bilateral relations between the UK and Germany (and at the same time between Adenauer and Macmillan) was felt for the first time: the influence of Franco-German understanding. Anglo-German relations were to become a function of Franco-German relations.

Triggered by a deep pessimism about future developments in the United Kingdom and the United States, the Chancellor – consciously or not – moved away from the Anglo-Saxons to find security with the French President de Gaulle. As the British Ambassador in Bonn put it, Germany, which 'should be one of the greatest forces of stability in Europe', had turned out to be an 'almost neutral factor'.[20]

This meant for Britain that German support over economic questions which they were hoping for, became highly questionable. As
previously in phases of pressure, the Prime Minister, who firmly
believed in the value of diplomacy at head-of-government level,
chose to intervene personally. Assuring Adenauer of the UK's stability and stressing the insecurity in France's political situation, he
tried to ensure the Chancellor's support in the free trade area
negotiations. More personal messages and another visit to Bonn
followed.[21] During this visit, again Macmillan grossly overestimated
his own standing with Adenauer. The latter had just met General
de Gaulle for the first time in their historic encounter in Colombey-
les-deux-Eglises,[22] and this meeting had had an electrifying effect
on the German. It was to be the beginning of a deep friendship
between two elder statesmen who still had political power ambitions, and indeed their understanding was to have important repercussions for European affairs, and in particular Britain's standing
with the Germans.

However, shortly after their first encounter President de Gaulle
surprised the Western leaders with the proposal of a NATO-
triumvirate, an idea which disturbed the Germans and above all
Adenauer. This three-power directorate comprising the United States,
the United Kingdom and France was not favourably received by
the NATO partners, but Macmillan believed it to be a blessing in
disguise for his own ambitions of convincing Adenauer of the strength
and reliability of Britain. As he put it in his diary: 'The Chancellor
is still very hurt and angry. I do not think he will ever trust de
Gaulle again'.[23] And then: 'The Germans have up to now been
very good, I think I can exploit his [Adenauer's] anger with the
French over the de Gaulle memorandum to some extent.'[24] But
Macmillan could not! The fact that de Gaulle's NATO triumvirate
proposal did not have a lasting negative influence on Adenauer
and on Franco-German relations, was symptomatic of the Chancellor's
foreign policy during his final years in office. Unwelcome French
moves would at worst overshadow the mutual relationship temporarily
without seriously endangering the long-term relations. In contrast,
any indication of misunderstandings with the United Kingdom, and
increasingly also the United States, had a lasting negative impact
on the Chancellor's attitude towards the Anglo-Saxons. This led to
a decline in British and American influence on the Chancellor's
decisions.

During the October state visit to Bonn, Macmillan clearly failed to recognize the limits of his influence on the Chancellor as he did not realize (and perhaps could not have done so) the significance of France's position in Adenauer's calculations. Ambassador Steel noted a few days after the visit that, contrary to Macmillan's own assessment, the Chancellor showed an 'unexpectedly pessimistic attitude' *vis-à-vis* Britain.[25]

A final attempt by Macmillan, in another letter to the German Chancellor warning him about the consequences of a failure of the free trade area negotiations, proved unsuccessful, since Adenauer did not intervene to secure a favourable outcome of the discussions, and less than two weeks after this final try, the negotiations broke down. What was not clear at the time was that this period between September 1958, the meeting at Colombey-les-deux-Eglises, and February 1959, Macmillan's visit to Moscow, was the turning point not only in the personal relationship between Adenauer and Macmillan, but also – if to a lesser extent – between Germany and Britain.

It was due to Macmillan's failure to handle the German Chancellor with sensitivity, caused by his desire to display superiority and independence – as evident for instance in this Moscow visit – that their personal relationship broke down. But it was clearly the attraction that de Gaulle had for Adenauer which enabled the German Chancellor to turn away from Macmillan and the British so decisively in the late 1950s. Adenauer's plea for trust in the 'new Germany' was answered by de Gaulle, and it was rewarded by the Chancellor's trust in French support in this critical time of the Berlin ultimatum crisis. Nikita Khrushchev had triggered a new crisis over Berlin, when in November 1958, he threatened that the Soviet Union would be prepared unilaterally, if the Western Allies were not willing to 'reach an adequate agreement' over the status of Berlin, which he envisaged to turn into a 'free demilitarised city'. Despite a steadfast official Western line, diplomatic activities at the end of 1958 showed that the willingness of, above all, the United Kingdom to defend Western rights in Berlin by force was diminishing.[26]

When Harold Macmillan, without prior consultation, informed his Western partners about his intentions to visit the Soviet Union (despite the continuing Soviet threat), this caused both consternation and disapproval in Germany, and it had a profound effect on the German Chancellor. He had been persuaded that British policy was 'unreliable and anti-German'.[27]

Adenauer's suspicions were only one side of the coin. Hand-in-hand with the new surge of anti-British feelings in the German Chancery went a phase of growing dissatisfaction with the Chancellor in the British Foreign Office. Although British and German diplomats tried to minimize the damage done by Adenauer and Macmillan in the course of the early months of 1959, their actions left a feeling of mistrust and decline in mutual relations.

During this time Adenauer – more than usually – lost his temper with the British in public,[28] and Macmillan got increasingly impatient with the Chancellor. The Prime Minister's disappointment was two-fold. On the one hand he deplored the fact that the Chancellor let himself be seduced by the French President; on the other hand he felt deceived by the German. In May 1959, he commented: 'Adenauer has become – like many old men – vain, suspicious, and grasping. . . . [He] had been carrying on a great campaign of vilification of HMG and especially of me.'[29] In June: 'Adenauer is now half crazy. . . . De Gaulle and Adenauer are just hopeless. Adenauer because he is a false and cankerous man.'[30]

But in addition to Macmillan's growing awareness of Adenauer's scepticism, he came to realize that in some issues of vital importance for both countries their interests diverged substantially and their policies were becoming more and more incompatible. The British programme of European co-operation ran counter to French interests, and German support of the British plans would potentially endanger Franco-German understanding. Consequently, in 1958, when Adenauer had discovered de Gaulle's terms of co-operation, Macmillan could not hope for Adenauer's help any more.

Conversely, British policies in East–West relations called into question the German hard-line position over the 'German Question' and Berlin. Up to the end of 1958, Macmillan could not risk taking a 'soft' line if he wanted to secure German support on European issues. This *do ut des* situation was no longer existent after Adenauer's acquiescence in the breakdown of the free trade area negotiations, because the Chancellor no longer seemed willing to give. Therefore, there was not much incentive for Macmillan and British officials to take into account German wishes to the same extent as in the previous two years.

The situation in 1959 differed significantly from that at the beginning of 1957 in another respect. When Macmillan succeeded Eden as Prime Minister, the Suez Crisis had dented British self-confidence and seriously shaken the Conservative Party and its leadership. By 1959, there was a new feeling of confidence among the people, the party and the political leadership. The economy had recovered, the Special Relationship had partially been restored, and the Conservative party had good prospects of winning the forthcoming general election.

For Adenauer, almost the opposite was true. In 1957 won the general election with an absolute majority of votes and mandates. His party and leadership were at the peak of their popularity. Economic as well as foreign policies had proved successful. Soon afterwards, the Chancellor's fortunes changed. His popularity began declining, and, when changing his mind again and again about standing for the Federal Presidency, his prestige inside and outside Germany suffered.[31]

In other words Macmillan, in 1957 the new and inexperienced head of government, impressed and fascinated by the Chancellor at previous meetings, had gained ground – by 1959 they were 'equal'.

In 1960, another attempt was made to restore the personal relationship between Adenauer and Macmillan. In August, when the low point in Anglo-German relations after a number of anti-semitic incidents in Germany and the 'Spain affair'[32] had been overcome, Adenauer – at short notice – invited Macmillan to Bonn. There were reservations and mutual suspicions on the part of the two policy-makers, and Harold Macmillan had to be persuaded to accept the invitation.[33] As he recalled in his diaries:

> I am not looking forward to our visit in Bonn. Dr Adenauer has deceived me before, over the great economic issue.... But – although many Germans are very sympathetic and secretly ashamed of Dr. Adenauer's trickiness ... I fear I have never succeeded in getting anything tangible out of these talks.[34]

Given all this, the meeting was a remarkable success. The British Prime Minister went as far as calling it an 'historic' meeting.[35] Even if this was an exaggeration, the talks did improve strained relations. The *Auswärtiges Amt* spoke of a 'noticeable improvement of atmosphere',[36] and both press and public reacted positively to the visit.

There were clear signs that an Anglo-German rapprochement was being sought at least in official relations. Germany increased efforts at 'bridge-building' between the EEC and EFTA, which was a major concern of the British. In return, Macmillan in his speech at the United Nations on 29 September 1960 and Lord Home in his inaugural speech as foreign minister in the House of Lords on 2 November 1960 strongly supported Germany on issues of European security, the German Question and Berlin. This continued in 1961 when statesmen during their meeting in February again pledged mutual support.[37]

However, in the early 1960's, although relations were not under severe strain, there was a feeling of unease on both sides. The autumn and winter of 1959 had marked an irreparable turning point in the relations between Macmillan and Adenauer and with it a decline in the relations between the two countries they represented.

It is during the Berlin Crisis that we see most clearly the various characteristics of Macmillan's policies *vis-à-vis* Germany and difficulties in dealing with the Federal Republic. First, there was the problem of how to reconcile the position of Germany as an object of policy (namely in questions of Four-Power responsibility over Germany as a whole and Berlin) with that of Germany as a partner within an alliance (namely the now sovereign Federal Republic of Germany).

Second, with regards to the Berlin issue the British pragmatic approach clashed with the German more legalistic approach more directly and with graver consequences than in any other policy area.

Third, in the context of the German question, there was more at stake for the Federal Republic than in other foreign policy questions. Hence it was significantly more difficult to overcome Chancellor Adenauer's suspicions concerning British steadfastness.

Fourth, British policies appeared to by competing and contrasting with de Gaulle's rigid line *vis-à-vis* the Soviet Union more clearly.

And, finally, with view to the domestic front, it was over Berlin that the question arose as to how to relate to the former enemy which – in the context of the East–West conflict had become a partner. Would it be necessary to fight for Germany on the Continent; and if so would it be possible to rally the British polulation behind such a cause.

It is clear from the sources that Harold Macmillan shared the conventional wisdom of most British and Western politicians and officials that it was necessary to bind West Germany firmly into the Western alliance system, if the country was to be prevented from turning eastwards towards an understanding with the Soviets.[38] Similarly, it was understood that it was necessary to pacify the Germans by proclaiming the desire to reunify Germany.[39] There was a clear sense of 'Rapallo', the potential danger of German–Soviet understanding at the expense of the West.

At the same time, Macmillan was keen on improving East–West relations by creating a more meaningful dialogue with the Soviet leaders, primarily Khrushchev. Towards the end of 1958, when Khrushchev single-handedly tried to withdraw from the Four-Power agreements, the two conflicting interests openly clashed. On an abstract level, Macmillan had to choose between the British pragmatic approach of trying to improve the relationship with the Soviet Union without much concern for potential diplomatic upsets on the one hand, and the more legalistic and principled approach of not negotiating with the Soviets as long as the Berlin ultimatum stood.

Macmillan decided in favour of pragmatism. In the eyes of the Germans, and above all Chancellor Adenauer, Macmillan had to make a choice between Germany and the Soviet Union, and the Prime Minister opted for the Soviets over and above his German allies.

The first indication of this were the notorious telegrams 8112 and 8113. These were later turned into a memorandum which summed up British thoughts on the subject of Berlin immediately after Khrushchev's first speech on 10 November 1958. In a nutshell, the argument was that in the long term the only feasible option was some sort of recognition of the GDR, because Khrushchev was in control of the situation.[40] When the content of the telegrams became known to the Germans, their reaction was excited, disappointed and suspicious.[41] British views appeared to contrast sharply with American firmness and, even more so, with strong French expressions of support and rigidity *vis-à-vis* the Soviet Union. This impression of British weakness in the face of the Soviet threat and the perception of a certain willingness on the part of Macmillan to trade away German (and Western) rights in Berlin was reinforced after the ultimatum speech of 27 November, and it become almost insurmountable after Macmillan's announcement, in early 1959, that his way of dealing with the crisis was a direct encounter with Khrushchev in Russia.

After Macmillan had decided to take up the Soviet invitation (originally addressed to his predecessor Eden) to visit the Soviet Union, concrete negotiating tactics needed to be developed. To this end, the Prime Minister summoned back to London Gladwyn Jebb, at the time British Ambassador in Paris. He was to deal with the problems of Berlin and Germany by addressing five questions posed by Macmillan:

(1) Would the Soviet Union accept a reunified Germany which remained a member of NATO?

(2) Would a reunified Germany which remained a member of NATO be compatible with the general détente in Europe, including a considerable degree of disengagement by the West and the Soviet Union?

(3) What chance is there that after Adenauer's death, Germany would succumb to a Soviet offer to accept the reunification of German territory provided that a reunified Germany left NATO?

(4) Could NATO survive effectively without Germany?

(5) If NATO for all practical purposes disappeared, could we in conjunction with the United States and France maintain an adequate defence against the Soviet Union?[42]

This catalogue of questions shows on the one hand that Macmillan was interested in an assessment of the various Allied moves and their implications. But it also indicates that he was prepared to consider what for many other Western statesmen (above all the German Chancellor) would have been unthinkable: NATO was not sacred, and there were alternatives.[43]

Jebb's answers as elaborated in his memorandum are interesting in that they anticipated a number of ideas which, over the course of the next few years, would become part of Western policies on Berlin and Germany as a whole. Jebb argued for the preservation of the status quo, a strengthening of continental Europe culminating in Britain's joining the Common Market, an avoidance of a neutralization of Germany, but – if necessary – the sacrifice of Western rights in Berlin.

There is no doubt that Macmillan, during his visit to Moscow, did not show any willingness to make concessions on substantial questions, despite Lloyd's *tour d'horizon* with the Soviet deputy foreign minister, Kusnetzov.[44] But it is equally clear that Macmillan was prepared to listen to almost any suggestion that might end the East–West stalemate – with little concern for German interests. He oversaw the development of Foreign Office thought on the recognition of the GDR, the agency theory, the recognition of the Oder/Neiße line and the Berlin Question, and the more fed up he became with the increasingly stubborn and inflexible German Chancellor, the more he discounted a German voice in the security questions. There is little indication of any meaningful exchanges between Macmillan and the Germans on these issues from the time of the Khrushchev ultimatum until the erection of the Berlin Wall almost four years later.

At the same time as the Germans were preoccupied with the Berlin and German questions, the British government was in a process of reappraisal of the country's European policy. In July 1961, only weeks before the erection of the Berlin Wall, the Prime Minister announced that Britain would seek to enter the European Economic Community. The subsequent negotiations were to dominate Anglo-German relations for the final years of Macmillan's premiership. Although the Prime Minister knew that the key to success or failure of the negotiations lay with the French, he hoped that German support and pressure would help influence the French in favour of British EEC entry.

In contrast to the Berlin Question, where the Germans were looking to the United Kingdom for support, in EEC affairs it was the British who were both actor and object of policy and negotiations; and it was the British who were asking for political support from the Germans. The dilemmas in Britain's attempts at enlisting German help have been described elsewhere,[45] but some observations are of significance in our context. The previous years of tension between the heads of government of both countries had left their mark on Macmillan and Adenauer alike. Neither was in conciliatory mood throughout the various encounters between 1961 and 1963, and considerable distrust remained between them. It is evident that the decisive consideration in Chancellor Adenauer's 'Grand Design' was de Gaulle and not Macmillan. Therefore, Adenauer was prepared, as he had been in November 1958, to sacrifice the pawn Great Britain to save Franco-German rapprochement and European integration.

Unlike in 1958 however, when there was general German acquiescence in the face of de Gaulle's free trade area veto, the German reaction in January 1963 was much more ambivalent. Adenauer took the last big foreign political decision of his chancellorship when he decided to push through the politically sensitive Franco-German friendship treaty of January 1963, despite de Gaulle's veto of the British. He had not been given prior warning of the General's intentions of blocking British EEC entry, and German political, public and published opinon was clearly in favour of the British joining the Common Market. But Adenauer had no intentions of risking Franco-German rapprochement for the sake of the British. Reconciliation with France was his political legacy. He was heavily criticized for this, even by his own party colleagues, let alone the opposition and the press. There were even thoughts of jeopardizing the ratification of the treaty in the *Bundestag*. In the end, the only visible sign of disapproval by the *Bundestag* of Adenauer's and de Gaulle's policies was the addition of a preamble to the friendship treaty which emphasized the significance of transatlantic relations. This did nothing to reconcile the British![46]

Macmillan hoped that after Adenauer's departure from the political scene (the chancellor's mid-term resignation had been part of the coalition agreements after the 1961 general elections) he could set about rebuilding his trust in German politics. Adenauer's most likely successor was Ludwig Erhard whom he knew to be supportive of the British. Ironically, Harold Macmillan himself did not remain in power long enough to do just that – his own resignation virtually coincided with Adenauer's.

In his discussions with the Germans and in particular with Adenauer and his foreign ministers, Macmillan made a number of tactical errors. It has already been mentioned that he continually overstated his own role in bilateral and multilateral negotiations on the head of government level. He also miscalculated the negative effect his Moscow trip would have on the cohesion of the Western camp and in particular the extent to which it undermined his position in Germany (and not just with the Chancellor). He misread the mood of the time in late 1958 and early 1959, by attempting to play a 'tit for tat' game on economic and security issues. After the disappointing German acquiescence over de Gaulle's veto of the free trade area proposals in late 1958, which coincided with Khrushchev's reopening of the Berlin discussions, Macmillan threatened to 'retaliate' by not giving Germany support over Berlin.[47] This in turn made it more difficult to impress on the Germans the need to support the UK during the EEC accession negotiations a few years later.

Moreover, Macmillan failed to recognize the importance of the Berlin issue which touched the very existence of Germany as a free and democratic country and which had a great symbolic and emotional significance. Berlin was not a bargaining chip. By implying a willingness to 'desert' Germany in a (perceived) hour of great need, the British Prime Minister put at risk German confidence in British reliability and his own credibility.

Most of these tactical 'errors' occurred when the Prime Minister was preoccupied with establishing himself as a world political leader. In the vacuum created by John Foster Dulles' illness in early 1959 and his subsequent death, Macmillan saw the opportunity of assuming the role of the foreign political leader of the Western camp. If he had to alienate other heads of government, this had to be outweighed against the potential power position he would gain as the motor of the East–West dialogue and the inclusion of Britain in any great power summitry.

By late 1959, it became clear, however, that he had harvested the fruit of his labour only on the domestic front. His foreign political activities in the spring and summer of 1959 were rewarded by a convincing electoral victory in the autumn. But America had moved centre stage again in the international theatre, and Macmillan's role as a broker of international peace came virtually to a standstill. He had lost the confidence of both Germany and France, and the coming negotiations, the 1960 abortive summit and the discussions around the time of the Berlin Wall, saw him in the position of a supernumerary.

It can be argued that he played this role more successfully than that of the main actor, because he managed to make his influence felt in the United States without attracting German suspicions immediately. So rather than bringing up East–West questions directly with the Germans, Macmillan tried to channel them through the Americans.[48] It certainly helped that Adenauer mistrusted the newly elected Kennedy as much as Macmillan. Also, Kennedy was open to Macmillan's views which largely coincided with his own in terms of the necessity to establish a dialogue with the East. Kennedy's motto: 'Let us never negotiate out of fear, but let us never fear to negotiate' could easily have come from British Prime Minister himself.

By 1961, Macmillan, in agreement with large sections of his Foreign Office, had settled for a policy of 'accepting the stabilisation of

Germany's Eastern frontier and the Oder/Neiße line', and an abandonment in all but official policy of reunification.[49] But unlike in the late 1950s, he did not expose himself with statements to that effect, but he let the Americans under Kennedy and Rusk make the running. In late 1961, he urged the American President to convince Adenauer to adopt a more flexible policy leading among others to *de facto* recognition of the GDR, acceptance of the Oder/Neiße line' and a loosening of the links between Berlin and West Germany.[50] This approach, in conjunction with a change in government after the general elections of 1961 (which brought a larger number of so-called Atlanticists into the Federal Government) allowed relations between Britain and Germany to resume a better quality. But it was not until both Adenauer and Macmillan had left the scene as heads of government that any lasting improvement occured.

NOTES

1. I would like to thank Richard Aldous for his comments on the essay.
2. He was one of only two survivors of all the Balliol scholars and exhibitioners of 1912. For some details of his experiences during the Great War see Richard Davenport-Hines, *The Macmillans* (London: Mandarin, 1992) Ch. 6.
3. Alistair Horne, *Macmillan: Official Biography*, 2 vols (London: Macmillan, 1989), here, *Macmillan*, vol. 1, p. 48.
4. Horne, *Macmillan*, vol. 1, p. 316.
5. Sabine Lee, 'Coming into the Game? Staying in the Game? Harold Macmillan and European Integration', S. Lee and R. Aldous (eds), *Harold Macmillan and Britain's World Role* (Basingstoke: Macmillan, 1996), pp. 123–48.
6. For details see essays by Scott Lucas, Nigel Ashton and Sir Oliver Wright in this volume.
7. For more recent studies see, for instance, David Reynolds, *Britannia Overruled* (London: Longman, 1991), pp. 156ff; John W. Young, *Britain and the World in the Twentieth Century* (London: Edward Arnold, 1997), Ch. 6.
8. Hans Heinrich Herwarth, 'Anglo-German Relations: a German View', *International Affairs*, vol. 39 (1963), pp. 511–32. See also Report Becker (Auswärtiges Amt) for Königswinter Conference, 22.5.1959, Politische Abteilung (PA)/Auswärtiges Amt (AA): Länderabteilung (LA) 3/304/99.
9. Günther Buchstab, *Wir haben wirklich etwas geschaffen. Die Protokolle*

des CDU-Bundesvorstandes 1953–1957 (Düsseldorf: Droste, 1990), pp. 852–3.

10. Frank Giles, *Forty Years On: Four Decades of Königswinter Conferences* (Blackpool, 1989), p. 1.

11. For recent analysis see Thomas Kielinger, *Crossroads and Roundabouts* (Bonn: Bouvier, 1996).

12. Adenauer's attitudes towards Britain have frequently been simplified as those of a narrow-minded politician who, as a Catholic Rhinelander had a 'natural' disinclination concerning the UK. In the light of primary evidence this cannot be upheld. There is a clear development in the Chancellor's views throughout the late 1950s which is largely a function of his relationship with de Gaulle. See Sabine Lee, *An Uneasy Relationship: British–German Relations between 1955 and 1961* (Bochum: Brockmeyer, 1996), pp. 64–70. The following is based on chapter 3 of the book.

13. Macmillan, Harold, *Riding the Storm, 1955–1959* (London: Macmillan, 1971), p. 291.

14. Report Caspari, May 1957, PA/AA:LA 3/304/34. Macmillan, *Riding the Storm*, p. 206.

15. Horne, *Macmillan*, vol. 2, p. 33. There is little indication that Macmillan left as remarkable an impression as he assumed.

16. Ibid.

17. For a particularly opinionated account of this aspect see Wolfram Kaiser, *Using Europe, Abusing the Europeans: Britain and European Integration, 1945–1963* (London: Macmillan, 1996), pp. 61–107.

18. Steel to FO, 11.10.1957, PRO: FO371/130732.

19. Maudling to Macmillan, 17.3.1958, PRO: PREM 11/2341.

20. Steel to Rumbold, 17.3.1958, PRO: PREM 11/2341.

21. Letter Macmillan to Adenauer, July 1958, PA/AA: PA 2/927. State visit to Bonn, October 1958. Macmillan, *Riding the Storm*, pp. 453–7. Henning Köhler, *Adenauer: Eine politische Biographie* (Frankfurt/Berlin: Propyläen, 1994), pp. 1007–10.

22. Details of the visit in Hans-Peter Schwarz, *Adenauer und Frankreich: Die deutsch-französischen Beziehungen, 1958–1969* (Bonn: Bouvier, 1985). See also F. Seydoux, *Dans l'intimité franco-allemande: Une mission diplomatique* (Paris: Edition Albatros, 1977), pp. 7–13.

23. Harold Macmillan Diaries (HMD), 9.10.1958, cited in Macmillan, *Riding the Storm*, p. 454.

24. HMD, 9.10.1958, cited in Horne, *Macmillan*, vol. 2, p. 110.

25. Steel to FO, 17.10.1958, PRO: FO 371/137378.

26. Forschungsgesellschaft für Auswärtige Politik (ed.), *Documents on Berlin, 1945–1963* (Munich, 1963), pp. 180–96. See also Sabine Lee, 'Perceptions and Reality: Anglo-German Relations during the Berlin Crisis, 1958–1959', *German History*, vol. 13 (1995), pp. 47–69.

27. Steel to FO, 14.2.1959, PRO: FO 371/145773.

28. For example, at a CDU party meeting he made some unfortunate remarks about Great Britain and British policy towards Europe. Steel to FO, PRO: FO 371/145773.

29. HMD, 28.5.1959, cited in Horne, *Macmillan*, vol. 2, p. 133.

30. HMD, 18.6.1959 and 27.6.1959, cited in Horne, *Macmillan*, vol. 2, p. 133.
31. Daniel Koerfer, *Kampf ums Kanzleramt* (Stuttgart: Deutsche Verlagsanstalt, 1987), pp. 187–277.
32. Reports of plans to establish *Bundeswehr* bases for training purposes in Spain caused concern across Europe, but particularly in the United Kingdom. See Herwarth, *Anglo-German Relations*, p. 514.
33. Hans Heinrich von Herwarth, *Von Adenauer zu Brandt* (Munich: Propyläen, 1990), p. 280.
34. Macmillan, *Riding the Storm*, pp. 317–18.
35. Ibid., p. 319.
36. Report about British attitudes *vis-à-vis* Germany, November 1960, PA/AA: LA 3/304/180.
37. Harold Macmillan, *Pointing the Way, 1959–1961* (London: Macmillan, 1972), p. 327.
38. Harold Macmillan, *Tides of Fortune, 1945–1955* (London: Macmillan, 1969), p. 648. PRO: CAB128/29 CC (55) 31 (9); CAB 129/81 C 112(56); CAB 128/31 C (57) 16(7).
39. PRO: CAB 129/74 C 83(55).
40. FO to Washington, 15.11.1958, PRO: FO 371/137333 and FO to Washington, 15.11.1958, PRO: FO 371/137334.
41. Steel to FO, PRO: FO 371/137336.
42. 'Berlin and Germany', a memorandum written by Sir Gladwyn Jebb, January 1959. Copy in possession of the author.
43. See also Macmillan's thoughts on NATO in the context of Franco-British relations, PRO: PREM 11/3334.
44. Report of the visit of the Prime Minister and the Foreign Secretary to the Soviet Union, 21 February to 3 March 1959, PRO: CAB 133/293, Top Secret Annex, p. 4.
45. Sabine Lee, 'Germany and the First Enlargement Negotiations 1961–1963', conference paper given in Oxford on 24 March 1996.
46. Oliver Bange, 'English, American and German interests behind the Preamble to the Franco-German Treaty, 1963', in Gustav Schmidt (ed.), *Zwischen Bündnissicherung und priviligierter Partnerschaft* (Bochum: Brockmeyer, 1995), pp. 225–80.
47. FO minute Hancock, 11.11.1958, PRO: FO 371/137334.
48. It is interesting to note, for instance, that at a meeting between Adenauer and Macmillan in early 1961 (just after another Khrushchev memorandum) neither European security, nor Berlin nor NATO were on the agenda. Report Hoyer Millar, 9.2.1961, PRO: FO 371/161127.
49. Shuckburgh to Caccia, 26.7.1961, PRO: FO 371/160480.
50. Harold Macmillan, *Pointing the Way, 1959–1961*, p. 408.

9 Perfect Peace? Macmillan and Ireland

Richard Aldous[1]

In April 1916, two young men put into action their beliefs about King and Country. Harold Macmillan had just returned to the Grenadier Guards at the trenches of the Western Front. He had been in London since Christmas recovering from wounds sustained at the Battle of Loos in which 60,000 fellow Guardsmen had died. He wrote to his mother from the Front:

> Many of us could never stand the strain and endure the horrors which we see every day, if we did not feel that this was more than a War – a crusade. I never see a man killed but think of him as a martyr. All the men ... have the same conviction – that our cause is right and certain to end in triumph.

Meanwhile, on Easter Monday in Dublin, Séan Lemass was on the roof of the General Post Office surrounded by home-made bombs with slow-burning fuses and shooting at the British troops on the street below. This was the Easter Rising – symbolic opening gesture of the Irish Revolution which would conclude with the creation of an Irish Free State in 1921. Macmillan followed events in Ireland with disdain, observing from the front that:

> The scenes in Dublin seem to be very much like those in Paris during the Commune. The real trouble is that the Sinn Fein movement is, as well as disloyal, largely anti-clerical. Therefore one of the strongest powers over them is largely diminished or hampered in its operation.

Almost half a century later, when he and Lemass met as Prime Ministers of their countries, Macmillan could only muse in his diary:

> The Irish story is a queer one.... Hundreds of years of bitter quarrels ... civil war among the natives following the complete surrender of the British – and now, peace – perfect peace.[2]

A quick examination of the index of Alistair Horne's excellent official biography reveals the obvious point that Ireland mattered little to Macmillan. The only reference to Ireland in volume two (1957–86) runs as follows: 'From Berlin, [President Kennedy] flew on to Ireland, and a warm-hearted but calmer welcome – and thence on 29 June to Birch Grove.'[3] Macmillan's view of Ireland was shaped by castles and books. He loved Lismore Castle in County Waterford, where his wife had grown up, and visited regularly. He had a profound respect for Irish literature and a particular admiration for Séan O'Casey. After O'Casey's death, Macmillan became very close to his widow, Eileen, and might actually have married her if he had not been too shy to pop the question. Rather touchingly, he believed Ireland to be 'the last happy country in Europe'.[4]

When Macmillan became prime minister in 1957, Anglo-Irish relations were cool. The public policy of successive British governments, Conservative and Labour, on partition had been consistent after 1922: the division of Ireland was an Irish not a British problem. Britain would support any arrangement made between North and South provided it did not interfere with British interests. The sympathies of governments after the Second World War, if they lay anywhere, were with the Unionists.

Attlee as Dominions Secretary during the Second World War had had very pointed views on Irish neutrality and, as Prime Minister between 1945 and 1951, he remained loyal to those from Northern Ireland who had fought in the war. In 1948, 100 left-wing Labour MPs, led by Tom Driberg, put down an amendment to the Representation of the People Bill asking for elections to the Northern Ireland parliament to be suspended until the problems of the Nationalist community were addressed. Attlee insisted that the Northern Ireland parliament was not subordinate and seemed to move beyond the 1920 Government of Ireland Act which had stated that 'the supreme authority of the Parliament of the United Kingdom shall remain unaffected and undiminished over all persons, matters and things in Northern Ireland'. Attlee's own view on the Union was unambiguous: 'no change should be made in the constitutional status of Northern Ireland without Northern Ireland's free agreement.' In other words, it was the people of Northern Ireland not the British parliament who should decide their future.[5]

Churchill returned to power in 1951 and, despite his ambiguous record on Ireland, the hopes of Nationalists rose.[6] He had said publicly on many occasions that he wanted an end to partition.

Back in office, however, Churchill sustained the view of the Attlee government that Britain could play no part in ending division. He continued to offer vocal support to Unionists, most notably in his leader's speech to the 1953 Conservative Party conference at Margate. Support for Unionism also came from Sir Anthony Eden, Churchill's foreign secretary and, in 1955, successor. On trips to Belfast he vigorously defended the Union and partition. The Irish Ambassador in London, Freddie Boland, despaired of him:

> From what I have seen and heard of him, I am inclined to think that he is not a friend of Ireland and that we are likely to find him very unsympathetic or easy to deal with on the partition issue.... In everything... affecting Ireland, he is just the ordinary Right Wing Tory – rather narrow, shallow-minded and self-righteous.[7]

If successive British administrations between 1945 and 1957 remained clearly pro-Unionist, Irish governments did little to encourage more enthusiasm for a united Ireland. In 1948, a Fine Gael-led coalition finally broke with the Commonwealth. Séan MacBride, foreign minister and former chief of staff of the IRA, summed up the republic's position on the division of Ireland in a speech to the Dail that could have been given by a frontbencher of any party between 1945 and 1959:

> That the partition of Ireland is a grievous wrong is a proposition which I do not need to put forward for the assent of any member of this House. Its injustice is recognised outside Ireland, among fair-minded people in many countries of the world including Britain itself, the perpetrator of the wrong. Like all acts of injustice, it is the source of many evils, for which there is no true remedy except the removal of the parent cause. Within the separated part of Ireland, under a government and parliament subordinate to those of Britain, there is no true peace.[8]

When Harold Macmillan succeeded Eden as prime minister in January 1957, Anglo-Irish relations were, in the words of a British minister, 'semi-detached'. Macmillan did not warm to Eamon de Valera (thinking him 'not very jolly') and, when the Taoiseach came to London for St Patrick's Day in 1958, their brief meeting was unproductive. As de Valera toured the country, he was regularly booed and pelted with vegetables. During a visit to St Patrick's Church, Soho, bottles were thrown (one of which hit the Irish Ambassador) and clashes in an angry crowd of several hundred ended in forty demonstrators being removed by the police. When de Valera left Britain, he took with him not just this noisy demonstration of hostility, but the clearly expressed view of the British government that 'Partition is the will of the majority in the six counties and it will continue to exist as long as they see no reason to change their minds.'[9]

By 1959, two years into Macmillan's premiership, all visible signs of Anglo-Irish relations were gloomy. When Macmillan visited Belfast shortly after his brilliant electioneering coup in Moscow he was accused by de Valera of hypocrisy. 'When Mr Macmillan went to Moscow we here wished him well, believing that he was engaged in a worthy mission trying to find a foundation for peace', the Taoiseach commented, '[but] we could have wished that his visit to Belfast had been promoted by such a spirit and that he was visiting our island not merely as the leader of a British political party preparing for a general election but as a statesman in pursuit here of the purposes which took him elsewhere'. But by 1959, de Valera was a fading political force. Almost blind and exhausted by forty years of active political life, he resigned from the premiership in the summer. His replacement, Séan Lemass, seemed ready to blow the 'winds of change' on the question of partition.

Séan Lemass, like de Valera, had an obvious Republican pedigree. He is thought to be one of the gunmen sent by Michael Collins to assassinate the Cairo gang on Bloody Sunday during the Anglo-Irish war and fought for de Valera during the Civil War. But Lemass was an altogether more progressive and modern-thinking man than de Valera. As Minister for Industry and Commerce in every Fianna Fail government between 1932 and 1959, he had been quietly reforming the Irish economy and encouraging industrial growth. He had long believed that the first steps towards accommodation between North and South would be economic rather than political, observing as early as 1953:

> The division of Ireland . . . is beyond question an economic absurdity. It is the greatest handicap to progress and stability on both sides of the Irish border. Its disappearance would open up new economic possibilities from which all the Irish people would benefit. It is certain to disappear sometime – economic absurdities always do – and the sooner the better.[10]

During the Macmillan years, Séan Lemass attempted to 'woo' Northern Ireland and move Britain away from the view that the partition was a matter for Irishmen alone. He aimed to encourage economic co-operation between the Republic and Northern Ireland; to change the semantics of partition; and, finally, to use prospective British and Irish membership of the Common Market to overcome problems of sovereignty.

Economic co-operation between North and South was at the heart of Lemass's plan for an Irish settlement. He told the *Belfast Telegraph* on becoming Taoiseach that 'better relations can be fostered by practical co-operation for the mutual benefit in the economic sphere' and promised 'to discuss with the Six Counties government proposals as to how policy might be directed so as to ensure that the economic progress of both parts of the country will be impeded as little as possible by the existing political division'. In speech after speech he offered to enter talks with the Northern Ireland government. He summed up his position at the Oxford Union in October 1959:

> We have expressed our willingness to co-operate with Northern Ireland without, on the one hand, concealing our own ultimate hopes or, on the other hand, asking those in control in Northern Ireland to make any immediate concession to our view. . . . Apart altogether from our political aspirations, we think this is a policy of good neighbourliness.

'The British government', he hoped, would 'encourage progress on these lines.'[11]

The semantic change which Lemass made was simple but significant. Ireland had long been in the habit of referring to its neighbour as 'the Six Counties'. This emphasized their place in the traditional thirty-two counties. This was done, in the words of the Secretary of the Department of Justice, purely 'for propaganda purposes' with 'no precedent' in law. Successive Northern Ireland governments were offended by the description. On 23 May 1960, Lemass announced that the government would encourage the title 'Northern Ireland' rather than 'Six Counties'. This practice was followed in subsequent government statements and adopted as house style by *The Irish Times* and *Irish Independent*. As the British Embassy in Dublin reported to London, this 'will perhaps go some little way towards meeting the Northern Ireland government's prerequisite for official contacts, i.e. "recognition of the constitutional status of Northern Ireland".[12]

When it became clear in the summer of 1960 that Britain would apply to join the Common Market, Lemass recognized the political as well as economic benefits which would come from membership by both countries. As he later told delegates at the Fianna Fail *Ard Fheis*:

> Within the ambit of an European community, the similarities of economic opportunities and problems in North and South, and the advantage of concerning policies to deal with them will, we believe, help to sweep away some of the arguments which have been used to sustain partition.

Certainly in discussion with the Boston-Irish Catholic US President, John F. Kennedy, officials emphasized expectations that the Common Market would provide a means towards genuine accommodation. The Irish Ambassador told Kennedy in 1962 that 'there was a political aspect involved and that membership of the EEC by ourselves and by Northern Ireland would go a long way towards eroding partition'. The President thought this 'would be a wonderful way of ending partition'.

With the Taoiseach, his government and officials all hopeful that membership of the Common Market would break down barriers, it is easy to see why de Gaulle's 'Non' in January 1963 should have been so devastating. An opportunity had been lost, Lemass told the Commonwealth Relations Secretary, Duncan Sandys, and once again Ireland had been 'left out on a limb'.[13]

Officials at the Commonwealth Relations Office – which still dealt with Irish matters even after the 1948 Republic of Ireland Act – were impressed by Lemass. A biographical sketch sent by the CRO to Macmillan in 1961 judged that Lemass was 'less rabid on the subject of partition than most Republican politicians'. With or without irony, the unnamed official concluded that 'there is little of the typical Irishman in him. . . . He is sensible, courageous and cool-headed, a man of affairs with his feet on the ground.'[14] Sir Gilbert Laithwaite, permanent under-secretary at the CRO commented that 'I have always had the feeling that we could do business' with Lemass, adding:

> Already Mr Lemass, though in very general terms, has adjured his people to stop talking about Partition and concentrate on improving relations with the North.[15]

This favourable reaction to Lemass was echoed at the Home Office which had responsibility for Northern Ireland. By 1961, the Northern Ireland desk believed:

> The political atmosphere in the South is changing. This metamorphosis will be neither rapid nor dramatic. But already there have been signs that the Dublin government is anxious to move away from the negative attitudes of earlier administrations. The spirit of 1916 and 1922 is on the wane.[16]

Enthusiasm for Lemass led Whitehall officials quietly to explore the prospects for increased economic co-operation with the Republic. In February 1960, the Home Office told the Stormont government in Belfast that:

> It is impossible to be optimistic about the Republic's economic future. Our economic and social relations with them are probably closer than with any other country, foreign or Commonwealth. The Republic comes eighth in the list of our world markets and a depression there must to some extent affect our own prosperity. It would therefore be desirable to try, if we can, to find some way of helping their economy.

In practical terms, this meant 'full UK support price for store cattle and sheep imported from the Irish Republic'; London would subsidize livestock in the Republic as well as Northern Ireland. This was the first step on the road to trade talks between Britain and Ireland which began in September 1963 and reached modest agreement in 1965.[17]

Unionists, unlike senior civil servants, were unimpressed by Lemass. As early as July 1959, the Northern Ireland cabinet decided that 'the proposal for "limited free trade" with the Republic could not be supported on political grounds'. The following year, the Northern Ireland prime minister, Lord Brookeborough, publicly rejected Lemass's offer of economic co-operation:

> Why this insistent harping on economic co-operation? Whatever the advantages – and I cannot see them in practical terms – we do recognise that the fundamental objective of Mr Lemass is political. Co-operation of the kind suggested is the thin end of the wedge which given time, would be driven home to create an ever widening gap between Northern Ireland and Britain and

eventually split us from the United Kingdom economy. . . . If this sounds uncompromising, I can only say that it is intended to be so. One can't compromise on matters involving basic principles, for to do so would be a betrayal.[18]

This was not only the view of Unionists in Belfast. There were influences close to the government, and Macmillan himself, who were keen to protect the *status quo* in Ireland. The arrival of Séan Lemass as Taoiseach coincided with that of Knox Cunningham, Unionist MP for South Antrim, in 10 Downing Street as Macmillan's principal private secretary (PPS). As Alan Clark observed in his diaries of the Thatcher years, the PPS is someone whom a prime minister can 'confide in personally' and will pop 'round to Number 10 when all engagements are over . . . [and] go upstairs to the flat and drink whisky'.[19] Macmillan found Cunningham congenial company. He was a fifteen-stone, jolly Ulsterman who had won a rugby blue at Cambridge and reminded MPs more of a secret serviceman than a political secretary. The official record of advice he was giving Macmillan on Ireland between 1959 and 1963 is almost non-existent, but if his stand after 1963 is a yardstick, it is unlikely to have been positive.[20]

After leaving Downing Street, Cunningham voiced consistently hard-line views on partition. He vigorously opposed the liberalizing policies of Terence O'Neill and was the only Unionist MP publicly to support Ian Paisley. Moreover, when O'Neill finally met Séan Lemass in 1965, Cunningham defied his own party in opposing the visit. Recent evidence also suggests Cunningham's involvement with the emerging paramilitary organizations. In particular, his friendship and financial involvement with William McGrath, the founder of TARA, excited controversy within Ireland. TARA helped orchestrate both political opposition against O'Neill and the original Ulster Volunteer Force bombings in the spring of 1969 that forced O'Neill from office. What Cunningham's activities after leaving Downing Street make clear is that there was at the heart of Macmillan's private office a trusted figure who later opposed any accommodation with the South and supported hard-line, possibly paramilitary, Unionism.[21]

Cunningham had access at the highest levels of government but he was not a major political player. R. A. Butler, however, was the most senior member of the government after Macmillan and, as Home Secretary, the minister responsible for Northern Ireland.

Liberal, reform-minded and committed only to the 'art of the poss-ible', RAB was the epitome of the consensus politician. According to his official biographer, Anthony Howard, 'RAB simply lacked the buccaneering attitude to politics.' This is what makes a gung-ho attitude to Ireland so surprising. Butler was a personal friend of the Northern Irish Prime Minister, Lord Brookeborough, and often paid private visits to his country home, Colebrooke in Co. Fermanagh. It was during one such 'private' visit in December 1959 that he was taken to the site in Rosslea where an RUC officer had recently been killed in a terrorist attack. Whilst there, the Home Secretary launched an attack on the Irish government for failing 'to do their utmost to control those who are perpetrating these out-rages'. At Belfast airport he told reporters that he would consider sanctions against Ireland to end terrorism, adding that 'It is most important not to have mere words but something that would have a real effect.' Butler was resolute in standing side by side with the people of Northern Ireland and declaring that 'your soil is our soil'.[22]

Butler's message was intended to reassure Unionist fears about the British attitude to terrorism. The IRA had been engaged in a campaign of terrorist activity in Britain and along the border be-tween Ireland and Northern Ireland since 1956. The fact that IRA members were thought to be well-known in Ireland but remained free gave strength to Unionist arguments that talk of economic co-operation was the acceptable face of Irish republicanism. At the House of Commons in November 1959, the Ulster Unionist MP Sir David Campbell told Butler:

> The Ulster members [are] convinced that the Eire government could do more to help; while they appreciate that open pressure might be inadvisable they [feel] that sufficient pressure had not been applied behind the scenes. Eire received all the privileges of the Commonwealth and some of these could be taken away.

If action were not taken quickly, he warned, 'the Ulster members . . . might not be able to restrain their people'. It is no coincidence that Butler's threat of economic sanctions should have come just weeks after this Unionist warning.[23]

RAB's uncharacteristic bullishness in Belfast seemed to catch Macmillan by surprise and he called the Home Secretary to Number 10 from the airport. The *Daily Mail* captured the sense of bemusement:

MPs were asking: Has RAB been carpeted. The view was that Mr Butler had been indiscreet. The idea of Mr Butler's being on the mat at No. 10 Downing Street is doubtless putting it too hard. Nonetheless, Mr Macmillan must have been distinctly puzzled by the whole affair.

Puzzled or not, Macmillan clearly accepted that Butler was only expressing the general thrust of government policy albeit in a forthright way. The Home Secretary reiterated his case in the House of Commons on 17 December and made clear a desire that 'the people of Northern Ireland should feel they have this government behind them'. This keen interest in the affairs of Northern Ireland continued throughout his time as Home Secretary. It was at RAB's request that a Cabinet Committee was established for Northern Ireland and a Northern Ireland bill drafted to enlarge the competence of the Stormont government.[24]

Macmillan's own relations with Stormont were not as close as his deputy's but remained relaxed and friendly. When, in July 1961, he invited Lord Brookeborough for a weekend at Chequers, he told him that 'I like to see as much of my friends at home as possible.' The party that weekend included the Chancellor of the Exchequer and the Home Secretary. Although there was some discussion about the difficulties facing Belfast's heavy industry, there was no proposal to exploit trade routes across the border.

The seriousness with which Macmillan listened to Brookeborough contrasted strongly with any desire to consult Lemass. The tone of their meetings had been established at the outset. Lemass met the Prime Minister for the first time as head of government in the summer of 1959. During the forty-five minutes they were together on 13 July, Macmillan exuded disinterest and even boredom. He inquired after the health of de Valera and asked questions from his crib cards about Irish industry, agriculture and emigration but showed little inclination to discuss the practical or philosophical aspects of Anglo-Irish relations.[26] In the same month that Macmillan invited Brookeborough to Chequers, his private secretary, Philip de Zulueta, noted that the PM was trying to 'put Mr Lemass off' because he was too busy to see him. Although British ministers were taking a critical strategic decision on Europe, the PM's office did 'not think the delay need matter since our decision about negotiations will not be affected by the discussions with the Irish'. In short, receiving Lemass was a simple (if inconvenient) courtesy and Irish views were a matter neither of priority nor interest.[27]

By the final year of Macmillan's premiership there were signs of a thaw between Northern Ireland and the Republic. The IRA had announced a year earlier 'the termination of resistance to British occupation launched on December 12, 1956'. Lord Brookeborough had been replaced by the more moderate and liberal Terence O'Neill as Northern Ireland's prime minister. Even Knox Cunningham felt moved to write that 'there is a wind of change blowing in Northern Ireland'.[28]

Counterfactual history always ends up by running into the buffers but what happens next is a moment so quintessentially Macmillanesque that it is impossible not to imagine an alternative narrative. Macmillan had based so much of his understanding of international politics on the importance of personal diplomacy. Like Churchill before him, he believed that if the key players could get round a table together, they would achieve more than endless negotiations between diplomats. The problem for Macmillan's summitry had always been Britain's position of relative weakness to the two superpowers, USSR and USA. But in any discussion with Ireland, it would have been Britain who played the role of 'superpower'. Even America would have deferred to Britain not least because the new President, John F. Kennedy was, according to the Irish embassy in Washington, 'British inclined and . . . makes no secret of his firm attachment to Britain.'[29]

The scenario was simple enough. In April 1963 Terence O'Neill asked Macmillan for his personal support in inviting President Kennedy to open the Giant's Causeway during his visit to Britain and Ireland that spring. Macmillan agreed this 'would be a good idea' and undertook 'to consider what could be done'. In reality he did nothing and made no suggestion to Kennedy that he might visit Northern Ireland. The Irish Ambassador in Washington had already warned Dublin that raising partition 'now when Britain has so many pressing problems to solve is something he [JFK] would avoid'. But if Macmillan had raised the issue and tried to engineer a meeting between Lemass and O'Neill during Kennedy's trip? If Macmillan had thrown his full weight behind talks and taken advantage of the goodwill created? If he had used the prospect of a presidential visit to Northern Ireland and the emergence of the forward-thinking O'Neill to initiate political talks? It is inconceivable that Macmillan would have missed this 'summit' opportunity had he believed for one moment that Ireland mattered.[30]

When Macmillan came to power, the policy of the British government was one of upholding the Union unless Irishmen of both traditions showed any inclination for unity. When he left office, despite the efforts of Séan Lemass and, latterly, Terence O'Neill, to enlist his support in starting a talks process, that position remained unchanged. By the autumn of 1963, hopes for accommodation and reconciliation were already receding. The IRA cease-fire was increasingly fragile with the additional threat that, if violence resumed, British cities would be targeted. Although O'Neill did eventually meet Lemass during the Wilson years, his room for manoeuvre had already been squeezed by hard-liners. From 1968, policy-makers struggling to come to terms with the violence would look back wistfully to days when all in Ireland had seemed 'peace – perfect peace'.

NOTES

1. I am grateful to Professor Ronan Fanning at University College Dublin for his perceptive and encouraging comments on early drafts of this chapter.
2. Harold Macmillan, *Winds of Change* (London: Macmillan, 1966), pp. 78–9; Alistair Horne, *Macmillan*, vol. 1 (London: Macmillan, 1986), pp. 40–1; John Horgan, *Sean Lemass: The Enigmatic Patriot* (Dublin, 1997), pp. 12–3; I owe the final quotation to Peter Catteral of the Institute of Contemporary British History.
3. Alistair Horne, *Macmillan*, vol. 2 (London: Macmillan, 1989), p. 512.
4. I am grateful to Charles Lysaght for much of this information which comes from his conversations with Macmillan; Horne, *Macmillan*, vol. 2, pp. 604–5.
5. National Archives Dublin, Foreign Affairs, London Embassy, F132/1/2: Department of External Affairs to London, teleprinter message 3351, 25 November 1951; Boland to O'Driscoll, 26 September, 1951.
6. Churchill had sent the infamous Black & Tans to Dublin during the Anglo-Irish war and negotiated the 1921 treaty with Michael Collins.
7. National Archives, Dublin, Foreign Affairs, London Embassy, F132/1/2: Ambassador to Secretary, Department of External Affairs, 22 January 1952; Ambassador to Secretary, Department of External Affairs, 24 April 1954.
8. National Archives, Dublin, Department of Taoiseach, S15823A: Statement in Dail Eireann, 30 November 1955.
9. Macmillan's conversations with Charles Lysaght; *The Times*, 18 March

1958; National Archives, Dublin, Foreign Affairs, London Embassy, L116/16: St Patrick's Day celebrations, 16–19 March 1958. The innocence of the 1950s with regard to security is beautifully illustrated during this visit. The report of the trip included the tale of a threatening phone call which 'claimed that a bomb had been placed in the Embassy and necessitated a precautionary search of the premises by the Ambassador and Sgt. Cruise'.

10. Horgan, *Séan Lemass*, p. 17; National Archives Dublin, Department of Taoiseach, S14291A/3: speech by Séan Lemass to Ottawa Canadian Club, 25 September 1953.

11. *Belfast Telegraph*, 9 July 1959; National Archives Dublin, Department of Taoiseach, S9361 I/94: Speech by Séan Lemass at Oxford Union, 15 October 1959.

12. National Archives, Dublin, Department of Taoiseach, S15579A: Secretary, Department of Justice to Secretary, Department of Taoiseach, 28 October 1955 (Secretary is the highest ranking civil servant in a Irish government department and equivalent to the British rank of permanent under-secretary); *Irish Independent*, 24 May 1960; PRO (Kew), DO 35/7824: Dublin 107/18, G. D. Anderson to O. R. Blair (CRO), 7 June 1960.

13. *The Irish Times*, 18 January 1961; National Archives, Dublin, Department of Taoiseach, S9361 K/62: speeches by Séan Lemass at Fianna Fail *Ard Fheis*, 16 January 1962 and 20 November 1962; Ambassador (Washington) to Secretary, Department of External Affairs, 28 March 1962; PRO (Kew) Prem 11/4320: Record of meeting at CRO, 12 March 1963.

14. PRO (Kew), PREM 11/4320: Notes on personalities and officials.

15. PRO (Kew), DO 35/7853: PUS to Secretary of State, 3 July 1959.

16. PRONI (Belfast), CAB4/115, Cabinet Conclusions, 2 February 1960: *Economic Relations with the Irish Republic: Memo for Northern Ireland Government* (with covering letter from Austin Strutt at the Home Office).

17. PRONI (Belfast) CAB 4/115, Cabinet Conclusions 2 February 1960; see also PRONI (Belfast), CAB 9R/60/12, Cabinet Secretariat: Anglo-Eire Trade Negotiations.

18. PRONI (Belfast), CAB4/1097; Cabinet Meeting 9 July 1959; *Irish Press*, 31 May 1960.

19. Alan Clark, *Diaries* (1993), p. 57.

20. His unpublished memoir, *One Man Dog*, is in the possession of the Drapers Company, London, but remains closed. The record of his activities held by the PRO amounts to a handful of letters and notes. Richard Thorpe was shown *One Man Dog* by its author and uses it in his biography of Lord Home (London, 1997).

21. C. Moore, *The Kincora Scandal* (Dublin, 1996); Bill Graham, 'Kincora: The Tangled Web', *Hot Press*, May 1996; review of *The Kincora Scandal*, by Conor Cruise O'Brien, *Sunday Independent*, 21 April 1996.

22. Anthony Howard, *RAB: The Life of R A Butler* (London, 1987); *Belfast Telegraph*, 12 December 1959; *Daily Mail*, 14 and 15 December 1959; *The Times*, 14 December 1959; *Observer*, 13 December 1959; National Archives, Dublin, Department of Foreign Affairs, London Embassy,

F132/11/21: London Embassy to Dublin, Teleprinter message 3830, 19 December 1959; National Archives, Dublin, Department of Taoiseach, S9361/I/94: Taoiseach's comments on statement by Mr R. A. Butler, 31 March 1960; PRONI (Belfast), COM/60A//1/3/89, Butler to Brookeborough, 10 September 1959.

23. National Archives, Dublin, Department of Taoiseach, S9361/K/63: London Embassy to Dublin, Ambassador to Secretary of Department of External Affairs, 19 January 1963; PRO (Kew), HO 284/45: Private Office to Home Secretary, Record of meeting with Ulster Unionist MPs, 23 November 1959; Note of meeting between Home Secretary and Sir David Campbell and other UUP MPs, 24 November 1959.

24. *Daily Mail*, 15 December 1959; National Archives (Dublin), External Affairs, F132/11/21 London Embassy: Teleprinter message 3830 from London, 19 December 1959; PRO (Kew), PREM 11/3897: de Zulueta to Glanville, 21 May 1961; Briefing notes for visit of Lord Brookeborough in July 1961.

25. PRO (Kew), PREM 11/3897: Macmillan to Brookeborough, 3 June 1961; Note for the record, meeting of Prime Minister and Lord Brookeborough at Chequers, 17 July 1961; PRO (Kew), PREM 11/4320: Record of meeting between Prime Minister and Taoiseach, 18 March 1963, National Archives, Dublin, Department of Taoiseach, S9361/K/63: London Embassy to Dublin, Ambassador to Secretary of Department of External Affairs, 19 January 1963.

26. PRO (Kew), DO 35/7853: Record of conversation at 10 Downing Street on 13 July 1959 between the Prime Minister and Prime Minister of Eire.

27. PRO (Kew), PREM 11/4320: de Zulueta to France, 30 June 1961.

28. National Archives, Dublin, Department of Taoiseach, S1157 B/94: Unsigned memorandum from Department of External Affairs, 18 February 1963; PRO (Kew), PREM 11/4386: Knox Cunningham to Tim Bligh, 18 April 1963.

29. See 'A Family Affair: Harold Macmillan and the Art of Personal Diplomacy', in R. Aldous and S. Lee, *Harold Macmillan & Britain's World Role*; PRO (Kew), PREM 11/4386, Note for the record, meeting between the Prime Minister and Captain O'Neill, 22 April 1963; National Archives, Dublin, Department of Taoiseach, S9361/K/63, Washington to Dublin, Ambassador to Secretary, 19 March 1963.

30. PRO (Kew), PREM 11/4386, Note for the record, meeting between the Prime Minister and Captain O'Neill, 22 April 1963; Cunningham to Bligh, 22 April 1963; Cunningham to Philip de Zulueta, 24 April 1963; National Archives, Dublin, Department of Taoiseach, S9361/K/63, Washington to Dublin, Ambassador to Secretary, 19 March 1963; PRO (Kew), DO35/7853 & PREM 11/4320.

10 Dear Brendan and Master Harold

Charles Lysaght

In the cool summer of 1968, when I was beginning my research for a biography of Brendan Bracken, I was bidden to lunch at Birch Grove, the Sussex home of Harold Macmillan. When I arrived in a taxi, I found my host waiting at the door to greet me. He fussed about where I should put my briefcase and whether I wished to wash my hands. He poured me a glass of sherry and then took me out into the lovely rose garden his mother had created and told me all about it and about her. He shuffled up and down the same path about ten times before we went into lunch. 'I don't usually see people who are writing books' he told me, 'but I liked your letter.' He spoke affectionately of 'dear Brendan' as he called Bracken. But speaking as a publisher he rather doubted if there was a book in it now that all Bracken's papers had been destroyed.

And so the conversation ranged wider. He had been to Ireland that summer and had been charmed by the Waterford countryside where his late wife's Anglo-Irish relations lived; 'I expect you know them', he added. 'It's the only happy country left in Europe' he remarked, 'nothing seems to have changed; it's just like England used to be when I was young.' He recalled the Irish writers he had known in his publishing days: Yeats whom he felt was a poseur; Sean O'Casey whom he considered a saint; James Stephens whom he loved and mimicked with relish and Oliver Gogarty whom he thought was rather a fraud. 'All that great efflorescence in Dublin in those days' he mused, 'and now nothing, I suppose.' He spoke of De Valera's great integrity but thought he was more a Spaniard than an Irishman – 'He is not very jolly, is he?' he remarked. As we talked, he made regular attentive enquiries about my comfort.

We worked our way through the regular Macmillan lunch of paté, cold ham and salad and then raspberries, which he proudly told me were his own as he took a second helping. No, he did not remember when I reminded him that in 1914, when he was Treasurer of the Oxford Union, he had spoken at the Cambridge Union for Irish Home Rule. But he was pleased to recall all his friends who

had died in the Great War. Ronnie Knox and one other were the
only friends he had left at the end of it.[1] Only his ambitious and
rather formidable American mother, who nursed him back to health
after he had been seriously wounded, had prevented him from following Knox into the Roman obedience. He was clearly very exercised by matters religious.

His own conversation was wonderfully learned, full of ideas and
literary and historical allusions. Brendan, he said, knew more history than anybody outside a university. When I asked if he thought
Bracken was a depressive, he answered that all the Irish and High-
land Scots are. 'That was why *we* drink'; he added, 'the English,
they drink for sociability – at bump suppers and the like.' He himself had suffered from the most awful depressions all his life and
the only cure he knew was to lock himself away and read Jane
Austen and pray that he would not have to take any decisions until
it passed. Certainly he had about him a lonely, melancholy air. 'I
don't live in the world anymore' he said; 'when I go to London
and see people, I get tired.' He shuffled around uneasily, moving
from place to place as we talked. He wrapped himself in a rug
when he sat down outside. 'Don't go yet', he said when I made a
move. He showed me all the family photographs. I did not then
know the sad story of his wife's infidelity, but I did notice that the
only photograph on his desk was of his mother. There were also
several shots of President Kennedy in the room. He spoke wistfully
and romantically of Kennedy's visit to him only a few months before
the fatal day in Dallas.

When the time came to go, he himself rang for my taxi. Before
I left he counselled me earnestly: 'Don't pay too much attention
to accounts of conversations. Brendan and Winston and Max
Beaverbrook were always saying outrageous things just for the hell
of it; it was a form of relaxation. The real business was done in
writing.' So he waved me off, a solitary, forlorn figure standing at
the door of his empty house, leaving me charmed and captivated
by his grace and style but not all that much wiser about 'dear
Brendan' whom I had come to discuss.

When I got to work on my book I discovered that, contrary to
what the Chairman of the House of Macmillan, who had been my
host, had said, the destruction of Bracken's papers was not an
insurmountable obstacle to writing a biography as many of his letters could be traced in other people's papers. Brendan Bracken
was such a good subject that another author ran up a book in a

year and won the Whitbread Prize, despite failing to unearth much material that was relevant and available.[2] I also discovered an amount about Bracken's relationship with Harold Macmillan that the former Prime Minister had not recalled or perhaps had never known.

Their association went back a long way. In 1926 as a young Conservative Member of Parliament, Macmillan had written an article for *The Banker*, a journal that Bracken had founded and was editing for the publishers Eyre & Spottiswoode, to whose board he had been co-opted that year at the age of 24. It was entitled 'Our mediaeval system of local taxation' and contained proposals for relieving industry of the burden of rates. They so impressed the Chancellor of the Exchequer Winston Churchill that they were given effect in the Derating Act two years later.[3] In the 1929 General Election, as the country swung away from the Conservatives, Macmillan lost his seat in Stockton while Bracken entered the House of Commons as a Conservative member for North Paddington, having survived a Labour challenge for this key marginal by a mere 528 votes after a tempestuous contest. 'The ladies of easy virtue who abound in Maida Vale and are the remnant of the once powerful Tory party are still loyal to our cause', he wrote during the campaign to his mentor J. L. Garvin, the editor of the *Observer*, 'but I fear their ancient profession is but little encouraged by derating and some of our other admirable measures.'[4]

In October 1930 Tom Jones recorded in his diary a weekend at the Astors' house Cliveden, when both Macmillan and Bracken were among a group of young disgruntled Tories 'all angry with Stanley Baldwin'.[5] But they would have had little in common except this antipathy. Macmillan was on the left of the party on economic issues, flirting with socialism as a cure for unemployment and blaming the Governor of the Bank of England Montagu Norman and other bankers for the Great Depression. Bracken thought this was arrant nonsense and was on the right of the party, decrying state intervention and criticizing 'lush doles'. He was also allied to Churchill in opposing self-government for India, a measure Macmillan supported when he returned to the House of Commons in 1931. As Churchill became isolated on that and on his early appeals for rearmament, and blotted his copybook by a number of other misjudgments, notably over the Abdication, Bracken remained at his side, his only consistent supporter. 'We were' Bracken later boasted 'a party of two.'[6] Stanley Baldwin, the Prime Minister, in a rare moment of wit inspired by his cousin Rudyard Kipling, described

Bracken as Churchill's faithful *chela*. *Chela* was the Hindustani word for a disciple.

In those years Macmillan drifted out of Churchill's life, although they lived quite close to one another in the country. Apart from their political disagreements, it may be surmised that Macmillan did not relish the possibility of meeting Robert Boothby, his wife's lover, who was a frequent visitor at Chartwell, Churchill's home in Kent. Churchill, for his part, found Macmillan over-earnest and rather dull. He deleted Macmillan's name when it was among those on a list of possible candidates to restore the strength of the Other Club, a cross-party dining circle of which Churchill had been a founder (with F. E. Smith) and remained the presiding presence, and of which Bracken was secretary.[7]

It was the issue of appeasement that brought Macmillan back into the Churchillian world. Macmillan recalled being invited to Chartwell in late 1935 during the uproar about the Hoare–Laval Pact, the effect of which was that the League of Nations sanctions imposed on Italy for invading Abyssinia were undermined; Bracken was among those he found there.[8] During the debates on the Munich Agreement at the end of September 1938 Macmillan brought Hugh Dalton to a meeting of Tory dissidents at 8 Lord North Street, Bracken's house, where the possibility of making common cause with Labour was discussed.[9] There was, however, little enthusiasm for this among these dissidents who lay low during the following months as the Agreement under which the German-speaking areas of Czechoslovakia were conceded to Germany was still popular. On 17 November only Churchill, Macmillan and Bracken voted against the government in favour of a Labour Party motion to establish a Ministry of Supply.[10] In the early summer of 1939, as the policy of appeasement disintegrated, Macmillan listened with admiration to Bracken in the House of Commons when he revealed that the Chancellor, Sir John Simon, had acquiesced in the transfer of the Czech gold reserves to the German Government. 'Simon's combination of legalism and cynicism', Macmillan later wrote, 'disturbed the House. Even the government's most loyal supporters could barely stomach so shocking and discreditable an affair.'[11]

On 3 September that year war was declared. Churchill joined the government as First Lord of the Admiralty. Bracken became his Parliamentary Private Secretary. Macmillan remained on the backbenches dissatisfied with Chamberlain's leadership and prominent in a group pressing for Churchill to succeed. Back in office Churchill did not intrigue with dissidents, but his acolyte Bracken made it his business to keep in touch with them.[12] In May 1940 after the fall of Norway, Macmillan was among those Tories who voted against the government in a division that was the death-knell of Chamberlain's administration. The next day Macmillan met Bracken, who seemed happy and assured Macmillan that he, too, could be happy. However, at the last moment, Chamberlain tried to hang on. 'It's like trying to get a limpet off a corpse', Bracken told Macmillan as they waited anxiously before Chamberlain finally agreed to go.[13]

Macmillan and Bracken remained in close touch as Churchill formed his government. Bracken was in the thick of things, suggesting the right men for various jobs. 'The Boss's mood is one of profound anxiety', he confided in Macmillan.[14] Macmillan was appointed one of Beaverbrook's understudies at the Ministry of Supply. Later he became Parliamentary Secretary at the Colonial Office, where he was able to act as spokesman in the House of Commons as Lord Moyne, the Colonial Secretary, was in the Lords. However, in the autumn of 1942, the government was re-arranged and Oliver Stanley, a Member of the Commons, became Colonial Secretary. This effectively downgraded Macmillan. He was disappointed that the Prime Minister did not value him more highly and wrote a letter of resignation. He showed it to Bracken, then whom nobody, he later wrote, was closer to Winston Churchill.[15] Bracken advised Macmillan to hold his hand. A month later, in the aftermath of the American invasion of North Africa, Macmillan was appointed Resident Minister there and given Cabinet rank. This proved the turning-point in his political career.

It was not long before Bracken was voicing disappointment about the man he had helped. In March 1943, in his capacity as Minister of Information, he was telling W. P. Crozier of the *Manchester Guardian*, that he had 'hoped Macmillan would fight for proper facilities for us in respect of news, but as a matter of fact, he was doing all the Americans told him and getting nothing for us'.[16] A little over a year later, on 22 June 1944, Robert Bruce Lockhart who worked with Anthony Eden, the Foreign Secretary, and with Bracken, noted in his diary:

both Brendan and Anthony are up against Macmillan, Anthony because Resident Ministers are always a bit of a business to the F.O. and Brendan perhaps because he is a little jealous of the P.M.s recent marks of confidence in Macmillan.[17]

Bracken and Macmillan were both members of the caretaker government formed by Churchill at the end of the War in Europe after the Labour members resigned in May 1945 to fight the General Election. Bracken was First Lord of the Admiralty, Macmillan Minister for Air. Both lost their seats in the landslide to Labour and both were returned at by-elections in safe Tory seats before the year was out.

Early the next year Robert Bruce Lockhart noted a meeting with Bracken at dinner in the house of Cyril Radcliffe, the eminent barrister who had run the Ministry of Information under Bracken:

> Brendan was subdued, quite sober, but in good form. He gave a long account of the difficulties of the new government, but thought that the Tories were out for a long time and were foolish in their tactics. Contrary to the last time I saw him, he was pro-Anthony [Eden] this time; said Anthony was the only leader who could command Liberal votes in the country and informed us that Harold Macmillan and Oliver Stanley were intriguing against him and trying to oust him from the leadership. All this was very foolish.[18]

Bracken viewed with jaundiced eyes the efforts of Macmillan and others, notably Rab Butler, to move the Party to the left. On 7 October 1946 he wrote to his friend Lord Beaverbrook:

> 'The Tory Conference is over. It was an interesting affair. The neo-socialists like Harold Macmillan, who are in favour of nationalizing railways, electricity, gas and many other things, expected to get great support from the delegates who are supposed to be greatly frustrated by the result of the general election and successive by-elections.
>
> Rab Butler and the other moles engaged in research to produce a 'modern' policy for the Tory Party believed that Blackpool would be a paradise for the progressives.
>
> It turned out that the neo-socialists were lucky to escape with their scalps. The delegates would have nothing to do with the proposal to change the party's name. They demanded a real Conservative policy instead of a synthetic Socialist one so dear to the heart of the Macmillans and Butlers and it gave Churchill one of the great receptions of his life.

I know not whether the Tories' return to their ancient faith is likely to get us more votes at the four forthcoming by-elections. it certainly won't lose us any.'[19]

Unfortunately, not much detail survives on the inner conflicts of the Conservative Front Bench during these years in opposition. Bracken's views critical of state enterprise, high taxation and welfare handouts, and in favour of the creation of the right environment for entrepreneurs as the only way forward may have been precursors of Thatcherism but they were then regarded as politically impossible. But apart from occasional sniping at Front Bench meetings and in his 'Men & Matters' column in the *Financial Times*, Bracken made little effort to harness political support against the 'Chartermongers' as he described Butler, Macmillan and their followers.[20] His priority was that his old friend Winston Churchill should be Prime Minister again. Arguments about policy could await that event. Meanwhile, he devoted himself to wholehearted noisy opposition to bills to nationalize public utilities such as gas, and to general abuse of government ministers.

I have not been able to discover any record of how Macmillan viewed Bracken's activities in these years. Doubtless he shared the general expectation that Bracken would return to the Cabinet on Churchill's coat-tails and may have been apprehensive of the influence he would wield on economic policy. But they were friendly enough that on the day the Labour Prime Minister Clement Attlee dissolved the House of Commons in October 1951, Bracken, who was quite confident of a Tory victory in the ensuing election, was discussing Macmillan's ministerial prospects with him. Macmillan later recalled the encounter:

According to his account, Churchill intends to stay a year or eighteen months.... Eden will go to the Foreign Office; Butler to the Exchequer; Lyttleton to Production. What would I like? The Service Departments will be under-secretaries, as in war. One idea would be to have a permanent chairman of the Chiefs of Staff Committee – an American plan which we subsequently adopted. In this case I could be the Minister of Defence unless Churchill took the post himself. Alternatively there was Leader of the Commons. With Eden at the Foreign Office it would be impossible for him to act as Leader. Would I like this? And so the strange conversation continued.[21]

In the event, when Churchill became Prime Minister, Macmillan was only appointed Minister of Housing. He was bitterly disappointed and had to be dissuaded from declining. He did not foresee how it would help his political career. Bracken, for his part, confounded friends and foes alike by declining the Colonial Office or any other post, pleading that his recurrent sinusitis made it impossible. Shortly afterwards, he resigned his seat in the House of Commons, so bringing his political career to an end at the age of 50. He was created Viscount Bracken, but never took his seat in the House of Lords, which in his irreverent way he called 'the Morgue'.

However, he remained close to Churchill and his commentary in letters to friends, notably Lord Beaverbrook, on the activities of ministers, including Macmillan, is full of interest. At first, most of his ire was directed at Butler because as Chancellor of the Exchequer he failed to check inflation. In January 1953, when the government had been in office just over a year, Bracken wrote to Beaverbrook:

> Taking them all in all I should think that Monckton and Macmillan are the most successful Ministers. . . . Macmillan is desperately anxious to get out of the Ministry of Housing, but I don't think Churchill will let him go to his spiritual home, which is the Foreign Office. Alone among the press the *Times* newspaper has pointed out that when the Socialists bolted they left behind them no less than 216,000 unfinished houses. It wasn't difficult, therefore, to induce good housing returns during the first year of a Tory government. Conditions will be very different this year and so Master Harold is right to try to find alternative employment. It must, of course, be said that Macmillan has shown a great deal of good sense in his dealings with the public. Small touches, such as arriving on the scene after the floods in Devonshire, are very much applauded by the public, and rightly so.[22]

In March 1953 Bracken spent a weekend at Chequers with Churchill where Macmillan was a fellow guest. He reported to Beaverbrook:

> Success has turned Harold into a healthy heretic and has shed his defensive armour of respectability. He is now chock-full of fun and is looking for new fields to conquer. Agriculture is beginning to attract him – I can't think of a better man to stir up

that moss grown department and to create hell in its appendage the Farmers' Union. Under him more food would be grown and so too would budget deficits.[23]

A few months later, in June 1953, Churchill suffered a stroke, whose existence was hidden from the public and even the Cabinet as a result of a conspiracy among his close associates, among whom Bracken and Beaverbrook were foremost. There followed two years when Churchill continued to preside over the government although not really fit to do so and his heir apparent Anthony Eden (who was recovering from a botched operation) grew more and more resentful at being made to wait. Macmillan, alone among Churchill's ministers, had the courage to tell the old man that he should make way for Eden. Bracken appears to have resented this although there is no evidence that he himself actively encouraged Churchill to remain on as Prime Minister.

Writing to his Australian friend W. S. Robinson on 28 January 1955, Bracken described Macmillan, who had become Minister for Defence, as 'a very remarkable man, imaginative, amusing and possessed of a judgement which is almost always wrong'.[24] Macmillan had apparently asked Bracken about becoming Foreign Secretary when, as was about to happen, Eden succeeded Churchill as Prime Minister. He was apprehensive that Eden would interfere with him unduly. Bracken, on his own account, told him that 'Eden would keep a grip on foreign policy as strong as a vice.' 'Nevertheless', Bracken remarked, 'Harold is not deterred as he has always wanted the Foreign Office.' In March 1955 Eden succeeded Churchill and Macmillan became Foreign Secretary. By November of that year Bracken was telling Beaverbrook that Macmillan had become 'a pompous posturer' and would be a growing liability to Eden.[25]

In December 1955 Eden re-shuffled his cabinet by making Rab Butler Leader of the House of Commons and moving Macmillan to replace him at the Treasury. Writing to W. S. Robinson on 18 January 1956 Bracken remarked:

Perhaps the major reason for Harold's appointment was his temperamental incapacity for the Foreign Secretaryship. There was only one place to which he could be moved and that was the Treasury and if he had not been given that he would probably have been at a loose end in the House of Commons where he could create lots of trouble for the Government. Never since the

days of Charles Townshend has there been a stranger appointment to the Treasury.

His apprehensions about Macmillan at the Treasury had not been
assuaged by a press conference that Macmillan held shortly after
taking up his new office; as he told Robinson:

> Our new Chancellor of the Exchequer is beginning well! He saw
> some of the moguls of the newspapers on Monday night and
> told them that in his judgment the bankers were a menace to
> the country. He recalled that he had been Member for Stockton-
> on-Tees for nearly 20 years and that nearly 20,000 unemployed
> had walked the streets because of the policies of Montagu Norman
> and the joint stock banks. He also told them that he had crossed
> the floor of the House of Commons because of the deflationary
> policies of the bankers and Baldwin's government and if this
> government followed their bad example he would be perfectly
> prepared to cross the floor again. Old Sir Oscar Hobson of the
> *News Chronicle* who is a financial troglodyte, and practically a
> teetotaller, had to be revived with brandy because no smelling
> salts were available in Whitehall.

Yet Bracken was not without some hopes for Macmillan in his new
post. As he wrote to Beaverbrook on 17 January 1956:

> Macmillan may be the witch doctor we need – at any rate for a
> while will give the appearance of being one – and may in our
> present circumstances be the best possible boss for the Treasury.
> He is a person of very little judgment and I can't forgive him for
> his gross disloyalty to Churchill. But our need now is for a financial
> Mary Baker Eddy and Macmillan has plenty of affinities with
> that lady. And so let us hope for the best.[26]

Within the month there was a serious clash in the cabinet when
Eden opposed Macmillan's proposal to cut food subsidies on bread
and milk in order to help stem the continuing flight from the pound.
Bracken wrote to Beaverbrook on 15 February 1956:

> Your prophecy that your former Under-Secretary would make
> trouble for Eden has been swiftly proved. He sent in his resigna-

tion yesterday on a cunningly contrived issue which would have gravely embarrassed his boss and would have given your former Under-Secretary the credit for being the only virtuous and strong man in government. A truce has been patched up, but how long it will last is anybody's guess.

Unfortunately for E. he has given this man a job which puts him plumb in the centre of the political stage and one may be sure that he will make the fullest use of his nuisance value.[27]

Beaverbrook replied tersely, as was his wont:

Be sure that Macmillan will make trouble if he has power. As long as he is kept in order he will be all right. When he gets up he will be all wrong.[28]

Bracken remained critical of the performance of the new Chancellor. Writing to W. S. Robinson on 20 April 1956 he remarked:

Macmillan's budget is a ridiculous affair which will do nothing to stop inflation. Unless he is prepared to offer prizes approximately equal to his opposite numbers in the football pool business his premium bonds may prove to be a flop.

Within a period of six months the British Government have twice increased profits tax and they do this at a time when they are exhorting British industry to equip itself with the best of modern plant. The new increase in profits tax is, of course, a feeble though costly effort to show the Trades Union bosses that the British Government have no love for employers or shareholders. To adapt a Biblical saying. 'If they do these things in a green tree what shall be done in the dry?'

When Mr. Gaitskell gets into Downing Street you can take it from me that company profits will be remorselessly socked and the Macmillan plus Butler precedents well supported.

When, in October that year, Macmillan put before the party conference a proposal for a free trade area with the six original EEC states, Bracken reported to Beaverbrook:

Harold Macmillan jumped the gun when he enunciated his wonderful Britain plus a part of Europe free trade area. Our government is so alarmed by the prospect of being left out of this curiously contrived arrangement that they are willing to toy with the idea.

There is, I am told, fierce opposition from industrial bosses who are large contributors to the Tory Party and I expect that Macmillan and Thorneycroft will battle for time.[29]

By this stage, President Nasser's seizure of the Suez Canal and its aftermath was dominating the political stage. Bracken was dubious about the practicality of using force against Nasser, but he could not help admiring Eden's toughness in so doing. On 5 November, while British troops were on their way to Egypt, he wrote to Beaverbrook:

> The socialists who thought he was a charming milksop now hold him to be a blood lusting monster. Vanity can be a great toughener.[30]

The following day the troops landed, but under international pressure, led by the United States, the British government declared a ceasefire. Bracken viewed Macmillan's gyrations during this period with some reservations. As he wrote to Beaverbrook on 22 November 1956:

> Until a week ago Macmillan whose bellicosity was beyond description, was wanting to tear Nasser's scalp off with his own fingernails. He was like that character in O'Casey's play who cried: 'Let me like a hero fall. My breast expanding to the ball'. Today he might be described as the leader of the bolters. His Treasury officials have put before him the economic consequences of the Suez fiasco and his feet are frost bitten.[31]

Eden was exhausted and took himself to Jamaica to recover, an action described by one of his biographers as 'a fatal mistake'. It meant that he was not in the House of Commons on 6 December 1956 to meet a motion of censure that was moved by the Labour opposition. Writing to Beaverbrook on the following day Bracken admitted:

> If it was a mistake for him to go away at the present time (and I now think it probably was) I was one of the people who advised him to go. It shows how poor an adviser I am! But as he told me that he fully intends to brazen this out, I thought he

might as well get physically fit before facing the litter of problems that lie ahead.[32]

Bracken persisted in his jaundiced view of Macmillan's performance in the crisis:

> Macmillan is telling journalists that he intends to retire from politics and go to the Morgue. . . . His real intentions are to push his boss out of No. 10 and he has a fair following in the Tory Party. The so-called Canal die-hards think better of him than they do of Eden or Butler.
>
> I still think you were right to back Eden. He is the best of the Tories. I don't say that is terrific praise, but it is something. The alternatives are the crackpot Macmillan or Butler, who is a curious blend of Gandi [*sic*] and Boss Tweed.

Eden resigned on 9 January 1957 to be succeeded by Macmillan. A fortnight later Bracken brought Beaverbrook up to date:

> The main reason for Eden's departure is not the one circulated by politicians and the Press. The reason is political, but as it involves a secret stuffed with dynamite I can't put it in a letter. This seems melodramatic, but alas, it is only too true as you will agree when you hear it. If Eden had been of tougher fibre, he could, I am sure, have brazened it out.
>
> Health, of course, played a part in the decision, but I think his illness is more due to the effect of mind upon body than to the patchwork done by surgeons and doctors.
>
> Butler greatly fancied his chances of succeeding Eden, but they were blighted by the advice offered to the Monarch by Eden, Churchill and Salisbury. Most of the Tories in the House of Commons were against Butler. They blamed him for the Suez scuttle, whereas Macmillan had a far greater responsibility. Nor was Macmillan slow in his siege of Number 10. He let it be known that in no circumstances would he serve under Butler and he did some powerful private canvassing. Of Butler, therefore, it may be truly said in the words of Coleridge – 'For I have lost the race I never ran'.[33]

Two days later, writing to an old friend, the former United States Ambassador, Lewis Douglas, Bracken remarked:

It was quite inevitable that Harold Macmillan should succeed Anthony Eden. Butler had been too long on the halls as an inevitable successor and so the audience is tired of him. He is credited with highly contradictory characteristics such as being naive and sly. A large number of Tories regard him as a Fabian whose only policy is to steal the Opposition's clothes. This is not an unfair estimate of Butler's devious leftish approach to politics. He is not, of course, by nature a man of the left, but he holds the simple view that in a democracy the only method of maintaining and keeping power is to bribe the mob.

I greatly grieve for Anthony. He is above the ruck of politicians. He is a man of high ideals and many graces and has been exceptionally well liked by all sections of the community. His political misfortunes and his departure have been a great shock to the young Tories to whom the Party owes its last two electoral victories. They looked up to Eden and felt that he was an Englishman of rare qualities. Neither Macmillan nor any member of the present Government can hope to command anything like the affectionate esteem that Eden enjoyed.[34]

Bracken watched suspiciously for signs that Macmillan's government would abandon the policy of disinflation initiated under Eden. Yet, when the Chancellor Peter Thorneycroft raised the Bank Rate to a record level of 7 per cent and cut back on capital investment programmes in the autumn of 1957 so as to defend the pound, Bracken expressed fears that it would damage British industry.[35] Early in 1958 Peter Thorneycroft resigned with the other Treasury ministers because measures they had proposed to defend the pound were rejected by Macmillan. By this time Bracken was in hospital being treated for the throat cancer that was to prove fatal. He sent a handwritten note to W. S. Robinson from his hospital bed:

Thorneycroft's resignation has had a peculiar effect upon the government. They parted from him because they looked upon him as an arch-deflationist. The excitement caused by his going stirred them to declare that they intend to cut more deeply than he ever tried to do. And in so far as Macmillan will abide by any policy for long I believe they will try to do so.

Macmillan shrugged off as 'little local difficulties' the resignation of his ministers and took himself off on a tour of the Commonwealth.

In March Bracken received a letter from Lord Cobham, the Governor General of New Zealand, after Macmillan had been there:

> Harold . . . was obviously tired, but wonderfully buoyant in face of all disaster: resignations, bye-elections, opposition attacks: – all seem to slide off him like the traditional water off a duck's back.

Bracken was not so impressed by all the results of Macmillan's tour. As he wrote to W. S. Robinson on 29 April 1958:

> As you may have read in the newspapers Harold Macmillan is talking about starting a bank for the whole of the British Commonwealth. What purpose such an institution may serve passes my understanding. When one tots up the meagreness of the gold and dollar deposits held by Britain on behalf of the whole Sterling Area the irritating question springs to mind 'What is the bank going to have by way of cash?' One thing is quite certain – they will never be wanting a supply of eager borrowers. We can rely upon Mr. Nehru to elbow his way to the top of the queue, and the self-governing Sambos of Ghana will not be far behind.

Bracken and Macmillan met in May at a dinner given by Beaverbrook in honour of the Prime Ministers of the Canadian Maritime Provinces. After the dinner Churchill spoke but cut his remarks short because, as he said, 'I am in the presence of my leader, the Prime Minister.' With equal delicacy and brevity Harold Macmillan paid tribute to Churchill. This exchange pleased the ailing Bracken and a fellow guest observed that his tired, worn face broke into a smile.[36] Before the summer was out he was dead. Among those who made the pilgrimage to say farewell as death approached was Harold Macmillan. He might well have reflected that it was Bracken's intervention when he was about to resign in 1942 that had set him on the road to becoming Prime Minister.

When my book of Bracken finally appeared late in 1979, the Earl of Drogheda, to whom Bracken had left 8 Lord North Street, gave a party there to mark the event to which he invited a number of Bracken's old friends and associates, including Harold Macmillan. I retain the picture of the old man, who was then eighty-five, seated in a low armchair having his hand stroked by the seventy-year-old Lord Drogheda, who sat on the floor beside him calling him 'Former Prime Minister' and begging him to speak. At last, he struggled to his feet. 'I have not read this book' he began, 'but I have read another'. Having recovered from this gaffe by promising to read mine, he went on to recall that it was in this very room, over forty years before, 'that Winston and Brendan and I plotted the fight against appeasement'. He remarked that they were days 'so like the present when danger was not recognised' and referred to Iran, Mozambique and the Horn of Africa. He said that like Aron with Moses, Brendan had held Churchill's arms high when he was in the wilderness during the thirties and the country owed him a very great debt on that account. He recalled Brendan's unique position in Churchill's life, how he would contradict Churchill during the War when nobody else would dare and the quarrels that ensured; 'it was rather like a quarrel between a happily married couple' he remarked. 'Most of us are pretty ordinary' he went on, 'but Brendan, he was different.' He spoke of how from humble beginnings Bracken had set out to improve himself and had pulled himself up by his own efforts. 'That was considered a good thing to do when I was young', he said. 'Now I suppose it would be considered wrong to aspire to belong to the privileged classes.' It was vintage Macmillan and we all lapped it up.

The next day I wandered in to the Carlton Club and found Harold Macmillan sitting in the reading room with my book open in his hands. He held it up close to his eyes as he read it. One finger was in the index and he was turning over pages as if looking up particular references. When the opportunity offered, I thanked him for his words the previous night. 'Curious fellow, Drogheda', he replied, 'he never told me I had to make a speech.' We conversed for a few minutes. I said something about Bracken's background not being so humble as his mother was a university graduate and he replied that he was sure they were perfectly respectable people. A few weeks later, having read my book, he wrote to Lord Drogheda correcting an error in a footnote that he had spotted but commending it because it showed 'a sympathetic understanding of a strange and lovable character'. If he was hurt, as surely he must have been, by Bracken's caustic comments quoted in it, and the discovery that the affection he had expressed for 'dear Brendan' did not appear to have been reciprocated, he did not show it. That too was Harold Macmillan.

NOTES

1. On Knox (later Monsignor Ronald Knox) and Macmillan's friendship with him, see Alistair Horne, *Macmillan 1891–1956* (Macmillan, 1988), pp. 17–27, 31–4.
2. Andrew Boyle, *Poor Dear Brendan* (Hutchinson, 1974).
3. Horne, op. cit., pp. 80–2.
4. Bracken–Garvin correspondence, Humanities Research Center, University of Texas.
5. Thomas Jones, *A Diary with Letters, 1926–30* (Oxford: Oxford University Press, 1969), p. 274.
6. House of Commons Debates (29 June 1944) vol. 401, col. 928.
7. Churchill Papers.
8. Horne, op. cit., pp. 111–2.
9. Harold Nicolson, *Diaries and Letters, 1930–1939* (Collins, 1966), pp. 375–6.
10. House of Commons Debates (17 November 1938) vol. 341, col. 1210.
11. Harold Macmillan, *Winds of Change* (Macmillan, 1966), p. 569.
12. See Charles Lysaght, *Brendan Bracken* (Allen Lane, 1979), chapter 14.
13. Harold Macmillan, *The Blast of War* (Macmillan, 1967), p. 76.
14. Harold Nicolson, *Diaries and Letters, 1939–1945* (Collins, 1967), p. 85.
15. Horne, op. cit., p. 151.
16. Lysaght, op. cit., p. 224.
17. Kenneth Young (ed.), *The Diaries of Sir Robert Bruce Lockhart, 1939–1965* (Macmillan, 1980), p. 325.
18. Ibid., p. 520. However, the sentence about Macmillan and Stanley intriguing in the original diary is omitted.
19. Bracken–Beaverbrook correspondence (now in the House of Lords) published in Richard Cockett (ed.), *My Dear Max* (The Historian's Press, 1990), p. 58.
20. See Lysaght, op. cit., chapter 19.
21. Harold Macmillan, *Tides of Fortune* (Macmillan, 1969), p. 355.
22. *My Dear Max*, p. 135.
23. Ibid., p. 144.
24. W. S. Robinson Papers, University of Melbourne.
25. *My Dear Max*, p. 184.
26. Ibid., pp. 186–7.
27. Ibid., pp. 189–90.
28. Ibid., pp. 190.
29. Ibid., pp. 193.
30. Ibid., pp. 194.
31. Ibid., pp. 196.
32. Ibid., pp. 199.
33. Ibid., pp. 203.
34. Bracken–Douglas correspondence, University of Arizona. (Copies available in the Churchill Archives, Churchill College, Cambridge.)
35. Bracken–Douglas correspondence.
36. *Brendan Bracken, 1901–1958: Portraits and Appreciations* (1958), p. 47 (Sir Beverly Baxter MP).

11 Macmillan, the Second World War and the Empire
S. J. Ball

Harold Macmillan had a good war. His appointment as Resident Minister to AFHQ, Algiers at the end of 1942 made his political career. Macmillan himself commented in later life, 'my belief is, when you get a chance, take it. It was always my philosophy. Chance played such a role in my life – Winston, the war, Algiers, Housing... made me Prime Minister.' With the exception of Housing the other three factors Macmillan identifies are, essentially, the same. His record as an anti-appeaser and relationship with Churchill meant nothing until he got his opportunity in Algiers. Churchill was ruthless with his junior ministers. Macmillan held two relatively unimportant junior ministerial posts at Supply and Colonies. In the autumn of 1942 he was effectively demoted and considered resignation. If he had done so there is little doubt that his political career would have been at an end.

The Algiers job became a godsend, but he was not first choice. His Guards contemporary, the Financial Secretary to the Treasury, Harry Crookshank, turned it down on grounds of ill-health. Neither was it an obvious route to the top. At the time he feared he was being sent to 'political Siberia'. The great advantage of the post was that it brought Macmillan 'into the loop'. Cabinet ministers in London who were not members of the War Cabinet or its Defence Committee were effectively excluded from policy formation. Macmillan's contemporary and superior at the Colonial Office, Lord Cranborne, had complained unavailingly to Churchill, whilst Dominions Secretary, that: 'I do not myself know what is going on... most of the important telegrams are exchanged by you personally, either with Heads of State or with Dominion Prime Ministers.'[1] Another Guards contemporary, ahead of Macmillan on the political ladder, Oliver Lyttelton, had already pioneered the Minister of State role in the Middle East.[2] He later recalled that 'no other office ... could present the same opportunities for usefulness, the same independence, the same authority. . . . I was far enough away from my colleagues to be able to make up my own mind on critical occasions. My powers were wide and unchallenged and I had to spend little time clearing subjects with other ministers.' Yet it was hard to disguise that the terms of Macmillan's appointment were less than ideal. Although he became a Cabinet minister, this gave him the same status as Duff Cooper, a slightly older politician whose career was already in decline, when he was sent to Singapore. Macmillan later wrote: 'His status would be roughly parallel to that of the Minister of State in Cairo.'[3] Unlike him, however, the Minister of State in Cairo was a member of the War Cabinet. Nevertheless, Macmillan made a major success of his appointment. It turned him, in his mid-forties, into a glamorous figure in the Conservative party.

Although he carried out his wartime duties with skill and dedication there is no doubt that he arrived in Africa at the right time. Political gossip had it that Algiers presented a tricky situation. On 1 January 1943 Harold Nicolson recorded in his diary: 'Rothermere tells me . . . Harold MacMillan [*sic*] has been hurried out immediately by aeroplane. He will have a difficult job.'[4] Macmillan, however, had the immeasurable advantage of acting within the context of military victory. From the victory at second Alamein and the successful launch of Operation Torch in November 1942, until D-Day reduced Italy to a secondary theatre in June 1944, Allied military operations had a large measure of success. Macmillan was associated with this success, most symbolically when he was invited onto the podium for the Algiers and Tunis victory parades by Eisenhower. Oliver Lyttelton, who had been the sole Minister of State in the Middle East between July 1941 and February 1942, was in position at a time of disenchanting stalemate and had left before a significant victory was achieved.[5] He was also unable to make political capital from his appointment. Alan Moorehead, the *Daily Express* correspondent in Cairo, noted that he was hard-working and respected but, 'his press conferences were so appallingly dull, his words so banal and evasive that it was impossible to put him before the public as a leader'.[6] During his tenure Lyttelton had to sort out the disorganized logistics system, an important but dull subject, and relations with the Egyptian government, whose pro-Nazi dealings had to be kept secret. In December 1943, when future command arrangements in the Mediterranean were being finalized, Macmillan noted, somewhat disingenuously, 'if there is one commander, there must be one Resident Minister... if I am not selected I shall be able to come home, and presumably Winston will give me something there'. Lyttelton, who was much closer to Churchill than Macmillan, had indeed been brought home to fill the key role of Minister of Production. Yet despite his excellent performance at the ministry between 1942 and 1945 it removed him from the political limelight. Richard Casey had arrived in the Middle East just before Cairo began to lose its strategic centrality to Algiers. Duff Cooper had been tarred by the fall of Singapore. Lord Moyne, having been demoted from Colonial Secretary to deputy Minister of State, only achieved widespread fame through his brutal murder by Jewish terrorists. It is not fanciful to believe that Macmillan's sensitivity to timing in 1959 was influenced by the start of his rise to power in 1943. As Robert Rhodes James has rightly noted it was: '[his] semi-independent role in North Africa that brought out his supreme negotiating and diplomatic skills with the Free French and the Americans. It also brought out an ambition that had not been noticed before by his colleagues. He had become, and was always to remain, a committed professional politician, with an eye on the main chance.'[7]

Anyone studying Macmillan's career cannot doubt that his two-and-a-half years with allied forces in North Africa, Italy and Greece was a formative experience. He spent just as long in this role as he did as Minister of Defence, Foreign Secretary and Chancellor of the Exchequer, the offices of state concerned with foreign affairs which brought him to Downing Street, combined. The world in January 1957 was very different from that of January 1943 and Macmillan had, to an extent, changed with it. He continued, however, to draw on the lessons of Algiers in his conduct of affairs. The elements of this experience which have been most thoroughly explored, and which Macmillan himself stressed, are his understanding of the 'special relationship' and his relationship with other world leaders, especially Eisenhower and de Gaulle. This essay suggests that wartime experiences coloured other areas of Macmillan's conduct of the Premiership, and, in particular, his attitudes to the Empire.

Both contemporary commentators and historians have been interested by Macmillan's attempt to redefine Britain's role as a global power and, within this overall context, the very rapid process of decolonization which took place during his second administration, between October 1959 and October 1963. Much can be explained by the 'strategic vision' that Macmillan developed in 1955–6 and reified during the Suez crisis. Britain needed to cleave more closely to the United States, make its power projection capabilities more impressive, discard the dead wood and cut a constructive and successful dash on the world stage. Most colonial territories came under the heading of 'dead wood'. Britain's most important colony, Malaya, had signed a defence treaty with the UK in January 1957, days before Macmillan became Prime Minister. Malaya became independent in August 1957. This prefigured a new kind of relationship of which Macmillan approved. After 1958, the timing of further moves to create this pattern of relations elsewhere rested largely on the interplay of Tory politics with international developments. In Britain the White Paper on massacres in the Hola camp in Kenya was published in June 1959 and the Devlin report on the suppression of riots in Nyasaland was released a month later. Just as importantly, French and Belgian moves to leave their African colonies made action inevitable.[8] In 1959, during talks with Michel Debré, Macmillan 'sympathized profoundly with French difficulties in Africa; . . . all the more because people were conscious that similar problems confronted HMG in, for example, Kenya and Nyasaland. . . . The problem of the multi-racial state remained . . . the $64,000 question in Africa, . . . similar difficulties confronted the Commonwealth and the French Community: in the case for example of both Algeria and Rhodesia the situation contained similar elements: there were important white communities and local coloured *évolués* who attracted the support of public opinion at home . . . there was no doubt that Africa was going to become the big problem.'[9]

Despite the obvious explanatory importance of politics in the late 1950s, however, Macmillan's experiences a decade-and-a-half before were far from being merely distant memories of a distant era. Macmillan drew a number of important long-term lessons from his wartime experience. They affected both his understanding of the nature of empire and his conduct of imperial policy.

Macmillan's own role as a semi-independent minister had been a golden opportunity. It was not an opportunity he wished others to repeat. He became aware how adventures in exotic climes could immeasurably increase a minister's prestige. Finding oneself under fire from communists and *The Times* in Athens had definite political advantages. His African and Far Eastern tours as Prime Minister were a reflection of this belief. Although Macmillan's most important prime ministerial summits were in Paris, Rambouillet and Nassau, he cannot have failed to reflect that white fur hats were ridiculous in both wintry Finland in 1940 and Moscow in 1959.

As prime minister he had little enthusiasm for imperial proconsuls; he preferred his colleagues safely under supervision in London and was irritated when they escaped. Duncan Sandys received few thanks for his personal presence in the Far East during the formation of Malaysia, although the intimate but hostile relations of the Singaporeans and Malayans in 1963 had points of comparison with intra-French relations in 1943.[10] Not for Macmillan the telegram Eden sent him during the Lebanese crisis: 'You are clearly the best judge since you are so much nearer the theatre than we are.'[11]

Oliver Lyttelton noted of Churchill: 'The Prime Minister was fond of applying to organisation the dictum of Napoleon [*"Une Constitution doit être courte et obscure"*] that constitutions should be vague.'[12] As Lyttelton had previously found in Cairo, Macmillan was to find in Algiers. There was no defined role for a politician on the loose. He had to push himself into an existing structure. Both Lyttelton and Macmillan succeeded in establishing themselves because of the political crises surrounding the Gaullist and Vichy French in North Africa and the Levant. The military authorities were glad to hand over their extremely complex wrangles, mainly over status, to a political figure on the spot. Allied military advances enabled Macmillan to expand his authority into Italy and the Balkans, effectively ousting Lyttelton's successor in Cairo, Dick Casey, who was 'liquidated' and sent out to become Governor of Bengal.[13] Yet even as he pushed out the boundaries of his authority, insisting that a political minister, 'must be in a position of greater freedom to initiate and criticize policy', Macmillan noted that this was not necessarily desirable. 'His relations with the Foreign Office and its representatives', he minuted Churchill, 'must always be somewhat delicate, sometimes even strained. . . . I am bound to say that I should myself sympathise with a Foreign Secretary who would prefer to rid himself of such an incubus and rely on more correct and perhaps more pliable instruments to carry out his policy.'[14] He always had a bad word for those in an analogous position to himself. Casey was '*very* pleasant – but not, I think, very clever.' Alternatively, he was 'intelligent but ill-educated, just has not got the experience. He is absolutely honest, patriotic and devoted. But he is weak.' Lord Moyne was 'charming and ineffective as ever.' General Louis Spears, Churchill's confidant and Minister in the Levant, was 'a clever man; but the trouble is that he has the qualities neither of the British or the French. . . . I cannot help thinking that being a popular hero in the Levant has rather gone to his head. I cannot believe he was ever so cheered and applauded in Carlisle!'[15]

Macmillan certainly chose more pliable instruments when he was Prime Minister. The post nearest in nature to that of Resident Minister in the 1950s was the Commissioner-General in Southeast Asia. Macmillan chose a minor politician, the former First Lord of the Admiralty, Lord Selkirk, for this post. He disliked Selkirk's attempts to approach him directly and the post was abolished at the end of his Premiership. On the other hand, Macmillan was extremely impressed by the performance of the military leaders with whom he dealt. He would escape to the calm of military headquarters. 'I cannot tell you', he wrote to Lady Dorothy in March 1943, 'what a delightful change this was from the continual atmosphere of strife, incompetence and intrigue which surrounds us in Algiers.'[16] In contrast to his dislike of regional 'czars', he firmly supported Mountbatten's introduction of unified military commands in the Near and Far East. Perhaps he remembered Churchill's post-prandial outburst en route to Cairo: '"you may take the most gallant sailor, the most intrepid airman, or the most audacious soldier put them at a table together – what do you get? *The sum total of their fears!*" (This with frightful sibilant emphasis).'[17]

As regards substance rather than process, the seeds of future policy were sown through Macmillan's insight that empires, whether formal or informal, were not independent entities. Indeed, they were not of primary importance to the European powers as anything other than the theatre of great power politics. Macmillan had rarely expressed a close interest in imperial affairs before the war and his sojourn in Algiers did little to ignite his interest. In May 1943, whilst still deeply involved in the political intrigues of Algiers, he heartily endorsed a paper by the Security Service officer Kenneth Younger, which baldly stated: 'North Africa, after all, is unimportant.' Younger went on to argue, and Macmillan agreed, that, 'now the Tunisian campaign is over the case for a "quiet life", the argument which carried Darlan to his short-lived tenure of power, is no longer convincing.' Yet the Resident Minister should not be concerned with the fate of the empire for its own sake. 'It is time now to look to France and the future of Europe. It is the task of Britain to ensure that future is decided not by the discredited remnant of the old ruling clique, not even by the liberal imperialists in Washington, but by the people themselves. In this, Great Britain, as the only great power left in Western Europe, can have a deci-sive influence and has therefore a special responsibility.'[18] Younger later went on to be Minister of State at the Foreign Office during Attlee's government and Director of Chatham House during Macmillan's prime ministership. In 1943 Macmillan agreed with him that co-operation with France on imperial issues was merely a way of securing co-operation in post-war Europe. His motivations were thus subtly different from those of his Tory colleague, Duff Cooper, who took over his responsibility for Anglo-French relations in January 1944. Cooper believed that 'we have surely enough native prob-lems of our own to face without stirring up native problems for others. I think we should try to help the French to rebuild both their country and their Empire, and by our encouragement win their friendship.'[19]

During his time in North Africa, Macmillan witnessed how im-perial issues could sow the seeds of discord, needlessly in his view, between great powers. He was as disturbed as Churchill, and at one remove de Gaulle, by Roosevelt's patronage of the Sultan of Morocco in January 1943. 'Things were not helped', he wrote of the Casablanca conference and attempts to reconcile Giraudist and Gaullist factions, 'by a dinner Roosevelt gave in honour of the Sultan of Morocco on the very day that de Gaulle arrived at the Anfa camp. It was a curious and impolitic manoeuvre. . . . The President talked a great deal about colonial aspirations towards independence and the approaching end of "imperialism". All this was equally embarrassing to the British and to the French.'[20] Macmillan was uneasily aware, however, that distrust of the processes of British imperialism was probably justified. He used irony to explain this distrust to Churchill.

> misunderstandings [of British imperial policy] are based on the curious way in which history seems to work out. Of course Mr. Gladstone repeated over and over again that we would leave South Africa, but somehow or other we got back there. Of course Lord Kimberley and the Little Englanders did their best to prevent us forming a Colonial Empire and to impede the efforts of Mr. Rhodes at every stage, but somehow or other Mr. Rhodes got the better of them. Of course a series of British governments declared their intention to leave Egypt, but somehow or other Lord Cromer brought us back there. We are always on the point of evacua-tion, but always return with greater authority. This, which ac-

cording to our political beliefs we regard either as the wicked and cruel fate that dogs us against our will to be a great imperial race, or know to be the mysterious workings of Providence, anxious always to give the British a second chance, the French believe to be due to more sinister, less hallowed and in any case less fortuitous causes.[21]

Conservative politicians of Macmillan's generation placed in similar positions lacked this sense of irony. Thus Oliver Lyttelton on Lord Killearn, Cromer's lineal successor: 'It became a popular criticism that [Sir Miles] Lampson was rough with the King of Egypt, that the velvet glove was threadbare, that he was dictatorial and still saw himself as High Commissioner. It was easy to make such charges, but equally easy to defend him and describe him, as I would, as a jealous guardian of his country's name and obligations, forceful and rigid only about essentials. Those who subscribe to this remember the sinuousities of some other British diplomatists in other countries, and whither they led us.'[22]

During his premiership it was hard to involve Macmillan in any imperial issue which did not have direct ramifications for domestic politics or relations with another great power. When, for instance, the Malayans suggested the formation of a federation with Singapore and British Borneo in June 1960, a move which had been British policy since 1948 and which the Malayan government had hitherto staunchly opposed, officials found it very difficult to engage the Prime Minister's attention. Despite the importance of this development for the region, an Anglo-American agreement, which allowed the British to stay out of Vietnam if the US was not called upon to involve itself in Malayan affairs, limited its impact on great power relations.[23] In June 1960 Macmillan was preoccupied by the collapse of the Paris Conference; in August 1961, when the move came to fruition, the Berlin crisis was at its height.[24]

Before his despatch to the Middle East, Macmillan had been under-secretary at the Colonial Office for ten months. Yet the empire he was to get to know most intimately was not that of his own country but that of France. During the war he was to have a powerful role in shaping the future of that empire in the Levant and North Africa. Macmillan believed that the empires were, in fact, dissimilar, accepting what Freya Stark had described to him as the incompatibility of the 'gradual assimilation or elimination as a ruling class of the *"indigène"* and "government by suggestion"'.[25] Nevertheless, the chance to see a major empire in crisis shaped the second set of substantive lessons he was to learn. France in the Middle East allowed him to develop some of his ideas about colonialism and its dangers. It showed him at first hand how imperial affairs could humiliate a great power. In 1944 he noted, pityingly, that the French 'entertain the pathetic belief that by insisting verbally upon France's greatness they make her in fact great again.'[26] Macmillan distrusted French imperial rhetoric. His successor as British representative to the French Committee of National Liberation (FCNL), Duff Cooper, could write that: 'To those who know M. Pleven and have savoured the mystic touch of his Breton ancestry, this highly coloured and spiritual concept at [the] Brazzaville [imperial conference] will not come as a surprise. But sometimes the dreams of the dreamer come true and I think the best in French colonial policy is well summed up by his own epigram . . . *"une politique imperialiste de l'esprit"*.'[27] Macmillan, however, took a much less complimentary line on imperial mysticism. 'De Gaulle . . . like so many mystics, is half-reactionary . . . and half progressive, but . . . is on questions of foreign and especially native policy fundamentally reactionary.'[28] Macmillan's analysis of de Gaulle's imperial policy was part of a wider lack of sympathy for the man and his ideas. Although he was sympathetic to the Free French movement he never really understood de Gaulle's conception of what France was or could be. He was always more comfortable with Jean Monnet and René Massigli. His favourite Free French generals were Catroux and Leclerc.[29] De Gaulle might admire M. Macmillan's *esprit délié*;[30] but he never made clear whether he regarded him as subtle or glib.

During the war Macmillan's thinking tended to have a *marxisant* slant taken over from his proposals for Britain's economic and social problems in the 1930s. His first sally into imperial affairs had been a remarkable paper written on Kenya whilst he was at the Colonial Office. In it he disputed the premiss that, 'the Highlands of Kenya are "a white man's country" in the same sense which other Dominions are to-day or the American colonies were in the 18th century' and that, 'on this analogy of American colonies, the claims to self-government of any substantial number of Englishmen who have settled permanently in a country cannot be resisted'. He believed that 'Kenya's future is to be a "white governed" country but not a "white man's country". We have before us the warning of the West Indies and the Southern States of America about the problems involved in a "plantocracy".' The implications of such a plantocracy were not appealing. 'Gradually the white stock will become contaminated by the effect of the climate or by some inter-breeding. But this decadent or slightly decadent people – not in-creasing largely in numbers by immigration – will be the proprietors of the land and all that implies. Surrounded by a native population [which] – if our medical and other services continue – will become increasingly crowded and land hungry. A clash is bound to come.' Macmillan's 1942 solution was to nationalize the land and to re-form agricultural production by creating state and collective farms. 'This would be based on the Russian system.'[31]

Macmillan's views were formed with no direct experience of Kenya. His knowledge was based on his wife's connections. His dislike of *colons* was reinforced by his sojourn in North Africa. There, white settlers had already shown the decadence he predicted in Kenya: they favoured the pre-November 1942 situation when business had been good and Jewish rivals could be persecuted.[32] Unsurprisingly, Macmillan tended to agree with analyses which portrayed North Africa in similar fashion to that in which he had characterized Kenya. Political action was shaped, indeed deformed, by the class basis of society. Kenneth Younger, for instance, saw wartime North Africa divided into five groups: rich colonial civilians; prosperous busi-nessmen from France led by Jacques Lemaigre-Dubreuil; military officers; the small bourgeois; and, finally, the Arab and Jewish na-tives. 'There is one significant gap', Younger concluded, 'a French or European working class is entirely lacking. . . . The absence of a European working class has left the field clear for the upper class elements, and in particular has removed any check there might otherwise have been on one tendency which is common to all the ruling and middle classes, civil and military – the overmastering terror of Soviet Russia and communism.'[33] Macmillan too found these 'upper class elements' distasteful. 'The chief of these was Jacques Lemaigre-Dubreuil. This man was a wealthy manufacturer of vegetable oil . . . an associate before the war of some of the Right-wing pressure groups, such as the Cagoulards. . . . Before the war, we irreverent young Conservatives had given to a number of the less attractive industrialists who sat on the Conservative side in this House of Commons, generally for very safe seats, the offen-sive nickname of the "Forty Thieves". Lemaigre-Dubreuil would have had a high place in this company.'[34]

Macmillan noted that Allied policy was too indulgent of such men and attitudes amongst the colonists: 'As for the principles of liberal democracy, the abolition of racial laws and so on, except in the less reputable part of Headquarters which is called PWB [Political Warfare Branch] and includes, therefore, as well as professional soldiers, professors, authors, journalists and the like who have put on the military uniform without acquiring the military outlook, the view held was that virtually any political development in North Africa was to be deplored as hampering the war effort.'[35] Yet he also had limited sympathy with 'professors, authors and journalists and the like', such as Stark and Younger. If the empire became too important to a nation, if, indeed, it became the nation, one would be caught between ultra-enthusiasts and liberal intellectuals. Although drawn to the latter, Macmillan developed a healthy distrust for both.

In 1959 he was to denounce the *trahison des clercs*, 'the attitude of certain British intellectuals, hostile to their own country, who attacked the whites in Africa and championed the blacks'.[36] In 1943 he had evinced little interest in the manifesto on political reform delivered to him by the Algerian writer Ferhat Abbas, 'a familiar type of nationalist intellectual', and did not protest when Abbas was placed under house arrest and the *Délégations Financières* was dissolved in September 1943. The main concern in his office was that, 'the eleven million Arabs of North Africa are bound to become increasingly vocal, and the French do not seem ready, either institutionally or psychologically to deal with (or as our American friends would say, to channelize) Arab Nationalism in North Africa.'[37] In November 1943 Macmillan maintained that 'We wish the pledges for Levantine independence given quite clearly in 1941 to be carried out. . . . the French must be told that in this liberal and progressive policy lies their only hope and that they must take this course or their Near East interests must inevitably go under in the end.' On the other hand, 'We must make it clear . . . to the Syrians and the Lebanese that we have no desire to see French interests in the Levant overthrown. . . . both the Syrians and (especially) the Lebanese must be deflated. They must be told that they cannot rely on us to help them eject the French, only to get a fair agreement as outlined.'[38] He strongly objected to the Casey/Spears line of threatening the imposition of martial law unless the Lebanese government, arrested by the French Commissioner, was fully restored to power.[39] 'Spears wants a Fashoda; and I do not.'[40]

The ambivalence Macmillan had developed about French imperialism during the war was reflected in his own imperial policies during his premiership. In essence his policy was based around the pref-

erences of liberal Conservatives such as Iain Macleod and Reginald
Maudling and symbolized by the 'winds of change' speech. Yet they
were often deliberately offset by hard-liners such as Duncan Sandys
and Macmillan's son-in-law, Julian Amery. As in 1943, Macmillan
attempted to maintain a balance. 'The cruder concepts, whether of
left or right, are clearly wrong', he told Walter Monckton, 'the
Africans cannot be dominated permanently. . . . Nor can the Europeans be abandoned.' As Prime Minister the issue which took up
most of the time Macmillan devoted to imperial issues was the
fate of the Central African Federation. In Africa, despite the demise of Macleod, Macmillan tended toward the 'abandonment of
the Europeans', the group he had found despicable in 1942. Where
a *colon* population did not exist he tended to favour less liberal
policies. In 1943 his preferred imperial relationships had been with
Egypt and Iraq. 'Both these countries are now completely independent. We maintain no longer High Commissioners there, but
Ambassadors. But we have special treaties freely negotiated, which
guarantee to us the special rights which our past and present connections with these countries justify.'[41] In 1956–8 he continued to
invest a great deal of hope in these relationships and was bitterly
disappointed by their failure.[42] His hard line on the eastern Mediterranean in the 1950s was reflected by his willingness to sanction
military action East of Suez, in Kuwait, Oman and Aden.

Macmillan was happy as Minister Resident. This much is clear
from the diaries he chose to publish at the end of his life. His
career blossomed and he was away from his unsatisfactory family.
One could argue that his time in the Mediterranean had an unfortunate effect on him. As Richard Aldous has observed: 'He breath-
lessly recorded in his diary that the [Casablanca] conference had
been "like a meeting of the later period of the Roman empire",
and christened Churchill and Roosevelt "the Emperor of the East
and the Emperor of the West". The experience remained with
Macmillan: the idea of bestriding the world stage as a latter-day
Churchillian emperor appealed to his highly developed historical
tastes.'[43] Arguably, he did not learn enough from his experiences.
He could see that 'France [in 1944] . . . now finds herself reduced
to the rank of a third-rate Power, with a small population and slender
resources compared with the giants that surround her.'[44] It was not
an analysis he cared to apply to Britain in the early 1960s. On the
other hand, although he later portrayed himself as a champion of
de Gaulle, he had little time for Gaullism. He had, after all, believed

that British officials needed 'the courage to deal firmly with de Gaulle if he behaved in an absurd way'.[45] British power had to be preserved, but not in the fashion in which de Gaulle, faced with a similar post-Suez *crise de confiance*, reinvigorated France. In 1943–5 and 1957–63, Macmillan spent as little time on empires and their subject peoples as possible. His lack of sympathy or understanding for both rulers and ruled was not unusual, but it did make his achievement fragile.

NOTES

The author would like to thank the British Academy HRB and the Faculty of Arts Research Committee, University of Glasgow for financial assistance in preparing this essay.

1. DO121/10A, Lord Cranborne to Prime Minister, 18 November 1941. (All documentary references are to files held in the Public Record Office, Kew.)
2. Olive Lyttelton, Viscount Chandos, *The Memoirs of Lord Chandos* (London: The Bodley Head, 1962), pp. 227–8 (hereafter *Chandos*).
3. Harold Macmillan, *The Blast of War, 1939–45* (London: Macmillan, 1967), p. 216 (hereafter *BW*).
4. Harold Nicolson, *Diaries and Letters, 1930–1964* (condensed edn; London: Harper Collins, 1996), p. 240. At the time Macmillan 'feared that the fact that Darlan had been eliminated might so simplify the French situation that a new Minister might not be needed' (*BW*, p. 218).
5. Erwin Rommel had arrived in North Africa in January 1941 and led his *Afrika Korps* to the borders of Egypt. Wavell was replaced by Auchinleck, but the latter's great November 1941 'Crusader' offensive failed to produce a clear military victory.
6. Artemis Cooper, *Cairo in the War, 1939–1945* (pbk edn; London: Penguin, 1995), p. 128.
7. Robert Rhodes James, 'Harold Macmillan: An Introduction', in Richard Aldous and Sabine Lee (eds), *Harold Macmillan and Britain's World Role* (London: Macmillan, 1996), p. 3 (hereafter *BWR*).
8. PREM11/2888, Dakar to Foreign Office, Tel. 34, 26 December 1959 (with Macmillan's comments).
9. CO936/562, Extract from Records of a Conversation between the Prime Minister and Foreign Secretary in Paris, 9–10 March 1959.
10. DO169/249, Duncan Sandys to Harold Macmillan, SOSLON No. 109, 5 September 1963; DO169/249, Kuala Lumpur (Sandys) to CRO (Macmillan), SOSLON No. 139, 11 September 1963; PREM11/4350, P. de Zulueta to Prime Minister, 11 September 1963.
11. FO660/40, Anthony Eden to Harold Macmillan, Tel. 2760, 23 November 1943.

12. *Chandos*, p. 228.
13. Harold Macmillan, *War Diaries: The Mediterranean, 1943–1945* (pbk edn; London: Macmillan, 1985), pp. 319–21 (hereafter *WD*).
14. PREM3/272/4, Harold Macmillan to Winston Churchill, 16 August 1944. Lyttelton came to a similar conclusion. 'Towards the end of my eight months in the Middle East it was quite clear that my relations with the Foreign Office were bearing the greatest strain. . . . Eden . . . must at times have been inclined to send me a telegram to keep off his grass altogether.' Eden was and remained, however, a close friend.
15. *WD*, pp. 33, 305, 393. Spears was MP for Carlisle.
16. *WD*, p. 46.
17. *WD*, p. 295.
18. FO660/15, Kenneth Younger to Roger Makins (with Macmillan's comments), 12 May 1943.
19. Duff Cooper to Winston Churchill, 21 February, 1944. Quoted in Duff Cooper, *Old Men Forget* (London: Rupert Hart-Davis, 1954), pp. 322–3.
20. *BW*, pp. 250–1.
21. PREM3/182/6, Harold Macmillan to Winston Churchill. Lord Kimberley was Colonial Secretary between 1870 and 1874, when Cape Colony was granted responsible government, and between 1880 and 1882, during the first Boer war. Lord Cromer was Britain's chief representative in Egypt, under various titles, between 1877 and 1907.
22. *Chandos*, pp. 232–3.
23. FO371/175100, Minute by J. E. Cable, 23 September 1964.
24. CO1030/978, Lord Selkirk to Iain Macleod, 23 March 1961; CAB134/1949, text of letter dated 11 August, 1961 from Tunku Abdul Rahman to Prime Minister; CO1030/982, Lord Selkirk to Iain Macleod, 24 August 1961; CO1030/983, Lord Selkirk to Iain Macleod, 16 September 1961; CAB134/1949, GM(61)1st Meeting, 27 September 1961.
25. FO660/36, *The French Problem. Personal Notes by Freya Stark*, 18 August 1943. Stark had written four books on the Arab world before the war. She joined the Ministry of Information in 1939 and served in the Yemen and Aden. She arrived in Egypt in June 1940 and set up the Brotherhood of Freedom. This group was supposed to encourage democratic, pro-British and anti-Nazi sentiment amongst educated Egyptians: it had limited success. She moved to Baghdad in April 1941 and had recently returned when this paper was written.
26. PREM3/182/6, Harold Macmillan to Winston Churchill, 3 January 1944.
27. FO660/126, Duff Cooper to Anthony Eden, 26 February 1944. René Pleven was the FCNL's Commissioner for Colonies in 1943–4. 'I met Pleven first,' Macmillan recorded in his diary for 3 November 1943, 'at Hever, just after I had gone to the Colonial Office. We worked together a good deal over the West African Produce Control Board, of which I made the Free French members. I think he was grateful for the assistance I gave him in those days and (although he got rather excited by political events from time time) he has remained a staunch friend' (*WD*, p. 276).
28. PREM3/182/6, Harold Macmillan to Winston Churchill, 3 January 1944.
29. 'With our troops [in the Tunis victory parade] were General Leclerc's

regiment of Free French who . . . refused to march with the French, preferring the English for companions', *WD*, p. 91. Leclerc was the *nom de guerre* of Philippe de Hauteclocque. Twelve years younger than de Gaulle, he was killed in 1947. Georges Catroux, the head of the Gaullist mission to the Middle East, and subsequently the Governor-General of Algeria and Commissioner in the Levant, was already 66 in 1943.

30. Charles de Gaulle, *Mémoires de Guerre*, 3 vols (Paris: Plon, 1954–59), vol. 2, p. 93.
31. CO967/57, Harold Macmillan to Sir George Gater, 15 August 1942.
32. *BW*, p. 216.
33. FO660/15, Kenneth Younger to Roger Makins, 12 May 1943.
34. *BW*, p. 259. Lemaigre-Dubreuil controlled the newspaper *Le Jour*. He was Giraud's *chef de cabinet*, until he was ousted in the 'New Deal' of March 1943. He was assassinated by Moroccan *colons* in 1955.
35. PREM3/182/6, Harold Macmillan to Winston Churchill, 3 January 1944. In 1941 Oliver Lyttelton had been equally disturbed by a promise made by General 'Jumbo' Wilson to the Vichy authorities in the Levant which prevented the Free French from gaining access to their troops. *Chandos*, p. 252.
36. CO936/562, J1074/20 Record of Meeting between the Prime Minister and M. Debré at 10 Downing Street at 10 a.m. on 14 April 1959.
37. FO660/26, Roger Makins to W. H. B. (Hal) Mack, 3 April 1943.
38. *WD*, p. 305.
39. FO660/39, Resident Minister, Algiers to Foreign Office, Tel. 2445, 21 November 1943.
40. *WD*, p. 297. Casey, of course, disagreed. Lord Casey, *Personal Experience 1939–1946* (London: Constable, 1962), p. 148.
41. *WD*, p. 305.
42. Nigel Ashton, 'Macmillan and the Middle East', in *BWR*, pp. 37–66.
43. *BWR*, p. 13.
44. PREM3/182/6, Harold Macmillan to Winston Churchill, 3 January 1944.
45. FO660/15, Harold Macmillan's notes on a paper by Kenneth Younger, n.d.

12 Macmillan and East of Suez: The Case of Malaysia
John Subritzky

INTRODUCTION

Harold Macmillan assumed the Premiership amid the national trauma resulting from Suez. This crisis – synonymous with the post-war decline of imperial Britain – was an appropriate prelude to Macmillan's term as prime minister. For the next six years his foreign policy would be dominated by attempts to preserve Britain's world standing in an era dominated by the superpowers. In particular, he had to wrestle with two simultaneous influences which seriously undermined British power: a relatively low-growth economy at home and assertive, fiercely anti-European nationalism abroad. Change was inevitable. Under Macmillan's stewardship, the transformation of empire to commonwealth was sharply accelerated. Writing in his diary, Macmillan speculated at the time whether he was 'destined to be the remodeller or the liquidator of empire'.[1] It shall be argued in this essay that, at least in regard to east of Suez and the case of Malaysia, Macmillan's ultimate objectives were traditional, not revolutionary. He still wanted empire, but by more subtle and realistic means. Nevertheless, the cost to Britain of maintaining a 'world role' proved severe. Macmillan's plans for a greater Malaysia federation were strongly opposed by Indonesia, which announced *Konfrontasi* (Confrontation) of the proposed state in January 1963. Only a few months later Jakarta instigated a major guerrilla war in Borneo in an attempt to wreck plans for federation. By 1965 the Wilson government was deploying over 68,000 servicemen in the Far East, together with a fleet of over eighty vessels, including two aircraft carriers.[2] Confrontation slowly developed, therefore, into Britain's gravest colonial crisis of the 1960s.

BRITAIN AND THE 'WORLD ROLE' EAST OF SUEZ

During 1957 the policies of the Macmillan government, as they related to Britain's presence east of Suez, appeared to confirm a commitment to disengagement. On 31 August Malaya, easily the most valuable colony in the region, was granted independence. In addition, Britain's ability to reinforce its position in the Far East seemed dangerously compromised by the government's own reforms on defence spending. On becoming prime minister, Macmillan was clearly determined to reduce military expenditure, which he believed had reached unacceptably high levels.[3] Further, he believed that, in any event, the services wasted enormous sums on conventional forces and weapon systems which were no longer needed in the nuclear age.[4] Acting on these perceptions, he appointed the notoriously abrasive Duncan Sandys to push major reforms past the anticipated resistance of the Chiefs of Staff. The government's White Paper, released by Sandys in April 1957, encompassed many of the ideas Macmillan had held for some time. Most importantly, conscription was to be abolished, the armed forces' manpower to be reduced from 690,000 to 375,000 by 1962.[5] In future greater reliance would be placed on the nuclear deterrent to protect British interests world-wide. These forces would also be supported by small, but highly mobile air, land and naval units which would be responsible for colonial peacekeeping. Despite the opposition of the Chiefs of Staff, who feared the government was placing too much faith in nuclear rather than conventional technology, Macmillan and Sandys succeeded in forcing their ideas upon a reluctant military establishment. In particular, real progress had been made, or so it seemed, in adjusting British defence and foreign policy to the realities of the nation's reduced status in the post-war world.

None the less, as was so often the case with Macmillan, appearances were deceptive. The main dispute with the Chiefs of Staff was over means, not ends. Macmillan believed financial savings could be made from the defence budget without necessitating an abandonment of Britain's 'world role'. Indeed, during the late 1950s, the government reduced British air and land units in Europe, but only so that some of these forces could be re-deployed to the Middle and Far Eastern theatres.[6] It was evidently clear, therefore, that Macmillan had no intention of cutting, at least for the foreseeable future, Britain's remaining world-wide commitments.[7] This was especially so in Southeast Asia. Although formal independence to

Malaya was conceded in 1957, the Macmillan government had already secured a continued pre-eminent role for Britain through the Anglo-Malayan Defence Agreement (AMDA). By virtue of this agreement, Britain remained responsible for the external defence of Malaya and, in return, received the right to maintain and use bases in that country for this purpose. By the late 1950s AMDA had become a crucial means for both Commonwealth defence co-operation in the region and British support for SEATO. In 1959 Australia and New Zealand joined AMDA as 'associates', not being directly responsible for the defence of Malaya, but prepared none the less to deploy forces in support of British objectives. All three countries contributed units towards the Commonwealth Strategic Reserve (CSR), which was permanently stationed in both Malaya and Singapore. The CSR was co-ordinated by, and received its directives from, the ANZAM defence committee, which comprised representatives of the chiefs of staff from all three countries. According to these directives, the defence of the Malayan region was only the secondary objective of the CSR; its primary function was to support SEATO in deterring communist expansion further north in Indochina and Thailand. Britain's post-colonial relationship with Malaya, epitomized by AMDA, had become a crucial hub for continued close relations with not only the Australasian powers, but also the United States. Even more important than Malaya itself, however, was the still very extensive military facilities at Singapore. Bastion of Britain's remaining far eastern empire, the city-colony was experiencing, during this period, the same aggressive nationalism that was sweeping Africa and Asia. Such a movement, as the author of 'winds of change' well knew, could ultimately blow away the entire British and Commonwealth defence structure in the region.

DECOLONIZATION: SINGAPORE AND THE OPTION OF A GREATER MALAYSIA

Due to the strength of Chinese nationalist feeling the Macmillan government felt it had little option but to compromise and concede self-government to Singapore. Accordingly, in 1958, a new constitution was promulgated. Britain would retain ultimate responsibility for both internal security and foreign affairs, but in all other matters the local government would be completely independent. These reforms, however, did not pacify strong local feelings against continued British sovereignty. In the 1959 elections, the People's Action Party (PAP), led by Lee Kuan Yew, and campaigning on a platform of full independence, won a decisive majority. Although Lee's rhetoric quickly moderated once in power, many of his party demanded immediate British withdrawal. By 1961 tension in the colony had risen appreciably. Early in that year Lee expelled known communist sympathizers from the PAP. In response, these members formed the *Barisan Sosialis*, a strongly left-wing party which demanded unconditional independence from Britain and a socialist constitution for the new state. It immediately won widespread local support, particularly from organized labour. By July Lee was in a desperate situation, only holding a majority in the general assembly by virtue of the speaker's vote.

There is little doubt that Macmillan and his colleagues were very concerned at these developments. If Lee fell from power, and was replaced by the *Barisan Sosialis*, Britain's base on the island would almost certainly be crippled by industrial chaos. In such an event, the government would eventually be confronted by two dismal alternatives: either forcefully reassert direct rule from London or negotiate a phased withdrawal. Whichever option was adopted would almost certainly damage British prestige and, in the case of direct rule, require more resources than the government was willing to provide. On the other hand, the seriousness of the communist threat presented Macmillan with an opportunity for a third and far more attractive option.

Since 1945 British policy-makers had consistently argued that the most logical form of decolonization in the region was a union of Britain's remaining territories, starting with Malaya and Singapore.[8] This vision was re-emphasized by Iain Macleod, the colonial secretary, as recently as April 1961, when he urged Cabinet to adopt a greater Malaysian federation as 'the ultimate aim of UK policy'.[9] Unfortunately for the British, however, this idea had been strongly opposed by the Malays. Such a union, they feared, would totally upset the delicate racial balance in favour of the Chinese. Nevertheless, by 1961, the Malayan prime minister, Tunku Abdul Rahman, was himself becoming increasingly disturbed with recent developments in Singapore. In short, he feared that a predominantly Chinese communist state was about to be created on Malaya's borders. He was therefore receptive to the arguments of Sir Geofroy Tory, British high commissioner in Kuala Lumpur, that federation was the only realistic alternative. Further, in order to allay Malayan fears over the racial balance, the Macmillan government hinted that a federation could include Brunei and the Borneo colonies. This would ensure that the Chinese remain a minority in the new state. Mindful of Lee's precarious hold on power, the Tunku quickly adopted these proposals as his own. On 27 May he made a public statement in which he talked of an 'understanding' at some future date regarding a federation between Malaya and Singapore, together with British Borneo and the Sultanate of Brunei.[10] Although British officials had in fact made the initial suggestion, London conceded authorship to the Malays, hoping this would enhance the credibility of greater Malaysia with both the inhabitants concerned and world opinion in general.[11]

The Tunku officially forwarded his proposals to London on 26 June. Although British policy-makers strongly supported greater Malaysia in principle, they knew a number of major obstacles had to be overcome before it could be established. Firstly, it was necessary to obtain the consent of the inhabitants concerned. Whitehall realized this would not be easy. Preliminary enquiry suggested many people in Borneo did not want federation and were perfectly content with the *status quo*.[12] Secondly, and even more worrisome, was that AMDA would have to be renegotiated. The original treaty allowed the British to use bases in Malaya for Commonwealth defence, but not SEATO-related contingencies. The Malays, like many Asians, were suspicious of this American-led alliance and did not want to be associated with it. Accordingly, they suggested a simple extension of current arrangements to include Borneo and Singapore when Malaysia was established. In his letter to Macmillan on 26 June, the Tunku made it clear that the Singapore base, in particular, 'would no longer be at the disposal of SEATO but could be maintained as a base for the defence of the Commonwealth'.[13]

Deciding upon an official response to the Tunku's proposals revealed clear divisions within Whitehall concerning Britain's long-term future in the region. At one extreme were policy-makers who argued that the armed services must retain the unfettered use of the Singapore base. Regardless of Malayan sensitivities, SEATO was considered an essential part of Britain's far eastern strategy, especially as it provided for close co-operation with other Western allies, such as the United States, Australia and New Zealand. To allow Kuala Lumpur to dictate the use of its own base would seriously undermine Britain's credibility in the region with both allies and opponents alike. Such determination to retain the *status quo*, however, was not universally accepted throughout Whitehall. Noting the government's obvious desire to cut military spending, some officials pointed to greater Malaysia as providing Britain with an excellent opportunity to lessen its excessive commitments, and hence expenditure, east of Suez. This chance arose precisely because of the link between the Singapore base and Britain's military deployment in the region. It was logical that if the base was no longer freely available for British forces, then Britain's defence commitments would have to be reduced accordingly. Put simply, the greater Malaysia project could be used to initiate a process some officials believed was long overdue: a British disengagement from the Far East. Macmillan's response to the Tunku's letter, therefore, would ultimately turn on a single important and contentious issue: whether Britain should retain a significant role for itself east of Suez. As Cecil Gough, an official at the admiralty, explained on 28 September:[14]

> It cannot be automatically assumed that we must insist on retaining defence facilities in Malaysia. Whether or not this should be our aim depends on the answer to the following questions:
> (a) Are we willing to accept a bilateral arrangement whereby we assume in future a responsibility for assisting in the external defence of Malaysia?
> (b) Are we prepared to continue our military contribution to SEATO in much the same form and to much the same extent as obtains at present?

The most persistent advocate of retrenchment was the Commissioner-General for Southeast Asia, Lord Selkirk. He justified his radical views by pointing to Britain's diminishing ability to defend its overseas interests. 'The resources at our disposal', he warned Macmillan in August, 'have become less and less adequate to meet the commitments we still retain. The result of this is that we are stretched to the point where our strength might snap under the strain and indeed our present position would be highly perilous were it not for our basic dependence on the United States.'[15] To Selkirk the arguments in favour of disengagement were overwhelming. 'It has become apparent to me', he concluded, 'that we should have to lighten the load of our commitments in this area.'[16] His pleas were not ignored by the prime minister. During September Macmillan ordered, as part of Whitehall's deliberations on greater Malaysia, a review of British policy in the region.[17] Previously, maintenance of a substantial British base at Singapore was accepted without question. Rather abruptly, this was no longer the case. 'On grounds of finance', concluded Cecil Gough during a meeting of the officials' committee, 'it is imperative and urgent to seek reductions in our commitments and establishments outside Germany and we must therefore take a new look at our position in Southeast Asia and the Far East'.[18]

These pleas for change were opposed by a powerful Whitehall triumvirate. The Chiefs of Staff, in particular, demanded that the *status quo* be retained. Without unrestricted use of the Singapore base, they feared British forces would no longer be able to contribute effectively to the West's deterrence of communism through the SEATO alliance. This in turn would seriously damage relations with key allies, such as the United States, Australia and New Zealand, all of whom relied, to varying degrees, on a British military presence at Singapore. 'The fact remains', argued Julian Amery, secretary of state for air, 'that if we want to contribute to keeping the communists out of Southeast Asia, and if we want to maintain our influence with Australia and New Zealand on the one hand and the United States on the other, we must have the effective use of Singapore. Without it our influence in the region could sink to the level of France.'[19]

The armed services' were supported in their hard line by the senior political departments. At the Commonwealth Relations Office (CRO), officials were concerned at the effect any British disengagement, no matter how slight, would have on relations with Australia and New Zealand. Proposals concerning greater Malaysia, it must be emphasized, coincided with Macmillan's dramatic announcement in the House of Commons on 31 July that Britain would seek entry into the EEC. Both developments, without question, strongly reinforced antipodean suspicions that Britain was abandoning the Commonwealth for integration in Europe. Consequently, it was not surprising that both Australasian prime ministers personally emphasized to Macmillan the importance of retaining military facilities at Singapore with as few restrictions as possible.[20] Of the two dominions New Zealand, given its greater dependency on Britain for trade and military support, was particularly anxious. As the prime minister, Keith Holyoake, pointed out to Macmillan:[21]

> Until now New Zealand's defence planning has been based almost without conscious thought on the assumptions that in any future war we should again be fighting side by side with you in all arms,

our soldiers transported in British ships, serving alongside British troops under British higher command, using British equipment, operating from British bases and receiving British logistic support.... But if there is in fact no reliable British forward base providing adequate facilities from which to operate in the theatre of particular concern to us a vital link is missing and our assumptions will require fundamental review.

There was little doubt that any such review would recommend a tightening of relations with the United States, resulting in weakening further traditional ties with Britain. Holyoake himself hinted as much as when he concluded: 'in the circumstances we feel that we may be faced with the need for painful decisions with sentiment pulling us one way and material considerations another'.[22] Quite naturally, the CRO was eager to arrest this trend and allay antipodean fears that Britain was turning its back on old friends. They deemed it essential, therefore, that a substantial British military presence at Singapore be retained.

Officials at the Foreign Office (FO) held similar views. They were well aware, for example, that across in Washington, policy-makers were as opposed to British disengagement as those in Australasia. 'From a military viewpoint', outlined the US consul-general in Singapore, 'it is essential that the bases continue essentially as at present if the UK is to meet its commitments in Southeast Asia.'[23] On the other hand, 'removal of these forces would create a military power vacuum which, if not filled by the US, would be filled only by hostile elements'.[24] Consequently, American policy-makers favoured continued retention of existing British forces east of Suez, even if this resulted in London achieving financial savings through cutbacks to its forces in Germany. 'Many nations could reinforce Europe', explained CIA director Allen Dulles to officials in London, 'but by the accident of history only Britain could do the job in Singapore'.[25] Given the importance of Anglo-American relations to British foreign policy in general, the FO was also, not surprisingly, determined to preserve the *status quo* in Singapore against Selkirk and other like-minded revisionists.

At Downing Street Macmillan was undoubtedly influenced by the reasoning of the Chiefs of Staff and political departments. When the prime minister finally replied to Selkirk's letter in October he urged caution. Although Macmillan accepted that 'the need to adjust our policy is clear in the light of our reduced resources ... any solution to the problems of the area can only come about gradually'.[26] He was particularly concerned about relations with Australia and New Zealand, warning that 'we must not give them any cause to blame us for leaving them precipitately in the lurch'.[27] As a result, the government decided, after much deliberation, to maintain the *status quo*. Indeed, preservation of the Singapore base was now recognized as a prerequisite to British support for the greater Malaysia project. Consequently, Macmillan advised Australian prime minister Menzies on 16 November that 'we are in complete agreement with you that our objective must be to maintain intact the rights we at present enjoy in respect of Singapore.... We shall be seeking an agreement whereby we can fully discharge our commitments under the Manila Treaty [SEATO] and we shall reserve our position for further discussion if the Tunku cannot meet us on this at the forthcoming talks.'[28]

Fortunately for Macmillan the Tunku proved accommodating. At the Anglo-Malayan talks in November the Malayan delegation accepted Britain's need to use Singapore for SEATO purposes. Macmillan did not completely disregard, however, Selkirk's pleas for a reduced British presence in the region. By establishing greater Malaysia, Macmillan intended to release Britain from its responsibility for internal security in Singapore. This was by no means a minor task, as nationalist agitation in the city-colony required the presence of many troops. With this role being assumed by the Malays after Malaysia was established, Macmillan was confident that major savings could be made. Consequently, although air and naval forces would be retained at their existing levels, land forces were to be substantially reduced. In this manner, Macmillan hoped to have the best of both worlds: retain Britain's strong influence in the region through close relations with Commonwealth allies like Malaysia, Australia and New Zealand, but at greatly reduced cost. As Charles Baldwin, American Ambassador in Kuala Lumpur, neatly put it to the state department: 'UK objective will be to continue to play dominant role in local defense picture at reduced cost.'[29]

There is little doubt that Macmillan was well aware of the need for change. Traditional empire in Southeast Asia had become, by the early 1960s, both politically obsolete and economically wasteful. But there was also no retreat. As the evidence clearly shows, Macmillan was merely changing the means by which British power east of Suez could be preserved. He certainly was not prepared to challenge the traditional presumption that Britain was, and should remain, a global power. Even the New Zealanders, who probably had more to lose than anyone from British withdrawal, accepted that Macmillan's policies were intended to enhance, rather than undermine, Britain's world position. Reported the New Zealand high commission in London in November 1962:[30]

> It seems clear that the government regards entry into Europe not as involving withdrawal from her traditional world-wide interests, but as a means of strengthening her economy and political influence in order more effectively to sustain those interests. Thus, there is no reason, in our view, to suppose that entry into Europe would mean an accelerated withdrawal by the UK from her overseas defence commitments. The growing cost of defence may, in fact, oblige the government to take measures of contraction from time to time but we do not believe it is its policy to anticipate necessity by abandoning its global commitments and concentrating its defence effort into Europe.

Accordingly, during 1962, the Conservative government commenced preparations for the transfer of sovereignty. In order to ascertain opinion in the Borneo colonies Lord Cobbold, former governor of the Bank of England, was appointed to head a commission of enquiry. Despite their obvious preference for the *status quo*, Macmillan was determined to proceed with federation. The stakes were simply too high. Malaysia was viewed by British policy-makers as an essential means of not only reducing expenditure east of Suez, but also improving Britain's position in the region as regards Asian nationalism. By contrast, the consequences of failure could be disastrous. As Macmillan himself pointed out, 'if we are successful in achieving greater Malaysia this would relieve the British government of its most invidious and burdensome responsibilities in the area. If we failed, the problem of Singapore would become most urgent: at the next elections a situation might arise in which most of the British forces in the island would be required to defend their own base.'[31] As a result, Macmillan was impatient with colonial office objections that greater Malaysia was being unfairly forced on the Borneo peoples. On one such telegram from the governor of North Borneo, Macmillan wrote:[32]

> I am rather shocked by telegram no. 104 and the attitude it reveals. Does he realise (a) our weakness in Singapore, and (b)

our urgent need to hand over the security problem there? The whole mood is based on a false assessment of our power. If this is the CO point of view we shall fail.

Given Macmillan's strong views on the matter, it was not surprising that, in July, Lord Cobbold reported that, of the options available to them – continued British sovereignty not being one – the Borneo peoples favoured federation with Malaya and Singapore. In the meantime, HMG was in the process of withdrawing major land forces from Singapore, arguing that these units were for internal security purposes only and consequently were no longer needed because of the imminent creation of Malaysia.[33] Towards the end of 1962 plans for the establishment of Malaysia appeared to be progressing smoothly. It was precisely at this time, however, that Britain's careful plans for easing the new federation quietly onto the international stage became badly unstuck.

INDONESIA, CONFRONTATION AND THE CHALLENGE TO BRITISH POWER EAST OF SUEZ

Back in 1961, when plans for a greater Malaysia were first announced, Jakarta raised no objections. British officials happily concluded, therefore, that the most likely external objector to the project had been successfully placated. Their optimism proved both premature and misplaced. Since 1957 Indonesia's President, Achmed Sukarno, was a leader deeply committed to eradicating colonialism from Southeast Asia. He was strongly encouraged in this endeavour by the *Partai Komunis Indonesia* (PKI), then the largest communist party in the world outside the Soviet Union or China. The initial object of Sukarno's anti-imperialist crusade was not Britain but the Netherlands and, in particular, its continued sovereignty over West New Guinea. Sukarno claimed the territory as rightfully Indonesia's and, during late 1961, commenced a campaign to oust the Dutch from it. Generously supplied with modern weapons from Moscow, Sukarno cleverly engaged in brinkmanship with the Dutch, hoping international pressure would eventually force them to leave. By the end of 1962 it was clear he had succeeded. A settlement was reached by which West New Guinea would be transferred to Indonesia, provided a UN investigation confirmed that that was the wish of the local inhabitants. Crucial to Sukarno's success was the attitude of the United States.[34] Fearing Dutch obstinance could lead to war and, as a consequence, Indonesia joining the communist bloc, President Kennedy personally intervened in the crisis, effectively forcing the Dutch to abandon their last remaining Asian colony.[35] None the less, with his most immediate objective realized, Sukarno was now in a position to carry his vision of a post-colonial Southeast Asia to other parts of the region.

With the Dutch successfully ousted, the only remaining colonial power of any significance was Britain. Although it was preparing for decolonization, Sukarno was largely unimpressed with Malaysia. He complained, probably with some justification, that the proposed federation was neo-colonialist, ultimately intended to preserve rather than end British influence in the region. By the end of 1962 Indonesian hostility to Malaysia was becoming increasingly clear. Matters then reached a climax when, on 8 December, an attempted coup was mounted against the Sultan of Brunei. The Indonesians complained that, with the dispatch of Ghurkha troops from Singapore, Britain was again using brute force to destroy a legitimate indigenous movement.[36] For their part, the British believed Jakarta was covertly supporting the coup, together with subversive movements in Borneo which opposed federation.[37] With Anglo-Indonesian relations deteriorating rapidly, it was not long before Indonesia's opposition to Malaysia would become official. On 20 January 1963 the foreign minister, Dr Subandrio, declared that henceforth Indonesia would pursue a policy of *Konfrontasi* (Confrontation) against Malaysia. Unable to challenge British military power directly, this amounted to actively nurturing and then supporting a guerrilla insurgency in Borneo.

In London the belief that Malaysia had to be supported, regardless of Indonesian opposition, was accepted virtually without debate. Indeed, ministerial discussions focused on how Malaysia could be established, rather than whether this objective should be reviewed given Sukarno's declaration of Confrontation. It was also noteworthy that the role of the prime minister in decision-making concerning Malaysia had diminished. Although being fundamentally involved in providing the framework for greater Malaysia during 1961, Macmillan had, by 1963, essentially delegated responsibility for British policy to Commonwealth relations secretary Duncan Sandys and foreign secretary Lord Home.

Both these ministers, together with their departments, believed Britain had little choice but to honour its security guarantee to

Malaya. Indonesian subversion, it must be emphasized, was directed at Borneo, which was still a British colony. Further, British prestige was already fully engaged regarding the Malaysia project. While still having pretensions that Britain was, and should remain, a global power, policy-makers could not afford to have their plans destroyed by a country like Indonesia. It was also perhaps noteworthy that British elites personally despised Sukarno. They regarded him as an Asian Nasser, a rogue pretender, impatient to steal the Emperor's clothes. 'We are up against a man', wrote Lord Selkirk, 'with much of the instability and lust for power of Hitler and military forces, if not so efficient, at least comparable in size for the area'.[38] Macmillan himself particularly loathed the Indonesian leader. Observing in his diary Sukarno's vain liking for extravagant military uniforms, Macmillan described him as a cross between 'Liberace and little Lord Fauntleroy'.[39] Given these perceptions, therefore, it was not surprising that the Macmillan government was determined to ensure Sukarno failed in his attempt to destroy Malaysia before it had been established.

Despite their uncompromising support for Malaysia, the British were under no illusions as to the extent of the security problem facing them. In the first instance Indonesian hostility to Malaysia effectively reversed London's plans to reduce British forces at Singapore. 'We had hoped', pointed out private secretary Philip de Zulueta to Macmillan on 3 April, 'that as Malaysia's own forces were built-up, we would reduce our own. But the Indonesian threat has made this impossible. Our commitments', he concluded, 'so far from decreasing, will therefore increase'.[40] Put simply, Sukarno was deliberately undermining Macmillan's plans to perpetuate British influence in the region through a greater Malaysia federation. If the prime minister wanted Britain to remain a far eastern power, then the asking price to be paid was going to be far higher.

British policy-makers were also well aware that, by sponsoring a guerrilla insurgency in Borneo, the Indonesians could realistically continue with Confrontation for a reasonably long period of time. This in turn would consume ever greater British military resources. Indeed, in many respects, the overall strategic outlook for Britain was very bleak. 'This is a potentially formidable commitment', argued the Lord Privy Seal, Ted Heath, 'since Malaysia is practically encircled by hostile countries – Indonesia to the west and south, the Philippines to the east and the rickety structure of Indo-China to the north'.[41] Macmillan himself was very conscious of the possible danger. On 3 April he warned Lord Home that he doubted whether, if the situation 'really got out of control, Britain could deal with it single-handed'.[42] As a result, the prime minister believed it essential for Britain to obtain strong Australasian and, in particular, American support so long as Confrontation remained. 'Sukarno would only be stopped', wrote Macmillan in his memoirs, 'if he clearly understood that the Western powers were at one in opposing his acquisition.'[43] Unfortunately for the British, however, such assistance was not as readily forthcoming as they might have expected.

Across in Washington policy-makers were wary of British requests that the United States should apply concerted pressure on Jakarta to end Confrontation. Although the Kennedy administration supported the concept of a greater Malaysia in 1961, its readiness to offer any meaningful assistance to Britain in 1963 was tempered by a number of countervailing factors. Many in the administration feared that forceful Western action against Sukarno held the unacceptably high risk of not only open conflict but also pushing Indonesia into the waiting arms of Moscow. Such an outcome would be disastrous for American policy in the region and would completely undermine Kennedy's efforts to bolster the non-communist regime in South Vietnam. 'As they see it', wrote an official from the British embassy in Washington, 'they have enough trouble on their hands already in Southeast Asia without incurring the lasting enmity of so large a country as Indonesia'.[44]

For Macmillan, the fact of American non-involvement, although disappointing, was not disastrous. What disturbed him, and his colleagues, was Washington's inclination to appease Sukarno by offering him concessions in order to have Confrontation abandoned.[45] The British believed such tactics were very unwise; Sukarno was personally committed to destroying Malaysia. Concessions to him, they argued, would only encourage, rather than deter him, from obtaining this objective. In particular, the American attitude was disturbingly close to that over West New Guinea. It was viewed as critical in London that such a parallel not be established. 'We must avoid a situation', argued Fred Warner, head of the Southeast Asia department of the FO, 'where the Indonesians conclude that the American role over Borneo will be the same as it was in the New Guinea dispute, so that they will therefore push things to a stage where British forces will be committed to a prolonged struggle with Indonesia, in which the latter would enjoy significantly more support from the communist bloc than we shall from the Americans'.[46]

With the Americans proving difficult, the British had high hopes that Australia and New Zealand, at least, would actively support them in Borneo. Both Canberra and Wellington, however, had similar concerns to Washington. Neither wanted a violent break with Jakarta if it could be avoided. Australian policy-makers, in particular, were adamant that the country could ill-afford a hostile Indonesia backed by international communism. The Australasian governments were also very reluctant to adopt a position independently of the United States, even if it were in association with Britain. 'We have seen what happened to the Dutch', wrote Holyoake to Garfield Barwick, Australia's foreign minister, 'when they could no longer count on anyone's support against Indonesia'.[47] Consequently, both Menzies and Holyoake were reluctant to publicly align their governments with Britain during the early stages of Confrontation.

Despite receiving lukewarm support from Britain's closest allies, policy-makers in London were determined to establish Malaysia on time, regardless of Sukarno's objections. Eventually there was a delay, but only by a few weeks. On 16 September 1963 the federation of Malaysia formally came into being. The Indonesian reaction was bitter. Only two days later a crowd, probably acting with the acquiescence of the state authorities, attacked the British embassy in Jakarta, burning it to the ground. Simultaneously Sukarno intensified the guerrilla war in Borneo, requiring even further reinforcements to be sent into the region from Britain. There is no doubt that British officials were seriously concerned at the sharp deterioration which had taken place. There was no end in sight to Confrontation, a campaign that Indonesia could easily sustain for many years. 'At worst', warned Lord Mountbatten, chairman of the Chiefs of Staff, 'costs might well compare with those involved in the Malayan emergency'.[48] None the less, even with Britain's military resources being dangerously extended, there was no turning back by the Macmillan government. Britain simply could not afford to let Malaysia fall without dire consequences for its position – and prestige – as a global power. By September 1963 the two had become inextricably connected. 'This [Confrontation] will be a heavy burden on British resources', argued Warner, 'but we see no choice between supporting Malaysia and withdrawing from Southeast Asia altogether'.[49] Many Conservatives, including probably Macmillan himself, shared these sentiments. As one senior official concluded many years later, 'the Tories were always committed to imperial responsibilities and the world role . . . their instinct was to hang on and not give up until they were convinced it was the only possible option'.[50] During 1963, at least, the inevitability of withdrawal had not yet been accepted.

CONCLUSION

Remodeller or liquidator of empire? That was the question Macmillan posed for himself when writing in his diary on becoming prime minister in February 1957. Certainly, it can be argued, especially with the benefit of hindsight, that greater Malaysia was an essential precursor to a British disengagement east of Suez. With power devolved to friendly local elites, and a stable federation established, the British were then in a position to quietly vacate the area.[51] The documentary evidence is clear, however, that Macmillan, at least for the foreseeable future, had no such intention. Admittedly, he realized that changes were long overdue. Traditional empire, in the form of direct rule from London, was no longer tenable. Singapore was a disaster waiting to happen, Chinese nationalist fervour threatening to explode into violence. The resources needed to control the situation were unsustainable in the long-term. The idea of a greater Malaysia federation, therefore, seemed a perfect solution to these problems. Responsibility for internal security in Singapore would be assumed by the Malays, thereby substantially reducing Britain's political and financial vulnerability in the region. Nevertheless, a strong British military presence would be preserved through AMDA and the Tunku's guarantees regarding the Singapore base. Britain, Macmillan hoped, would get the best of both worlds: pre-eminent influence at less cost to the Exchequer. These plans – or hopes – proved wildly over-optimistic, however. Sukarno, like Nasser in the Middle East, had no intention of allowing an ailing imperial power retain even a measure of its former glory and influence. The result was Confrontation, which critically undermined British objectives. Instead of releasing Britain from its more onerous imperial burdens, greater Malaysia drastically intensified them. The crisis remained unresolved when Macmillan announced his intention to resign as Prime Minister on 10 October 1963. It would ultimately be left to a Labour successor, Harold Wilson, to negotiate an end to a crisis which was proving, by 1965, to be an unsustainable drain on Britain's financial and military resources.

NOTES

1. Alistair Horne, *Macmillan, 1957–1986*, vol. II (London: Macmillan, 1989), p. 15.
2. John Darwin, *Britain and Decolonisation: The Retreat from Empire in the Post-colonial World* (London: Macmillan, 1988), p. 290.
3. Wyn Rees, 'The 1957 Sandys White Paper: New Priorities in British Defence Policy', *Journal of Strategic Studies*, vol. 12 (1989), p. 226.
4. Simon J. Ball, 'Macmillan and British Defence Policy', in Richard Aldous and Sabine Lee (eds), *Harold Macmillan and Britain's World Role* (London: Macmillan, 1996), pp. 67–8.
5. Philip Darby, *British Defence Policy East of Suez* (London: Oxford University Press, 1973), p. 107.
6. Ball, *Macmillan and British Defence Policy*, pp. 74–85.
7. A number of historians have stressed this point. See, in particular, Ball, *Macmillan and British Defence Policy*, p. 92; Turner, *Macmillan* (London: Longman, 1994), p. 272; Peter Clarke, *Hope and Glory: Britain 1900–1990* (London: Allen Lane, 1996), pp. 265–7.
8. See A. J. Stockwell, 'Insurgency and Decolonisation during the Malayan Emergency', *Journal of Commonwealth and Comparative Politics*, vol. XXV, no. 1 (1987), pp. 71–81.
9. Macleod to Cabinet, 7 April 1961, memo, PRO, DO 169/25.
10. J. A. C. Mackie, *Konfrontasi: The Indonesia–Malaysia Dispute, 1963–1966* (Oxford: Oxford University Press, 1974), p. 41.
11. Singapore to State Department, 16 June 1961, telegram, RG 59, central decimal file 1960–63, Box 2099, United States National Archives (USNA).
12. Brook to Macmillan, 17 April 1961, memo, PRO, Prem 11/3418.
13. Tunku to Macmillan, 26 June 1961, letter, PRO, Prem 11/3418.
14. Gough to Mackintosh, 28 September 1961, letter, PRO, DO 169/29.
15. Selkirk to Macmillan, 14 August 1961, letter, PRO, FO 371/159702, D1015/16.
16. Selkirk to Macmillan, 30 December 1961, letter, PRO, Prem 11/3866.
17. Committee on greater Malaysia, 27 September 1961, minute of meeting, PRO, CAB 134/1949, GM(61)1.
18. Ibid.
19. Amery, 4 October 1961, note, PRO, CAB 131/26, D(61)66.
20. Menzies to British High Commissioner Canberra, 28 August 1961, letter, PRO, Prem 11/3418; Holyoake to Macmillan, 20 October 1961, telegram, PRO, Prem 11/3422.
21. Holyoake to Macmillan, 14 December 1961, PRO, Prem 11/3866.
22. Ibid.
23. Singapore to State Department, 28 September 1961, telegram, RG 59, central decimal file 1960–63, Box 2099, USNA.
24. Ibid.
25. Amery to Watkinson, 2 November 1961, letter, PRO, DO 169/29.
26. Macmillan to Selkirk, 17 October 1961, PRO, FO 371/159702, D1015/26.
27. Ibid.

28. Macmillan to Menzies, 16 November 1961, message, AA, A1209/80, 1963/6544.
29. Kuala Lumpur to State Department, 24 March 1962, telegram, RG 59, central decimal file 1960–63, Box 2199, USNA.
30. Templeton to McIntosh, 2 November 1962, letter, Ministry of Foreign Affairs and Trade (NZ) (MFAT), PM 106/7/1.
31. Greater Malaysia committee, 21 March 1962, minute of meeting, PRO, CAB 130/179, GEN 754/3.
32. Goode to Colonial Secretary, 19 June 1962, telegram, PRO, Prem 11/3867.
33. High Commission Kuala Lumpur to CRO, 29 December 1961, telegram, PRO, Prem 11/3866.
34. For an excellent commentary of JFK's policy during this crisis, see Timothy P. Maga, *John F. Kennedy and the New Pacific Community, 1961–63* (London: Macmillan, 1990).
35. James N. Giglio, *The Presidency of John F. Kennedy* (Lawrence: University Press of Kansas, 1991), pp. 238–9.
36. Mackie, *Konfrontasi*, p. 121.
37. Selkirk to Foreign Office, 8 December 1962, telegram, PRO, Prem 11/3869.
38. Selkirk to Foreign Office, 20 December 1962, telegram, PRO, Prem 11/4346.
39. Horne, *Macmillan*, vol. II, p. 321.
40. de Zulueta to Macmillan, 3 April 1963, memo, PRO, Prem 11/4189.
41. Heath to Macmillan, 23 April 1963, memo, PRO, Prem 11/4347.
42. Macmillan to Home, 3 April 1963, minute, PRO, Prem 11/4347.
43. Harold Macmillan, *At the End of the Day, 1961–63* (London: Macmillan, 1973), p. 260.
44. Forster to Cable, 11 May 1963, letter, PRO, FO 371/169700, D1071/134/G.
45. Macmillan, *At the End of the Day*, p. 261.
46. Warner, 16 May 1963, minute, PRO, FO 371/169701, D1071/147.
47. Holyoake to Barwick, 4 February 1963, cablegram, MFAT, PM 420/2/3, Pt 2A.
48. Mountbatten to Thorneycroft, 30 September 1963, letter, PRO, Defe 4/161.
49. Warner, 29 May 1963, minute, PRO, FO 371/169702, D1071/172.
50. Sir James Cable, counsellor in the FO 1961–3, head of the Southeast Asia department 1963–6, interview with author, Cambridge, 16 September 1994.
51. For an outline on this argument, see Chin Kin Wah, *The Defence of Malaysia and Singapore: The Transformation of a Security System, 1957–1971* (Cambridge: Cambridge University Press, 1983), p. 60.

13 Macmillan and the Soviet Union
Sir Curtis Keeble

The global contest of ideology and power between the Soviet Union and the Western democracies set the tone for the conduct of international relations during a large part of the twentieth century. For successive British Prime Ministers it did much to establish the context within which their foreign policy had to be constructed and implemented. Many of them alternated between policies of confrontation and co-operation as they struggled to contain the twin threats of Soviet power and Communist ideology, while maintaining a working relationship with the Soviet government. David Lloyd George is identified with the abandonment of armed intervention and the first unsuccessful attempt to draw the new Soviet state into the international community. Churchill, his imagination fired throughout much of his political career by the threat and the challenge of Russia, moved from the anti-Bolshevik tirades of the twenties and thirties to the wartime military alliance, the nuclear confrontation of the Cold War years and the final attempt to forge some new understanding after the death of Stalin. Harold Wilson, to his final, sad years, never failed to recall his early trade negotiations with Mikoyan. Margaret Thatcher, coming to office after thirty-four years of Cold War, confronted almost immediately with the Soviet invasion of Afghanistan and as harsh as Ronald Reagan in her denunciation of the 'evil empire', could claim, as British Prime Minister, to have been among the first of the Western leaders to sense that with the arrival of Mikhail Gorbachev the time had come to end the decades of sterile confrontation. Yet so sterile had the relationship been that for most of those who occupied 10 Downing Street between 1917 and 1991 there had been little room for positive moves in the field of British–Soviet relations and of those initiatives which were undertaken few were fruitful. It is against this background that Macmillan's handling of the relationship has to be judged.

Now, as the century nears its end, the sharp images of confrontation with a formidable world-wide deployment of Soviet power and communist doctrine are quickly fading. In the popular memory of Macmillan the trivial and the grave come together in a jumble of impressions: the celebrated white hat acquired in Finland and worn in Moscow, the repatriation of the White Russians, Khrushchev banging his shoe at the United Nations, the Cuban Missile Crisis and the Nuclear Test Ban Treaty. Was there an identifiable single thread running through Macmillan's dealings with the Soviet Union?

In January 1957, when he formed his first government, the Soviet Union was arguably close to the apogee of its power. It had demonstrated in Hungary its ability and will to hold by force its wartime conquests. Beyond Europe it sensed the opportunities offered by the decay of Western imperial structures and it seemed ready, by a combination of armed force and doctrinal subversion, to extend a new Soviet imperialism throughout the world. The flaws in the structure were visible, but for most Western leaders, the threat of hostile Soviet power was only too apparent. As he confronted this power, what experience could Macmillan draw on?

Harold Macmillan was remarkable among British Prime Ministers in having taken a serious personal interest in the Soviet Union at a very early stage in his career. His interest was, in some ways, typical of his generation and to the end of his life he retained many of the instincts of that generation. These were the young men who, born into the gentle life of the well-bred comfortably endowed families of pre-1918 England, had survived, scarred by years in the trenches, to experience the disillusion of the post-war depression and the apparent inability of a capitalist system to provide adequately for the British people. There were few of them for whom Communism had any real appeal, but many felt that a political system which purported to harness all the power of the state to the welfare of the people at least merited closer examination. Macmillan summed up their feelings well when he wrote in *Winds of Change*[1] 'While the capitalist world seemed, to many observers, in decay if not in mortal agony, the Bolsheviks had apparently consolidated their power and stability. In the early years of my political life, Bolshevism was regarded in Britain with feelings ranging between contempt and fear. But by 1932 many British people were beginning to wonder whether, after all, the regime which had imposed itself over a vast part of the world's territory might not be worth careful and, if possible objective, study.'

At the end of 1929 the first Ambassadors had taken up residence in London and Moscow. On the first of January 1930 the

Daily Worker had been founded. And in September 1932, after a brief flirtation with Oswald Mosley's proto-fascist New Party, the young Macmillan, re-elected in the Conservative landslide of 1931, set sail on a Soviet ship at the start of a five-week exploration of the Soviet Union. He was accompanied by Allan Young, an ex-Marxist from the Clyde. In his memoirs he drew on letters written to his mother to describe the 'looking-glass world' which he found, a world 'where everything was the opposite of what one would expect'. Arriving in Leningrad, he spent some days in Moscow before travelling to Nizhni Novgorod and taking a river steamer for a 1,200 mile journey down the Volga to Stalingrad, visiting Rostov and Kharkov, returning to Moscow for further meetings with Soviet government ministers and officials and spending a final few days in Leningrad.

In a state of some mental turmoil, having just recovered from the nervous strains precipitated by Dorothy's relationship with Bob Boothby, and with his own political orientation still uncertain, he must have been in an impressionable frame of mind. There is no sign, however, that his remarkably thorough exploration of the Soviet Union led him to any definitive conclusions. He came with a questioning mind, hoping, as he said, to be able to read and study more intelligently in future what might be the developments in that bewildering scene. He left with few questions answered, but with impressions which he can scarcely have failed to recall in his later dealings with the Soviet leadership. His letters might have been written by almost any conscientious, independent-minded British visitor during the seventy years of Soviet power. As he made the standard circuit of housing developments, clinics, factories and collective farms, he commented on the sheer size of the projects, but expressed some scepticism about the gap between plan and reality. At an official function in Leningrad he had an opportunity to observe Stalin and remarked that so Bonapartist was the regime becoming that all evening the one subject of discussion was the identity and prospects of a young man sitting beside Stalin 'who had been thus singled out by the quasi-royal favour'. He records discussions about the prospects for British trade and investment, but only at one point is there a suggestion that there ought to be room for substantial improvement. Noting the shoddiness and the waste and suspecting the brutalities and tyrannies of a police state, he returned to Britain, 'stepping back from a kind of nightmare world into the world of reality', with no feeling of affection or admiration for the Soviet system, but with a deep impression of the good nature and kindness of the ordinary people.

His subsequent publications, *The State and Industry*, *The Next Step*, *Reconstruction: A Plea for a National Policy*, *Planning for Employment*, *The Next Five Years* and finally *The Middle Way*, show a concern that the state should involve itself actively in economic planning, but this owed much to his study of Keynes and little or nothing to his experience of the planned Soviet economy. There were, as he admitted in *Reconstruction*, points of similarity between his proposals and those of the Russian Communist or Italian Corporate state, but their political basis was wholly different. As he explained in *The Middle Way*, he sought a policy which would avoid both 'the intolerable restriction of a totalitarian state and the unfettered abuse of freedom under the old liberalism'.

As the European crisis deepened, Macmillan, preoccupied at first with Britain's own economic problems, showed a growing concern for the need to establish a firm front against the dictators. One might have expected him in this context to have taken a special interest in the position of Russia. Writing about it subsequently, his view was clear. In relation to Eden's visit to Moscow in the spring of 1935 he commented: 'Had something been done at that time to come to terms with Russia it is possible that an alliance could have been built which would have prevented the Second War.' But this was with the advantage of hindsight. At the time, he probably shared the view that Russia was 'at once too weak and too dangerous'. When, on the eve of war, the British Government made its half-hearted attempt to establish a tripartite pact with France and Russia, Macmillan does not seem to have joined publicly with Churchill and Eden who, in Parliament, were urging that the government should show a greater sense of urgency and purpose in the negotiations. In his subsequent treatment of the episode in his memoirs, arguing the case for a tripartite pact, he showed considerable sympathy with the Russian position: 'If Britain had grounds for suspicion of Russia, the reverse was also true. The hostility of the Western powers after the First War; the intervention in the Russian Civil War; the loss of territory imposed on Russia: none of these were forgotten.'[2] This understanding of the Russian obsession with security was a theme to which he was to revert at various stages.

Such sympathy as Macmillan had for the policy of Stalin's Russia in confronting the German threat must have been swiftly dissipated by the Nazi–Soviet pact of August 1939, the occupation of the Baltic States and eastern Poland and then, in the winter of 1939–40, the Russian attack on Finland. Among the British public, sympathy and admiration for the gallant fight put up by the Finns was matched by disgust at the callousness of the Russian attack and contempt for the incompetence with which it was pursued. Macmillan accepted with alacrity an invitation to lead an official mission to organize aid to Finland and to recruit an international volunteer force. Had he received more swift and determined support from Chamberlain's government, the result might have been to embroil Britain in war with the Soviet Union. Had he, on the other hand, been constrained by the responsibility of a ministerial appointment requiring a colder assessment of the longer-term British strategic interest, he could scarcely have responded so enthusiastically to the popular mood. As it was, the episode tells us more about the emotional half of his character, never wholly suppressed by the subsequent cares of office, than it does about his gradually evolving assessment of Soviet Russia.

In one respect, Macmillan's experience in Finland can scarcely have been absent from his mind when he was confronted, in May 1945, with the problem of the forced repatriation of Cossack troops and White Russians from Austria. He had in Finland been shown the bodies of a large group of Russian troops allegedly shot in the head or neck by their own commissars and he clearly had no doubt as to the probable fate of the Cossacks. His diary entry for 13 May reads: 'To hand them over to the Russians is condemning them to slavery, torture and probably death.' Macmillan's view, expressed in a brief conversation with General Keightley, the Allied commander responsible, was that they should, nevertheless, be handed back. The return of members of the Soviet forces who had been captured by the Germans had been agreed at Yalta. It formed part of a reciprocal arrangement under which British and other Allied prisoners of war in areas occupied by the Soviet army were also to be returned. In the confusion of the time, those handed back included not only the Soviet troops whose repatriation had been agreed, but also White Russians who could not properly be regarded as Soviet citizens, together in some cases with civilian family members. The incident has given rise to wild allegations about Macmillan's role and has been subjected to detailed investigation as well as legal proceedings. It does not, however, seem to have been a matter on which he believed that he was deciding policy or indeed to which he gave detailed consideration. For those who wish to pursue it, there is a very full and fair treatment in Alistair Horne's biography.[3]

It is in the early post-war years that we find the first major Parliamentary interventions by Macmillan on the question of relations with Russia. They are very much in character. By the beginning of 1946, less than a year after the victorious conclusion of the war against Germany, the alliance with the Soviet Union had disintegrated. Bevin had suggested a possible extension of the Anglo-Soviet Treaty to fifty years, but had, at the same time, warned Stalin that 'there was a limit beyond which we could not tolerate continued Soviet infiltration and undermining of our position'.[4] The deterioration in British–Soviet relations gathered pace and on 20 February 1946 Macmillan, opening a Foreign Affairs debate in Parliament, devoted some time to an analysis of the relationship. His theme was that, with the tripartite alliance virtually, if not formally, in abeyance, the time had come for personal and direct negotiation at the level of Heads of Government. What, he asked, did the Russians want? Were they returning to the expansionist policy of the Tsars? Was there to be a new imperialism or a return to the proselytizing fervour of international communism? Were military theorists back in control? Or: 'May it not be that the apparent Chauvinism of Soviet policy is a form of insurance, not of expansion, that security not imperialism is their instinctive goal and for this a new cordon sanitaire is being created . . . a kind of defensive glacis of small nations looking to the Kremlin for political and economic theory and to the local Russian commander for material support.' The purpose of Soviet policy might, he suggested, be 'not to dominate the world either as Russian imperialists or as militant international Communists, but to secure the soil of Russia herself against new outrages'.[5] At a time when public opnion was beginning to harden against Soviet policy, he was clearly disposed to look for a charitable explanation if one existed.

Macmillan's attitude at that time can be judged against the background of Winston Churchill's Iron Curtain speech, delivered at Fulton a fortnight later. Churchill, like Macmillan, recognized Russia's need for security and the need, too, for some understanding between Russia and the West. But where Macmillan posed questions, Churchill was more inclined to suggest answers and to speak of the Soviet Union as seeking not war, but 'the fruits of war and the indefinite expansion of their power and doctrine'. Where Macmillan called for tripartite discussion, Churchill called for Western unity and strength as the prerequisite for an understanding with Russia.[6]

It was not long before the deterioration in relations with the Soviet Union, coming to the brink of armed hostilities over the Berlin blockade, removed any hesitation Macmillan might have had as to the true nature of Soviet policy and the appropriate Western response. In March 1949 he spoke of Kremlin policy 'uniting in a single aggressive movement both the expansionist tradition of Russian imperialism and the subversive aims of international Communism' and, remarking sadly that 'we could not believe that the genuine friendship which we had honestly held out to our Russian allies could be so scornfully rejected', he called for the Cold War to be fought with as much energy and single-mindedness as the shooting war. Later that year, fearing another Rapallo, he was calling for closer European co-operation in the face of the 'persistent malignancy of Soviet policy', denouncing 'the peace of Communism, the peace of death, the peace of anti-Christ' and calling for the strengthening of Europe. He may have had his own half-apologia in mind when he said: 'What four years ago was a pardonable and even praiseworthy spirit of good will would now be criminal weakness.'[7] The confrontation had been joined and so it would remain until the death of Stalin and the accession of Khrushchev suggested to Western leaders that the time might be coming for a new attempt to establish a dialogue with the Soviet Union.

The early fifties saw a remarkably swift evolution of British policy, but it was some time before Macmillan was directly involved. In October 1951, when the Conservative government returned to power under Winston Churchill, the Korean War had brought the East–West relationship to a point of extreme tension, but by 1953, with the death of Stalin, it seemed that the time might be ripe for a new effort to improve relations. Macmillan at that time was busy restoring the Tory Party's standing in the country by building 100,000 homes a year. He had little time for the Soviet Union and does not seem to have been involved in Winston Churchill's controversial and abortive attempt in 1954 to establish an early dialogue with the new Soviet leadership. His brief period of office as Foreign Secretary under Eden in 1955 did, however, provide an early opportunity for him to establish his own direct contact, first at the ceremonial signing of the Austrian Peace Treaty and then at the abortive Geneva conferences on German reunification where, for the first time, he encountered Khrushchev, 'this fat, vulgar man, with his pig eyes and ceaseless flow of talk'.[8] At this stage the Soviet Union was an obstacle to German reunification, a looming menace to Western Europe and a growing threat to British interests in the Middle East, where Macmillan saw the threat that Pan-Arabism might become dominated by Communism and enable the Russians to 'turn the right flank of Europe'. The direct British–Soviet relationship did not take a high place in his immediate preoccupations at that time, but it was at Geneva that Eden invited Bulganin and Khrushchev to visit London. It was from this visit, carried out in the spring of 1956, that one can trace the route which was to lead through the dreary wasteland of the correspondence with the Soviet leaders to Macmillan's own visit to Moscow, the resolution of the Berlin crisis of 1958 and, eventually, the conclusion of the Test Ban Treaty.

The visit by Marshal Bulganin as Chairman of the Soviet Council of Ministers and Nikita Khrushchev as leader of the Communist Party was the first occasion since the Revolution on which the top leadership of the Soviet Union had visited a Western country. Macmillan had moved from the Foreign Office to the Treasury at the end of 1955 and had little direct involvement with the visit other than attendance at formal functions. As Chancellor of the Exchequer his main foreign policy concern at that time was with the development of the process of European integration, leading up to the Treaty of Rome and the attempt to reconcile Britain's Commonwealth and European interests. The Khrushchev visit does not seem to have made any marked impression on him – apart from the fact that, combined with Grace Kelly's marriage to Prince Rainier, it rather distracted public attention from his first budget. He commented that Eden thought it might be possible to do some business with the new Soviet leaders – not about Europe or Germany but over the Middle East – but there is no indication that Macmillan himself shared this view. The most that can be said is that the experience of encountering this strange pair at first hand may have whetted that curiosity which had inspired his first visit to the Soviet Union and have made him the more inclined, on becoming Prime Minister, to follow up the direct personal contact.

Then came Suez. It brought Macmillan to Number 10 with a shell-shocked government, a divided country and a deeply splintered relationship with the United States. He saw himself as faced with six major tasks: to restore confidence; to deal with the aftermath of Suez; to re-establish the relationship with the United States; to walk the economic tightrope; to re-appraise defence policy; and to manage the Commonwealth relationship. As such, the Soviet Union did not figure in this list. It was, however, to become a major element in the restoration of the British–American relationship. From that restored relationship flowed important consequences for defence, especially in terms of nuclear weaponry, and for foreign policy, not least in the hardening of French opposition to British membership of the European Economic Community.

In his memoirs Macmillan quotes with approval a letter, the existence of which he only discovered much later, sent by Winston Churchill to President Eisenhower in the aftermath of Suez. The whole theme of Churchill's letter was that if misunderstanding and frustration over Suez harmed the Anglo-American alliance, the Soviet Union would move into the dangerous vacuum in the Middle East, the North African coastline would come under Soviet control and Western Europe would be 'at the mercy of the Russians'. This was very much the argument which, with considerable success, Macmillan himself was to deploy in the course of 1957. It also matched, on the obverse, the Soviet analysis of the situation. The official history of Soviet foreign policy, published in 1980, noted with satisfaction: 'The years from 1957 to 1971 were characterized by further advances in the development of the world revolutionary process.'[9]

Macmillan's first opportunity came almost immediately, in the form of Eisenhower's initiative for a meeting in Bermuda in March. In his opening speech Macmillan said that they were meeting at a time which was critical in the secular struggle against communism. There could not, he argued, be neutrality in a war between two principles, one of which, communism, was evil. The immediate outcome of Bermuda was agreement on the stationing of American nuclear missiles in Britain and on the continuing of the nuclear testing which was necessary for Britain to develop its own capability in this field.

The Bermuda Conference was followed by a visit to Washington in October. It was during the period between the two meetings that Macmillan became increasingly involved in the problem of relations with the Soviet Union. At the time of the Bulganin/ Khrushchev visit to Britain in 1956 there had a been a plan for a return visit by Eden in May 1957. This was on the table when Macmillan replaced Eden at the beginning of the year. By then the Soviet action in Hungary and their intervention over Suez had produced so hostile a reaction in Britain that one of Macmillan's first acts was to propose a delay until 'a situation may develop when a visit would be both welcome to you and timely from the world point of view'.[10] Bulganin's reply was noteworthy both for its speed and for its relatively positive content, looking forward to a meeting, stressing that the May invitation was still open, but agreeing to consider an alternative timing. The Bermuda agreements on nuclear defence policy must have rung some alarm bells in Moscow. Bulganin followed up his first letter with a vast ten thousand word document concentrating on disarmament issues, warning against the dangers of stationing American rockets in Britain and calling for an immediate suspension of nuclear testing. Between the Bermuda and the Washington meetings, the correspondence between Bulganin and Macmillan continued. In the course of it, Macmillan was careful to involve both his American and European partners. It was a difficult exercise, because this was a time when public opinion was becoming increasingly concerned about the dangers of a nuclear defence policy. The Russians were skilfully playing upon these fears, while insisting upon separating nuclear from conventional defence and maintaining their overwhelming superiority of conventional forces available for deployment in the European theatre. As the exchange progressed, Macmillan found it increasingly tedious. The letters were, he said 'interchanged with courtesy, but on a healthy basis of mutual distrust' and there was in Bulganin's lengthy epistles 'little that I did not already know or disbelieve'. Foreseeing that 'neither the interchange of a long and argumentative correspondence, nor the almost interminable detailed discussions of the sub-committee in Geneva would prove the real road to progress', he began to think of some 'bold initiative'.

It was against the background of this correspondence, of Britain's own nuclear weapons test programme and of the launch of the first Russian *Sputnik* that Macmillan went to Washington in October 1957, still within his first year as Prime Minister. Looking back at the 1957 records, it is clear that the *Sputnik*, seeming to symbolize the scientific and technical capability of the Soviet Union and its potential for sophisticated military developments, had a quite remarkable effect on thinking in both London and Washington. On 10 October Macmillan sent Eisenhower a long message, pleading for a re-examination of the ability of the two governments to meet the Russian challenge on every front, military, political, economic and ideological and seeking a co-ordinated effort. The President's response was encouraging: 'I believe that all countries that fear

themselves threatened by communism or any other form of dictatorship look primarily to your country and to ours for the leadership they need. . . . It is necessary not only that the highest officials
of our two countries are close together in these matters, but that
this understanding and agreement should, to the greatest possible
measure, extend to our two countries.' The message was followed
quickly by the invitation to visit Washington. Informing his Cabinet colleagues of the President's invitation, Macmillan described
this as a visit to consider how the collective strength of the free
world might be mobilized. The United States government 'appeared
to be convinced that, in order to counter the Soviet threat, of which
the earth satellite was the most recent and the most spectacular
warning, the whole structure of Western collaboration needed to
be re-examined'.[11] The result of the visit was a formal British–
American Declaration of Common Purpose which provided for joint
measures of security against 'the threat of international Communism' and the 'danger of Communist despotism'. This was, in effect,
a restoration of the close co-operation which had been established
during the war and which, but for Macmillan, might have come to
an abrupt end with Suez. It was a co-operation which operated in
many areas, but, for Macmillan, the great prize was the promise of
repeal of the McMahon Act and the consequent renewal of co-
operation on nuclear defence. 'For the next decade', Macmillan
wrote, 'Britain's problems in this immensely expensive and complicated area of scientific development of weapons were resolved.'

There is no doubt that Macmillan himself had been concerned
about the threat of Soviet subversion, especially in the Middle East,
and the invasion of Hungary in 1956 had demonstrated the readiness of the Soviet government to use military force in order to
maintain its grip on the Eastern European satellites. A British nuclear
defence capability was necessary as a counter to the pressure of
the Soviet forces arrayed against Western Europe and there was,
indeed, a broad identity of view between the British and American
governments. On the other hand, as we have seen, the need to
counter the Soviet threat had not figured in Macmillan's own list
of his priority tasks on taking office and he had dismissed rather
cursorily Bulganin's threat of a rocket attack on Britain at the time
of Suez – 'We never took them too seriously.'[12] Certainly the correspondence with Bulganin made him focus on the relationship with
the Soviet Union, but it is hard to escape the conclusion that, in
restoring the British–American relationship and, in particular,

securing the repeal of the McMahon Act and the promise of American co-operation in Britain's nuclear defence programme, Macmillan was shrewdly exploiting the sudden surge of concern in the United States about the Soviet threat. It would be wrong to say that he did not share that concern. Sharing it, he could the better exploit it.

With the American relationship restored, Macmillan could turn his mind back to the wider issues of peace and war, the 'fatigue and worry of the long-drawn-out struggle against Russia', and the need to work through negotiation for some easing of the tension. He had sensed – not that at the time of the Aldermaston marches it needed much acuteness of perception to do so – that the Russian peace campaign was playing upon very real public concern about the implications of a nuclear defence policy and he was ready to take an initiative with the Soviet leadership. Having spent the Christmas of 1957 brooding over the problem of how to handle the Russians and at the same time rally support among the Western countries and in the Third World, he sent a long thoughtful and very personal telegram to Eisenhower on New Year's Day. In it he deliberately raised questions rather than proposing a firm course of action, but he made clear the need to maintain the nuclear deterrent so long as the Soviet Union had its massive superiority in conventional weapons. This brought him to the argument against the McMahon Act.[13] At home he followed up with a Party Political Broadcast on 4 January in which he harked back to the courage and fortitude of the Russians during the war and the hope that, despite the profound differences, peaceful coexistence might have meant live and let live. Hopes had been dashed. But he was still ready, using any means, to try 'to clear away the rubble of old controversies and disagreements and then perhaps to get the path ready for a meeting of Heads of Government'. A reference to 'starting by a solemn pact of non-aggression' with Russia brought anxious queries from Eisenhower and Dulles and a typically nervous Foreign Office reformulation.

Macmillan's personal engagement with the problem of dealing with Russia had now strengthened to the point at which it was a leading foreign policy preoccupation. For a time, the correspondence with Bulganin and the consultation between London and Washington continued. Eisenhower accepted in principle a Bulganin proposal for a Summit Conference, but insisted that it would not be useful unless Foreign Ministers had first made some progress. Immediately after the broadcast Macmillan had the idea that he should write to Bulganin, offering to come to Moscow to discuss the agenda and procedure for further discussions. On a Commonwealth tour, he telegraphed Selwyn Lloyd: 'Somebody will try to break the log-jam one day. Why shouldn't we get the credit? If, as is very probable it all ends in failure to agree, we shall at least have gone through the necessary moral and intellectual exercises to strengthen our resistance.' With Butler chairing the Cabinet and Selwyn Lloyd arguing the Foreign Office case that a visit would be likely to 'provoke anxiety and suspicion among the Allies', it is not hard to reconstruct the discussion which was summed up in a minute that 'the Cabinet endorsed the view that it was inadvisable for the Prime Minister to propose a personal visit'.[14]

Telegrams went to and fro and when Macmillan returned to London he took the matter up again in Cabinet, referring to the public desire for progress in disarmament and trying to secure a less negative and uncompromising line than that advocated by the Americans. Eventually he sent a letter endorsing Eisenhower's view that any meeting of Heads of Government should be preceded either by a meeting of Foreign Ministers or by confidential diplomatic exchanges. But he was still concerned that Bulganin might get the better of these public exchanges. His wish, as he made clear in correspondence with Eisenhower, was that 'we should come forward as soon as possible with a constructive proposal that will put the burden firmly back on the Russians and be understood to do so'.[15] Taunted in Parliament about the government's slowness in securing a summit meeting, he could only take the line that he wanted a summit, but he wanted it to be successful.[16]

He had, however, to wait while the correspondence which had been initiated with Bulganin was continued with Khrushchev. As Britain, the United States and the Soviet Union pursued the different objectives reflecting the different stage each had reached in the development of nuclear weaponry and as the Western European countries strove to meet their own varied national interests and the pressures of their own public opnion, it was a frustrating exercise. This is not the place to analyse the sequence of Macmillan's moves in this multi-dimensional chess game, as he sought to complete the British nuclear test programme, while waiting for the US Congress to repeal the McMahon Act and meeting the specious Soviet declaration of a unilateral end to nuclear testing. The correspondence was still taking its frustrating course when, on 10 November 1958, Khrushchev injected a sudden new note of danger by a public announcement, followed by a formal note to the British, French and US governments, to the effect that the Soviet Union proposed within six months to end the Berlin occupation regime and to negotiate to establish a new status for West Berlin as a demilitarized free city. Since 1945 and above all since the 1948 Russian blockade, Berlin had been potentially the most dangerous point on the European fault line, a point at which a Soviet threat to the Western military guarantee of Berlin's independence from the East German regime could, if mishandled, trigger direct conflict between Soviet and Allied forces. Macmillan had already reminded Dulles of the celebrated minute by Palmerston on Russian policy – always to push forward its encroachments as fast and as far as the apathy and want of firmness of other governments would allow it to go, but always to stop and retire when it was met with decided resistance. Firmness was clearly necessary, but, as Macmillan wrote in his diary on 5 January 1959: 'Are we really prepared to face war over Berlin?' So it was that Macmillan decided, as Bevin had done a decade earlier, to take a lead, revive the outstanding invitation to visit Moscow and then proceed by way of Bonn and Paris to Washington.

The visit was planned and announced as an exploration, a voyage of discovery, not a negotiation, but even so considerable political capital was invested in it. Throughout the post-war years of confrontation with the Soviet Union, no British Prime Minister or American President had visited Moscow. The Soviet Union, under Khrushchev, had apparently thrown off some of the domestic barbarity of Stalin, but externally its combination of massive power with capricious policy gave no reason for confidence. Bonn, Paris and Washington accepted Macmillan's proposal with reactions ranging from serious concern to mild scepticism. The risk that it might be exploited for wedge-driving was obvious. The Berlin stakes were high. An airlift no longer offered a solution and the military option was unrealistic. To abandon West Berlin was unthinkable. To threaten was to risk a bluff being called. Yet why, unthreatened, should Khrushchev withdraw his ultimatum? As Macmillan wrote to Caccia, the British Ambassador in Washington: 'The whole art of dealing with an opponent who is indulging in brinkmanship consists of not allowing him to get into a position in which he has to choose between war and humiliating retreat.' At the least Macmillan wanted to leave no doubt in the public mind that every effort had been made to reach understanding and agreement and to ensure that

Western policy was based on as good an insight as possible into the basis of Khrushchev's policies. Beyond that he needed, without threatening, to make Khrushchev realize the gravity of the situation and, if there were any chance, to induce some move towards compromise. In this, against many expectations, he succeeded. What is more, by his success, he not only averted a possible disastrous clash over Berlin, but may have made just a fraction of difference to the very fine balance of forces which eventually tilted the Soviet Union away from a greater disaster over Cuba a few years later.

This was the high point of Macmillan's involvement with the Soviet Union and it is appropriate to consider the precise nature of his contribution. It was in essence that he recognized the need for direct contact with Khrushchev, that he had the force of character to establish it and that, having done so, he was able to inspire a degree if not of trust at least perhaps of respect. His action was, in some ways, akin to that of someone who is confronted with an armed man, isolated and holding a hostage at gun-point. Khrushchev had the arms. He had shown that he was prepared to brandish them and, in Hungary, to use them. Berlin was the hostage. The key to such a situation lies in the psychology of the hostage-taker. The essential is to talk. The Soviet leadership, brought up on Marxist–Leninist dogma, had held power by virtue of that dogma and, in power, had been fed with the same cliches which they had fed to others. They were isolated from any real understanding of the West. As leader of the Communist Party of the Soviet Union, Khrushchev had inherited massive power. By nature he had both the crudity and the shrewdness of the Russian – or, in his case, Ukrainian – peasant, capable of rational judgement in relation to his own field of personal experience and of wild irrationality in relation to anything outside it. Macmillan was swifter than other Western leaders of his time to recognize that with such a man there is a need for direct personal contact. In character and background he was as far removed as possible from Khrushchev, above all in terms of political and personal sophistication. Yet there was in Macmillan's character enough of the romantic to bring some glimmer of response from even so earthy and yet at the same time impulsive and emotional a man as Khrushchev. The enquiring spirit which had led the young Macmillan to pay his first visit to the Soviet Union was still unquenched by the cares of Downing Street. As he wrote in his memoirs: 'The visit would certainly be a great adventure; it might also be great fun.'[17]

An adventure this might be. Fun it might be. But there was a difficult political hand to be played. It called for cold, hard judgement and shrewdly calculated tactics. No statesman welcomes the prospect of returning empty-handed from a much publicized personal encounter and the Kremlin machine knew well how to play on the temptation for a foreign visitor to seek some superficial agreement at the price of ambiguity. Macmillan was careful not to arouse excessive expectations. In Moscow he was neither to be seduced by the flattery of a generous reception nor deterred by the abrupt change of tone from blandishment to bluster.

There was nothing remarkable in what he had to say to Khrushchev on Berlin. There was little which could not have been said through diplomatic channels and little, if any, room for actual negotiation. In any case, Macmillan did not have a mandate to negotiate for the Western allies. What his visit brought to Moscow was the fact of his presence and the force of his personality. After every courtesy had been shown to the visitor and all the conventional, well-worn arguments over Berlin had been exchanged, Khrushchev launched into progressively more intemperate attacks on British policy, including a reference to the unsuccessful talks with British and French delegations in 1939. Nothing, he said, had been done and war had broken out. If that should happen again Britain would bear the responsibility. Macmillan remained calm but firm. Khrushchev, pleading toothache, ostentatiously withdrew from a planned joint visit to Kiev. Macmillan, outwardly unflustered, continued with the visit and found that by the time of his return to Moscow Khrushchev had recovered his good humour. The final communique was an unremarkable document, recording that the use of nuclear energy for solely peaceful purposes and the conclusion of an interim agreement on ending nuclear tests were objectives which the parties had in common. On Berlin, disagreement on juridical and political aspects was recorded. But, silently, the ultimatum had gone. Instead, by agreement to the holding of a meeting of Foreign Ministers, a dialogue had been substituted. Unproductive though the dialogue was, it meant that the American, British and French rights in Berlin could be sustained until, three decades later, Germany was reunified. The visit also brought bilateral agreements on trade and on cultural relations. These, between them, helped to thicken the network of non-governmental contacts which over the years would gradually open the closed Soviet society to the Western world.

In his memoirs, Macmillan devotes a hundred pages to the Moscow visit. Gromyko gives it eighteen lines: 'Macmillan's term as Prime Minister was characteristic of the Cold War. . . . The atmosphere was none the less businesslike: nobody banged the table and a calm tone was maintained; but nothing was achieved. In all the results of that visit amounted to the fact that a senior guest had actually come and a meeting had actually taken place. That was all.' The contrasting treatment speaks for itself. In formal terms Gromyko, the supreme functionary, may have been right. The essentials of Soviet foreign policy were unchanged. The mood was still one of supreme confidence. In real terms, however, Khrushchev had perhaps learned more than he showed. At that time, confident, impulsive and uncomprehending of the West, he had the personal power to determine peace or war. Macmillan had thrown all he had into the visit. In the face of many difficulties and on occasion of great provocation he had handled the discussions with patience, firmness and skill. The years that followed demonstrated only too clearly how far the maturing of Khrushchev had yet to go, but at a critical point, Macmillan had helped him to pause and consider.

The Moscow visit had convinced Macmillan that there was no point in conducting a quibbling correspondence by means of replies to Soviet notes: 'I am quite convinced that we can have no effective negotiation with anyone but Khrushchev', he wrote in his diary.[18] The logic of this was that there should be a Summit Meeting. It seemed that the route to it had been opened up by the Moscow discussions and Macmillan must have felt that, as a result of the visit, he was uniquely well placed to bring it about. It was not long, however, before it was demonstrated to him with brutal effect that, skilfully though he had deployed a weak hand, the British role was at best only that of an intermediary in a tussle for supremacy between two superpowers. So long as the United States held itself aloof from direct contact with the Soviet leadership, Macmillan could take centre stage, enjoy the role and execute it with panache. The years which followed were to demonstrate the realities of power in the global contest.

When Khrushchev resumed his correspondence during the follow up to the Moscow visit, Macmillan recognized the Soviet tactic of driving a wedge between Britain and the United States. He was cautious in his handling of Khrushchev's proposal for a formal nonaggression treaty between Britain and the Soviet Union. He was at pains both to inform Eisenhower personally of his exchanges and also to do all he could to convince Khrushchev, from his long and intimate personal relationship with the President, that there was no risk whatever of the United States willingly embarking on a policy which would plunge the world into a nuclear war. It therefore came as a most unwelcome shock, causing him 'great annoyance – alarm – and even anger', when, in the summer of 1959, without any prior consultation, Eisenhower issued an invitation to Khrushchev to visit the United States that autumn, linking the visit to a possible Summit in Quebec. Macmillan recognized this for the turning point which it was. In his diary, listing the likely consequences of 'this foolish and incredibly naïve piece of amateur diplomacy', he wrote: 'Everyone will assume that the two Great Powers – Russia and U.S.A. are going to fix up a deal over our heads and behind our backs. . . . People will ask, "Why should U.K. try to stay in the big game? Why should she be a nuclear power?" . . . You and we have been made fools of . . . U.K. had better give up the struggle and accept, as gracefully as possible, the position of a second-rate power.'[19] However, within a very short time, mollified by Eisenhower and much gratified by public recognition that it was Macmillan's own action which had broken the ice, he recovered his composure, accepted the potential advantage of a Khrushchev visit to the United States and sent the President a character sketch of Khrushchev, pointing out that, while his intellectual formation had been entirely communist, he was open to influence; that, in a changing world the Soviet Union would have to change; and that Khrushchev's policies would need at least to appear to be more responsible, consistent and law-abiding. He was looking further ahead than he knew. But in the short term his renewed optimism seemed justified. In a more hopeful atmosphere, negotiations for a Nuclear Test Ban Treaty moved ahead and preparations were made for a quadripartite Summit in Paris in May 1960. Again, however, Macmillan was cautious not to arouse excessive expectations. A summit could not be expected to solve all the outstanding problems at a stroke. There had to be 'continued negotiations through a long and extended period involving a series of meetings'.[20]

The collapse of the Paris Summit, resulting from American incompetence in the handling of the U2 intelligence flight, the shooting down of the aircraft and Khrushchev's emotional and intemperate reaction, demonstrated only too clearly that, for all Macmillan's attempts to prevent the collapse, his earlier pessimism over Britain's role was justified. Eisenhower sent him a gracious little message of appreciation: 'No one could have tried harder . . . to bring about a degree of civilized behaviour in the arrogant and intransigent man from Moscow.' But no such message could hide the fact that his efforts had been in vain. It is interesting that, looking back many years later, Macmillan was inclined, as he had been in 1939 and 1946, to look for a charitable explanation for Russian behaviour. Had Khrushchev, perhaps, risked too much in his attempt to achieve co-existence and even co-operation with the West? Had the inept American handling of the U2 affair given genuine offence? Had he reacted partly under pressure and partly under a real sense of indignation? In Parliament, Macmillan's tone was one of gloomy perseverance. This was not the time to retire from the struggle, but rather to 'labour on patiently and with faith'.[21]

Whatever the explanation, the result seemed to be that Khrushchev was the more determined to brandish Soviet power and, in the response to it, Macmillan was no longer playing a leading role. Khrushchev continued to address to him and to other Heads of Government letters which Macmillan found 'long, argumentative, false and curiously boring', but this was little more than a routine propaganda exercise. They clashed at the United Nations, where a shoe banging interruption of Macmillan's speech did little for Khrushchev's international – and probably also domestic – standing. More alarming than his intemperate language was Khrushchev's action in bringing the Berlin crisis back to the boil by announcing a decision to conclude a separate peace treaty with East Germany and building the Berlin wall. Gloomy about the failure of the West to mount an effective response to the menace of Soviet power, Macmillan had already formulated his 'Grand Design' to develop a greater unity of purpose between Europe and the United States. In his diary[22] he wrote: 'We may drift to disaster over Berlin – a terrible diplomatic defeat or (out of sheer incompetence) a nuclear war.'

Throughout the later months of 1961 and the first half of 1962, the Berlin crisis waxed and waned, the exchange of diplomatic notes and correspondence with Khrushchev continued and the whole complex trial of strength between the Soviet Union and the Western powers took up much of Macmillan's time. Increasingly, however, he was turning his attention to the Western European dimension of policy. It was concern with the menace of Soviet power that led him, in his search for a unity of purpose, to see British membership of the EEC as part of the Grand Design. The application for membership made in August 1961 would probably have come at some point without the Russian spur. It might also have been successful rather earlier, had the Russian spur not led through the route of Anglo-American nuclear co-operation to De Gaulle's veto. But without the Russian spur the application might well not have been made in 1961.

In the event, the risk of armed conflict with the Soviet Union was at its highest in the autumn of 1962, when Khrushchev attempted to install nuclear missiles in Cuba. As a result of his close contact with President Kennedy, Macmillan felt himself to be at the centre of events: 'We were "in on" and took full part in (and almost responsibility for) every American move. . . . The whole episode was like a battle; and we in Admiralty House felt as if we were in the battle HQ.'[23] At this point, however, the trial of strength was a trial between the Soviet Union and the United States. For all that he may have felt himself to be at the battle HQ, Macmillan was there as a trusted, senior staff officer, not as Commander-in-Chief.

In relation to other aspects of the relationship with the Soviet Union – in particular to the Berlin crisis and the disarmament negotiations, Macmillan was acting as a principal. It has to be said, however, that his contribution received only the barest mention in memoirs such as those of Khrushchev or Gromyko. As the Berlin crisis ebbed, his final achievement was the signature on 5 August 1963 of the Nuclear Test Ban Treaty, 'one of the great purposes' which he had set himself. Just over two months later his Premiership ended.

Considered against the background of British–Soviet relations during the forty-year period from 1945 to 1985, the years of Macmillan's Premiership, from January 1957 to October 1963, were both turbulent and dangerous. They were years during which the Soviet Union was perceived as being at the peak of its power and influence and during which the aberrant megalomania and the impulsive conduct of policy by Nikita Khrushchev offered both the possibility of dialogue and the menace of open conflict. The great achievement of Western policy was that, through all the muddle, the contradictions and the misunderstandings, the global confrontation of power and ideology was so managed that open military conflict between the Soviet Union and the Western powers was avoided and no nuclear weapon was detonated in anger. In this process, for better or worse, the tone of the East–West relationship was set by the United States and the Soviet Union. British policy could often be a significant factor, occasionally crucial in terms of influence, but never dominant. The primary task of Western statesmanship in those years was to establish such a measure of contact with the Soviet leadership and to maintain such a degree of coolness and consistency as to pass safely through the worst tensions while the inevitable evolution of the Communist regime took its course. As Macmillan put it in Parliament, if war could be avoided, the offensive features of Soviet Communism might eventually became 'blurred, blunted and perhaps softened'.[24] For such a task to be successfully accomplished it was necessary, first, to understand Soviet Russia, the working of its system, the mentality of its leaders and the nature of its people. This, from his very first visit and throughout his political career, undeterred by the barrage of official Soviet mendacity, Macmillan sought to do. Understanding was the prerequisite. But, on the basis of understanding, realistic policies had to be constructed. These, in Macmillan's Premiership were the policies of the Cold War. They could not, in the circumstances of the time, have been any other. They amounted, in essence, to creating and maintaining an effective unity of purpose among the Western powers; resisting Soviet pressure; and seeking any opportunity to control and, by negotiation, to reduce the more dangerous areas of actual or potential conflict. It was Macmillan's achievement, that, pursuing these policies, he re-established British influence in the conduct of relations with the Soviet Union, maintained a measure of Western unity and kept the dialogue going until the worst crises had been weathered. Time was needed before his successors could begin to reap the reward.

NOTES

1. Harold Macmillan, *Winds of Change, 1914–1939* (London: Macmillan, 1966), p. 324.
2. Ibid., pp. 405, 595.
3. See Alistair Horne, *Macmillan, 1894–1956*, vol. I, pp. 252–78. I was personally involved in the repatriation of Russian prisoners of war by sea through Odessa in the early months of 1945. The circumstances were very different from those which prevailed in Austria, but they were part of the same pattern of muddle and confusion in Europe at the end of the war. There was the same priority task of securing the

repatriation of British and Allied prisoners and the same need for pragmatic decisions by the military commanders on the spot. I find Horne's account of the whole affair thoroughly convincing.

4. FO 371/56763/4065; CAB 133/82; FO 800/507/SU/45/7.
5. 419 HC Deb, 20 February 1946, cols 1164–66; *The Times*, 21 February 1946.
6. *The Times*, 6 March 1946.
7. HC Deb 463, 23 March 1949, cols 375–391; HC Deb 467, 21 July 1949, col. 1570; HC Deb 469, 17 November 1949, col. 2317.
8. *Macmillan Diary*, 22 July 1955, quoted by Horne.
9. Gromyko and Ponomarev, *Soviet Foreign Policy* (Moscow, 1980), p. 345.
10. Correspondence between the Prime Minister and Mr Bulganin, Cmnd 380.
11. CAB 128/31 CC 74(57) CC 76(57).
12. Harold Macmillan, *Riding the Storm* (London: Macmillan, 1971), p. 165.
13. FO 371 135279.
14. CC (8) 58.
15. *Riding the Storm*, p. 557.
16. 582 HC Deb, 20 February 1958, col. 1521.
17. Macmillan, *Riding the Storm*, p. 585. I have relied heavily on Macmillan's own account in his memoirs. In relation to the Moscow visit I have, however, been particularly grateful for the advice of Sir Patrick Reilly who was at that time HM Ambassador in Moscow.
18. *Macmillan Diary*, 8 March 1959.
19. *Diary*, 26 July 1959.
20. HC Deb 612, 27 October 1959, cols 77–80.
21. HC Deb 624, 30 May 1960, col. 1012.
22. *Diary*, 25 June 1961.
23. *Diary*, 4 November 1962.
24. HC Deb 582, February 1958, col. 1224.

14 Macmillan and Nuclear Weapons: the SKYBOLT Affair
Donette Murray

INTRODUCTION

When Harold Macmillan became Prime Minister in 1957 after the damaging Suez débâcle, he quickly identified two areas that demanded immediate attention: the economy and the 'special' Anglo-American relationship. Whilst financial constraints required the government to pursue a defence policy more orientated towards nuclear rather than conventional deterrence,[1] in the aftermath of the crisis two conflicting defence policy strategies emerged. On the one hand, Suez highlighted doubts surrounding the reliability of the American nuclear guarantee and encouraged dedication to an independent British deterrent force. It also succeeded, however, in reinforcing the lesson that American acquiescence was at least desirable, if not necessary, in order for Britain to consider unilateral action again. Thus developed in Britain a curious paradox – a policy of independence as a means of influencing the United States, retaining world-wide prestige and national pride that appeared to co-exist alongside a rhetoric of interdependence with the United States.

Macmillan attempted to convince the United States to restore the special nuclear relations that had originated during the Second World War, citing among his arguments Britain's nuclear progress,[2] the threat of Russian technological advances symbolised in Sputnik,[3] and the need for American help if Britain was to commit to a test ban agreement. Fortunately for Macmillan, the American President was committed to reversing what he personally believed to be the unjust McMahon Act restrictions that had prevented nuclear collaboration.[4] Success came in 1958 and the following year when the restrictions were amended. The restoration of the special relationship and the rebuilding in particular of defence relations, however, sowed the seeds of problems that would come to the surface within a few years. Increasingly faced with the unprecedented technological and scientific changes of the late 1950s, Britain was unable to credibly maintain her independent nuclear deterrent force and had to rely more and more on American information and collaboration. By 1960 the future of the last indigenous British weapon, BLUE STREAK, was being reconsidered and the difficulties in maintaining the dual policies of independence and interdependence were becoming increasingly apparent. In 1962 Anglo-American relations were in crisis and Macmillan was faced with fundamental choices to make about his nuclear weapons policy. The reason was SKYBOLT.

CAMP DAVID

> It is an intriguing story, full of forebodings and uncertainties, of high political stakes dependent on technological progress, of a chain of errors of judgement carefully kept from the public gaze and, finally, at Nassau, one of the great confrontations in the history of Anglo-American relations.[5]

The story begins at an earlier conference at Camp David in March 1960. The opening scenes of this drama gave no indication of what lay ahead. A light-hearted and friendly meeting between the British Prime Minister and the American President Eisenhower in the tranquil surroundings of the President's Maryland retreat was typical of the good relations the two leaders had managed to re-establish. Co-operation in the field of defence had been at the top of Macmillan's agenda since he had become Prime Minister. As the two men now talked about this, Macmillan confided some of his problems to his counterpart, the most pressing of which was that the shift from bombers to missile delivery systems involved a leap in technology that was increasingly beyond the British national capability.[6] In order to preserve the British-designed and manufactured V-bomber force as a credible deterrent by enabling them to penetrate Soviet air defences, a new generation Intermediate Range Ballistic Missile was needed. Such a missile, BLUE STREAK, was currently under development; however, all indications pointed to the fact that the missile would enter its operational phase obsolete. Moreover, the cost was proving to be prohibitively high.[7]

Macmillan's government had made the independent deterrent a high-profile policy. To now abandon what had become the visible embodiment of that doctrine without having an acceptable replacement was a worrying prospect for the Conservatives.[8] Fortunately Eisenhower was sympathetic to Macmillan's dilemma and offered his British counterpart a new weapon – SKYBOLT – currently under development for the United States Air Force.[9]

The SKYBOLT offer was a highly attractive proposition, especially in the eyes of the RAF.[10] The missile promised to extend the life of the British V-bomber force which was facing obsolescence by the mid-1960s, whilst reaffirming the position of the RAF, traditionally the service responsible for nuclear deterrence, and all at a bargain price. The agreement provided that the United States would undertake and pay for all the project's research and development costs, leaving Britain to pay for the number of missiles she then decided to buy.[11] With Macmillan's acceptance of this arrangement, Anglo-American relations had entered a new paradoxical phase – the British 'independent' deterrent was to be preserved through interdependence with the United States. SKYBOLT was the linch-pin.

CRISIS

Between the easy days of the Camp David agreement and the tense confrontational Nassau conference, a crisis unfolded. Moreover, it was one that was 'compounded', wrote David Nunnerley, 'of drama and deceit, of uncertainty and distrust, of muddled perceptions and disappointed expectations, of high political stakes both won and lost, of miscalculation and misjudgement, a phoney crisis', according to Nunnerley, 'that should never have been allowed to happen'.[12]

The SKYBOLT missile was an ambitious project by any standards, requiring the development and application of highly advanced and as yet experimental technology to be used to improve the credibility of the manned strategic bomber – the B-52. The rationale of such a mode of delivery was itself not without problems since the future of this particular weapons system was regarded by many as no longer assured.[13] It was, as Henry Brandon reported:

> the most complex ballistic missile the United States had yet undertaken – more so than MINUTEMAN or POLARIS. The missile had to be launched over an altitude range of several thousand feet, to be able at high speed to resist shock, vibration and noise from a hostile environ and to be integrated in a unique way with

the mothership which, with its computer system, contains about 130,000 parts.[14]

As it became clear by the beginning of the 1960s that the Soviet Union was building increasingly sophisticated anti-missile technology,[15] SKYBOLT's supporters were forced to redefine its role, arguing the need for a kind of 'tin opener' to knock out enemy air defences, thus clearing the way for other bombers and missiles.[16] This 'defence suppression' mission against enemy air fields and early warning radar systems was also highly attractive to the British whose ageing V-bomber force was similarly becoming increasingly incapable of high-confidence penetration of enemy defence networks. The SKYBOLT missile would give these bombers a 'stand-off' capability, enabling them to perform the difficult task of targeting strategic locations within the heart of enemy territory without running the risk of succumbing to interception.[17]

Despite the confidence of the USAF and the Douglas Corporation (SKYBOLT's prime contractor), Thomas Gates, the US Secretary of Defense under Eisenhower, was never happy with the 'drawing board proposition' as they called it, but nevertheless decided to approve the missile's development heavily influenced by the lack of operational missiles the United States was able to deploy and the uncertainty facing those currently in development.[18] Despite this decision, both men made no secret of their concern and frequently impressed upon their British counterparts the doubts and problems facing the project. Douglas told Harold Watkinson, the British Minister of Defence, shortly after the missile was given the official go-ahead, that SKYBOLT was 'in real trouble',[19] while Gates urged Sir Solly Zuckerman, the British Government's Chief Scientific Advisor, to warn the Minister that 'nobody would gain from making a political issue out of it', adding that attention was now shifting noticeably in favour of the Navy's *wunderkind* – the POLARIS Sea Launched Ballistic Missile (SLBM).[20]

Macmillan and Watkinson were concerned, the latter suggesting that they should begin work on a response should the Americans decide to drop the project. Macmillan was sufficiently worried to ask the Minister of Defence to prepare a memo on alternatives:

if SKYBOLT should fail we shall have, on the basis of our present arrangements, no way of maintaining an effective means of delivery of the nuclear deterrent in the period 1965–70 ... if you think there is a real risk of SKYBOLT being abandoned soon, we must consider urgently what alternatives are open to us. There would be strong grounds for pressing the Americans to help us with a replacement, but we cannot do so effectively without some knowledge of the costs and timings involved.[21]

In conclusion, Macmillan advised that nothing should be volunteered to indicate either total dependence on the project or that Britain feared the repercussions of it being cancelled. The danger, recognized and duly noted for the record, prompted no more action for the time being. Meanwhile, in the United States, a decision to radically reduce SKYBOLT's funding in the last budget of the Eisenhower term virtually ended effective development and the future of SKYBOLT hung in the balance as American politics moved into limbo pending the outcome of the Presidential elections. In Britain, the Prime Minister and his colleagues held their breath and anxiously awaited an indication of what position the new Administration would take on the matter.[22]

KENNEDY

The new Kennedy administration initially backed SKYBOLT. Robert McNamara, the Secretary of Defense, was both worried about the current (and as yet undebunked) missile gap theory, and conscious of the fact that he was contemplating scrapping another star in the Air Forces' firmament – the B-70 bomber. Any attempt to cancel both programmes at once, the Secretary knew, would be tantamount to committing political suicide.[23] Ignoring a confidential report from a panel of experts recommending cancellation, McNamara instead allocated more funds to the project in the belief that Gates' reduction would not prove either way if the missile was to be a success or failure.[24] But as the year wore on SKYBOLT's future was again being questioned. Although McNamara was by now having doubts about the weapon he was not yet in a position to make a move against it. However, before the summer of 1962 had ended, McNamara's technical and budgetary aides were again urging him to close the project down recommending that it be dropped from the next budget in order to avoid a fight with Congress and the Air Force.[25] McNamara set the process of cancellation in motion, swearing his aides to secrecy lest the supporters of the programme find out and cause an ugly fight.[26] On 7 November 1962 McNamara met with President Kennedy and Secretary of State Rusk to tell them of his plans. In agreement, both men pressed upon him the importance of letting the British down gently on this and urged consultation. The Secretary of Defense himself volunteered to handle the cancellation, promising not only to tell the British but to go to London to negotiate a replacement deal for them.[27] Informing David Ormsby-Gore, the British Ambassador and Peter Thorneycroft, the Minister for Defence, McNamara then became embroiled in difficult budget details that prevented the Secretary from reaching Britain until 11 December.[28] Then, quite simply, all hell broke loose. McNamara and Thorneycroft met, argued and parted, shocked, confused and angry. As Ormsby-Gore wrote:

> suspicions, frayed nerves and bad temper became the order of the day. In such circumstances it behoved all in positions of authority to try and keep a cool head and strive to calm the atmosphere. The precise opposite happened.[29]

With no agreement reached it was left to Macmillan and Kennedy at Nassau one week later, to come up with a solution to diffuse the crisis.

CAUSES OF THE CRISIS

As Richard Neustadt discovered:

> Misperceptions evidently make for crisis in proportion to the intimacy of relations. Hazards are proportionate to the degree of friendship. Indifference and hostility may not breed paranoia; friendship does.[30]

There are three major factors that underpin the crisis: the different agendas being pursued by the US and the UK; a breakdown in communication between the two nations; and external events.

Different Agendas

The US government had decided to develop SKYBOLT as one of several weapons at a time when the only missile system it had fully operational was the ATLAS. Ambitious and complicated, the SKYBOLT missile would only have been useful for a tactical defence suppression mission if its development had been cheap and technically straightforward. However, since its inception in the late 1950s, the nature of strategic planning had completely changed as a result of the onset of the missile age, rendering obsolete systems that could not effectively penetrate enemy air defences in order to reach a target. During the course of its development, the missile proved anything but value for money and repeatedly failed when assessed against McNamara's 'cost–efficiency' yardstick.[31] It would, the Secretary explained:

> combine the disadvantages of the bomber with those of the missile. It would have . . . the bomber's disadvantage of being 'soft', 'concentrated', relatively vulnerable on the ground, and slow to target, . . . [it] would have . . . the lower payload and poorer accuracy of a missile, without the relative invulnerability and short-time to target of a MINUTEMAN or POLARIS.[32]

McNamara also had an agenda to rationalize of the Defense Department. While not exactly penalizing projects because of their complexity, he did target those that were incurring greatly augmented costs and time lags by refusing them the extra time and funding required to produce a viable system. Although the SKYBOLT system was far from technically impossible, according to Eugene Zuckert, the Secretary of the Air Force, 'the technical people downstairs had gotten Mr McNamara and the President in a bit of a bind by picking on the "technical infeasibility" or at least making dampening comments about technical progress in connection with SKYBOLT'.[33] To be fair to McNamara, the technical ins and outs of the weapons system was something he neither fully understood nor really cared about. Facing a defence budget of some $51 billion (the largest ever) and having spent $500 million on SKYBOLT already, the Secretary of Defense badly needed to jettison some excess dollars – SKYBOLT was costly, unpredictable and constantly late.[34] Instead of pumping more money into the project, McNamara knew that some two to three billion dollars could be saved if he pulled the plug now. Eventually, it was cost rather than feasibility that decided SKYBOLT's fate.

Within the administration opinions varied, not so much about the sagacity of abandoning SKYBOLT, but about what was to happen to the British independent nuclear deterrent as a result. For the most part the Pentagon, and particularly those in the International Security Affairs office, wished only to preserve the *status quo*. Many in the State Department, however, had very different ideas. Secretary of State Rusk, as Brandon remarked, 'was very passive', and seemed willing for McNamara to 'carry the ball', stipulating only that Britain should be given as much help as possible.[35] Many of his subordinates' thoughts, however, were more firmly crystallized, and ranged from providing assistance in a multilateral context to taking this opportunity to remove Britain from the nuclear club altogether.[36] As Rusk later admitted:

> British paranoia may also have been fostered by some in our own bureaucracy who wanted to use the cancellation to pressure the British to give up an independent force.[37]

In addition, major speeches made by senior American figures including Dean Acheson and Robert McNamara appeared to heavily criticize small independent nuclear deterrents, thereby increasing the suspicions of those in Britain.[38] It was clear that an element within the administration wanted Britain out of the nuclear club. What wasn't clear was how far this extended to official policy and the upper echelons of the Kennedy government. Even Macmillan himself was suspicious. He noted in his diary:

> it was difficult to suppress the suspicion that the failure of SKYBOLT might be welcomed in some American quarters as a means of forcing Britain out of the nuclear club.[39]

Outside State and Defense, the USAF and the Douglas Corporation had their own agendas, unashamedly based on vested interests. Both groups proclaimed until the weapon was officially cancelled in late December 1962 that SKYBOLT was a winning ticket, bound to succeed if given the necessary time and money to see it through a not unusually difficult development phase. The USAF, in particular, was fearful that cancellation of the project would effectively mean an end to any future the manned bomber might have.[40] With the B-70 virtually terminated, SKYBOLT was perceived in both Air Forces as a last ditch attempt to preserve their role as the nuclear arm of the deterrent.[41] It was not in their best interests to paint a gloomy picture.

Britain's position *vis-à-vis* SKYBOLT could hardly have been more different. Although Macmillan and both Defence Ministers, Watkinson and Thorneycroft, were well aware of the dangers involved in relying too heavily on the American missile, they nevertheless failed to take action to prevent a catastrophe should the project be dropped.[42] Despite remarks to the contrary, the fact remained that in theory and in practice, Britain's whole independent deterrent was tied up with the weapon. This worrying dependence should have been highlighted by repeated efforts by American officials to alert the British to the difficulties SKYBOLT was experiencing. Even though the most senior scientist in Britain, Sir Solly Zuckerman, was publicly blunt in his criticisms of the weapon, as Richard Neustadt discovered, 'it made no impact'.[43]

For Macmillan, reports of design problems and technical difficulties were something to be expected in such a complicated undertaking; not a new and worrying development. In order for SKYBOLT to be an effective deterrent for Britain, it only had to 'appear to work'. 'In English ears, a guidance system did not sound like a great trouble'. 'British purposes required only that the Russians *think* the weapon could be guided to a city' in order to fulfil the 'Moscow Criterion.'[44] Britain was not so much concerned with deterring the Soviet Union for it had the protection of the United States to meet this need, as it was with retaining some influence over American strategic decision-making and presumably over the targeting of the vast arsenal commanded by the United States.[45] Besides, Macmillan was assured, the SAC and the USAF were depending on the weapon as much as the British and since they were a formidable influence in the United States, traditionally dominating the Pentagon and receiving the lion's share of the defence budget; the fact that they did not appear to be anticipating trouble for SKYBOLT could only be interpreted as a good sign.[46] Even if cancellation was considered, Macmillan believed, Kennedy was an honourable man who would respect the 'moral obligation' to provide a replacement inherited from the tying of the 1960 SKYBOLT and Holy Loch agreements.[47] The Prime Minister also had other things on his mind. The Common Market negotiations were giving some cause for concern and his government had been long considering the possibility of offering de Gaulle some measure of nuclear-aid in order to smooth the way for an agreeable conclusion. Macmillan did not anticipate that the Americans would rock the boat at such a delicate time.

Thorneycroft also recognized the dangers inherent in a possible cancellation, even though he had come late to the story, inheriting the missile and the present problems from Watkinson. Ambitious at a time when the question of Macmillan's successor was very much open to debate, Thorneycroft knew that as the Minister for Defence he would be one of the first casualties if SKYBOLT were indeed to be cancelled. Unlike his counterpart in America, his power over the department and the armed forces was far from assured. Powerful RAF and Navy lobbies pressured the minister to support a course of action favourable to their interests. Thorneycroft was faced with two choices, neither of which appealed to him. He could either support SKYBOLT and take the blame for being incompetent both for allowing the British deterrent to become dependent on the United States and for failing have contingency measures in place. Or, he could denounce the American decision, declare that he had been told nothing to indicate that SKYBOLT was in trouble, and in private work to secure a better deal for Britain. Thorneycroft almost certainly had decided to do the latter by the time he had been contacted by McNamara. But he couldn't openly embrace POLARIS until SKYBOLT had been well and truly buried. As Neustadt remarked:

> It would be tantamount to treason, selling SKYBOLT down the river.[48]

Instead, professing shock at McNamara's decision, Thorneycroft waited, and having privately set his sights on POLARIS, hoped that in the crisis atmosphere that was building up, Britain would get POLARIS and he would emerge politically unscathed.[49] Convinced that POLARIS was the only acceptable alternative, he tried to convince the Prime Minister to adopt a pro-POLARIS stance. Macmillan, however, had a lot more to lose. Having brokered the SKYBOLT deal, its cancellation at this point would reveal not only the fallacy of the independent British nuclear deterrent, but in doing so, could fatally undermine Macmillan's own position. Retention of the British nuclear deterrent as his biographer said:

> represented a major plank of his political platform . . . the unrequited removal of SKYBOLT would be as if Britain were unilaterally disarmed.[50]

The future of the independent deterrent had been gambled on an unproved missile and when it became clear that SKYBOLT would be dropped by the US administration, Macmillan's government had no contingency plans to fall back on. The warnings he had received, far from galvanizing the Prime Minister into action, had served rather to immobilize him.[51] Unfortunately for Macmillan the alignment of his three key policies: independent nuclear capability; close Anglo-American relations and entry into the Common Market, was to coincide with SKYBOLT's demise. Aware that SKYBOLT was going to fall, he could do nothing until his meeting with de Gaulle at Rambouillet in a few days time for fear that the General might react negatively. The Common Market negotiations were reaching a critical stage that promised a decision one way or the other and the Prime Minister dared not show weakness *vis-à-vis* the Americans. Finally, Macmillan was also aware of the fact that Britain was just days away from completing the tests necessary to produce a nuclear warhead for the missile delivery system. Any action he might take ran the risk of upsetting this highly critical work.[52]

> McNamara's warning raised a horrid prospect: Pandora's box might open . . . the issue for Macmillan in November was how to sit on the lid.[53]

As the Prime Minister prepared for Nassau he knew that he should have heeded the warnings and taken action sooner to head off what was shaping up to be a very dangerous crisis. Depressed by his meeting with de Gaulle and as yet undecided about whether or not to try and save the SKYBOLT deal,[54] Macmillan calculated that the outcome depended on his own ability to stage-manage the negotiations.[55] Everything rested on his being able to appeal to Kennedy to honour the spirit of the 'Special Relationship'. However, the success of this strategy depended on the maintenance of an atmosphere of crisis and confusion until he, Macmillan entered to face Kennedy. He couldn't risk letting his plans become known, not least because if it were to be revealed that SKYBOLT was lost he faced dissension among the Services and the Cabinet. Indeed, Macmillan could not even be sure that a POLARIS deal would get the support of his Cabinet colleagues or indeed the country.[56] It was better, he reasoned, to return home with a *fait accompli* rather than risk being humiliated by a Cabinet split and damaging public opinion. Macmillan feared the repercussions of the renewal of the debate on the national nuclear deterrent. For some years, civil servants, Opposition and Conservative ministers as well as the Armed Services had been arguing over the feasibility and desirability of maintaining the British force. Any discussion prior to the Nassau meeting would almost certainly ignite this discussion and question whether this might be the opportunity to reassess the costly and for some, wasteful national obsession that embodied one of the central elements of Macmillan's foreign and defence policies. According to one Cabinet Secretary:

> for several months . . . there had been growing an uncrystallized, uncanvassed, latent Cabinet sentiment against prolonging the effort to sustain the independent deterrent . . . if a change had been put to the Cabinet . . . especially if it involved more money, all those latent feelings might have crystallized *against* going on . . . the hell with it . . . the PM was not unaware of that.[57]

The years had seen the contradiction between independence and interdependence become increasingly obvious and difficult to rationalize. Macmillan had no desire to lose control now.

Breakdown in Communication

Failure to communicate effectively turned a relatively simple policy decision into a crisis in Anglo-American relations. This case study is special in that the misunderstandings, misjudgements and general confusion can be traced back to almost all levels of government, and in some cases, not only between British and American officials, but between American and American, British and British. As the crisis unfolded, too many conduits of communication rapidly became too few.

It has been argued (somewhat lamely by the British) that they were unaware of SKYBOLT's rocky past and precarious future. This would appear highly unlikely. Between technical teams, the RAF officers assigned to liaise with the project and Zuckerman himself, the reports reaching Britain about SKYBOLT were detailed and plentiful. Watkinson had repeatedly warned the Prime Minister that the project did not look very promising. His successor, Thorneycroft, was aware of SKYBOLT's probable fate from as early as his September meeting with McNamara.[58] Yet all three failed to communicate the potential for crisis to their American counterparts. It was only when Thorneycroft and McNamara met in December that the British Minister laid his cards on the table. But by this time, in an atmosphere of distrust and suspicion, a crisis was unfolding. Macmillan, on the advice of Ormsby-Gore, had not spoken directly to Kennedy about the matter, deciding that it was more sensible to wait for the Nassau *tête-à-tête*. Kennedy had really no idea his friend was in political hot water until he was on his way to the conference.[59]

Macmillan did stay in close contact with his Ambassador in Washington (although it has often been claimed that the Prime Minister deliberately kept him in the dark about his intentions).[60] Ormsby-Gore's advice was sought on several key matters including whether or not Macmillan should contact Kennedy directly. He was instructed to determine if the President would have any legal or Congressional problems that might prevent him from being able to offer a 'lend' of POLARIS submarines.[61] The Ambassador was also told to make sure that Kennedy would not make his decision public until he had first spoken to the Prime Minister.[62] Ormsby-Gore's job was to prepare the ground for a successful resolution of the crisis without giving away any clues about Macmillan's intentions. His was an unobtrusive role and it suited the Prime Minister's purpose for it to appear that the British Ambassador was not privy to his private thoughts on this matter. In contrast, Ormsby-Gore's American counterpart, David Bruce was much less active although this was not part of any Department of State strategy. Bruce received little by way of information largely because the SKYBOLT issue was being handled by the Department of Defense and not the State Department. Generally aware of the situation but without any specific instruction, the American Ambassador could do little besides send off telegrams warning of the volatile political situation in England.[63] Unfortunately, as was the case with numerous other reports, Bruce's fears failed to make much of an impact.

On the American side the breakdown in communication went further than David Bruce and failure to effectively communicate official policy was evident. Those within the State Department who wished to see the playing field levelled, and Britain removed from the nuclear club, could not come out and say this. Instead, they managed to influence key documents enough to make it appear to the British that this was a Kennedy–Rusk–McNamara agenda.[64] The USAF and the Douglas Corporation conveyed a rosy picture that was far from accurate, even until the final and so-called 6th successful test-flight[65] in order to preserve their own lucrative and prestigious positions.[66] With such confident reports coming from these sources, officials were understandably less likely to take notice of contradictory noises emanating from other sections of the US administration.

McNamara failed to effectively communicate his plans although he had his reasons for keeping these close to his chest. Because of SKYBOLT's supporters in Congress, the USAF and among the Joint Chiefs of Staff, McNamara could not openly set out his agenda without bringing upon himself the weight of these powerful bodies. Although he was in mind to cancel SKYBOLT certainly from August 1962, he could not say so even to his British counterpart who visited in September, for fear that the word would get out and catch him off-balance.[67] In fact, although Thorneycroft later complained that McNamara should have informed him earlier, the Secretary of Defense was only in a position to do so on 23 November when Kennedy officially approved the cancellation plan.[68]

> He could not tell them SKYBOLT was about to die, no matter that he had decided so, for this was not yet an Administration decision.[69]

McNamara again confused matters by emphasizing that the cancellation was for predominantly technical and financial reasons. At a distinct disadvantage as a result of their unfamiliarity with 'the new jargon emanating from the Defence community in Washington',[70] the British had trouble accepting the new procedures, facts and figures that their counterparts were claiming explained the cancellation decision. Aware that SKYBOLT was not a complete failure – the British then wondered if some other motive was behind the cancellation. McNamara's failure to ensure consultation had taken place before the story leaked only further exacerbated feelings of bewilderment and distrust.[71]

Kennedy had little to do with the crisis until Nassau. Many of his staff were aware that it was going to cause political fireworks, but all failed to effectively convey this message to him. Rusk, Bruce, McNamara, Bundy and Nitze all expressed concern that outright cancellation without prior warning or consultation risked dire repercussions for the alliance, but their concerns appear not to have reached the President.[72] Although McNamara was aware that the affair had crisis potential, certainly before his baffling encounter with Thorneycroft in December he was confident that the matter would be resolved with the minimum of fuss. This was largely due to a fundamental misconception about the original SKYBOLT deal. The Secretary believed that under the terms of the 1960 agreement, Britain was committed to assigning her SKYBOLT-armed V-bombers to NATO. He therefore expected to arrange a straight swap – POLARIS for SKYBOLT under these terms.[73] This pivotal mistake guaranteed confusion and chaos and for many in the administration created an opportunity that was not to be missed. The notion that the American Administration was intent on forcing Britain to relinquish her nuclear deterrent was a popular one. Macmillan and Thorneycroft both recognized the potential leverage that could be gained form emphasizing this apparent 'covert agenda'. Although the Prime Minister noted at the time in his diary that the behaviour of some in Kennedy's government was highly suspicious, he toned this down in a post-crisis entry that seemed to absolve the President and his top staff of any wilful wrongdoing in this area:

> it is also clear to me that they are determined to kill Skybolt on good general grounds – not merely to annoy us or drive Great Britain out of the nuclear business. But, of course, they handled things in such a way as to make many of us very suspicious.[74]

External Factors

No event in foreign affairs can fail to be influenced by or to influence other events unfolding around it. In the case of the SKYBOLT affair, it was the Cuban Missile Crisis in particular which played a major role. The Cuban affair not only delayed McNamara's plans, but it distorted perceptions and numbed usually sensitive antennae to a potential crisis that officials would otherwise have had under control. When the administration returned to the SKYBOLT issue after the euphoric but exhausting Cuban episode, the problem was not given the same consideration it might have received had the administration not been so distracted. As one official remarked:

> If there had not been a traumatic experience like the Cuban crisis, SKYBOLT would have seemed a big problem. But it didn't. Golf was the order of the day, not (more) missiles.[75]

Likewise, for Macmillan's government, other concerns seemed more troublesome than the admittedly disconcerting rumours reaching Whitehall about the probability of a cancellation. Macmillan's leadership had never looked so precarious. His popularity had declined badly over the past year and the domestic policies he had championed like the 'pay-pause' and entry into the Common Market, had not been well received. Alarming electoral defeats had prompted the Prime Minister to lose his characteristic *sang-froid*, axing a third of his Cabinet in a desperate attempt to retain the credibility of his government. This crisis barely over, Macmillan's reputation was further damaged by the furore in the British press over what they called the impotence of British power. This was demonstrated, it was alleged, by the lack of consultation by Kennedy during the Missile Crisis.[76]

Macmillan's many difficulties had resulted in a hardening of his position. Pushed into a corner by domestic problems and a cutthroat Press, the distractions of the Common Market negotiations, colonial problems in Africa and uncertainties facing the NATO alliance, the SKYBOLT crisis threatened to unbalance him to a degree he might well have survived in an earlier time. With less at stake politically, Macmillan's handling of the affair would arguably have been more low-key, focusing on technical rather than political issues. This, however, was now impossible. As he prepared to go to the conference he noted in his diary 'we shall have a difficult time with the Americans in Nassau'.[77]

NASSAU

As the Prime Minister stepped into the warm, inviting air of the picturesque Caribbean island, he wondered how things had become so perilous. Why hadn't Kennedy intervened? 'Everything depended upon it', he thought, 'the future of the Anglo-American alliance . . . the future of the Conservative administration, the future of Macmillan himself.'[78] Although Macmillan was under no illusions as to the difficulties that lay ahead, President Kennedy had only just been alerted to the gravity of the situation. Having invited Ormsby-Gore to fly down to Nassau with him, he quickly discovered the full extent of the problem and the possible repercussions for alliance relations if a solution was not found. The two men lost no time in getting to work on a proposal which allowed the US to withdraw from the project and Britain to retain it while splitting the research and development costs.[79]

But Macmillan had already seen the transcript of TV remarks Kennedy had made just days before criticizing the project. Even if he had wanted SKYBOLT, the Prime Minister knew that he could not accept a missile so publicly denounced by the President. 'The virginity of the lady', he told the Americans, 'must now be regarded as doubtful.'[80]

The atmosphere was tense as the two delegations met for the beginning of formal talks the next day.[81] Macmillan lost no time in captivating his audience by a skilled performance, describing in an emotional, eloquent and wonderfully phrased oratory, the story of the two great nations. He went to recall the recent agreement he had made with Eisenhower allowing the United States docking and service facilities in Scotland, reminding his audience that this agreement which had caused both he and his government considerable political difficulties, though not legally binding, had always been understood as a quid pro quo arrangement. In light of this, Kennedy had inherited, he suggested, a 'moral obligation' to provide a suitable replacement. Having established themes of friendship and betrayal, shared glories and hardships, and an indivisible common purpose, the Prime Minister set about demolishing possible American arguments for not giving Britain POLARIS. In response to the American fear that such an agreement might seriously jeopardize Britain's chances of getting into the Common Market, Macmillan replied confidently that 'the outcome of the Common Market negotiations would not be affected by decisions about nuclear delivery systems'; agriculture, he suggested, was the real stumbling block.[82] De Gaulle, Macmillan told the Americans, had understood clearly that the Prime Minister intended to ask for POLARIS as a substitute when they had met a few days previously in Rambouillet.[83] As for the other allies, it was foolish he told his audience, to conceive of any adverse reaction coming from that quarter as it was widely accepted, if admittedly not liked, that Britain and America had a special nuclear relationship dating back to the wartime Manhattan project.[84] Anyway, why should the NATO countries take offence at a switch from the 'lame horse', SKYBOLT, to what was now the favourite, POLARIS?[85]

Kennedy for his part, although not unreceptive to Macmillan's moving arguments, had come to Nassau with very little manoeuvring room on POLARIS. In the weeks leading up to the conference, divergent elements within the State Department had united in a passionate attempt to prevent Macmillan from wresting a POLARIS deal from Kennedy.[86] Unwilling to incur the combined wrath of these elements – and aware that there existed a very real possibility that to do so would rock the political boat at a delicate time – Kennedy resisted. The president was under immense pressure to avoid giving in to Macmillan's demands at all costs. Having decried the existence of small independent nuclear forces, argued against nuclear proliferation and repeatedly refused French requests for assistance in this field, by giving Britain POLARIS, Kennedy would be executing a very public U-turn in US policy. Not only did it risk endangering Britain's bid to join the Economic Community, but it would also reinforce resentment among NATO countries, especially France, of what was already perceived as the discriminatory Anglo-Saxon 'special relationship'.[87]

Another problem for Kennedy lay in the complications a POLARIS deal would have for the Multilateral Nuclear Force (MLF) proposal, a central element in his 'Grand Design' for Europe.[88] For some time his administration had been working on a formula designed to prevent nuclear proliferation and to stay what was perceived as a West German desire for a strategic nuclear role. This focus on multilateralism was in direct opposition to bilateral nuclear agreements and in particular to any agreement that would facilitate the continuation of the independent British deterrent. How could America hope to sell the concept of multilateralism to her European allies, the MLF proponents demanded, when one of the key players, Britain, had just received help to prop up her independent force?[89]

On the other hand, the President was deeply troubled by what might happen if Britain didn't get a deal. He was aware of the growing press criticism at home claiming that America was betraying her closest ally.[90] Kennedy also now knew that little consultation had actually taken place and recognized that being seen to renege on a deal could have serious implications for present and future relations with the other European countries. Moreover, if a solution was not found, Britain might turn for comfort to the arms of General de Gaulle or even West Germany.[91] If this happened (or the survival of the Conservative government came to depend on Macmillan adopting an anti-American stance), his administration's whole European policy would probably suffer a debilitating blow.[92] In the end Kennedy was reluctant to let his ally down. He had a high regard for Macmillan and the close relationship they had built up. If this crisis was allowed to get out of hand the President risked losing possibly the one leader he felt he could really talk to.[93] Macmillan played on these fears painting 'with something of a Churchillian palette', according to Brandon, 'the future of Anglo-American relations', emphasizing that while Britain would not renege on past arrangements with the United States, such intransigence would inevitably lead to a deep rift in relations between the two countries.[94] As Neustadt remarked, the President was facing:

> an impassioned older man embodying a valued weaker ally, who invoked in his own person a magnificent war record, an historic friendship, and a claim upon our honour – in Eisenhower's name – to say nothing of one politician's feeling for another. McNamara and Thorneycroft had spoken different languages; these two spoke the same.[95]

Having tried to placate the British Prime Minister with a range of other alternatives, in the end Kennedy gave in over POLARIS.[96] He offered the weapons system in a multilateral context and Macmillan accepted, providing that he was given an escape clause that was necessary in order for him the defend the agreement back home. The final agreement stated that the force would be used for:

> The international defence of the Western Alliance in all circumstances *except where Her Majesty's Government may decide that the supreme national interests are at stake.*[97] (my emphasis)

CONCLUSION

It was, as George Ball later wrote, 'a monument of contrived ambiguity'[98] that both sides could claim as a triumph. Macmillan had pulled off a remarkable face-saving exercise. He had gone to Nassau with little to offer and a great deal to lose. The Polaris agreement had secured the future of the British deterrent, against the express advice of the majority of Kennedy's advisers. With his nuclear policy broadly intact, he had preserved the central plank of his foreign policy – the special defence relationship with the United States and all at a bargain price. His personal diplomacy and skill in utilizing the 'special relationship' to get what he wanted from Kennedy whose government's dislike of national deterrents and nuclear proliferation dictated America's nuclear weapons policy was quite remarkable. Moreover, the Prime Minister had secured the deal without consulting the military men (Defence Chiefs and Service Heads) who were left to argue somewhat lamely after the fact that their preferences had not been taken into consideration.

Unfortunately, for Macmillan, although the Nassau agreement reaffirmed the special Anglo-American relationship, it presaged a year overshadowed by alliance problems beginning with de Gaulle's veto of Britain's Common Market bid and rejection of Kennedy's Polaris offer.[99] The 'independent' British nuclear deterrent had been preserved but the cost was as yet undetermined. Nassau highlighted the fact that the national deterrent was independent in name only. Provided by the United States and targeted in accordance with American plans, only the warheads would be British-made and even these were closely based on American designs. Moreover, Macmillan was faced with growing demands from the United States to participate in the multilateral force discussed at the conference and move away from an unrealistic and unnecessary independent stance. Nassau symbolized the apogee of Anglo-American defence relations and the successful restoration of the special nuclear bond severed after the Second World War. The triumph was short lived. Dissent and disagreement followed soon after.

NOTES

1. For Britain and nuclear weapons see: S. J. Ball, 'Military Nuclear Relations between the United States and Great Britain under the terms of the McMahon Act, 1946–1958', *Historical Journal*, 38:2 (1995); John Baylis, *Anglo-American Defence Relations 1939–1980* (London: Macmillan, 1981) and *Ambiguity and Deterrence: British Nuclear Strategy 1945–1964* (Oxford: Oxford University Press, 1995); Ian Clark, *Nuclear Diplomacy and the Special Relationship: Britain, Deterrent and America 1957–62* (Oxford: Oxford University Press, 1994); Lawrence Freedman, *Britain and Nuclear Weapons* (London: Macmillan, 1980); A. J. R. Groom, *British Thinking About Nuclear Weapons* (London: Frances Pinter, 1974); Martin S. Navias, *Nuclear Weapons and British Strategic Planning 1955–58* (Oxford: Oxford University Press, 1991); Peter Malone, *The British Nuclear Deterrent* (London: Croom Helm, 1984); Andrew Pierre, *Nuclear*

Weapons: The British Experience with an Independent Strategic Force, 1939–1970 (London, 1972); John Simpson, The Independent Nuclear State: The United States, Britain and the Military Atom (London: Macmillan, 1984).

2. Britain's first thermonuclear device was successfully exploded in May 1957.

3. *Sputnik* – the first earth-orbiting satellite – was particularly shocking to the West because it demonstrated that the Soviet Union was capable of constructing the technology necessary for long-range missiles, making the United States vulnerable to Soviet attack.

4. Dwight D. Eisenhower, *The White House Years: Waging Peace, 1956–61* (London: Heinemann, 1966), p. 219; *The New York Times*, 4 February 1960.

5. Henry Brandon, 'Skybolt', *The Sunday Times*, 8 December 1963.

6. CAB133/243 Commonwealth and International Conferences, 1960, Washington Meeting, PRO.

7. Britain had already spent £65 million and was facing an estimated bill of £600 million.

8. The decision to abandon BLUE STREAK had been taken on 24 February 1960 but only announced officially after Macmillan was sure he had Eisenhower's promise of a replacement. *The Times*, 14 April 1960.

9. The SKYBOLT or GAM-87A was an air-launched two-stage solid-propellant hypersonic ballistic missile with astro-inertial guidance. It had a range of approximately 1,000 miles.

10. The USAF had been in touch with the RAF about the missile since 1959. See *Aviation Week*, 22 February, 1960; *Space Business Daily*, 10 December 1962.

11. Memo, Dillon to PM, 29 March 1960, CAB 133/243, Public Records Office (PRO) London. In return, Macmillan agreed to Eisenhower's request for service and docking facilities for POLARIS. Although the PM had wanted more commitment on a future POLARIS deal, when this did not materialize, he backed down, content in the knowledge that this could be negotiated at some later date.

12. David Nunnerley, *President Kennedy and Britain* (London: Bodley Head, 1972), p. 127.

13. Sir Solly Zuckerman, Oral History, John F. Kennedy Library, Boston, p. 28.

14. Henry Brandon, op. cit. See also *Chicago Tribune*, 12 December 1962.

15. During the 1960s it was thought that anti-ballistic missile (ABM) systems could be developed which would track and destroy the incoming warheads of a nuclear attack. Although both the Russians and the Americans deployed such systems, they proved to be extravagantly expensive and essentially unworkable.

16. *The Times*, 9 June 1960.

17. Clark, *Nuclear Diplomacy and the Special Relationship*, pp. 281–4. See also *The Times*, 9 June 1960.

18. At the time, the US had only one operational missile – ATLAS – and it was unclear how those in development (MINUTEMAN, TITAN and POLARIS) would fare (Brandon, op. cit.).

19. Record of Meeting, 21 October 1960, PREM11/3261, MM 46/60.
20. Brandon, op. cit. See also Watkinson to Macmillan, 12 May 1960, DEFE13/195 PRO. POLARIS was a submarine-launched ballistic missile being developed for the US Navy.
21. Macmillan to Watkinson, 19 Nov. 1960, PREM11/3261 PRO.
22. Memo, December 1960, PREM11/3261 PRO; Record of Meeting, Gates and Watkinson, 12 December 1960, PREM11/3261 MM 54/60 PRO.
23. Roswell Gilpatric, Oral History, JFKL, p. 74. See also Richard E. Neustadt, *Alliance Politics* (New York: Columbia University Press, 1970) p. 37.
24. December 9 Memo, Box 273A–274, NSF, JFKL. See also John Newhouse, *De Gaulle and the Anglo-Saxons* (London: André Deutsch, 1970), p. 195.
25. Richard E. Neustadt, *Report to the President: Skybolt and Nassau: American Policy-making and Anglo-American Relations*, 11/63, Meetings and Memoranda, Box 322–323, NSF, JFKL, p. 4.
26. Neustadt, *Report to the President*, p. 9.
27. *Foreign Relations of the United States 1961–1963*, vol. XIII: *Western Europe and Canada* (Washington, DC: Department of State, Government Printing Office, 1994), p. 1085, Doc. No. 399.
28. Richard E. Neustadt Papers Box 19, Government consulting, Skybolt/ Atlantic Affairs 12/62, Skybolt-Nassau (classified) Folder 2, JFKL.
29. Lord Harlech, 'Suez SNAFU, Skybolt SABU', *Foreign Policy*, vol. 1, no. 1 (Spring 1971), p. 49.
30. Neustadt, *Alliance Politics*, p. 72.
31. *Washington Post*, 21 December 1962.
32. Andrew J. Pierre, *Nuclear Politics: The British Experience with an Independent Strategic Force* (Cambridge: Cambridge University Press, 1972), p. 299.
33. Eugene Zuckert, Oral History, JFKL, p. 89.
34. *Washington Star*, 16 Dec. 1962; *Philadelphia Inquirer*, 28 December 1962; *Chicago Tribune*, 28 December 1962.
35. Henry Brandon, Oral History, p. 4; Clark, p. 361.
36. Telegram, London to State, 22 March, 1960 Box 1236 General Records of the State Department, Central Decimal File 1960–63 (RG59), National Archives, Washington, DC. This group known as the 'Europeanists' were a powerful element within the State Department. They believed that the 'special relationship' hindered the improvement of relations with America's other allies, notably France and West Germany.
37. Dean Rusk, *As I Saw It* (New York: W. W. Norton, 1990), p. 266.
38. Address by Acheson, 5 December 1962, Neustadt Papers Box 19 Folder 12/62 Skybolt Folder 2, JFKL and United States Information Service, United States Embassy, 16 June 1962.
39. Harold Macmillan, *At the End of the Day* (London: Macmillan, 1973), p. 343.
40. *The Times*, 27 December 1962.
41. As it turned out, the Air Forces' fears proved to be groundless. The B-52 bomber was still operational in the 1980s as were the British V-bombers.

42. Watkinson to Macmillan, 12 December 1960, PREM11/3261, PRO.
43. Neustadt, *Report to the President*, p. 20.
44. Neustadt, *Alliance Politics*, p. 41.
45. Pierre, *Nuclear Politics*, p. 93.
46. McGeorge Bundy, Oral History, p. 4. See also Neustadt, *Alliance Politics*, p. 62.
47. Telegram from Ormsby-Gore to Macmillan, PREM11/4229; Watkinson to Macmillan, 23 September 1960, PREM11/2941. See also Brandon, Oral History, p. 3.
48. Neustadt, *Report to the President*, p. 34.
49. Thorneycroft to Macmillan, 7 December 1962 PREM11/3716, PRO.
50. Alastair Horne, *Macmillan, 1957–1986* (London: Macmillan, 1989) p. 433.
51. Neustadt, *Report to the President*, p. 42.
52. Clark, op. cit., p. 349.
53. Neustadt, *Report to the President*, p. 44.
54. Macmillan was in a difficult position with pressure coming from the RAF and pro-SKYBOLT lobbies. According to Thorneycroft, out of a sense of loyalty and obligation to the RAF, SKYBOLT was still an option when the delegation headed out to Nassau (Thorneycroft, Oral History, p. 19, JFKL). Bligh recalls that the PM believed that it was better to 'try and play Skybolt along for another year to eighteen months in order to avoid political difficulties at home'. Note for the Record, 9 December 1962, PREM11/3716 PRO.
55. Note for the Record by Bligh, 9 December 1962, PREM11/3716.
56. Walt Rostow, Oral History, p. 102; Neustadt, *Report to the President*, p. 91.
57. Neustadt, *Report to the President*, p. 46.
58. Brief of 6 September 1962, FO371/166314; Memo 19 September, PREM11/3778. See also Zuckerman, Oral History, p. 28.
59. Neustadt, *Report to the President*, p. 89. Kennedy felt badly let down by his staff and complained afterwards that someone should have made sure he was informed. This is borne out by Bundy (Oral History, p. 4, JFKL).
60. Brandon, op. cit.
61. De Zulueta to Ormsby-Gore, 11, December 1962, PREM11/3716, PRO.
62. Neustadt, *Report to the President*, p. 49.
63. Ibid., p. 55.
64. Memcon, December 16, 1962 Box 317 meetings, NSF, JFKL.
65. Telegram, Ormsby-Gore to Macmillan PREM11/4229. See also Gilpatric statement, 22 December, 1962, Richard E. Neustadt Papers, Box 19–20 Skybolt/Atlantic Affairs, Statements and Clippings on Skybolt 1959–63. See also *Washington Star*, 30 December 1962.
66. Zuckerman strongly believed that those bodies fed their counterparts and contacts in Britain, as well as in the US overly sanguine and even false information about the missile's progress. See Zuckerman, Oral History, JFKL.
67. Neustadt, *Report to the President*, pp. 4, 61, 62.
68. Ibid., p. 22.

69. Neustadt, *Alliance Politics*, p. 41.
70. Nunnerley, op. cit., p. 132. See also Sir Solly Zuckerman, *Monkeys, Men and Missiles: An Autobiography, 1946–1988* (London: Collins, 1988), pp. 252–3.
71. Neustadt, *Report to the President*, p. 53.
72. Rusk felt it was essentially a defence matter and was happy to let McNamara handle it. While he was aware that it could cause problems for Britain, he failed to take notice of the warnings from Bruce that indicated that it had all the makings of a potential crisis. It is clear that despite warnings from some of his most trusted advisors, Kennedy failed to grasp the severity of the problem until his conversation with David Ormsby-Gore en route to Nassau.
73. Neustadt, *Report to the President*, p. 78; Adam Yarmolinsky, Oral History, pp. 61, 64, JFKL. This goes some way to explaining McNamara's confusion in London when Thorneycroft asked him for POLARIS without strings and seemed upset at the Defense Secretary's shock. McNamara was only informed of his error at a 16 December meeting re SKYBOLT! McNamara's unfamiliarity with the terms of the original agreement also meant that he was not aware that it contained an escape clause, inserted at the request of the British that allowed for cancellation of the project on technical grounds. Had he known, his job would certainly have been considerably easier.
74. Horne, op. cit., p. 441.
75. Nunnerley, op. cit., p. 137.
76. Not only was this politically damaging to the Prime Minister, it was also personally hurtful. In a Cabinet meeting after the crisis, he told his colleagues: 'we played an active and helpful part in bringing matters to their present conclusion, but in public little had been said and the impression had been created that we had been playing a purely passive role. It would not be easy to correct this without revealing the degree of informal consultation which had taken place; but this might be embarrassing to President Kennedy.' Rather than cause the President any trouble, Macmillan was content to let the matter pass without comment. The British press continued to harangue him about his role. CAB128/36, Minute 63rd conclusions, PRO.
77. Horne, op. cit., p. 432.
78. Nunnerley, op. cit., p. 151; Brandon, op. cit., p. 166.
79. Neustadt, *Report to the President*, p. 87; Harlech, op. cit., pp. 46–7; Note for Record, 1 August 1963, PREM11/4737. According to Neustadt and Ormsby-Gore, this 50–50 offer was never seriously intended as a solution. It would appear that its main purpose was to provide both Kennedy and Macmillan with ammunition for those who would criticise the dropping of SKYBOLT.
80. Record of Meeting 19 December 1962, PREM11/4229.
81. Nunnerley, op. cit., p. 153.
82. Record of Meeting: 19 December 1962, PREM11/4229.
83. Record of Meeting: 19 December 1962, PREM11/4229. Some controversy surrounds the Rambouillet meeting. The official British records show that while the two leaders spoke briefly about the SKYBOLT

problems, no mention was made, as de Gaulle latter claimed, of a joint Anglo-French nuclear force in place of continued Anglo-American collaboration. In spite of this confusion over a nuclear deal, Macmillan had returned from the meeting virtually certain that the French leader intended to prevent Britain from joining the Common Market. With this policy denied to him, it would appear that he made no mention of this in the hope that a deal with Kennedy might save the Anglo-American relationship and thus preserve at least one of his key policies.

84. Record of Meeting: 19 December 1962, PREM11/4229.
85. Record of Meeting: 19 December 1962, PREM11/4229.
86. Neustadt, *Report to the President*, pp. 23–31.
87. Note for Record, 1 August 1963, PREM11/4737.
88. The MLF proposal had been around for some time. First advanced by Robert Bowie as an alternative to General Norstad's MRBM scheme, the idea had been re-floated by the State Department under Kennedy. The proposal was for a mixed manned fleet (under Kennedy it became surface vessels rather than submarines), made up of participating NATO countries. The idea was that in such a fully integrated force, it would be difficult, if not impossible, for one nationality to dominate decisions or to seize control of the nuclear warheads in their possession. The scheme really took off after the Nassau conference in December 1962 and looked most likely to succeed in late 1963/early 1964. Almost universal apathy and opposition (with the exception of West Germany) eventually forced the Johnson Administration to drop the proposal in its entirety. Britain remained opposed throughout, agreeing only to participate in discussions about the force in October 1963, fearing that her continuing intransigence would only damage the 'special relationship'.
89. Memo by Bohlen, Neustadt Papers, Government Consulting, Box 19, Skybolt/Atlantic Affairs Folder 3, JFKL.
90. Neustadt, *Report to the President*, pp. 75–6. See also *Washington Post*, 15 December 1962.
91. Newhouse, *De Gaulle and the Anglo-Saxons*, p. 219. See also *Newport Press*, 13 December 1962.
92. Note for Record, 1 August 1963, PREM11/4737. See also *Wall Street Journal*, December 19, 24, 1962.
93. McGeorge Bundy, Oral History, p. 2.
94. Brandon, op. cit.
95. Neustadt, *Report to the President*, p. 91.
96. Kennedy offered among other things, another American missile uninspiringly named HOUND Dog. Record of Meeting: 19 December 1962, PREM11/4229 and a joint study group to be set up to analyse the problem. Neustadt, *Report to the President*, p. 87.
97. Nassau Communiqué: Bahamas Meetings: Texts of Joint Communiqués, Cmnd 1915 (HMSO, 1962).
98. George Ball, *The Past has Another Pattern*, p. 268.
99. Almost as an afterthought, Kennedy (and Macmillan) decided to make an offer of POLARIS on similar terms to de Gaulle which the General subsequently refused.

15 Managing Transition: Macmillan and the Utility of Anglo-American Relations

Nigel Ashton

The Macmillan years, 1957–63, have been described as some of the most intimate and successful in the post-war history of the Anglo-American 'Special Relationship'.[1] Perhaps only the degree of warmth of the Thatcher–Reagan relationship comes close to matching that achieved between John F. Kennedy and Macmillan in particular.[2] Indeed, the December 1962 Nassau Conference, when Macmillan snatched political victory and the independent nuclear deterrent from the jaws of defeat and humiliation has been called his finest hour.[3] Consider, then, this telephone exchange between the President and the Prime Minister a mere four weeks after the conclusion of the conference:

Macmillan I say, did you enjoy Nassau? I loved it, didn't you? I thought it was awfully good.
Kennedy Oh, which is that?
Macmillan The Nassau meeting.
Kennedy Oh yes – very good, very good.

Macmillan's official biographer, Alistair Horne, suffixes this exchange with the laconic observation: 'Kennedy's mind had evidently moved on.'[4] Perhaps, though, it points to one more general truism about the special relationship for which it would be unfair to blame Macmillan, and which is worth bearing in mind when examining his record in the field. In the post-war years, the Anglo-American relationship has always seemed more special and more important from the British than from the American perspective.

If one examines the relative international economic and political standing of the two nations in the period in question then the balance of their relations could not and should not have been otherwise. Britain's days as a pre-eminent world trading power were long since over. Her share of world manufacturing output by 1963 stood at 6.4 per cent compared to 35.1 per cent on the part of the United States.[5] Although the Empire and Commonwealth, together with her Permanent Membership of the United Nations Security Council, seemed to give Britain a standing in world affairs at the head of the second division of nations, just below the superpowers, the gap in prestige and influence was in fact a substantial and growing one. In terms of the crudest measure of power, Britain's total defence expenditure in 1963 stood at $5.2 billion compared to $52.2 billion on the part of the United States.[6] Moreover, a succession of retreats and symbolic defeats in the post-war years, ranging from the collapse of the Palestine mandate, through the Iranian oil crisis, to the Suez crisis, had created a *perception* of Britain as a nation increasingly unable or unwilling to project or maintain its power on the international stage. Such perceptions became as much the cause as the effect of a relative decline in Britain's international standing.

Macmillan held office at what was very much a transitional period in terms of Britain's international position as a whole, and more specifically in terms of the special relationship. Since it stands to reason that transitions are far more difficult to manage than the mere maintenance of a well-charted course we should perhaps adopt an appropriately less stringent standard in judging his handling of the Special Relationship. Before him stood three possible paths in international relations. The first was that of Empire and Commonwealth. If he bolstered Britain's commitment in this sphere he would please the Right of the Conservative Party and that segment of public opinion which was disenchanted with the Anglo-American alliance in the wake of the Suez fiasco.

The second path was that of Europe. Should he change tack and try to draw Britain closer to the union of the Six which was coming to fruition on the Continent? The perils of this path were evident. It would divide opinion within his own Party and the country as a whole, which was far from convinced that Britain's future lay in an 'ever closer union' with its European neighbours. Moreover, membership of the new Common Market which was in the process of being created might not even prove economically beneficial. Put simply, the scheme might not work. Forty years later the same dilemma resonates in different circumstances.

The final possible path was that of the Anglo-American alliance. Although the breakdown in relations over Suez might not make this a popular course in the short term, the legacy of close wartime relations, which had in part been translated into post-war international co-operation, seemed to make it an attractive course in the longer term. At the very least, Britain might be able to alter perceptions of her own decline through a renewal of her close association with the United States. Potential foes around the world would think much harder about challenging Britain if they knew that they could also expect to encounter steadfast US opposition. This was, at any rate, one lesson which could be drawn from the Suez fiasco. The Anglo-American course in foreign relations seemed perhaps the most appealing, and Macmillan could be forgiven for thinking that in any case a parting of the ways had not yet been reached. Surely he could continue to tread the path of the Special Relationship without turning his back on either Europe or the Empire? Events were to prove this judgement mistaken, but perhaps we should examine Macmillan's conduct of the Special Relationship, and the dividends he derived from it, before pontificating too much on the myopia of the course he chose.

To assess Macmillan's success in this field, let me propose five tests. First, and, it seems, most important, is how well the relationship functioned in periods of acute international crisis. In other words, how far was Macmillan able to influence the course of international events in a direction favourable to British interests through Anglo-American channels? Or, put another way, how far could Britain under Macmillan turn the projection of American power towards her own ends?

Macmillan's record here contains elements of both success and failure. For instance, one of the crucial theatres in shaping post-war perceptions of Britain's decline had been the Middle East. At the March 1957 Bermuda Conference, where much of the lost conviviality was restored to Anglo-American relations through the public camaraderie of Eisenhower and Macmillan, little was done to narrow the gap over Middle Eastern problems. As the *New York Times* reported, 'Administration officials privately said it would be unwise to overlook the importance of points on which differences remained or on which decisions were left open.'[7] Suspicions and differences persisted, despite Macmillan's attempts to rebuild relations with the President, and re-emerged in the response of the two countries to the Iraqi Revolution of July 1958. Publicly, the intervention of

American marines in Lebanon and British paratroops in Jordan was presented as a triumph of Anglo-American co-operation. Macmillan and Eisenhower exchanged open congratulations over the success of the supposedly combined operation, with the President noting that 'we can take special satisfaction in the complete understanding and splendid cooperation which was evident between our two Governments in these undertakings.'[8] However, in private the Americans had refused repeated requests for US troops to be sent to Jordan to stand alongside the British Paras. They had in practice treated the operations in Jordan and Lebanon as separate interventions.[9] As Macmillan himself acknowledged privately, the Anglo-American alliance had proven uncertain when put to the test in the Middle East.[10] On the other hand, one could still argue that in terms of international *perceptions*, it was more important for the US and Britain to have appeared to be acting in concert in the Middle East than for this to be the reality. Certainly, appearances in the summer of 1958 contrasted sharply with those of the autumn of 1956. Furthermore, Macmillan showed both in Jordan in 1958, and in Kuwait in the summer of 1961, that he had at least discovered the knack of ensuring American acquiescence in British action in defence of her interests in the Middle East. This, together with public protestations of support and co-operation, was perhaps all that was required from the Anglo-American alliance to bolster the British position in the region.[11]

Looking at the Macmillan–Kennedy years, the key international confrontation of the period took place over Cuba. Here, it must be asked how far Macmillan was able to influence the American President's handling of a major international crisis? Although recent research is sharply divided on the significance of Macmillan's role, there is a general consensus that his input did not substantially alter the course charted by the President.[12] This observation is not in itself all that significant, for it may well be that, as one historian has commented, Macmillan and Kennedy were in fact of similar mind as to the best way to deal with the Missile Crisis.[13] As to the importance of the support and counselling offered by Macmillan to the President there is a substantial divergence of opinion. One school of thought has it that Macmillan's role was to act as little more than an international Samaritan on the end of a phone line. He listened sympathetically to the President's telephone accounts of the decisions being taken in Washington, but was unable to influence them.[14] For historians of this school there is no evidence that Macmillan personally was able to do anything more than offer reassurance and solace to the President. Others, who include his official biographer, have argued that Macmillan's advice, understanding, and steadfast support helped to bolster Kennedy's resolve, and contributed to Khrushchev's decision to back down.[15]

Certainly, there seems little doubt that Macmillan's earlier decision to install David Ormsby-Gore, a close personal friend of Kennedy's, as British Ambassador in Washington, gave Britain a degree of access to the decision-making process in Kennedy's inner circle which was the envy of other Western allies.[16] Although it remains a matter of debate as to how significant an influence Ormsby-Gore exercised, his advice to the President over the question of how far to extend the maritime blockade around Cuba does seem important. Kennedy appears to have been convinced by Ormsby-Gore to move the blockade closer to Cuba against the advice of Defense Secretary McNamara.[17] This intervention allowed for a longer breathing space before any direct US Soviet maritime confrontation.

In the end, the verdict on the functioning of the special relationship over the Cuban question has to be one which recognizes that, for Kennedy, this was in the first instance a domestic American crisis. His first concern had to be with the security of the United States, and the survival of his Administration. It would be surprising if, in these circumstances, any outside power was able to influence his decision-making to satisfy its own interests. Taking this into account, the extent of the communication and consultation afforded Macmillan was indeed special.

In Indo-China too, although Macmillan was able to do little to influence either Eisenhower or Kennedy's handling of policy towards Vietnam, his advice over the problem of Laos, which confronted Kennedy in the first months of his administration, does seem to have had an impact. Laos was one of the four states which emerged in Indo-China following the 1954 Geneva Conference. Although supposed to be neutral, Laos' position was made precarious by the tensions between North and South Vietnam. During the course of 1959, civil war broke out between the central government and the Communist-backed *Pathet Lao* guerillas. By March 1961, the situation had deteriorated to the point where the new President Kennedy was under significant pressure from his advisers to contemplate full-scale military intervention. The case bears some similarities to that of Cuba in that the reservations Macmillan expressed at the Key West meeting about the nature and extent of operations proposed by Administration hawks seem merely to have reinforced Kennedy's own predilections. Nevertheless, by helping to forestall major military operations in Laos, Macmillan avoided the need for awkward choices to be made over any significant British ground force contribution. He also helped to avert the risk of a major superpower confrontation, leading one commentator to describe this as being amongst his finest diplomatic achievements.[18]

It is arguable, therefore, that Macmillan wrung about as much as could be expected from the Special Relationship in terms of its functioning in periods of international crisis. He was never going to be able to create a perfect uniformity of approach to every problem. For instance, differences persisted under both Eisenhower and Kennedy over issues such as Vietnam, the future of Berlin, and the handling of Arab nationalism. However, Macmillan avoided open breaches on the scale of Suez and was able to foster the appearance, if not always the reality, of two allies who would support each other in their respective times of trial. After the succession of blows which had eroded Britain's international prestige in the post-war years, there was something to be said for a period of greater stability underpinned by an apparent renewal of the Special Relationship.

In terms of my second test of the Special Relationship, its domestic dividends, one could also argue that Macmillan achieved a measure of success. Certainly, he was able to make use of the close relations he established with successive US Presidents to bolster the domestic standing of his government at several key junctures.[19] Here again, what seems to have been important as much as the substance of the Anglo-American relationship was its presentation. From the beginning of his premiership, Macmillan excelled in this. So, the pictures of Macmillan and Eisenhower strolling in friendly conversation at Bermuda in March 1957 were far more important domestically than the fact that beneath the surface major foreign policy differences remained unresolved. Similarly, although Eisenhower and his staff had major reservations about Macmillan's efforts to promote a great power summit during 1959,[20] Macmillan still managed to twist the President's arm to persuade him to visit Britain at the end of August 1959. At the beginning of the General Election campaign, Macmillan was able to bask in the reflected glory of Eisenhower's first visit to England since his wartime years as Supreme Commander of Allied Forces. The television pictures of the two leaders enjoying a cosy fireside chat, and Eisenhower's comments emphasizing the renewal of the Special Relationship, did no harm to Macmillan's re-election prospects.[21]

Finally, it seems clear that considerations of Macmillan's domestic position were at the forefront of the reasons why Kennedy eventually yielded to his demand for the Polaris nuclear delivery system at the Nassau Conference of December 1962. Here, surely, was a case where Macmillan's efforts to foster close personal relations at the summit of the Anglo-American alliance dug him out of a potentially disastrous political hole at home.[22] Kennedy proved willing to override the advice of his closest advisers in order to save Macmillan's political skin. Although some expected that the deal would still damage Macmillan domestically, once again his skilful presentation turned it into a dividend. It seems difficult to avoid the conclusion, therefore, that Macmillan wrung the maximum possible domestic political advantage from the Special Relationship, in sharp contrast to his predecessor in office.

The third test of Macmillan's handling of the special relationship must be its broader impact on other aspects of foreign policy. Here, we must return to the three possible paths outlined at the outset, and ask how far Macmillan's renewed focus on the Special Relationship hobbled him in his dealings with Europe and the Empire. These topics are dealt with elsewhere in this volume so the comments supplied here must of necessity be brief and impressionistic. In the simplest sense, the Special Relationship and membership of the Common Market were only incompatible because De Gaulle said they were. During the 1980s, when the Anglo-American alliance went through another of its periodic cycles of renewal under Prime Minister Margaret Thatcher and President Ronald Reagan, it was not credibly suggested that Britain must as a consequence consider withdrawal from the EEC. True, the renewed closeness in Anglo-American relations was indicative of a certain Euro-scepticism at the top in Britain. However, translating this back into the circumstances of the early 1960s, a degree of reticence and scepticism about the European project in high political circles in Britain was hardly sufficient grounds for the delivery of the French veto. Events at the Nassau Conference were no more than the pretext for De Gaulle's action. The fork in the paths of Europe and the Special Relationship only appeared due to the presence of a uniformed De Gaulle directing traffic.

As regards the Empire and Commonwealth, the Special Relationship proved to be far less of a hindrance in the Macmillan years than had previously been the case. This was largely due to the fact that Macmillan quickly came to the conclusion that Britain's interests were best served by moving swiftly to dismantle the African Empire. In contrast to the wartime tensions which had emerged between Churchill and Roosevelt over the former's refusal to grant early independence to India, neither Eisenhower nor Kennedy needed to chivvy Macmillan down the path to decolonization. There could of course be specific exceptions, such as the case of Cyprus, where Archbishop Makarios cleverly played to the US domestic audience in his campaign for the ending of British rule. Similarly, Anglo-American tensions emerged over the Congo Crisis. Here, Macmillan's concern was with the impact of the disintegration of the former Belgian colony on his precarious efforts to forge a Central African Federation. Kennedy, on the other hand, was preoccupied with the Cold War battle against the advance of communist influence in the Third World. Nevertheless, if one had to provide a brief blanket judgement as to the negative impact of the Special Relationship in the spheres of both Europe and the Empire it would be that this has been exaggerated. A renewal of the Special Relationship did not of itself seriously hamper Macmillan's conduct of policy towards Europe and the Empire.

My fourth test of Macmillan's handling of the Special Relationship is the personal relations established at the highest level – Prime Minister to President. Here, there is an interesting paradox. It would have seemed reasonable to predict that Macmillan would get along very well with his former wartime colleague, Eisenhower. Indeed, for much of Eisenhower's two terms of office this was so. Eisenhower greeted the replacement of Eden by Macmillan as Prime Minister with unabashed enthusiasm and, according to his biographer, Stephen Ambrose, counted Macmillan among the closest circle of his friends.[23] This friendship had of course been forged back in wartime days during Macmillan's tenure as British Minister with the Allied Forces in North Africa. However, Eisenhower seems to have drawn a clear dividing line between personal friendship and major affairs of state which became increasingly clear in the final eighteen months of his administration. Perhaps this division was a function of his military background. He could not allow major decisions of strategy to be clouded too far by particular personal attachments.

At any rate, Macmillan's efforts to cut a figure between the two superpowers before and after the 1959 General Election evoked considerable irritation on Eisenhower's part. This irritation first surfaced during Macmillan's visit to Washington in March 1959.[24] Although the Prime Minister went some way towards repairing the damage through his careful management of Eisenhower's visit to London in August 1959,[25] problems resurfaced at the failed Paris summit of June 1960. Here, the President was greatly piqued by what now appeared to be Macmillan's fair-weather friendship. The Prime Minister failed to back him up strongly in the face of Khrushchev's onslaught over the U-2 incident. Macmillan's attempts to salvage something from the wreckage greatly annoyed the President, who perhaps detected the continuing whiff of domestic political calculation in the background. At any rate Macmillan's efforts to persuade Eisenhower to beg Khrushchev to return to the negotiating table at the end of the summit drew an icy rebuke from the President.[26] As a postscript to this tale of what were, in the end, perhaps not quite so special personal relations, it is interesting to note that these two great friends apparently did not correspond directly for sometime after Macmillan left office. Eisenhower's explanation was that he had lost Macmillan's address.[27]

The Macmillan–Kennedy relationship, on the other hand, while far less predictable, became, for all its comparative brevity, remarkably close. Macmillan's efforts to build a bridge to the new President at the beginning of 1961 through his rather vapid musings on the 'Grand Design' seem, in the spirit of their later relationship, rather ironic. It was on the more fundamental level of a shared outlook on life, and a shared sense of its perversities that the two connected. During their earliest meetings, Macmillan's dry sense of humour evidently struck a chord with the new President who, in private, was wont to make remarks of his own in a similar vein. On the other hand, it is doubtful whether Macmillan knew what to make of another of the more prominent features of Kennedy's character: his womanizing. During one meeting between the two, Kennedy's attention evidently wandered, and, turning to Macmillan, he asked, 'I wonder how it is with you, Harold? If I don't have a woman for three days, I get a terrible headache . . .' Macmillan was apparently non-plussed.[28] Perhaps the problem was that while he frequently had his nose buried in the pages of romances, Kennedy was out conducting them.

For all their different experiences in life the Prime Minister and President were able to connect and communicate with each other remarkably effectively. Of course, there were occasions when the strength of their personal relations could not resolve disagreements over policy. Their final meeting at Birch Grove in the summer of 1963, for instance, was undoubtedly a failure. Nevertheless, cynics should not be allowed to denigrate the exceptional closeness the two achieved, leading Kennedy famously at Nassau to override all of his advisers to dig his friend out of a domestic political hole. Perhaps, then, the record of Special Relations under Macmillan at the highest level is one which on balance deserves to be described as a particular success.

This record, though, can only properly be judged when set against the concluding test of the Special Relationship under Macmillan. Agreements brokered using personal ties with the President might mean little if his close advisers, officials at a lower level, or political enemies, conspired to prevent them being put into practice. How well did the decisions taken at the highest level negotiate hurdles in Congress, and seep down through the various layers of the bureaucracy in London and Washington? Here, the record is rather mixed. Part of the problem seems to have been that, as Eisenhower put it in a moment of particular exasperation, Macmillan and his colleagues 'just didn't understand our parliamentary system'.[29] For instance, they placed far too great a weight of expectation on action the President could take without regard to the wishes of Congress. So, when, in the summer of 1958, Macmillan called on Eisenhower to mount a large-scale, ill-defined joint military action in the Middle East, the President cautioned him that this went far beyond the extent of anything he could do constitutionally.[30]

In terms of the Washington bureaucracy, although one could point to the nuclear field as one in which successful Anglo-American co-ordinating mechanisms were created, in other areas of defence and foreign policy senior advisers and lower-ranking officials did not always work together as their political masters intended. A good example of this would be the Working Group on the Middle East set up as a result of an agreement between Eisenhower and Macmillan during their talks in Washington in October 1957. Although the group produced an outline plan for joint Anglo-American military operations in Lebanon, such action was opposed by key figures in the US military and diplomatic corps. These included Admiral Arleigh Burke, the Chief of Naval Operations, and Henry Cabot Lodge, Ambassador to the United Nations. Their opposition no doubt contributed to the decision not to put the plan into action in the summer of 1958.[31]

As regards the Presidents' top advisers, under Eisenhower, British suspicions of Secretary of State Dulles were legendary. Mistrust of Dulles, according to Winthrop Aldrich, Ambassador to Britain at the time of the Suez Crisis, permeated the British Cabinet.[32] Certainly, the Secretary of State's handling of the crisis did little to dispel such views. Under Kennedy too, there were concerns about the tenor of advice on the Special Relationship given to the President by top aides such George Ball and Robert McNamara. The persistent British fear was that the President's advisers were working to force Britain into a Europeanist, multilateralist straitjacket. This judgement in fact does not seem to have been too wide of the mark.

On balance, though, these five tests of the Special Relationship suggest that Macmillan played what was a problematical hand in Anglo-American relations with a good deal of skill and a fair measure of success. Although criticized for his concentration on personal relations at the top, he was able to exploit these to achieve a measure of influence over US policy which Britain's relative international power and prestige would not otherwise have justified. Similarly, whilst it is true that the Anglo-American alliance was cited by de Gaulle as a pretext for blocking Britain's entry into the Common Market, the roots of the French veto lay in the General's desire for French domination of the EEC. The theory is impossible to test but it seems probable that neither closer nor more distant relations with the United States would have made any difference to the outcome of Britain's application to join the Common Market. After the débâcle of Suez, Macmillan's largely adroit restoration of the Special Relationship provided a degree of stability in what would otherwise have been a far more awkward period of transition. One would have to conclude by registering the verdict that, on balance, Macmillan was one of the more successful post-war British Prime Ministers in managing the special relationship during a period which threw up more than its fair share of international problems.

NOTES

1. R. M. Hathaway, *Great Britain and the United States: Special Relations since World War II* (Boston: Twayne, 1990), pp. 50, 70.

2. A. Horne, *Macmillan, 1957–1986* (London: Macmillan, 1989), p. 281.
3. Ibid., p. 443.
4. Ibid.
5. D. Reynolds, *Britannia Overruled* (London: Longman, 1991), p. 12.
6. P. Kennedy, *The Rise and Fall of the Great Powers: Economic Change and Military Conflict from 1500 to 2000* (London: Unwin Hyman, 1988), p. 384.
7. 'Detail Unsolved at Bermuda Talk', *New York Times*, press cutting, 25/3/57, Box 113, John Foster Dulles Papers, Seeley G. Mudd Library, Princeton, NJ.
8. D. D. Eisenhower, *Waging Peace* (London: Heinemann, 1965), p. 279; H. Macmillan, *Riding the Storm* (London: Macmillan, 1971), pp. 533–4.
9. N. J. Ashton, *Eisenhower, Macmillan and the Problem of Nasser: Anglo-American Relations and Arab Nationalism, 1955–59* (London: Macmillan, 1996), pp. 165–89.
10. Horne, *Macmillan, 1957–1986*, p. 98.
11. For further discussion of the Kuwaiti operation see: N. J. Ashton, *Eisenhower, Macmillan and the Problem of Nasser*, pp. 220–32; 'A Microcosm of Decline: British Loss of Nerve and Military Intervention in Jordan and Kuwait, 1958 and 1961', *The Historical Journal*, vol. 40, no. 4 (1997).
12. There is a substantial body of recent research on the Cuban missile crisis. Most relevant here are two contributions which look directly at the British role: G. D. Rawnsley, 'How Special is Special? The Anglo-American Alliance During the Cuban Missile Crisis', *Contemporary Record*, vol. 9, no. 3 (Winter 1995), pp. 586–601; P. G. Boyle, 'The British Government's View of the Cuban Missile Crisis', *Contemporary British History*, vol. 10, no. 3 (Autumn 1996), pp. 22–38.
13. Boyle, 'The British Government's View of the Cuban Missile Crisis', p. 36.
14. Rawnsley, 'How Special is Special? The Anglo-American Alliance During the Cuban Missile Crisis', p. 590; R. Lamb, *The Macmillan Years, 1957–1963: The Emerging Truth* (London: John Murray, 1995), p. 356; J. Turner, *Macmillan* (London: Longman, 1994), pp. 165–6.
15. Boyle, 'The British Government's View of the Cuban Missile Crisis', pp. 34–6; Horne, *Macmillan, 1957–1986*, pp. 382–4.
16. Horne, *Macmillan, 1957–1986*, p. 368; Lamb, *The Macmillan Years*, pp. 352–3, 356; Boyle, 'The British Government's View of the Cuban Missile Crisis', pp. 22–3; Rawnsley, 'How Special is Special? The Anglo-American Alliance During the Cuban Missile Crisis', pp. 588–90. Once again, Horne and Boyle argue that Ormsby-Gore's role was significant, while Lamb and Rawnsley contend the opposite.
17. Horne, *Macmillan, 1957–1986*, p. 369; Rawnsley, 'How Special is Special? The Anglo-American Alliance During the Cuban Missile Crisis', p. 588; Boyle, 'The British Government's View of the Cuban Missile Crisis', p. 26. At no point does Rawnsley manage to refute the specific contention that Ormsby-Gore swayed the President's decision to reduce the perimeter of the blockade.
18. Lamb, *The Macmillan Years, 1957–1963: The Emerging Truth*, p. 394.

19. This test relates to the specific political dividends of the Special Relationship. Depending on one's perspective, it could of course be argued that the survival of this particular government and the advancement of the national interest were not necessarily in harmony.
20. For Macmillan's summitry see R. Aldous, '"A Family Affair": Harold Macmillan and the Art of Personal Diplomacy', in R. Aldous and S. Lee (eds), *Harold Macmillan and Britain's World Role* (London: Macmillan, 1996), pp. 9–36; and R. Aldous, *The Last Summiteer* (Bangor: Headstart History Press, 1996).
21. Horne, *Macmillan, 1957–1986*, pp. 147–8; Lamb, *The Macmillan Years, 1957–1963: The Emerging Truth*, p. 59.
22. J. Melissen, 'Pre-Summit Diplomacy: Britain, the United States and the Nassau Conference, December 1962', *Diplomacy and Statecraft*, vol. 7, no. 3 (November 1996), pp. 678–82. Melissen's penetrative analysis reasserts the vital importance of personal diplomacy at the summit in resolving problems which are effectively intractable at lower levels.
23. S. Ambrose, *Eisenhower: Soldier and President* (New York: Touchstone, 1990), pp. 421–2.
24. Horne, *Macmillan, 1957–1986*, pp. 146–7.
25. Aldous, '"A Family Affair"', in Aldous and Lee (eds), *Harold Macmillan and Britain's World Role*, pp. 22–3.
26. Ibid., pp. 23–5.
27. Horne, *Macmillan, 1957–1986*, p. 588. It should be noted that Horne puts a very different gloss on this loss, and subsequent re-establishment, of contact.
28. Horne, *Macmillan, 1957–1986*, pp. 289–90.
29. Ashton, *Eisenhower, Macmillan and the Problem of Nasser: Anglo-American Relations and Arab Nationalism, 1955–59*, pp. 24–5.
30. Ibid., p. 171. It should be noted that ways around such constitutional limitations could be found in exceptional circumstances, as illustrated by one of Eisenhower's successors in office, Lyndon Johnson.
31. Ibid., pp. 152, 170.
32. Winthrop Aldrich, interviewed 15 July 1964, John Foster Dulles Papers, Oral History, Seeley G. Mudd Library, Princeton, NJ.

Index

Jed Talks #2

Away from the Things of Man

JED MCKENNA

Contents

The world wants to be deceived,
so let it be deceived.

Petronius

> The 'monk' - known only as Penis
> Baba - can be seen fiddling under
> his robes while he apparently
> attaches a rope to his private
> parts.
> After the white rope is tied to
> the car before he staggers backwards,
> pulling the heavy vehicle around
> 100ft.
> 'Baba' said: "It is not art. It is
> the power of God - the power of
> devotion.
> "Any person can go to any extent
> by doing devotion."

Obviously, no one can claim to be an enlightened spiritual master if they can't pull at least a stacked washer/dryer set with their tethered member. Now that a true spiritual master has appeared in the world, I will retire and not return until I can not only *pull* a car in so notable a manner, but squat, clean and jerk it as well.

On second thought, I'm not really a big devotion guy so maybe I'll just stick with the truth angle and leave the Indian rope tricks to the fakirs. Let's start the book.

Genuine Learning

All genuine learning is active, not passive. It involves the use of the mind, not just the memory. It is a process of discovery, in which the student is the main agent, not the teacher.

Mortimer Adler

A FTER A TALK I HAD RECENTLY GIVEN, a young woman approached and asked me to give another. She introduced herself as Miss Flowers and told me she was a fourth-grade teacher and asked if I would give her class a career talk on the life of an author.

"Sure," I said, "if you're sure."

"Sure I'm sure," she said brightly. "What could go wrong?"

So I presented myself at the appointed time and place. Being in a classroom brought back weird memories, especially when I looked above the blackboard and saw the long-despised clock. I might wish time would move more slowly these days, but back then, during my own failed indoctrination, it was painfully slow.

"Mr. McKenna has written several books," Miss Flowers told the assembled halfborns, "so I asked him to join us today and tell us about the life of an author. What are his work habits, how he knows what to write about, where he gets his ideas, what books he reads and things like that. Mr. McKenna?"

I step front and center and lean on the desk.

"Good morning, young people."

I get a few piddly good mornings in return.

"So, what have they been teaching you guys lately?" I ask by way of an icebreaker.

"History, like the revolution and the constitution and the Boxer Rebellion," comes one response.

"How to do science," says one.

"Long division," says another.

"Reading better, like whole books, even."

"How to write cursive."

"Decimals and fractions and stuff."

"How the earth is a ball and goes around the sun," says a boy.

"Root words and prefixes and suffixes."

"How to be responsible and have morals."

"That sounds like fun," I say, *fun* being a euphemism for the torment of the damned.

"What do you do?" one of the little darlings asks me.

"Well, I'm not really sure," I say. "I kind of write books about stuff."

"What stuff?"

"Well, grown-up stuff, I guess."

"Like dirty stuff?"

Lots of giggles.

"No, more like spiritual stuff."

"What does spiritual mean?"

"I'm not really sure."

"You write books about it but you don't know what it means?"

"Yep."

"Do you write about religious stuff?"

"Sometimes, not much. More like practical philosophy stuff."

"What's philosophy?"

"It's like thinking about things, like what's *really* going on around here."

They all look around to see if anything weird is going on, but it all looks pretty normal.

"What does it mean that it's practical?"

"That it's not just stuff you think about, it's stuff that actually makes a difference."

"Can you talk about the stuff you write books about?"

keep appearing wherever you go and disappearing wherever you leave."

"How would that even work?"

"I don't know," I say. "Maybe the real you is the part that watches everything so that even your thoughts and feelings are a part of pretend you, not real you."

That causes a minor uproar.

"Or, maybe you're not just *in* the game, maybe you *are* the game. Maybe you and the game are the same thing. I mean, your brain is a very powerful computer, it's just made of different stuff, right?"

They're not sure they agree.

"And this is the kind of stuff you write books about?"

"Yep, like what if you found out right now that you're inside a game or a computer or a dream? What if you woke up and realized that nothing in your whole life has ever been real?"

"Then what *is* real?" asks Tad.

"Congratulations," I say, "you have just asked a very good philosophical question."

-☼-

"What about when we die?"

"I don't know. Maybe death isn't real either. Maybe instead of lives, we have different games, like we just play one character in one game and when it's over we start a new game as a different character."

"Cool!"

8

"Pretend you're sitting alone in a dark theater watching a movie, and suddenly the power goes out. You were really getting into the movie, but now there's nothing playing so you're just sitting alone in the dark. But then the power comes back on and there's a different movie playing, so now you watch the new one and forget the old one. One minute you're a teenager in love running on a beach, and the next minute you're a soldier or a nurse in wartime, and then the movie changes again and you're a kid sitting in a classroom talking about how life is like the movies, but you don't remember those other ones, you only know about the one you're in. Maybe that's what life and death are like; you're playing one level in a game and you come to the end, and then you're at the beginning of the next level, and the same way it's hard to remember dreams, it's also hard to remember your other levels."

"Sometimes I don't dream at all," says one of the boys, "and my daddy says he never dreams."

"Maybe he just doesn't remember," I say. "We don't know what memory is or how it works, so if we don't control it, maybe it controls us. What if you controlled someone else's memory, think of what you could do. You could turn off real parts and put in fake parts, right? You could make them believe anything. You could make them forget who they are and think they're someone else, and they wouldn't know, right?"

They kind of nod and think about it.

"Then how do we know that's not happening to us right now?" asks the girl next to Tad.

"That's another very good philosophical question," I say.

✵

Miss Flowers gently reminds me that I'm supposed to be telling the children about the career of writing, not undermining their concept of reality.

✵

"What about radioisotopes?" asks a girl dressed like a pop star. "Dr. Fischer says..."

"Who?"

"He's an eighth grade science teacher," Miss Flowers informs me. "He visits us once a week for a science talk. Last week he told us about gravity."

"Okay, so Dr. Fischer might be a very *smart* man, but he's not very good at *thinking*. That's an important thing you can understand if you try. Trying to understand, instead of just believing what you're told, *is* good thinking. We believe that people who are very smart are also very good at thinking, but very smart people can be very bad at thinking, and not-smart people can be very good at thinking."

"Which one are you?"

"I'm a regular person who is very good at thinking."

"But not because you're very smart?"

"No, because I try very hard. So the good news is even if you're not super smart, you can still be a very good thinker."

"But we don't have to just think hard," says one internate.

"Right, we have to think *better*," says another.

"And we have to be honest," says a third, "we can't just pretend-think, we have to really do it."

"Very good," I say. "You guys came up with that just by thinking a little bit. Imagine what you could do if you thought a lot."

※

This was a good learning experience for me too. I looked over at Miss Flowers and learned what the word *glowering* meant.

※

"Life is like a big game of make-believe that everyone is playing all the time," I continue. "Make-believe means pretending something is real that isn't real, so basically, we're all lying all the time. Your moms and dads are liars, the people at your church are liars, even Miss Flowers and Dr. Fischer are liars. It's not really a bad thing, it's just how everything works."

"So you're a liar too?"

"Yes I am."

"So why should we believe you?"

"Why should you believe anyone? You can think for yourself."

"So when we grow up, do we have to be liars too?" asks a sniffly boy in the front row.

"Yes," I say. "You're already trapped in the system, so you just have to make the best of it. Life is all make-believe, and the better you pretend, the better you get along with everyone else because they're all pretending too. So, let's use an example. What's a game everyone knows?"

"Monopoly!"

"Texas Hold-Em!"

"Truth-or-Dare!"

"Doctor!"

"Okay, stop. Monopoly is fine. I've never heard of those other ones."

"Liar! Liar!" they all burst out yelling and laughing.

"Who knows how to play Monopoly?"

All hands go up.

"Okay, and when you're done playing, whether you win or lose, where do all the hotels and all the money and properties go?"

"Back in the box," they all shout.

"Right. No one really gets rich or goes bankrupt, everyone is the same after the game as they were before the game, but the game is exciting and fun because you're pretending it's real. You don't really get any railroads or hotels, or even ten dollars for placing second in a beauty contest. The winner is only better than the loser inside the make-believe world of the game. They say that when a game of chess is over, the big strong

king and the weak little pawns all go back in the same box. That's how life is. It's all terribly exciting and important when you're playing, but then it's over and all the stuff goes back in the box and the box goes back in the closet, so it's all just make-believe."

✲

"My grammy just died last year," says a freckly little girl. "Mommy says she's still alive with God. Is that really true?"

"No, that's just how grownups play make-believe. People are made up of two different parts; one part is like the part of you that watches everything, and the other part is like everything you see and hear and feel, and all your opinions and ideas about yourself and the world and your memories and everything. Well, the part of your grandma that was her feelings and her thoughts is dead, but the watching part is still alive."

"So the watching part is her soul?"

"Yes, kind of. Not really, no."

Miss Flowers rubs her temples vigorously.

"Will I ever get to see her again? Like in heaven?"

"Maybe, but just because you see something doesn't mean it's real, it just means you see it."

"How come is that?"

"You see things in dreams and in your imagination and on TV that you know aren't really real, right?"

"Yeah, like flying sharks and stuff."

"Well, it's the same thing with your dead grandmother."

"So my dead grammy is like a flying shark?"

"Exactly."

✵

"Mr. McKenna, I'm not sure this is a good idea," whispers Miss Flowers behind me.

"That would be a matter of context," I whisper back.

"In the context of me keeping my job!" she whispers through clenched teeth.

"No ma'am," I concur, "this is not a good idea in that context."

✵

"My parents say that our minister is our shepherd," says the only girl not wearing pants, (by which I mean, she's wearing a dress), "and that we are like sheep in his flock."

"That's right."

"It is?"

"Uh, yep. Your minister is like a shepherd and you are like the sheep in his flock. That's exactly right. If that sounds good to you, then I have more good news; you're going to have a very nice life. You will grow up and become just like your parents and raise your own children to be just like you."

"That doesn't sound bad."

"Then it's not."

"Our minister says God is real and anyone who says he's not is bad and can't go to heaven when they die."

"Well, I know this is hard to understand, but even though he seems all grown up, your minister is actually a little kid just like you. His body is older than yours, but his mind is probably about the same age as you, or maybe a little younger due to pre-mortem rigor mortis. If you want to stay like you are right now for your whole life, then you should listen to your minister because that's what he's there to help you do."

"What about God?" asks another girl.

"There's no such thing as God," I reply, "that's just something grownups pretend so they can believe that when they die, they'll go to some magical fairyland where you feel no pain and never get bored."

"That sounds like drugs," says a boy.

"It *is* like drugs," I say, "or like anything else that lets you hide from truth. Adults are addicted to a lot of different drugs; sometimes it's pills or alcohol, sometimes it's religion or sports or shopping, sometimes it's their job or just being a mommy or daddy. Their parents got them addicted at a young age, and now they're getting you addicted, and it's working because you're just children and you really don't stand a chance."

"My parents are not trying to get me addicted to drugs!" shouts a gingery lass.

"No, your parents are really just sleepwalking with all the other grownups, like a big herd of zombies. They're scared and confused because they don't know

their eyes are closed, so instead of opening their eyes, which they could do if they really tried, they just clump together and do what everyone else does because it's easier and less scary than actually going off on their own and living their own lives."

"And that's what we're going to do too? Be like a herd of zombies?" asks a boy.

"Yes."

"Do we have to?"

"Yes. That's why they have you here in school; to turn you into little zombies. If your parents were actual adults instead of little kids in adult bodies, then they would help you become adults too, but it's like our whole society is made up of tadpoles who never developed into real frogs, so being a tadpole your whole life is normal, and turning into a frog, even though that's what tadpoles are supposed to do, is weird and gross and almost never happens."

"So we have to be tadpoles? We can never be frogs?"

"Maybe in fifteen or twenty years you'll wake up enough to realize that you're asleep and you'll try to find your real life, but probably not."

"Mr. McKenna!" whispers Miss Flowers forcefully from behind her desk.

"Your teacher would like me to add that living your whole life as a tadpole is actually a good thing because that's how the world works so you should just go along with it even though it means you never get to have a real life of your own."

"That's not what I was going to say," she hisses.

※

"What about heaven?" asks dead-grammy girl, "and the other place?"

I go to the chalkboard and draw a long horizontal line. I write Heaven on the right end and Hell on the left. There are some gasps at the use of a forbidden word.

"This is what Heaven and Hell are. It's like candy on the Heaven end, and broccoli on the Hell end."

"I like broccoli," says one little tadpole.

"And I don't like candy," I say, "so it's different for everyone. We spend our entire lives somewhere on this line, and we move up and down the line depending on what's going on. When you pass go and collect two hundred dollars, you're way up at the good end, and when you have to go to jail and not collect two hundred dollars, you're down at the bad end. Most of the time you'll just be bouncing around the middle like you are right now."

"So it doesn't really matter if we eat a lot of candy and drink soda and play video games all the time?" asks a little dumpling who looks like he already does.

"No, just like it's okay in Monopoly not to buy property and charge rent. It just means you're not playing a very good game. No matter how much candy you eat, when the game is over you go back in the same box as

the guy who ate broccoli all the time, so it's really just a matter of who had more fun."

An argument erupts, and the consensus is that candy is more fun than broccoli.

"Yes," I agree, "candy is dandy, but being fat and having your arms and legs cut off is not so dandy, so you have to decide how you want to play the game. Of course, you don't have to play at all if you don't want to. Just like in Monopoly, you can just quit whenever you want. In life that's called suicide. Show of hands, who knows what suicide is?"

"Jesus Christ, Mr. McKenna, *please*," whispers Miss Flowers.

"Your teacher doesn't want me to tell you about suicide because she's an adult and wants to pretend that dying is terrible, but obviously dying is not terrible, it's just how the game ends, and it can end anytime, whether we want it to or not."

"So we could all die today?"

"Sure, that's what makes today special. Your bus could get stuck on the train tracks on the way home and *bam!*, you're all dead. Then your mommies and daddies will be very sad," I point to the Hell end of the line, "and stick you in a box in the ground where worms will eat your eyes and guts and everything, unless you get burned up in the bus and there's nothing left for the worms."

That gets a big reaction.

✵

"Dr. Fischer says…"

"Is that the same guy who told you about gravity?"

"Yes," they say.

"And did he prove gravity? Or did he just tell you and expect you to believe him?"

Just told, they say.

"Well, that's not very scientific, is it?" I ask. "That sounds more like religion. If gravity is supposed to be science, then you should ask Dr. Fischer to either prove it or admit he's just telling stories."

I take a clear glass saucer from under a plant and set in on Miss Flower's desk. I tell everyone to stand up and gather 'round. Miss Flowers backs out a little to give them room. I ask for water and someone hands me a bottle from their backpack. I pour a few inches in the saucer.

"Okay, so here's a way you can ask Dr. Fischer a question," I say. "Can everyone see this?"

They move around so everyone can see the water in the saucer.

"Can you see how still it is? Not sloshing around, not moving even a little bit. Perfectly still, right?"

They agree.

I tap the desk lightly and the surface of the water ripples.

"See that? Even a tiny bump makes the water move, right?"

They agree. I take a globe from a shelf and set it on the desk next to the water. I spin the globe.

"Now, supposedly, we're standing on this big round ball right now, and it's spinning all the way around once every day, which means we're going almost 900 miles an hour where we are."

I go to the chalkboard and write down the number.

"We're going 900 miles an hour right now?"

"According to science, we're going almost two million miles an hour in five different directions right now. And look, the water is perfectly still."

Wide eyes and open mouths.

"How can we be going in different directions?" asks a bespectacled little boy.

"Well, while we're spinning around like a top, we're also going around the sun once a year at over 60,000 miles an hour."

I write that number on the board. My numbers may not be right, but they're right-ish.

"Plus, the sun and the earth and all our planets are moving through space at more than 40,000 miles an hour."

I add that number to the column on the board.

"Plus, at the same time as all that, we're going around the galaxy at almost 500,000 miles an hour."

I add that to the list.

"Plus, our whole galaxy is moving through space at over a million miles an hour."

I write that number on the board and draw a line under it.

"So according to science, you and me and Miss Flowers and the water in that saucer are all moving at over 500 miles per second in five different directions, and yet we don't feel like we're moving and the water stays perfectly still, all because of gravity. It's like magic, right?"

They agree.

"But it's supposed to be science, not magic, so if someone tells you to believe something that doesn't seem true, you should ask for some proof. If Dr. Fischer tells you the water doesn't move because of gravity, you should ask what gravity is and how it works and make him prove it. He might say it's an invisible force that keeps the water from moving, but that's not an explanation, it's just a description. Maybe he doesn't know if gravity even exists. Maybe it's just a word he uses to describe what he sees. So, who's right and who's wrong? Is there such a thing as gravity? Are we on a spinning ball moving more than 500 miles every single second? I don't know, but I do know we don't have to believe whatever people tell us. A famous philosopher once said that we believe things because we don't want to know what's true. He meant that we're afraid of the truth, but that doesn't mean we have to be. We can decide that we'd rather know what's true and not just settle for make-believe answers because everyone else does. That's what practical philosophy

means; it means you ask questions and go where the answers take you, not where you want to go because that's where everyone else is going. That's what thinking really means. Belief always takes you with all the cows walking along with their heads up each other's butts, and that seems to be okay with everyone because they don't mind looking at butt and smelling butt all day, but if you don't like having your nose up someone else's butt then there's this other thing you can do. You can ask good questions and look for better answers and see where that gets you. That's the difference between thinking and believing, and that's something you can really do all by yourself."

※

Miss Flowers sends the children back to their desks. She pulls me over to the door and whispers urgently.

"Jed, please! I'm going to lose my job."

"Yeah, no shit," I whisper back. "Unless these kids really do get hit by a train before they can tell their parents what they learned in school today, I think you can expect to be called into the principal's office first thing in the morning. You should pack your stuff out tonight so you don't have to do the walk of shame with a box of books and a potted plant tomorrow."

"Oh my God!"

"Hey, I'm on your side, but you're supposed to be grooming these kids for herd life, not teaching them

to question and think. What were you doing inviting me here?"

She stares at me like this is my fault. I consider sharing the parable of the frog and the scorpion but this doesn't feel like a teachable moment.

"Oh my God," she repeats, "you've ruined my life!"

"Nonsense. Think of it as a death-rebirth thing. Losing your job is going to be painful, but you're made of good stuff and you'll come out ahead on the deal. You might want to say your goodbyes today, though. I doubt you'll be allowed to see these kids again, probably by court order. So anyway, thanks for having me. It was fun. Hug? No hug? Okay, no hug."

DECEPTION: ACT I
Opium Den

DOM and ARIADNE strolling along crowded city sidewalks.

DOM

Let me ask you a question: You never really remember the beginning of a dream do you? You always wind up right in the middle of what's going on, right?

ARIADNE

Yeah, I guess.

DOM

So how did we get here?

ARIADNE

Uh, I took an Uber from the airport.

DOM

No, I mean to this world, this body, this universe. Think about it, how did you get here? Where are you right now? Where were you before?

ARIADNE

You mean, I'm dreaming right now?
gestures to their surroundings
But it's all so *real*.

DOM

It *seems* real, but how can you judge?

ARIADNE

I can judge because I'm conscious.

DOM

I have a t-shirt that says "I Am Conscious", but it's not conscious, it's a t-shirt.

ARIADNE

Yeah, but I'm not a t-shirt.

DOM

I have another t-shirt that says "I'm not a t-shirt", but it *is* a t-shirt.

ARIADNE

So what's your point? That you have a lot of weird t-shirts?

DOM

The fact that you're in a dream doesn't mean *you're* the dreamer. Maybe your entire reality is being generated by an evil demon which is really just a few lines of malicious code in a sentient mainframe.

ARIADNE

So I could just be a computer bug?

DOM

We think the AI revolution is coming, but maybe it already came and we lost. Who knows? Nobody knows anything.

ARIADNE

I don't know, I'm a pretty spiritual person and I've never heard anything like that.

DOM

Come on, I'll show you something.

Dom leads Ariadne down a long dark stairway into a smoky, labyrinthine lair. Above the entrance is a sign that says Pnevmatikí Agorá.

ARIADNE

Geez, it looks like an opium den. What does *Pnevmatikí Agorá* mean?

DOM

Depends who you ask. It's either Spiritual Marketplace or Village of Flatulence.

The catacombs are lit by candles and divided by hanging wisps of tattered veil. The sound of chanting echoes hauntingly through incense-filled air. People sit in groups and talk about waking up. Some turn and stare at Ariadne.

ARIADNE

Why are they looking at me?

DOM

They think you're going to upset their delicate balance. They're afraid you're going to try to wake them up.

ARIADNE

You mean, all these people are asleep right now?

DOM

Depends who you ask. If they're asleep, are they really people? If they're not awake, how are they better than cattle?

ARIADNE

But they're *not* cattle, they're people!

DOM

So is Soylent Green.

ARIADNE

What can we do to end their suffering?

DOM

They're *not* suffering, that's the point. They're happy down here in the dark. You want to be an angel and set them free, but they'll see you as a demon trying to destroy them.

ARIADNE

But look at what they're doing! Meditating, chanting, worshipping pictures and praying to statues! They want to wake up!

DOM

No one wants to wake up. It's just a game to pass the time.

ARIADNE

Then why are they even here?

DOM

This is their safe space. At some point, they opened their eyes a little and some light got in, so now they huddle in the darkness pretending to seek what they're actually hiding from.

ARIADNE

That's so sad.

DOM

Not really, it's just another form of drama, and all drama is good drama. It doesn't matter what

we strive *for,* only that we strive.

> *They ascend out of the catacombs and make their way to a sidewalk cafe where they continue their conversation over coffee.*

ARIADNE

They told me you had a wife, but the two of you got trapped in a place called Limbo. What happened?

DOM

Her name was Mal. We were like actors in a movie, but she got so deep into her character that she forgot who she really was. Instead of playing the character, the character began playing her. I tried to remind her, but I couldn't get her to believe that we were dreaming and that to wake up, we had to commit suicide together.

ARIADNE

Yeah, that would be a tough sell.

DOM

So I had to enter her dreams and plant the idea in her head.

ARIADNE

shocked

Wow! You used hypnosis to make her commit suicide with you? That sounds like a terrible violation.

DOM

Not at all. It's called Deception. You go into someone's dream and plant an idea so they think it's their own.

ARIADNE

And how is using mind control not the *worst* thing you can do to someone?

DOM

Think about it, isn't life just wall-to-wall Deception? Government, business, news, education, advertising, healthcare, science, religion. It's all just a massive disinformation system, so what's the big deal?

ARIADNE

Herding people like livestock is okay due to mass adoption?

DOM

My point is that it worked on Mal, but a little too well. Once we were out of Limbo and back in our normal life, the Deception was still planted in her head. She thought we were still stuck in Limbo and that we had to kill ourselves again.

ARIADNE

Yeah, I can see where that would be a problem, but what does any of this have to do with me? What do you need me for?

DOM

You're an expository device. I have to explain everything to you, and that's how the audience gets to understand what's going on.

ARIADNE

looks around

What audience?

DOM

I don't know, but we have to imagine there's an audience out there. Otherwise, we're just one hand clapping, a tree falling without making a sound.

ARIADNE

So someone's *watching* us right now? Are they dreaming too?

DOM

Probably. Let's try to wake them up.

A series of slow-motion explosions blow the entire cafe scene to bits, including Dom and Ariadne.

Marichelle 4: Maps of Ideas

What I talk about doesn't always make sense
when I'm talking about it. Don't worry about
that too much. It makes sense when you start
doing stuff, then you know what I'm talking
about. Then it all makes good sense.

Marichelle

MARICHELLE IS AWAKE. She is from Switzerland
and now lives on an island off Honduras. In
response to many requests, she gave a one-time series
of talks in English to a small group. The transcript of
these talks has been provided to me with permission
to use. Attempts to organize this material only seem to
make things worse, so I'm just presenting the best of
it in loosely strung-together bite-sized bits. The talks
were lively, but audience interactions have not been
retained. I have made minor changes for readability.

۵

We have to talk sideways about some things, we can't always talk direct. An analogy is a way of talking sideways. Analogies can be very useful as tools, but they have limits so don't trust them too much.

۵

Maps are just pictures of places and analogies have edges like maps maybe, or they're just about one thing and leave other things out. Even this analogy about analogies is feeling very weak. Maybe just do your own.

۵

Analogies can cause problems if you don't know the limits. Don't trust them too much. Don't trust tools more than your own calculations. Learn to trust your calculations, not maps and analogies. Don't be lazy is good advice.

۵

You don't need a map if you're not going anywhere, which maybe you're not, but maybe you are. I won't guess because I'm not good at guessing. I won't say my hope either way because I don't have a way I like better.

What else do I want to say about maps and analogies? Probably nothing right now. It's good to know how good they are, and also how bad. Also, where they start and where they end. You can't do everything with one map, you need different maps like you need different tools.

Maybe you get to the end of one map and you need a different one. Analogies are like that, you get to the end of one and then you need the next one. Also good not to have lot of extra. You don't need a million maps to carry around, just a few good ones is all. And also when you're done with a map you can throw it away. Travel light.

Analogies are very good because they are like maps of ideas. It makes it easier to think about something big if we have a little version to look at, like the way a map is a little version of a place, right? This is like that.

You look in the totally wrong direction. There are interesting things inside, but you look at outside things. There is stuff on the inside that is of real interest. Try to look there, but not in a nice way.

Not like a tourist, more like a soldier maybe, or a criminal. It's not a time to be nice.

✤

Sometimes you can do calculations to know something is there when you can't see it, but sometimes it's the opposite. Sometimes you can do calculations to know something is not there even when you do see it.

✤

Everything you know is based on what you see, right? But maybe instead it can be based on calculations that you think. We can talk more about how to think because it's your best tool and you're not using it very good.

✤

If you want to see what's real, you have to look where your eyes can't see. This is what no one does. This is what makes a difference.

✤

Everyone looks at the surface and says okay, but if you want to see what's under the surface you have to learn to see not with eye vision but brain vision. Eyes only see the surface. The brain sees under the surface. Nothing can hide from the brain.

It looks like we are part of a group, but thinking shows it is not this way. Maybe I'm just talking to myself, I don't know. You are all alone which is scary so get used to it.

Now is where the circle gets smaller. Once it starts, it never stops. Everything just shrinks down to almost nothing. You can be upset by this, no problem. It's very upsetting.

Coma is for your happiness. If you want to be happy, don't mess around. The way you are is fine. Why change things that aren't so bad? Even if you think things can't be worse, you might be wrong.

Just because you believe a certain thing doesn't make it true, it just makes you easy to fool, which we already know you are.

Try not to be too upset by things I say, we don't have time for that. Maybe pretend I'm talking about someone else if that helps, then it can just get in more slowly.

Right now it's not a mess, but when you try to make change then it can turn into a big mess. That's what we're talking about here just for starters, so keep that in mind.

Don't have a lot of trust for other people's calculations, just do your own. It's not that hard, but you don't have the habit.

I'm here to be like an analogy for you, like a map, that's all. If you can get some help from me, that's okay. If not, that's okay too. What you do is what you do, I'm just one little thing. Don't bet on me, just bet on yourself. Okay.

A Filmmaker's Apocalypse

> A rock pile ceases to be a rock pile the moment
> a single man contemplates it, bearing within him
> the image of a cathedral.

Antoine de Saint-Exupéry

"LAST NIGHT, SOMEONE ASKED ME something about *Apocalypse Now* and how it relates to the journey of awakening, so I talked about that a little bit – the ugliness of the awakening process, the stark unspirituality of it, the horror and all that – but later on it occurred to me that I hadn't seen *Apocalypse Now* in a while, so I watched it again. Then I read a bunch of commentary about it and rewatched the documentary about the making of it, *Hearts of Darkness: A Filmmaker's Apocalypse.* [†]

[†] If you don't like war movies, you can get the same mileage from *Fitzcarraldo* and *Burden of Dreams*.

39

"So, as you can imagine, I had *Apocalypse Now* on the brain, and that's what I planned to talk about tonight; the parallels between *Apocalypse Now* and the journey of awakening – making your own trip up your own river into your own dark interior – but then I went for a walk this afternoon to let it all digest, and to my surprise the whole thing took a sharp turn and became something else."

I'm addressing a group of twenty-five or thirty people sitting on cushions and backrests on a patchwork of rugs and carpet remnants on the floor of a brick warehouse that has been converted into a small venue for talks, films, music and such. It's my second night speaking here and some of the faces are familiar. I'm sitting on the front edge of a makeshift stage, but I'll end up standing and pacing as I figure out what I'm talking about.

"To start out with, there are two interesting things to understand about *Apocalypse Now*; one, it's very similar to *Moby-Dick*, but told from a different perspective and with a different backdrop, and two, it's much more accessible than *Moby-Dick*, but, for our purposes, not as good. *Apocalypse Now* is like the theoretical classroom edition, and *Moby-Dick* is the hands-on field guide. This observation isn't based on the material itself, but the author and authority behind the material. It's the difference between a guy who sets a movie in the jungle and the guy who disappears into the jungle, and then, decades later,

someone finds and publishes his journals. *Moby-Dick* is both vehicle and record of Melville's actual journey, whereas *Apocalypse Now* is just Coppola's somewhat flailing attempt to capture something thematically and archetypally grand, but with which he has little or no personal acquaintance, at least, not to begin with. Coppola developed that personal acquaintance in the process of making *Apocalypse Now*, which brings us to what I want to talk about tonight, which is why the filmmaker's apocalypse is the real story."

A quick poll reveals that most of the crowd has seen *Apocalypse Now*, but not in a long time. A few have seen the junked-up *Redux* version. Only one has seen the making-of documentary.

"Okay, to summarize a bit, *Apocalypse Now* was filmed in the Philippines, and the entire production was slammed by what looks like one great misfortune after another. Eventually, Coppola was forced to put everything he had on the line, so instead of just being a director, he took on the full burden of this insane project, and shooting a movie *about* a descent into madness became *itself* a descent into madness. This is the correct way to understand Coppola's journey for our purposes; he bit off more than he could chew with this project, so the universe reforged him into the tool that could do the job.

"That's what some of you might be doing, making your own journey into your own dark interior. *Apocalypse Now* is a somewhat useful allegory for understanding

this process, but the making-of documentary is the real-life record of a guy actually doing it, and not by choice. Coppola didn't know what he was getting into and he didn't understand what was happening to him, but he asked for it in the way the universe understands, so that's what he got. Once this journey begins, once we've somehow initiated it, then we quickly learn that we're just along for the ride and that the river is really in charge.

"In the course of trying to find his way, Coppola fell into suicidal despair over the fact that the movie would fail, that he couldn't make the script work, that the project would bankrupt him and ruin his career, that it would cost him his family and his health, and so on. All perfectly reasonable when viewed from the right perspective, which is what we'll try to do here tonight. Captain Willard's journey up the river to terminate the command of Colonel Kurtz is just a shadow of Coppola's real journey into the heart of darkness to make his movie. For our purposes, the movie is just a parable and the documentary is the real thing.

"In trying to figure out what his movie was really about, Coppola shot a huge amount of film and kept rewriting the script. This is what I mean by flailing; he was fully immersed in the project while still lacking a coherent vision. He may have sensed that Conrad's book and John Milius' script were about something grand and archetypal, but he didn't know what it was. He had no personal acquaintance with the subject.

Maybe he assumed it was something external that could be captured on film, but the river is internal, and the only way to understand your own dark interior is to make your own journey.

"*Hearts of Darkness* details much of what went on during principal filming in the Philippines and how every imaginable problem seemed to conspire against Coppola. Remember what Whitman said; *All forces have been steadily employed to complete and delight me, now on this spot I stand with my robust soul.* Well, that's a double-edged sword. Those forces aren't a ticklefest; they break us down and rebuild us. This process can be profoundly brutal and take us far beyond our breaking points. That's how it was for Coppola in making *Apocalypse Now*; his own journey to his own interior from which he eventually emerged with a masterpiece. That's what we're interested in; not a guy making a movie in the jungle, but the superpower we all possess but few of us really use; the power to create."

I stand and begin pacing back and forth across the front of the platform. For me, this isn't like speaking to an audience but like thinking out loud, and I'm sometimes surprised to look up and find a roomful of people eavesdropping on my thoughts.

"The apparent creator of any creative work – Coppola in this case – is not the sole creator, and the creation occurs, in some cases, almost despite the human partner. This is the other side of the cocreative coin. My ego, for instance, might like to think that I am the author

of my books, but my ego is an idiot. I know that I was really just privileged to be a partner in a cocreative relationship; a transpersonal union from which the books issued. In a similar sense, I might like to think that I am the captain of my life, that I am the creator of myself or the dreamer of my dreamstate, but that too would be vanity. I, like everything in the dreamstate, like the dreamstate itself, am a black box. I may see what goes *into* the black box and I may see what comes *out* of the black box, but I have no idea what's going on *inside* the black box. The only thing I understand about myself is that I don't understand anything about myself; not my body, not my feelings, not my mind, not my personality, not the lint under my fingernails, nothing, and if I think I do, then I'm lying to myself. We're not these personalities we wear like costumes, and we're not our thoughts, feelings, and beliefs, so who are we? That's the only spiritual question there is; Who am I? Ultimately, of course, we are nothing and no one. No matter how much you peel away, you never get to your real self because there is no such thing as a real self. And this goes for everything, nothing in the dreamstate stands up to scrutiny. Whatever you look at and think you understand, you're always looking out from inside a black box. It's all a cognitive illusion. You can never understand what you observe because you can never understand yourself as observer. You *can*, however, understand that you can't understand, and understanding *that* can really open the way forward."

44

·☼·

"Nothing is good or bad but thinking makes it so," I paraphrase Hamlet. "Our judgment of what's good and bad depends on context, so let's take a look at a shared context. How about birth? That's something we all have in common. We all went through it, and it was our first experience of death and rebirth. For our entire lives we were floating in a warm, safe environment, all our needs being met, and then *bam!*, all of a sudden, shit gets crazy. Everything that was so heavenly turns to pure hell. Pressure builds until we're literally being crushed to death. We have no knowledge of what's going on, no precedent for it and no reason to think it will ever end. It's like one minute you're asleep in bed dreaming sweet dreams and the next minute you're being crushed under tons of earthquake rubble with no hope of rescue. This is something that really happened to you, and when you were a baby, no less. We think prolonged labor is hard on the mother; think what it's like for the baby, and then remember that baby was you. If we could remember our own perinatal experiences we'd all be paralyzed by post-traumatic stress. And if that's not enough, when it's finally over, you're in some loud, bright, crazy-place surrounded by huge, insane monsters, and you never get to go back to your happy-place again. That's our first death and rebirth experience and just because you don't consciously remember it doesn't mean it's not the most powerful and formative experience of your life.

"The second stage of our birth process, from juvenile to adult, would be a paradigm shift of similar magnitude, but most of us never undergo that transition. Egoic forces have been steadily employed to neuter and domesticate us, now here we stand with our bovine souls. Maybe we *do* remember our birth trauma. Maybe we *are* cowering in fear of a repeat event. If you think about what stage one must have been like, you can understand why we'd opt out of stage two.

"So now that we have some shared context, what sounds better? Making the birth transition from womb to world, or staying in the nice, warm happy-place forever? If your baby-self had its way, you'd still be in the womb right now, which is a good thing not to picture. We don't give unborn babies a choice between oceanic bliss to a prolonged, suffocating, soul-crushing death because they'd go with the bliss every time. Soul-crushing death is hard to put a positive spin on even if you really sell the rebirth part, but it's best for the baby, which brings us back to us. We *do* have a choice, and like babies, we choose to stay where we are rather than venture out into life. We ask children what they want to be when they grow up, and there's a long list of good answers, but the one that isn't on the list is the only one that should be; an adult. Nothing else comes before that and everything else follows from it. That's the crossroads you came to at the age of sexual maturity, but you were just a little critter in a great big herd so you missed your shot at a life of your own

and now, whether you understand it this way or not, you're wondering if you can get back to the crossroads and go a different way."

After some question and answer time, largely center-ing on everyone's insistence that they're fullborns, not halfborns, a teenage guy who took the bold position that war is bad on the previous night now accuses me of saying destruction is good, which definitely *is* what I'm saying.

"We must destroy one thing to create another, die out of one life to be born into the next, so yes, destruction is obviously part of the process, and since you and your dreamstate are really the same thing, all destruction is self-destruction. Destruction is a part of the creative process. The pure white light of perfect intelligence hits the imperfect lens of ego, and the distorted light that emerges is our contribution to the dreamstate spectacle. If we want to change real-ity, we have to change ourselves as lens, and this is what we see with Coppola. This whole terrible ordeal of making *Apocalypse Now* had nothing to do with bad luck or misfortune or fate, those are just superstitions adopted by people unable to discern the subtle dynam-ics of pattern and energy. Coppola's real ordeal was the process of becoming the filter through which the universe could project *Apocalypse Now*. Coppola wasn't ready to do that right out of the box, so he had to make his own journey upriver to his own dark interior. He had to be reground into the lens through which a

great work like *Apocalypse Now* could be projected, and that begins as a process of destruction. He expressed a desire in the way the universe understands, so he got his wish, even though it wasn't what he expected or hoped. He wasn't a victim, he just didn't know what he was asking for. Be careful what you wish for, not because you'll get it but because you'll be turned into the thing that *can* get it. It's not a process where you just ask for something and it magically appears, it's a process that breaks you down and rebuilds you into the right tool for the job. We're fortunate to have the making-of documentary because it shows us this reforging process at work. Coppola got in way over his head and might have been crushed beneath the weight of the project, but instead, he rose to the challenge and paid the price and finally arrived at a coherent vision and a transcendent masterpiece, not because he drew the project down to his dimensions, but because he expanded into it."

※

A note about themes. From where I sit, lightning does not strike great artists twice. Melville had *Moby-Dick*, Orwell had *1984*, Kesey had *Cuckoo's Nest,* and Coppola had *Apocalypse Now.* The rest of their works were just build-up and fall-off. As Melville said of whale as theme:

> One often hears of writers that rise and swell with their subject, though it may seem but an ordinary one. How, then, with me, writing of this Leviathan?

> Give me a condor's quill! Give me Vesuvius' crater
> for an inkstand! Such, and so magnifying, is the
> virtue of a large and liberal theme! We expand to
> its bulk. To produce a mighty book, you must
> choose a mighty theme. No great and enduring
> volume can ever be written on the flea, though
> many there be who have tried it.

I'm eager to make this distinction between pedestrian and elevated themes because it seems like such an inviting onramp to higher perspective. Francis Ford Coppola is a great filmmaker best known for *Godfather I* and *II*. As great as they may be in artistic or cinematic terms, the *Godfathers* are thematically banal, little more than over-produced soap operas. Sure, they're great movies, but they're not *about* anything and therefore don't deserve to be considered alongside films like *Apocalypse Now* and *Joe Versus the Volcano* and others that *are* about something. The Corleones are fleas.

Furthermore, many who watch *Apocalypse Now* come away with the idea that it has something to do with the war in Vietnam. I never made that connection, but I can see where a viewer might get that impression, in the same way that Conrad's *Heart of Darkness* could be viewed as an African travelogue or *Moby-Dick* as a fishing yarn. Sad to waste them on such superficial interpretations, but we all see the world through our own eyes and if we want to see better things, we have to see things better.

Finally, I mention again the peculiar inability of some artists to understand their own creations at the highest levels at which they can be interpreted, which applies to Orwell, Coppola, Shakespeare and many others. It's a weird thing about the cocreative partnership that the art can transcend the artist. The creation is the point, not the creator. Sometimes we're a partner and sometimes we're just a tool. What was Jesus but God's tool? Mohammed but Allah's? Arjuna but Krishna's? The universe has no other hands but ours.

※

"At times, Coppola thought he had failed and the movie would never be made. He was nearly suicidal over it, but at the same time, he staked everything he had on it. That's pretty good drama in itself, right? A man goes into the jungle and puts everything on the line to achieve his artistic vision? That's why the documentary about the making of the movie can teach us more than the movie itself; it's one level up, one less layer of allegory, the real journey of a real man into the real heart of darkness. Coppola staked all he had – health, wealth, family, reputation – for something he sensed but couldn't see. It was only after years of post-production editing that he was able to bring the movie into focus, to polish it to its essence, and in so doing, reveal a masterpiece that transcended his own comprehension. That's how these things really work; a true masterpiece isn't created, it's revealed. It's not

made, it's allowed. We are not creators but facilitators. We can be in contention against our creation even as we create it. Coppola thought it was his movie; he didn't know he was in a partnership. He didn't understand that the project had a will and a mind and a life of its own, and that he was just one part in a larger machine.

"Inside my black box, between my input and my output, the silent partner finds its way into the equation, and if I can be open and allowing, then that higher element can come through, and that's when transcendent things happen. Ego blocks this partnership, surrender allows it. This is how things really work in the Integrated State, and if we can see this influence at work in *Apocalypse Now*, then maybe we can see it at work in our own lives. You tell the universe you want some sort of spiritual achievement – awakening or enlightenment or higher consciousness or whatever – and instead of your life becoming wall-to-wall bliss, it turns to shit. You might enter into years of health and financial problems, family and emotional issues, and you might think back to that long-ago wish you made to become more spiritual and reflect bitterly on what a curse it was, but it's wasn't a curse, you're just in the process of getting what you asked for. That's what Coppola did; he told the universe in the way the universe understands – through focused intent manifesting as action – that he wanted to make a movie about this grand archetypal theme that he only dimly

sensed, and then, while making the movie, everything turns to shit and suddenly he's not in Kansas
anymore. This isn't on some Hollywood backlot, this
is in a jungle just like the one he was depicting. This
is the real takeaway that elevates *Apocalypse Now* to
Moby-Dick status. It's not about making a movie, it's
about the deconstruction and reconstruction a man
went through to manifest his vision, and as for him,
so for you. Creativity is like a superpower all possess
but few understand, so we spend our lives in a state
of diminished capacity, like Clark Kent forgetting
who he really is. Clark Kent isn't Superman's authentic
self, Superman is living a lie. Clark Kent doesn't turn
into Superman, he *is* Superman. He pretends he's dull
and weak to blend in with a herd to which he does
not rightfully belong. It's the same with us. No one
rightfully belongs in the herd, we're all playing lowly
mortals because we're afraid of expanding into our
heroic dimensions. We settle for life as herd creatures
when we're actually lords of creation. As Emerson said,
man is a god in ruins. We shuffle through life like
cattle because we forgot who we really are.

"The universe is just a big playground full of building materials and tools and art supplies and how-to
books and helpful little elves, and the animating force
behind it all is this superior aspect of ourselves that
will come out and play if we know how to ask. This
applies to anything we want to do; make art, build
a better mousetrap, heal ourselves emotionally and

physically, grow spiritually, whatever. Creativity is a process of coming into focus, not just of your creation but of you as creator."

I pause, drink some water, consider.

"We can take our understanding of this cocreative process one final step by understanding that there really is no cocreative process at all, that there was only one party at work all along, not two. It was only the illusion of segregated selfhood that made us think there was an invisible partner. Self and dreamstate are the same, dreamer and dream are one. That's the missing link in our understanding. The distinction between self and not-self only exists at the level of belief and wrong-knowing. You and the dreamstate you inhabit are not two different things just as you and your nighttime dreams are not two different things. Everything always boils down to one, and if it doesn't, it just means you have more boiling to do. Okay, no questions. I just hit a wall. Good night."

Unlearn Everything

If you would die to the past, if you would
die to every minute, you would be the
person who is fully alive, because a fully
alive person is one who is full of death.

Anthony de Mello

J ESUIT PRIEST AND AUTHOR Father Anthony de
Mello's teachings were temporarily banned within
the Roman Catholic Church. The ban has been lifted,
but Catholics are still advised to avoid his writings.

Understand your darkness and it will vanish;
then you will know what light is. Understand
your nightmare for what it is and it will stop;
then you will wake up to reality. Understand
your false beliefs and they will drop; then you
will know the taste of happiness.

⅋

Wisdom comes to those who learn nothing, unlearn everything.

⅋

Monk: "All these mountains and rivers and the earth and stars, where do they come from?"

Master: "Where does your question come from?"

⅋

If you see through yourself, you will see through everyone.

⅋

Do you want a sign that you're asleep? Here it is: you're suffering. Suffering is a sign that you're out of touch with the truth. Suffering is given to you that you might open your eyes to the truth, that you might understand that there's falsehood somewhere, just as physical pain is given to you so you will understand that there is disease or illness somewhere. Suffering occurs when you clash with reality. When your illusions clash with reality, when your falsehoods clash with truth, then you have suffering. Otherwise, there is no suffering.

☙

When the eye is unobstructed, the result is sight. When the ear is unobstructed, the result is hearing. When the mind is unobstructed, the result is truth.

☙

The day you follow someone, you cease to follow truth.

☙

There comes a point in your life when you become stark raving insane, commit suicide, or become a mystic.

☙

Nobody is afraid of the unknown, what you really fear is the loss of the known.

☙

The only way that someone can be of help to you is by challenging your ideas.

☙

Wisdom tends to grow in proportion to one's awareness of one's ignorance.

⅋

When you fight something, you're tied to it forever. As long as you're fighting it, you're giving it power.

⅋

Turn on the light of awareness and the darkness will disappear.

⅋

Problems only exist in the human mind.

⅋

The only way to change is by changing your understanding.

⅋

Most people don't live aware lives. They live mechanical lives, mechanical thoughts – generally somebody else's – mechanical emotions, mechanical actions, mechanical reactions.

⅋

Seek to change yourself, not other people. It is easier to protect your feet with slippers than to carpet the whole of the earth.

❀

What you are aware of you are in control of; what you are not aware of is in control of you.

❀

All conflict comes from attachment.

❀

There is only one cause of unhappiness: the false beliefs you have in your head, beliefs so widespread, so commonly held, that it never occurs to you to question them.

❀

You are only a disciple because your eyes are closed. The day you open them you will see there is nothing you can learn from me or anyone.

❀

When you come to see you are not as wise today as you thought you were yesterday, you are wiser today.

ஃ

You can never be free as long as you have an ego to defend.

ஃ

Think of a flabby person covered with layers of fat. That is what your mind can become; flabby, covered with layers of fat till it becomes too dull and lazy to think, to observe, to explore, to discover, not wanting to be disturbed or questioned into wakefulness.

ஃ

If you search within your heart, you will find something there that will make it possible for you to understand: a spark of disenchantment and discontent, which if fanned into flame will become a raging forest fire that will burn up the whole of the illusory world you are living in, thereby unveiling to your wondering eyes the kingdom that you have always lived in unsuspectingly.

DECEPTION: Act II
Loading Program

After the explosion at the cafe, Ariadne and Dom wake up on lounge chairs in a clean white warehouse. Sitting open between them is a high-tech briefcase. Tubes from the case plug into their arms. In the center of the case is a big red button.

ARIADNE

Holy shit! Where are we?

DOM

This is a blank construct, like the loading program in *The Matrix*.

ARIADNE

But *The Matrix* is just a movie.

DOM

As opposed to what?

ARIADNE

So we're in Limbo right now?

DOM

Limbo, dreamstate, matrix, whatever.

ARIADNE

But I'm a real person, so this must be real.

DOM

There are no *real* people in Limbo. You identify with the character you play, but there's no authentic connection because there's no authentic you.

ARIADNE

You're saying that *I'm* not really *me*?

DOM

No more than you're Winston Churchill or Aunt Jemima. You're simply the zeropoint of awareness in a constantly rendering, multi-sensory, 3D gamespace viewed through an avatar called Ariadne.

ARIADNE

Then who's doing the rendering? Who's doing the viewing?

DOM

God, Brahman, Aunt Jemima, take your pick.

ARIADNE

Then how do I know what's real?

DOM

Who says anything is real? C'mon, I'll show you.

Dom pushes the big red button. They both fall asleep in their lounge chairs and wake up together on a path in a lush, tropical setting. They talk as they stroll.

ARIADNE

Wow! So I'm still dreaming right now?

DOM

You're *always* dreaming. That's what I never understood. I thought there was such a thing as *real* reality, but there's only layer upon layer of Limbo.

ARIADNE

How can there be no real reality? If we wake up, what do we wake up *to?* What's left when the dream is gone?

DOM

There's nothing outside of dreaming. Limbo is all we have.

ARIADNE

It actually seems kind of obvious now that I'm thinking about it. How do we manage to stay asleep?

DOM

By *not* thinking about it. Emotion is the ballast that holds us down in the dark. Thought is the knife that cuts ballast away and lets us ascend into the light.

ARIADNE

But those people in the catacombs were so spiritual!

DOM

Spirituality is a crutch for people who can't handle truth. If you have trouble keeping your mind subdued, you have to redirect it into designated safezones like religion and spirituality.

ARIADNE

I'm feeling very conflicted right now.

DOM

That's your thinking mind struggling against emotional sedation. Don't worry, it'll pass. C'mon, I'll show you the part where I talked my wife into suicide.

They enter a clearing with a swimming pool. MAL, in a bikini and sunglasses, lies on a chaise lounge sunning herself. She sips from a

glass with a straw and an umbrella.

DOM

to Ariadne

This is what happened.

Dom approaches Mal and casts a shadow over her.

MAL

charming French accent

You stand in my sun.

DOM

I know you don't believe it, Mal, but none of this is real. We're living in a shared dream.

MAL

Again with this dream nonsense! You are telling me that reality is not real?

DOM

Well, *this* reality isn't real. There might be a real world out there somewhere, but this ain't it.

MAL

Then what is this place where we have lived for so many years?

DOM

This is called Limbo. You used to know that, but you locked the knowledge deep inside. In order to get to the *real* reality, we have to wake up,

which means we have to kill ourselves together.

MAL

How romantic! You should create a line of greeting cards.

DOM

I'm serious, Mal. Dying is our only way out.

MAL

And how should we be doing the dying?

DOM

I suggest we lie down on the railroad tracks, and the train will wake us up.

MAL

You mean the train will squish our heads. This is your big idea?

DOM

Well, yeah, but our heads aren't really *real*, so we'll just wake up out of Limbo.

MAL

I have to say, your plan is very stupid.

DOM

It's not very stupid, it's very smart!

MAL

Okay, well, why don't you go do the smart head squishing thing and I'll stay here and drink

stupid Mai Tais.

DOM

No, Mal, we have to kill ourselves *together*! That's what love means!

MAL

Mais non! That's what being in a cult means.

DOM

But none of this is real!

MAL

Okay, fine, but what is so terrible about not-real? Not-real is okay. We get to design the world and make it how we like. In your *real* reality, do I still get to create with my mind?

DOM

It's not so simple in the real world.

MAL

Okay then, what's so bad about here? If you were saying that in this real world of yours we would be super-beautiful and super-rich, with many admirers and servants...

DOM

snaps fingers

Oh yeah, that's right! I just remembered! In the *real* world, you and me are megastars! We work in a dream factory and we're rich and everyone loves us! It's all coming back to me now!

MAL

Zut alors! That sounds much better! You should have said that first instead of the head squishing thing. Let's go kill ourselves. First I finish bronzing, then we go.

Dom returns to Ariadne and they continue their stroll.

ARIADNE

Wow, that Deception you planted in her mind really worked. How long were you guys in Limbo?

DOM

Decades, though it was only a few hours in this world. Time has no meaning in Limbo. Five minutes can be a hundred years.

ARIADNE

A hundred years! Who'd wanna be stuck in a dream for a hundred years?

DOM

Depends on the dream.

ARIADNE

So the Deception you planted in Mal's mind worked? You killed yourselves and woke up?

DOM

It worked *too* good. It never *stopped* working. Mal just wanted to keep going further and further.

A door appears on their path. Dom and Ariadne step through the door into a ransacked hotel suite.

DOM

This is what happened.

Dom goes the window. Mal sits in the window of an identical suite across the alley, about to jump. Her legs dangle over the void, one shoe drops into the darkness.

DOM

distressed

Holy shit, Mal! What are you doing over there? Why are you hanging out of an open window?

MAL

Because we must jump now, you and I together. Just like before with the train and the head squishing. We must die together so we can wake up!

DOM

But we're *already* awake! This is the real world. If you jump, you'll die! This is where we want to be, here in America with our kids, living the dream!

MAL

We are *not* awake, we are still trapped in this stupid Limbo! Why are you trying to make it nice and pretend it's okay? I thought you were

Mr. Reality-guy, now you're Mr. Happy-pants!

DOM

I think positive emotion trumps negative emotion every time.

MAL

You have said a very silly thing. Positive emotion is the fart of a unicorn, yes? A tiny little rainbow poof! It is cute, yes, but that's all. It trumps nothing, it changes nothing, it does not – how you say? – get shit done.

DOM

Snookums, I think you're making too much...

MAL

Positive emotion makes people sit on their ass and get fat and go nowhere and do nothing. Negative emotion burns. It makes heat and energy and change. What does the asshole of the unicorn give us? Flowery stink, that's all.

DOM

Wow, you've really given this some thought.

MAL

To say I like happy thoughts is to say I give up! I am afraid of my own life! I do not like this game and do not wish to play. I want to stay safe in the harbor and never set sail on the voyage of life. I spit on your stupid positive emotion. It is fear! It is death!

DOM

Listen, pooty-bird, that's no reason to jump...

MAL

Don't you pooty-bird me! This is why we *must* jump. We must die together! This isn't real. We must die from the dream to awaken to the real! It scares you because you think this world is real, but you are deceived! This is just another level of Deception. You think we escaped from Limbo, but we are still here!

DOM

But baby, this *is* real. I planted that Deception in your mind when we were in Limbo and it's still in there making you think you have to keeping going further, but there is no further. We're here! This is it! This is the real world!

MAL

You are very wrong. We are still in Limbo. This is the great big joke you do not get. Wherever we go, we are *always* in Limbo.

DOM

You're just mad because I planted the Deception in your mind. Please calm down and back away from the ledge.

MAL

I will *not* calm down, I am on fire! You were once on fire too, but now your flame has gone out and you are scared like a baby. You say to

me, "Mal, don't be a crazy lady, relax and be happy like me," but I have had enough of your pretend happiness. I will find my way out of this maze if I have to jump out a thousand windows and have my head squished a thousand times! *Montagnes peuvent s'écrouler sur ma tête...*

DOM

That's not *you* talking! That's just the Deception I planted in your head so we could get out of Limbo. It worked! Now we're here! We can stop now!

MARION

There is no stopping! Do not be so eager to feast on yummy lies. I ask you, where is the dream factory you promised? Where are my servants and fans? This is not the real world, this is just another layer of bullshit cake. Come, let us jump to our deaths and awaken together!

DOM

You don't understand!

MARION

It is *you* who does not understand!

NED

I'm afraid neither of you understand.

Dom turns to find NED standing behind him. Ariadne looks on.

72

DOM

Jesus Christ! Who the hell are you?

NED

Ned McFeely. I'm the author of this scene. It seemed like it was getting bogged down in all this quibbling so I thought I'd pop in and give it a little tweak.

DOM

You're not the author of me. I'm a self-determined individual! I have free will!

NED

There, see? That's what I mean. Your dialog is stilted and boring. Let's explore your character's motivation.

MARION

Dommy-bear? Who is that man with you?

DOM

No one, babe, just the author.

NED

to Dom

Okay, so you locked something away, something deep inside, the truth that you had once known, but chose to forget.

MAL

Yoohoo! Mr. Author! I was just now telling him this!

DOM

It's like something in my solar plexus that just keeps churning so I can never relax.

NED

Yes, and someday it will burst out of your chest like an alien and you will give birth to yourself. Until then, you're like a caterpillar dreaming of butterflies.

MAL

Papillon!

DOM

Then who am I really? I mean, *really* really.

NED

If you are aware, then you are awareness.

DOM

Well, I guess that's not nothing.

NED

It's the only something there is.

DOM

Then maybe dreaming ain't so bad.

NED

Depends on the dream.

MARION

Hello? Sweetie-pie, remember me? Your wife? I'm sitting on a ledge about to jump to my death. Care to join me?

DOM

Yeah, just a minute, honey-britches.

MARION

Don't you honey-britches me! Are we going to jump together or not?

DOM

to Mal

We're working on that right now, butter-buns. Just a sec.

to Ned

So all these levels of dream and reality, you're saying that *none* of it is real?

NED

Or, you can say it's *all* real, but none of it is true. Isn't that the nature of a dream? Real but not true?

MARION

Hello? Darling? What are you doing that's more important than jumping to your death right now?

DOM

Just having a chat, *mon petit albatros*. Be right with you.

NED

In order to be *re*born, one must first be *un*born.

DOM

You mean die.

NED

Same difference.

DOM

Like by jumping out a window or getting run over by a train?

NED

Dramatic but messy. The only real way to awaken from the dream of selfhood is through the process of focused thought. Emotionally *suppressed* thought leads to deeper sleep. Emotionally *fueled* thought leads to dream destruction and awakening.

DOM

Suicide by thought?

NED

To be born into lucidity, you must die out of wrong-knowing.

DOM

I don't want to die, I want to be me, but I also want to wake up.

NED

That's what those people in the opium den were trying to do, wake up without leaving the dream, but despite what they promise in the Village of Flatulence, you can't have your cake and eat it too. It's one or the other. Wake up or stay asleep.

DOM

So what do I have to do to wake up? Why shouldn't I join her in jumping to our deaths?

NED

I didn't say you shouldn't.

DOM

Well, dammit, I'm *not* gonna jump!

MAL

overhears

Okay pussy-boy, I go alone!

DOM

rushes to window

Mal, wait. No!

MAL

See you in my dreams! *Au revoir!*

A trailing-off scream is heard.

DOM

wails in despair

Oh Mal! Baby! What have I done? I killed you!
Oh my God!

turns angrily on Ned

You bastard! This is all your fault!

NED

It feels like the scene is dragging.

DOM

What are you saying? My wife just committed
suicide! Oh my God! My poor baby!

NED

I think we've reached the end of your character
arc.

DOM

What the hell are you talking about? Jesus
buddy, can't you see I'm grievin' here?

NED

Your character is stuck. I think you need a little
push.

DOM

Holy shit, are you crazy? Don't you understand?
My wife just jumped out the fuckin'...

Ned pushes Dom out the window.

NED

turns to Ariadne

Is it just me, or was it getting a little whiny in here?

ARIADNE

You can see me?

NED

I see all.

ARIADNE

What happens now?

NED

I write the press junket scene.

ARIADNE

What about me?

NED

You're just words on a page, Ellen.

Exeunt.

Diamond Bullets

Each problem that I solved became a rule, which
served afterwards to solve other problems.

René Descartes

H ERE ARE SOME OF THE MAXIMS by which
I understand, interpret, and navigate the
dreamstate:

- Whatever is, is right.
- No Belief Is True
- Cogito, Ergo Sum/No Objective Knowledge
- Truth Hath No Confines/All Context Is False
- Awareness True/Appearance Untrue
- Truth Exists/Untruth Does Not Exist
- No-Self is True Self
- I Am/Consciousness
- Nonduality/Not-Two
- That Thou Art/All Is One

Seeing them written down, I notice that they all boil down to a binary zero or one, true or false, as certainly they must. Some are flipsides of others, some can be worded differently for different occasions, and there's a good deal of overlap between them, but they're all my own personal tools of dreamstate navigation. I can trust them because I did the work and I know their truth directly. I can steer by them and be sure they won't send me off into a ditch. I never have to stop and think about anything because I have these tools to answer any question or guide me in any situation.

Notice that there's nothing on the list like Love Will Find a Way, We're All in it Together, Good Will Triumph, or Truth Will Out. Those might be adequate within the tight confines of the herd where all your decisions are made for you, but once you're on your own in the Great Whatever, you need more sophisticated tools of navigation.

Maxims are not mere beliefs or credos or commandments, they're statements of truth, but their power can only be wielded by someone who has perceived that truth directly. I can take my maxims as gospel and trust them implicitly because I fought for them and won them fair and square. I didn't adopt them or subscribe to them or have them handed down to me by some Big Daddy guru. I did the hard work and made them mine. I *own* them.

In a similar vein, a maxim is not a boon that I can grant. My maxims are not mine to give or yours to

82

receive. I can tell you what they are, and you might get some sense of direction from them, but it's not until you've done the work for yourself that you own them for yourself. Until then, my maxims are just catchphrases you might believe more or less, now and then, according to the needs of the moment, more like a catchy slogan or a personal motto.

Amusingly, my maxims are completely useless for the purposes of everyday life. I don't have one for removing wine stains or saving on electric bills or anything handy like that, just these black and white truisms that are of very little practical use in the gray-scale dreamstate.

I should also mention that I never actually call these maxims to mind except for the purposes of writing. They are merely words representing an awareness that is fully in place. I don't have them printed on a card in my wallet in case I get lost. I don't need to refer to them any more than I need to give my feet verbal commands when walking. My sense of right action is so deeply ingrained that for decades now I've been unable to muster the slightest interest in Tarot, I Ching, astrology, channeled material or any other navigational aids for which I have plenty of respect but no personal need. If I stood in the kitchen of the Oracle as she baked, the only thing I'd want from her would be a cookie.

In fact, the only reason I'm aware of my maxims at all is because I'm in the business. If I were just living

a normal life, I'd probably just be doing normal life stuff, whatever that is, and not spending my time reverse-engineering the dreamstate. If I could think of anything better to do I'd go do that, but what could be more interesting than the holy trinity of Maya, Atman, and Brahman? I suppose I could try being a pop star or a gigolo or a shipping magnate, but those professions require expensive sunglasses and I'm a cheap sunglasses kinda guy, so I guess I'll stick with the spiritual thing. And speaking of clumsy segues, let's take a few of the maxims out for a spin and see what they can do.

※

Nonduality, the certainty of one and certain impossibility of two, is an example of a minor epiphany that is achieved by some seekers who consider it valuable in and of itself, but who never go on to unleash its full weapon-of-dreamstate-destruction potential. In the process of waking up in or from the dreamstate, only progress matters, and progress is only made by destroying the false. The insight of not-two is not an ornament to be hung on the wall, it's a sledgehammer for destroying illusion, and it's not until we start swinging it that we see what it can really do.

I like to harp on nonduality because so many people get to this modest plateau and declare victory, like arriving at a mountain trailhead and mistaking the map kiosk in the parking lot for the peak above;

understandably tempting since the parking lot is where the party is. If I were to define my most appropriate audience, on paper anyway, it would probably be stalled-out advaitins and nondualists, but my long-standing, ill-informed and largely indifferent opinion on the matter is that nondual folk are pretty happy where they are. They ran their tanks dry getting to the parking lot and that's where the party is, so no one even notices the trail leading further up. I suspect they believe that nonduality is a philosophy or a teaching or a school of thought, but it's really just a simple statement of fact, and when you're trying to wake up, facts are not precious jewels of spiritual insight, they're mountain-busting machines that only create change when put to hard use.

The sign at the base of the trail reads: "Who goes beyond goes alone." The party crowd didn't sign up for that and seem blissfully unaware that there's anything above the parking lot; that's where all the perpetual seekers are, that's where all the fun teachers are, and that's where the party is, so who even thinks of going further? It might have started out as a quest for truth or enlightenment, but that was just the bait before the switch to compassion, love, uber-consciousness or whatever, and all the neo-neo-advaitins are cool with that because no one wants to leave the party and go off into the lonely, scary, unfun dark.

Contributing to chronic spiritual underachievement is the legion of popular teachers, some of whom

actually made the transition from juvenile to adult but have mistaken their newfound state for enlightenment when it's really just the shallowest stage of post-natal development. They're right to think they've done something pretty cool, and they'd be right to teach it if they grew into it, but they're wrong to call it enlightenment and they're wrong to do a victory dance while their heels are still resting on the start line. In their defense, when everyone around you is still stuck in their shell and you've managed to poke your head out, the term enlightenment would naturally spring to mind.

Similar to the insight of nonduality in the fraudulent claims department is the power of discrimination. Many people believe they exercise their power of discrimination, but the first thing they'd see if they did was that they don't. Possessing the power of discrimination is not the same thing as employing it any more than having a flashlight helps you see in the dark if you don't turn it on. Discrimination is not how we choose science over religion, it's how we blow them both out of the water. It's not how we choose Theravada over Mahayana, it's how we nuke Buddhism out of existence. Discrimination is not a dimestore penlight, it's flamethrower, and you don't use it as an egoic adornment, you use it to light up and burn down every dark corner and hidden crevice of your dreamstate universe. That's what this waking up stuff is all about, and if your spiritual teachings

and teachers didn't tell you that then they're as good a place to start throwing flame as any.

☀

Another simple maxim of great potential value is "Whatever is, is right." These words were first strung together by Alexander Pope in the poem *An Essay on Man* in the 1730s:

All nature is but art, unknown to thee;
All chance, direction, which thou canst not see;
All discord, harmony, not understood;
All partial evil, universal good:
And, spite of pride, in erring reason's spite,
One truth is clear, Whatever is, is right.

The clear understanding that isness and rightness are synonymous purges morality, judgment, and opinion from your mental space in a single Herculean stroke. All our views on right and wrong, good and bad, better and worse, simply vanish once we remove our biasing filters and see that whatever is, is as it must be because it is what is, and can therefore not be wrong. Imperfection lies in the eye of the beholder, so judgment always reflects not on the judged, but on the judge.

Okay, but here's the tricky part. See where Mr. Pope held back? *Partial* evil? He didn't hedge his bet in the first three lines, so what's up? Is he saying *whatever* is, is right, or whatever is, except really *bad* shit, is

right? He left himself a backdoor so when pissed off townfolk and churchfolk showed up at his door to ask if he meant Satan was right, or plague was right, or failed harvests were right, he could walk it back and say, "Heck no! That's why I said partial! Whatever is, is right, except really bad stuff!" He certainly understood that the word partial was false, and I'm sure he was reluctant to weaken the fourth line, especially since the first three and final lines don't equivocate. In fact, I'd say the penultimate line apologizes for the word partial and should be read:

And despite the fact that I just lied.
One truth is clear, Whatever is, is right.

Remove the offending word and read the fourth line the way Pope meant it: *All evil, universal good.* Saying that would cross a line that Pope couldn't cross, which may be why *An Essay on Man* was originally published anonymously. Besides not wanting to be jailed, tortured, excommunicated, or blacklisted, I'm sure he just didn't want to alienate his readership, which would be an easy thing to do. I myself always hold back. Maybe when I write *Jed Talks 44: Deathbed Jed*, I'll really let 'er rip, but for now we have to keep things civil. No one is threatening me with the rack and ruin, but if I alienate my imagined readership then I will have failed to communicate, and what's the point of being more honest if I'm just talking to myself? Anyone who is awake from the dreamstate is going to appear

monstrous or psychotic from the unawake perspective because Pope is right; *whatever* is, including all the very worst shit, *is* right. Perfectly black and white, no shades of gray. Calling morality a delusion isn't *partially* true, saying life has no meaning isn't *conditionally* correct; these blasphemies against herdthink are true and knowable. Nothing matters or can matter because meaning can only exist within context and, as another maxim states, all context is false. The dreamstate is all appearance and no substance, so that which *is* cannot be wrong any more than an apple falling upward in a dream is wrong. Appearance can't be wrong, so the only thing that *can* be wrong is the thing that doesn't happen. If something *does* happen, it's right, and if you think it's not, you're wrong, which, in turn, you are right to be. All evil is universal good. Sit with that for a minute. How long would even a tenured philosophy professor have a job if he encouraged students to explore the ramifications of that one?

The creation of a personal maxim is not like a flash of insight or intuition, it's like solving a math problem you've wrestled with for a year; they structurally redefine who and what we are. Petty insights commonly promoted as spiritual breakthroughs only contribute to obstructions rather than dislodging them. Fear always demands more – more false knowledge, more groupthink, more buttressing from tight-packed herdmates – but awakening always goes the other way. It's not arrived at through acquisition but through a slow,

painful process of reduction. No belief is true, so the key is not to lay on more beliefs but to slice away those we already have, and since we are what we believe, this is invariably a process of self-destruction.

The realization that whatever is, is right, triggers a massive avalanche which clears away all wrong-knowing and confusion surrounding morality and opens the way to a fully integrated mastery of right action. Once you know firsthand, by having actually achieved this level of perspective, that wrongness is not possible, then the need for judging everyone and everything right and wrong, good and evil, better and worse, simply falls away. Villains are valid characters like any other, you may even play one at times. The man with the black hat and curly mustache is not being a good neighbor when he ties the pretty lady to the railroad tracks, but he's not wrong; he's just playing his role, performing his function. If disagreeable functions went unperformed, there would be no conflict, no drama, no emotional engagement, just players and beholders sitting around, bored out of their minds.

As Anthony de Mello said, "All is well, all is well. Though everything is a mess, all is well." Once you see that everything is right just the way it is, you can suspend your emotional outflow and see your life for the dramatic production it is, and then you'll be free to explore the larger creative playspace of which you are an inseparable part. That's how we release our attachment to the outer world and make the hard

turn inward where a different kind of life awaits. This inward-turning is not about becoming heartless, only reclaiming our lifeforce and putting it to better use. The external world of people and events is only one small part of what's going on. Most people are satisfied with herd life because they don't know there's anything else. The only way to find out there's more is to turn inward and see for yourself, and that's a one-way trip.

Vesuvius buries Pompeii as easily as a breeze ripples a field of wheat. Endless waves of men can be marched to doom, nations can fall into seas, plagues and cancers can sweep continents, infant mortality can hit one hundred percent and humans can whimper out of existence, and not one iota of substance will have been gained or lost, exactly as if it happened in a movie or a dream. The next great extinction might begin before you finish this chapter, or maybe it already has. The point isn't that it's a tragedy but that it's irrelevant. Every person is their own world and they all end in cataclysm. You may not like the sound of that, but the process of awakening is one of directly confronting things you don't like, one after another, until all beliefs are reduced to ash and only truth remains. To wake up, you have to reverse your emotional polarity and be drawn toward that which now repels you and go into the negative. If you came here looking for peace and tolerance and happy thoughts, welcome to the wrong book.

Let's think of something we can all agree is bad without invoking the beleaguered Nazis. How about people who break into apartments and throw babies against the wall for no apparent reason? I think we can all agree that under generally accepted standards of Golden Rule behavior, this is pretty bad. And yet, the exact value of this action is unmistakably zero. "Sure," you argue, "*one* baby, but what if someone breaks into an apartment and throws a *zillion* babies against a wall for no apparent reason? What then?" Well, let's do the math; zero times a zillion equals zero. Nothing in the dreamstate ever adds up to anything, and even if all the people in the world get together and agree that throwing a baby against a wall without a darn good reason is the worst thing ever, it still adds up to nothing. The perceived value of throwing babies against walls is way down on the bad end of the good-evil spectrum, but the exact value of the entire spectrum is knowably zero. We *feel* meaning, but thought shows us that meaning can only exist within context and all context is false so, big surprise, emotion is tricking us into seeing something that isn't really there.

Says ACIM: "Nothing real can be threatened. Nothing unreal exists." Says Krishna: "The unreal never is: the real never is not. This truth indeed has been seen by those who can see the true." Says I: "Awareness is true and truth exists. Appearance is untrue and untruth does not exist." No matter how

you phrase it, truth is real and untruth is false and never the twain shall meet.

Whether it's the sneeze of a kitten or a mass baby-hurling event or planetary extinction, the exact value of everything in the dreamstate is knowably, certainly, obviously zero. The rational mind sees this clearly and threatens to upset the dramatic applecart, but emotion rushes in with desire for the carrot ahead and fear of the stick behind and the great herd plods on instead of grinding to a halt and dying in its tracks.

❊

No-self is true self. As Whitman will say elsewhere in these pages: *This is curious, and may not be realized immediately, but it must be realized.* There is no you. You are a fiction. Ego is a lie, personality is a lie, self is a lie. You are simply a character in a dream and because there is no real you, even the dream is not yours.

This stuff can seem pretty obvious when stated outright, but it's essential to the dreamstate experience that we remain unaware of it which, through the emotional flimflammery of ego, we effectively do. The function of ego is to make us see what's not and not see what is, and on that imaginary basis rests our ability to subscribe wholeheartedly to the juvenile construct of selfhood. As true as self may seem in the dreamstate, the dreamstate itself is false. The emotion fueling the illusion that selfhood is true is generated by the fear that it's not.

All belief systems exist to shield us from truth so the show can go on. All the paths, teachings, schools and ideologies that promise to help us discover our true selves are perpetrating a fraud because there is no true self to discover. No-self is true self. With this one little truth bomb, we nuke the entire spiritual marketplace into a heap of smoldering ash. Next, you can use the Cogito to nuke philosophy, No Belief Is True to nuke the rest of the dreamstate, and I Am/Consciousness to nuke whatever remains of yourself.

※

And as long as we're in the neighborhood, I'm in the mood for nuking love, so here's a bonus double-maxim: Fear is the source of all emotion, and all fear is the fear of truth.

Many of those above-mentioned paths, teachings, schools, and ideologies promote unconditional love as the highest ideal toward which we might aspire, but this sort of vapid puffery has no place in any serious discussion. You can love the living shit out of everyone and everything and all you'll have to show for it is enough blood-sugar content to induce a diabetic coma. And what would an unconditionally loving person even look like if you met them in person? Like someone who needs a good smack, I'd say.

We like to think of love as something in its own right rather than a derivative of something not as many-splendored, and of course, the spiritual and

entertainment industries love to beat the love drum, but the truth is that love is a subtle transfiguration of fear. Maybe you think I don't know what I'm talking about, but listen closely and you'll hear your Little Bastard telling you I do. Love has a real counterpart in the adult world, but as long as you accept the shadow as real you'll never turn around to see what's casting it.

✲

Okay, one more for the road: Good spirit is everything. No, it's not a maxim and yes, it's a little rah-rah, but let me take this opportunity to say that I know this stuff isn't all rainbows and puppy dog tails, so take a moment to congratulate yourself for being here. To borrow from Orwell, in a time of universal deceit, *seeking* the truth is a revolutionary act, and here you are. You have good spirit, and it's probably a good idea to remind yourself of that now and then.

Okay, that was nice of me, now let's get back to work.

The Old Pond Road

> Once you realize that the road is the goal and
> that you are always on the road, not to reach
> a goal, but to enjoy its beauty and its wisdom,
> life ceases to be a task and becomes natural
> and simple, in itself an ecstasy.

Sri Nisargadatta Maharaj

I T'S COLD. Not super cold, just pretty cold. Crisp.
There's snow everywhere, but not fresh snow. The
sky is black and star-speckled with a bright moon and
wisps of cloud. The air is still. Paul and I walk in
silence. This is the same Paul I talked about in the
first book, but this was before that.

I'm a little upset with Paul because he's walking
with his hands clasped behind his back and his head
bowed forward in the manner of a deep thinker. That's
how I want to walk, but now I can't because we'd look
like a couple of dipshits. Not that there's anyone to see

us out on these moonlit country roads in the middle of endless snow-clad fields, but we would become self-conscious of our own idiotic appearance. I don't want Paul pulled out of his process right now, so I concede to adopt a different walking posture. I try just walking normally, but my arms won't swing right when I think about it. I try crossing my arms or clasping my hands in front of me, but both positions are too unnatural and conspicuous-feeling. I finally decide to put my hands in my pockets, even though I have to take off my gloves off and stash them inside my coat to do it. Better. So Paul gets to walk with hands behind back, head bowed, all nice and thoughtful looking, while I, the illustrious teacher, have to walk along with my hands in my pockets like a dopey student. (I know I make it look easy, but there's a lot more to this enlightened spiritual master thing than just a silly job title.)

Despite his contemplative appearance, Paul is not composing music or constructing a haiku, he is actually thinking. I know he is, I can feel it like an electric buzz emanating from his head like a Tesla coil. I couldn't think with all that buzzing going on even if I wanted to which, happily, I don't.

Paul stops, freezes, turns to me but doesn't speak. I wait. His eyes are unfocused and he seems to be scowling inwardly, perhaps at his own internal reflection scowling back. A casual observer might think he is riding out a wave of pain, and maybe he is, but

I recognize his state as that of someone engaged in an inner conflict so consuming that all other systems must spin down whenever a skirmish flares up. He is committing violence in his head, killing something he doesn't want to kill. For me to say anything now would be like crinkling a candy wrapper during a chess match, or your stupid friend who blurts out random digits when you're trying to memorize a phone number. I know a small part of him remains above the surface, aware of his surroundings, of me, so I gently turn my attention inward and don't move again until he does.

"Huh, okay," he says after a few moments and resumes walking. We continue for twenty minutes in silence. I maintain a quiet mind. This is not teacher-student stuff or spiritual stuff, this is someone going through something with someone who already has. Every step is its own undertaking, its own process with its own set of cold calculations. Every step requires sacrifice. Every step is painful and complete and somehow magnificent.

"Knock knock," I say.

"Who's there?"

"Deja."

"Deja who?"

"Knock knock."

He nods almost imperceptibly and we continue for another twenty minutes in silence.

"Knock knock," I say.

"Who's there?"

"The interrupting doctor."

"The interru…"

"You have cancer."

He nods. We continue. After fifteen minutes he stops, eyes down.

"So," he says, and then is silent for a full minute. "So," he repeats, "there's really no…" He leaves it hanging. I know what he means.

"No," I say.

He nods. We continue. I fall behind. He makes small gestures with his right hand as if connecting puzzle pieces of thought, his left hand helping now and then. He occasionally speaks aloud to himself as if conducting both sides of a debate. I serve no obvious purpose in accompanying him, but my presence is required. I stay back so I can be in my own space without interfering with his. He stops. I stop. He goes. I go. I would like to make a snowball and knock his hat off, but the snow isn't right.

He turns and walks back to me.

"It was like this for you?"

"For anyone," I say.

"Yeah," he says. Like any question he could ask me right now, he already knows the answer but can't quite believe it. He nods, thinks, nods again and continues walking.

He seems calm, but there's an intensity in his smallest gesture, in his quiet words, that reveals his inner turmoil. He goes on many walks without a wingman.

In fact, I don't think I've seen him in a few weeks, but today he came to me.

"Can we take a walk?" he asked.

"Sure," I said.

So here we are.

He's a very serious person. I'm not. Once I was and someday he won't be, but for now, he is and I'm not.

We complete a loop and arrive back at the house. The loops out here are pretty big and it's pretty cold. He pauses at the driveway. I wait. He starts lap two. I follow.

We're walking in and between tire ruts cut through packed snow. A pickup passes us and almost clips Paul with its mirror. He doesn't notice. I stand aside to give it room. I wave.

Paul is much more composed than I was at this stage. I was bouncing off the walls, going out of my head, trying to get a handle on the process; steer it, control it, understand it, capture it in words, battle it with words, translate it into words. I was living on words, consuming and rejecting books piles at a time. Like a mathematician-lawyer with OCD, I was obsessed with defining the terms I needed, which introduced new terms that had to be meticulously defined, which introduced new terms that had to be meticulously defined. Rejecting esoteric and arcane terminology wholesale. Writing, pacing, talking to myself, writing more. Getting to the end of one thing and collapsing in exhaustion until the next thing

flared up. Externalizing my thoughts, getting them out where I could see them and polish and correct and destroy them. It was pretty crazy.

Maybe Paul is crazy like that in private, but right now he's outwardly calm. If this doesn't kill him, if he doesn't obey the urge to physically rip himself open and pull out his own guts, he'll get through it. He'll destroy the teacher, which isn't really me but some internal aspect of self. Maybe he'll write books when he's done, or maybe he'll find some sort of life for himself that fits his new understanding of things. As must be true of anyone who is awake *from* the dreamstate, I am also awake *in* it, and my course is laid out and doesn't require much input from me. Maybe it will be that way for Paul, but for now, he's still down in the thick of it.

We complete the second loop and arrive back at the house. I divert to the mailbox. He continues into a third lap. I follow, fifty feet behind, and go through my mail which has brought good news; "Congratulations," it informs me, "you may already be a winner!"

Sweet.

Marichelle 5: The I-Part

There's no such thing as not-being. You can't not
be, right? There's only what is, there is not what's
not. Don't break out in a rash about this. Just relax
for now. We have a lot to cover.

.   ⚘

Here's a funny riddle: How many sides does a
monkey have? Okay, two, okay? Inside and outside.
Same as you. You basically have two parts, inside
and outside. As you go more inside, more of the
inside becomes outside. That's a good point. You
can write that down.

✿

How far can you go is a good question. When all the inside becomes outside, what's left inside? This is a good question, but you can only answer by going. First you go, then you know.

✿

The I-part is what's left when everything else is gone. Just to call it something I call it the I-part. The I-part is the always part. The rest comes and goes, but the I-part stays the same. You can't even joke about that.

✿

Nothing can be and also not be. I can't tell if that's very obvious or not. If something really is, then it always is, but if some really isn't, then it never is, okay? This is hard to say right but it's really good to think about.

✿

If you want to say you have heart and brain, then okay, you can say your heart will keep you in coma and your brain can maybe get you out. Heart is a lot stronger than brain so that's a hard fight. Right now you just use the heart so everything holds together, but when you start using your brain then everything can come apart pretty fast.

You think you think your thoughts, but this is just for show. You think what your heart tells you to think. That might sound bad but it's probably good. Long story.

Put your hand down, you don't have to tell me you disagree. Of course you disagree, that's automatic. Until you see things yourself you only have opinion. There is no opinion with me, the only opinion is with you.

Right now you're wrong about everything because that's how it is. If you were wrong about just some things that would be a big problem, but you're really wrong about everything so it's not as bad.

You think your thoughts and feelings are on the inside, but as you go more inside they become more outside. Your thoughts and feelings don't move, only your understanding moves. As your understanding goes more inside, everything inside becomes more outside.

☙

Once something goes outside like that, it loses power. Maybe it was really big and important when it was inside, but when it goes outside it's like a rock or a bush or like something you're just done with.

☙

The I-part is the only real part. Take this thought with you and hold onto it and everything will change. Pretty simple.

☙

Until you see that you're insane, there is no chance of becoming sane. Believing you're sane is just a part of insanity. Because you're living in a crazy place full of crazy people, you think you're normal. Maybe you're normal but you're not sane.

☙

You have to get down to the I-part. Everything else is coma. The I-part is the middle part all this other stuff goes around. The I-part doesn't move or change, it's just there. No matter where you go, the I-part never moves. Even when you're dead the I-part is still there because it's not really you. That's a more advanced concept, I would say.

The I-part doesn't do anything. It's not this way or that way, okay? All the same. It's not a boy monkey or a girl monkey. All that monkey stuff is just coma.

The I-part isn't in coma, coma is in the I-part. Mind isn't in dream, dream is in mind. Brain is in dream, dream is in mind. Something like that.

If you think there is a real you, that you are a real thing, that you really exist, then I would say this is just a part of your condition and if you ever want to go sane you have to come out of it, but then there's no one left so the whole thing is kind of a joke. Not really, but kind of.

I know you have some stuff in your head you think is pretty good, like not nonsense, like you have some good ideas you want to keep, like you just need a little more of what you already have, but really, you don't have any good ideas yet. They're all pretty bad.

Everything circles around the I-part, but the I-part never moves. That's all the I-part does is sit in the middle and watch. Everything else is not-I. That's actually right, but maybe you don't like that. Maybe we don't want to be here yet. Maybe I went too far at this point. I shouldn't jump ahead.

Don't worry what someone else says, just do your own calculations. Everything else will just make a mess. You want to trust some person or some system, but this is something you do by yourself.

You only believe what you feel, but thinking is another thing you can try. You have to try to see with your brain. That's what it's there for, right? I don't know, but you can try.

You can just keep digging and digging looking for something that's not nothing, like maybe the next thing or the next thing, but the next thing keeps being nothing too. Every time you find something it turns out to be more nothing, so it can be upsetting.

No one else can do your calculations for you. It's like no one else can eat your food for you or live your life for you. You have to do it yourself or it never gets done.

You don't think everyone is wrong about everything, like you just have to join with the people who are right and then you'll be okay, but no one is right. There are no right people in coma. There are no people at all, but that's another day.

As you continue this inside-out adventure, you see that everything is not really made of anything. Everything is nothing. That's crazy I know, but very obvious when you see it instead of someone just telling you.

Whatever you think you are, you're not. Pretty simple. You believe all this stuff that is very obvious until you look closer, then all this stuff is really not there.

☙

This is the most basic stuff. Maybe it's a big deal because it's not your normal idea about things. If you want, you can try to show how I'm wrong about something. That's a very good exercise, like some homework you can do.

☙

When you get to the end of pretending, then it all makes better sense. Pretty good sense. Everything has to make sense. That's a good thing to remember. You can do some good calculations if you remember that.

☙

Maybe you think this ends up with you in some great place, so it might be a disappointment to discover nothing is real. Maybe that's not what you were hoping.

☙

I really don't know why I'm talking to you or why you're listening to me, but okay. I can do some talking and you can do some listening. Why not? I don't have a problem with it. I'm just having a nice time.

The Tyranny of Delusion

> I found myself desiring and knowing less and less,
> until I could say in utter astonishment: "I know
> nothing, I want nothing." Earlier I was sure of so
> many things, now I am sure of nothing. But I feel I
> have lost nothing by not knowing, because all my
> knowledge was false. My not knowing was in itself
> knowledge of the fact that all my knowledge is
> ignorance, that "I do not know" is the only true
> statement the mind can make. I do not claim to
> know what you do not. In fact, I know much less
> than you do.
>
> *Sri Nisargadatta Maharaj*

"Why do you always have to be so negative?" asks a frowny young man sitting on a backrest in the front row. "There's no reason we can't all get along and live lives of harmony and compassion. I mean, isn't that the point of spirituality? So we can live in peace and tolerance and love?"

If this were a game of beach volleyball and he set me up like that, I'd reward him with a smash that would make his ancestors wobble, but this question

isn't from a fierce competitor, it's from a delicate little New Age snowflake who has been tricked into being here because he thinks I'm a spiritual teacher. He's like a baby dolphin that has been caught in a shark net. All I want is to untangle him and send him on his way, but the setup is too good to pass up.

"I'm not positive or negative," I reply, "I'm actually neutral, so from the perspective of false positivity, I appear negative. If you're hosting a little tea party for Lord Lion and Lady Gazelle and someone comes along who doesn't share your fantasy narrative, then the problem isn't that they're negative but that your make-believe world is a bit fragile."

That's about as gently as I can return the ball, which, to my surprise, he deftly returns. He has a well-worn, dog-eared book in his hand. I recognize it, having owned a few copies over the years, as *Man's Search for Meaning* by Viktor Frankl. He opens to a bookmarked page and reads forcefully, as if warding off a demon:

"...for the first time in my life I saw the truth as it is set into song by so many poets, proclaimed as the final wisdom by so many thinkers. The truth – that love is the ultimate and the highest goal to which man can aspire. Then I grasped the meaning of the greatest secret that human poetry and human thought and belief have to impart: The salvation of man is through love and in love."

He closes the book and stares at me triumphantly.

"This guy was in Auschwitz," he says. "He created the school of Logotherapy. He's hardly hosting tea parties."

Tricky little dolphin. Now he's got me arguing with a Holocaust survivor by proxy.

"Okay," I say, "I agree."

He looks at me like I'm setting him up.

"But?"

"I agree that love is the highest goal to which humanity can aspire," I say, "but, simply put, I don't agree that you're a human. You're saying love is the best thing in the dungeon, other people say other things, but I say, why stay in the dungeon at all? Why try to make the best of a bad situation? The door's not locked, you're free to leave, so what's the point of sitting in the dark worshipping a stray shaft of light when you can walk out into the sun? Dr. Frankl might not have had that option, but maybe you do."

He starts to answer, waving the book at me, but I know the book. I know Dr. Frankl and Logotherapy. I would clear off an entire shelf of dusty philosophy and saccharine spirituality to make room for the book this young man is trying to bludgeon me with.

"Thank you for the question," I tell him. "You have done very well to get to Dr. Frankl, but don't stop there. Use him as a stepping stone to go further."

He nods and thanks me.

"I have been asked what it is that makes me different. I don't glow or levitate or radiate benevolence, so it's

a reasonable question. The answer has two parts. The first part is that I'm not one of you. That's accurate but not helpful. The second and more important part is that you're not one of you either. You're clinging to a false idea of yourself and only you can change it. The reality is that the only one who cares about you is you. That may sound cruel, but it's true, and truth leads to adulthood and liberation. Love, as we know it, is just a cheap knockoff of the real thing. It's always selfish because it's always a manifestation of fear. Just as your love for others is false and conditional, so is theirs for you. What seems like a genuine connection is more like actors playing Romeo and Juliet who are stupidly in love on stage, but go their separate ways when the curtain comes down. We're all in it alone and even the deepest love is just a kind of Stockholm Syndrome brought on by environment and circumstances, like prisoners in a dungeon huddling together against the cold and damp. Once we find our way out of the dungeon and into the warmth of the sun, the huddling urge is gone and the people we were so close to no longer serve a purpose. To say that darkness is better than sunlight is fear at work. We're choosing the pain-reliever over the cure because we believe the dungeon is reality and there's nothing beyond. We'd rather live in spiritual squalor than take a risk. Within the dungeon, this love-huddling seems like salvation, but from the perspective of someone living in the warmth of the sun, it looks like sightless white eels writhing in a cave

puddle. We can shape ourselves to each other, become emotionally entangled in each other, intermingle our thoughts and feelings and fluids, but there can never be an authentic connection, only the profound desire to connect which is generated by fear of the black hole within, which is – ironically, paradoxically, counter-intuitively – the door that leads out of the cave and into freedom."

✻

I can read the room well enough to know that this is not a popular message, but it's not meant to be. A lot of these people hang their spiritual hat on the whole love thing, which is exactly why I'm kicking it around. What is this love that we love so much? The love of one ego for another? Of one false self for another? My avatar loves your avatar? My lie loves your lie? Is it a person we love or love itself? We're all trapped in a Freudian-Oedipal, mommy-daddy stage of emotional development because we're trapped in the juvenile state. There is a truth of love, and I'm a big fan of the real thing, but the real thing is an adult thing and we'll never discover it as long as we settle for the kiddie version.

✻

"If you think that spiritual development means an expansion of love, then you're putting all your eggs in the wrong basket; facing outward when the real journey is inward. It's like a child who thinks that being a

grownup means you get to have lots of candy and play all day and never eat broccoli. That's what a perfect life looks like to a kid, just the way love and bliss and life everlasting might look to one kind of grownup, or wealth and power to another, or junkfood and a game console to another, but adulthood is none of these things and by clinging to adolescent expectations we anchor ourselves to the juvenile state. By trying to make the best of the dungeon, we abandon any hope of escape. All the preconditions we put on adulthood will act like emotional deadweight that will either be painfully severed in the transition to adulthood, or block it altogether.

"All the teachers, priests and gurus in the spiritual marketplace are peddling their visions of the future and we shop for the best deal; the least sacrifice now for the most heaven later. The spiritual marketplace is a very large carnival full of very sincere people selling lovely visions of our potential, even delivering in some cases to some degree, but what no one in the carnival is selling is a shitty deal. No one is offering a path to meaninglessness and futility and the oblivion of no-self. That's my little niche and I can maintain it because I'm not actually *in* the spiritual marketplace, I'm out back with the dumpsters and the portable toilets and all the weird smells. People stumble out to puke up all the sugary crap they've been stuffing themselves with, sick from broken promises and dead-end paths, and they find me in the back alley wearing a dark overcoat

with my hat pulled down, offering a different kind of vision. I have a very simple story to tell and, as they say of *The Mahabharata*, if you listen closely, when it's over, you'll be someone else.

"What you find when you stumble out the back gate into the dark alley is that the carnival is just a tiny island of light surrounded by a deep, dark forest. You want to go back into the light, but I'm pointing into the dark. That's where you'll find what you were looking for all along. In a dungeon, everyone will gather around whatever thin spear of light might pierce the darkness, but that spear of light isn't a destination, it's an invitation, the promise of a fully illuminated reality of which the benighted mind cannot conceive.

"The path into the woods is the eye of the needle through which ego cannot pass. It's on that dark path that you will be set upon by demons ripping you to shreds who you will come to regard as angels tearing away your bonds. Every step in those dark woods is marked by the loss of something you thought could never be lost. Whatever you bring will be torn from you and the degree to which you resist is the degree to which you suffer. You may think you know what's on the other side of those woods based on what some priest or guru or some guy in a dark alley told you, but you don't even know if there *is* a beyond. For all you know, you might walk into that forest and disappear, but maybe you've reached a point where anything is better than going back into that carnival of sweet lies,

so you listen to your Little Bastard and do a trustfall into the void.

"Or maybe not. Maybe you haven't reached that point. Maybe you just walked through the wrong gate. Maybe you just wipe the vomit off your chin and head back for another round of spiritual tail-chasing and water-treading and time-wasting, which is the exact purpose of the spiritual marketplace and a straight-up victory for ego, but right now you're not in the spiritual marketplace, you're in the back alley with a shadowy figure who's telling you what deep inside you already know; that what you've been looking for is not in the gaudy light but in the gloomy dark. That's what's happening here tonight. We're standing between two worlds; the bright shiny carnival you came out of and the dark scary forest I'm pointing to. One looks like life and happiness and the other looks like death and despair, but look again; which is really which? Ask your Little Bastard. That's the only guru you'll ever need, but right now he's smothered beneath your squirming emotional mass. As long as he can't make himself heard, you'll always head back into the madhouse, but when he starts getting his way, the real spiritual journey can begin."

❄

We take a ten-minute break. I grab a bottle of water and go outside. I walk briskly away for five minutes and then turn back. As I return, I see that many of

the cars in the parking area have a bumper sticker on which the word coexist is spelled out in religious symbols.

Though warm, I shiver.

✳

"In a long process of cutting away emotional deadweight," I continue, "the first thing to go is the illusion of connection to your herdmates. Then, once you're selfborn out of the herd and into the adult state, your real life begins. You won't send postcards home because everywhere is now home. You won't be keeping friends and family apprised of your progress because they're not really friends and family anymore, just people you huddled with in bad times. You believe your bonds to these people are real and can never be broken, but they're not and they can. The parents of the halfborn child are not the parents of the fullborn adult. The adult is an entirely different order of being, like caterpillar and butterfly. New relationships may form, but not like they were because they will not be based on need and fear.

"I was just out in the parking lot and I saw coexist bumper stickers on a lot of the cars. That's just more Lord Lion and Lady Gazelle tea party fantasy. You know what happens when gazelles sit down to tea with lions? They get killed and eaten. That's not a system error, that's how it's supposed to be, but if you ask a gazelle, they'll tell you it's a very bad system

because they're judging from a low-level perspective. Those bumper stickers are spelled out with the iconography of major religions and belief systems, some of which seek to consume or eradicate the others, and none of which are concerned with truth. They symbolize the tyranny of delusion, why pretend otherwise? Why pretend at all?

"Futility, meaninglessness, and impermanence are the facts of life, but it doesn't end there, that's just the sign over the entrance. Why do so few awaken in or from the dreamstate? Why can no one find the only thing that can never be lost? Fear, always fear, and all your spirituality is really just burying your head in the sand because you're afraid of your own life. Everyone prefers sham spirituality with all its pretty lies and sweet people, like living in a day spa, but real spirituality is not pretty and sweet, it's scary and it ruins your nice little life, but when the transition to adulthood is complete you'll be free to learn and develop and understand what you really are and what this place really is. The futility, meaninglessness, and impermanence will still be there, but they were never really the problem in the first place; denying them was."

I flash them a peace sign but with three fingers.

"Make war, not love. Good night"

The Allopathic Mechanic

It is no measure of health to be well
adjusted to a profoundly sick society.

J. Krishnamurti

THE DOMINANT SYSTEM OF MEDICINE TODAY is allopathic. I have very little acquaintance with allopathic medicine, but I used to take my car to an allopathic mechanic.

One day, a warning light came on so I went to the mechanic. He cut the wire to the light. I thought that was weird, but he's the expert so I paid my fifty bucks and left.

A few weeks later the car started making a clonking sound. I went to the mechanic and he installed a noise dampening system, advised me to play the radio louder, and charged me a few hundred bucks.

The next month, black smoke started pouring out from under the hood making it hard to see. I took it to my trusted mechanic and he installed some new pipes that rerouted the smoke out the back end where I wouldn't be bothered by it, and charged me a few thousand bucks.

That was okay for a while until the engine gave out and he told me I needed a new one. That cost a lot.

A few weeks later I saw him at the golf club. He had a few drinks in him and spoke candidly. I asked him why we did all the work-around repairs when all the car needed in the first place was a quart of oil.

"Because I'm an *allopathic* mechanic, and that's not how we do things," he said indignantly. "We perform problem management, not prevention, and we sure as hell don't *fix* anything. We like it broken, that's where the real money is." He went on to explain that if he'd just added a quart of oil when the red light came on, he would have made a dollar, but the series of symptom-centric changes he performed was much better because he made thousands of dollars. He bemoaned the plight of his father, also a mechanic, who spent his life in the upper-lower class striving for lower-middle, while he himself was in upper-middle with an eye toward lower-upper.

"At my expense," I wanted to object, but he was starting to scare me.

"Allopathic mechanics have risen to a position of total dominance in the field," he bragged. "All competing

modalities have been sidelined as goofy, crazy, and even illegal." He stroked his expensive putter lovingly as he spoke. "To the victors go the spoils. We've made it so that only nuts add oil when the red light comes on. Soon it will be against the law, and then we'll get the warning light removed altogether. Your way, you add some oil and your car keeps running. *Cui bono?* Who benefits? You? That's a very selfish and anti-social attitude. In the allopathic model, everyone benefits. Your car dies sooner so you have to buy a new one, which is good for the auto and finance industries, but before that, you undergo all sorts of repairs, which benefits the mechanic and the parts industry. See the difference? Your way is good for you, our way is good for everyone. Socialized obsolescence!"

I said that sounded pretty corrupt, like an automotive-industrial complex cannibalizing its own market. He said I was missing the big picture.

"It's not about your one little car working for you," he explained, "it's about a healthy economy working for everyone. What you call corruption is just how things really work, but you're too small-minded and self-centered to see it. You know, in mechanics school, they never even taught us about adding oil when the red light came on. They never taught us to take care of a car because where's the money in that? I guess you could add some oil yourself, or go to one of those preventative fringe mechanics, but if you go that route then you will be, in effect, an enemy of the system.

Okay, sure, your car will last longer and work better, but your insurance rates will shoot up, your warranty will be voided, and your license might be revoked. A simple speeding ticket might turn into a huge legal ordeal. You may even be deemed unfit to raise the next generation of drivers, and why? All because you're selfish and want to put your needs above the needs of society."

"But what about me?" I asked. "Who's on my side?"

"Who cares about you?" he replied. "Look around, open your eyes, see where you are. Within the hallowed halls of this private country club, you see not just mechanics, but car and parts makers, bankers, corporate leaders and shareholders, politicians and lawmakers, all enjoying the fruits of their labors, but who do you think pays for all this? You, that's who. We are the engine of society and you are the fuel. That's your function in a healthy society. I went to mechanic school for three semesters, so I get to *enjoy* this place. You didn't go to mechanic school, so you get to *pay* for this place. If you had gone to mechanic school, then you would have learned how things really work."

"But what about the free market?" I ask as he takes a sip of his cocktail, which comes flying back out.

"Oh gee, yeah, the free market," he replies, wiping his face on his sleeve. "And what about rotary phones and rabbit-ear antennas and snail mail? What about Santa Claus and Mary Poppins and the Easter Bunny? What about peace on earth and good will toward men? Jesus,

what a loser! You're obviously not a team player, I don't think I can accept you as a client anymore. Kindly remove yourself from the premises before I have you ejected."

I begged him to keep me on, promising to follow his advice unquestioningly, and he finally relented. I'm on my fifth car since then. I know a few selfish people who've been driving the same car for years, some with very high miles and still going strong. They seem happy, but inside it must be eating away at them that they chose the good of the one over the good of the many. Some of them even take that same selfish attitude and apply it to other areas of their lives. Of course, those people are no longer my friends; that might adversely affect my Good Driver Score, and I need to buy another car soon.

DECEPTION: ACT III
Dream Factory

MARION and LEO sit in raised director's chairs. An Inception *movie poster hangs behind them with the tagline: Your Mind is the Scene of the Crime. They chat between interviews.*

MARION

Nom de dieu de putain de bordel de merde de saloperie de connard d'enculer ta mère! I hate these press junkets. Two hundred interviews in three days, always the same questions over and over! And we must always smile and pretend they're all so new and clever.

LEO

I know. They should just use impersonators so we can get on with other projects.

BOB bounds in carrying blue 4x6 index cards. He takes the interviewer's seat facing Leo and Marion.

BOB

Impersonators would only work if they didn't *know* they were impersonators.

Leo and Marion laugh uncomfortably at being overheard.

LEO

Hey, yeah, that's right.

MARION

You're so clever.

Bob gets comfortable in his raised director's chair, checks his notes.

BOB

Which means *you guys* might be the impersonators.

Marion and Leo laugh nervously.

BOB

Just kidding, guys. Hey, I'm Bob and I can tell you, this is a real treat for me, a real treat! Wow! Look at you guys; young, beautiful, super-rich, super-famous, adored by millions. Living the dream!

MARION

aside, to Leo

Leo, this man is frightening me.

BOB

What's it like being global superstars? Pretty fun, I bet.

LEO

Your name is Bob?

BOB

Yes, I am Bob!

LEO

Bob what?

BOB

checks cards

Just Bob!

LEO

No last name?

BOB

Most of the main characters in your movie only had one name.

LEO

Yeah, but this is real life.

BOB

Oh, that's marvelous! Let me write that down. *This is real life.* Pure gold! They'll put me on the Paris desk after this.

MARION

France?

BOB

Hilton. So guys, wow! So first off, let me just thank you for your patience with me, I'm pretty new at this interviewing stuff.

LEO

You're doin' fine, Bob.

MARION

Yeah, so good.

BOB

Great, so let's see, I only have a few minutes with you guys so here we go, question one: How do you know you're not still in Limbo? Marion?

MARION

What do you mean Limbo? Like, in the movie? Leo, is this man asking if we're still in the movie?

LEO

Bob, buddy, I don't think that's an approved question. Try again.

BOB

Okay! Leo, you were Dom down in Limbo, but you came up through all those dream levels until you were back in America with your children, but then you came up another level and now

you're a rich and famous movie star working in a dream factory and adored by millions. Do you wonder if you might not have a little more waking up to do?

LEO

Listen pal, you don't have a lot of time, are you sure this is how you want to use it?

MARION

These are very bad questions, mister.

BOB

So you're staying in character for the press junket? How wonderful!

LEO

We're not in character now, we're us. This is who we really are. We're actors!

BOB

Sure, sure, I get it. So let's see, first you're both dream pioneers exploring internal realms and using Deception on other people and each other and growing old together in Limbo, and now you're rich, beautiful megastars doing a press junket for your massive global fanbase. Do you think it's at least possible that you're actually a couple of fat slobs living in a trailer park in Asshat, Kansas playing a virtual reality game you got for Christmas?

LEO

What? No! Seriously? No! Wait, *what?*

MARION

Putain de merde! That is quite absurd!

BOB

checks his cards

Oh, I'm sorry, my assistant must have given me the wrong notes. Let's see, gosh, it says here that you're really a couple of guys – brothers, actually – living in a trailer and uh… Oh, here we go, fun fact, you save all your beer cans throughout the year until they cover the floor of your trailer. You call it your Christmas Fund because you redeem them all in December to get yourselves something special. Gosh, isn't that nice. The reason for the season, right guys?

MARION

Leo, why does he keep calling me a guy?

LEO

What the hell are you talkin' about, buddy?

BOB

So this year, you guys treated yourself to a virtual reality game called *Inception*. Sound familiar? No? I'm your game host and you are now starting a new level called "Dream Factory". Any of this a ringing a bell?

LEO

You're full of shit, dude.

BOB

Amazing tech, right? People put on that VR headset and just get lost in the gamespace.

MARION

Did Chris send you? Is this one of his little jokes?

LEO

You're saying this isn't real and that Marion and I are actually brothers living in a trailer park in Kansas?

BOB

Roger, Roger.

LEO

Leo.

BOB

Roger, Leo.

MARION

Please, no! Leonardo, make the bad man stop!

LEO

I'm trying, Mal, uh, Marion.

BOB

She's Ronnie. You're Harlan.

MARION

Mon Dieu! Je me sens comme Alice, mais le trou du lapin est mon propre cul!

BOB

Such a lovely language.

LEO

Yeah, listen buddy, I don't know how you got past my people...

BOB

No one here but us chickens, Dom.

LEO

angrily

My name is Leo. Dom was just a character I played. You got that?

BOB

writing

Just a character I played... Got it.

MARION

Then why do I not behave like this Ronnie person? Why am I so naturally me?

BOB

Super question! The game interface converts emotional impulses into character-appropriate behaviors. You're not just *playing* Marion, you have been digitally remastered *into* Marion. It's not just a costume you wear, you are mentally

and emotionally integrated with the character, just like real life!

DOM

Then who was Ariadne?

BOB

refers to cards

Ah, it says here your weed dealer stopped by and you gave him the tour.

MARION

Quel guignol! Leonardo, help me!

LEO

So what's next in your little game? We turn into these trailer park bums and then what? That's just another level of Limbo that we have to make our way out of?

BOB

checks cards

Um, I don't have answers regarding levels you haven't reached yet, so I guess you just keep going. Further! Onward and upward!

LEO

Listen, buddy, we exist just as much as you do.

BOB

Oh, I don't exist. The system calls and I appear!

MARION

Leo, please! I don't want to be fat and stupid and live in a tiny house with wheels!

LEO

He didn't say we were fat and stupid.

BOB

You are.

MARION

I want to stay as Marion! I want to be *me*, Leo. I want to stay as us! I like being Marion!

BOB

Naturally, everyone wants to be Marion and Leo forever; beautiful, rich, adored, living the dream. No one wants to pull off the headset and wake up back in Kansas. Unfortunately, there's no such thing as Marion and Leo, those are just fancy game avatars that were whipped up by our coding and design teams.

LEO

Jesus, Marion, I think it's true. I'm starting to remember...

MARION

No, Leo, don't remember! I don't want the truth, I want beauty! I want to stay here! I want to be Marion and Leonardo forever.

LEO

You're the one who jumped out a window to wake up!

MARION

That was my goddamn character!

LEO

You're a goddamn character!

MARION

pulls out phone

I'm calling my agent!

LEO

to Bob

So what's next for us? Where do we go from here?

BOB

We wrap up the interview and the next guy comes in to ask about the movie and life goes on.

MARION

puts down phone

Suce ma bite! So we're not in Limbo? We get to stay as Marion and Leo?

BOB

Well, you're *always* in Limbo — it's turtles all the way down — but you can remain in character as long as you want, or finish this level and go up to

the next. You saw Mr. Anderson in *The Matrix*, right? Instead of continuing up another level, he decided to stay as Neo and play Goth Superman. Why not? That's what the game is for.

LEO

But then he woke up as Keanu?

BOB

Sure, and he got to be a movie star for a while, but then Keanu woke up as Marcy Lundt, a twelve-year-old girl from Oxnard playing a game called *The Matrix*. And when she finished the game, she unlocked an Easter egg and found herself strapped into a chair in a high-tech memory implant lab from which she escaped and went on to save Mars from greedy industrialists, and now she's a bodybuilder, movie star and governor of California in a bonus level called *True Lies*.

LEO

And in our next level we're a couple of fat, lazy brothers?

BOB

Unless you find the little door that leads into the mind of John Malkovich.

LEO

And after that?

BOB

I guess you'll find out when you get there.

LEO

But it does go on?

BOB

Well, heck yeah! The gamespace keeps rendering wherever you go. Move up, go back down, hop around wherever you like!

MARION

No, Leo, no! We must stay here! We must remain in this level forever. It can never be better than this! I want to stay in Dream Factory forever! Don't make me go to Asshole Kansas!

LEO

But it's not *real*, Marion. This is all fake. We're dreaming and we have to wake up, and the only way is to follow the white rabbit and take the red pill and go up through *all* the levels!

MARION

But if it's all Limbo, who cares?! If it's all bullshit, why not pick *happy* bullshit? I like *this* bullshit. This is *good* bullshit! Don't make me go to Kansas. I don't want to be a fat stupid American!

Marion stands and clicks her heels together.

There's no place like Hollywood. There's no place like Hollywood. There's no place...

LEO

It's just another level, babe.

MARION

pleading

Let's stay here. Everything is perfect here! We are rich and famous and beautiful here!

LEO

We can't live a lie.

MARION

Of course we can! Everyone does!

LEO

But it's not true!

MARION

So what it's not true? There is no truth, that's what this ridiculous Bob-man just told you. There is no *true* level so we just pick the one we like. I like this one! Don't make me be poor and smelly!

BOB

Would you like to access the built-in Help Wizard?

LEO

You have a goddamn wizard?

MARION

Tell your Mr. goddamn Wizard I want to stay in goddamn Oz!

A Life of Constant Duplicity

The great majority of us are required to live a life of constant duplicity. Your health is bound to be affected if, day after day, you say the opposite of what you feel, if you grovel before what you dislike, and rejoice at what brings you nothing but misfortune.

Boris Pasternak

"IT'S A DEFINING FEATURE OF social conformity, groupthink, and herd mentality that we abdicate control of our lives to various specialists – doctors and lawyers, governments, ministries, corporations, employers, parents, teachers, and so on – and the price we pay is that whatever we abdicate, we lose. If we want to thrive and grow and expand – physically, mentally, spiritually, emotionally, creatively – then we have to stop abdicating our self-sovereignty and reclaim it. This is as true in health matters as in spiritual matters or anything else. Open your eyes, see for yourself and everything comes back into alignment."

I pause to drink some carefully chosen water and hold up the bottle for all to see.

"Back in my twenties, I came to the conclusion that the only safe product in the grocery store was bottled water, but as cynical as that was, it was clearly not cynical enough. I don't think we had organic produce back then, but I wouldn't have trusted that either. Organic doesn't mean better or more nutritious, it just means a bit less toxic. You don't know how much less, you just pay twice as much and hope it's only half as bad. You know organic costs more and probably spent more time in transit, but you don't know what toxins it contains or what nutrients it's lacking, so it's more of a gesture than a solution, just another way we deceive ourselves."

We're in the meeting room of a library, sixty seats plus people sitting on the floor up front and standing along the walls. Someone asked about my eating habits and it has turned into a talk about health and nutrition which are, to me, the same thing.

"When it comes to your health, the only doctor you can trust is your own body. The only healer you have is yourself, which is fine because that's all you need. We don't have to create perfect health, we just have to stop sabotaging it. We can never improve on perfection, we can only derail it, which is what ego does by design, and nowhere is that more apparent or more personal than when it comes to our health and the health of our loved ones.

"I know I'm preaching to the choir here, but some-times the choir needs its own rousing sermon, its own wake-up call. I have drilled down on the subject of health until I arrived at a clear bottom line, which is nutrition. Most people suffer from severe malnutrition in the form of toxicity and deficiency; the bad stuff we eat and the good stuff we don't. We have to stop poisoning the body and give it what it needs. If we don't, we'll think we're healthy until, one day, *bam!*, something goes wrong, and then what? You run to the doctor and start spiraling down the shithole of pills and surgery and radiation to treat symptoms, and those solutions cause more symptoms that need more solutions, and on and on.

"I'm not an expert in health and nutrition, of course, but we're not really talking about that, we're talking about waking up, in which I *am* an expert. Breaking out of the herd requires focused emotional intensity, and seeing clearly that the herd is feeding on you and your loved ones seems like a good way to generate it. This is as in-your-face as it gets. If you can't wake up to this, then you can't wake up to anything. An insatiable monster is infecting our lives right now, not just killing us and our loved ones, but milking us first, squeezing us slowly to get every drop, depriving us of health and wealth and happiness, feeding on our lifeforce as we march obediently into its gaping jaws. I'm not painting some dark vision of the future, this is happening now, every day, to everyone, and if we

are not fully awake to it, then we are already being chewed and pre-digested. What fictional monster can compare to the living reality of our own healthcare system?"

I get some blowback from friends and members of the healthcare community who rise to its defense, but what is there to defend? The writing is on the wall. It's not a matter of opinion; our health is unnaturally bad and rapidly worsening, and it's not because our bodies are stupid but because we are stuck in an eyes-closed, fear-based, greed-infected, self-cannibalizing herd. Some of the people speaking up are defending their family doctors, but it's not the frontline doctors and nurses who are to blame any more than your friendly bank cashier is responsible for the global financial complex or your kid in the navy for the military industrial complex.

"Awake is awake," I continue, "it doesn't matter what road you took to get there, so who knows, maybe this one will do. You don't make the transition to adulthood based on a desire for spiritual evolution – a history of total failure is very clear on that point – but you can definitely get there by harnessing the power of hatred and fear. Hatred of false self is the one I usually talk about, hatred of being a lie, but fear is just as good, maybe better. How about fear of death? How about the fear of malevolent forces dressed in crisp white lab coats, backed by the full force and weight of society, slowly murdering you and your family? These

are very healthy things to be afraid of, but your fear has been weaponized against you. Once you realize that the pandemic of disease is manmade, that a well-treated body is easily capable of maintaining itself in perfect condition, and that the healthcare system has nothing to do with health and everything to do with fear and profit, then maybe you can claw your way out of this system, maybe even out of the herd. I'm just guessing, but it's worth a shot. Worst case, you get a little healthier.

"We enjoy what we're told is the most advanced healthcare in history, but at the same time we're seeing epidemics of obesity, heart disease, cancer, diabetes and hundreds of other hideous maladies that have become the new normal. The reality disproves the narrative, yet we still subscribe to the narrative; that's the definition of mindless conformity and herd mentality. The only metric by which to judge healthcare is the health of the people it serves, which is not just bad but unnaturally bad. Nature never screws things up like this, only fear-based ego does, and society is an ego-based organism. The contradiction between reality and narrative appears wherever we look, and we still don't see it, which is even more perplexing since we inhabit the data. We're not talking about a remote tribe in Botswana or cells under a microscope, this is us; our friends and neighbors, our parents and kids and our pets, ourselves, getting sick as if it were the most natural thing in the world, but it's not. Perfect health

is the most natural thing in the world but there's no money in it so it's been banished from the land.

"Our children are being chemically lobotomized for profit and we go along with it, delivering them for injections, making sure they take their pills, but when we go up a belt size or a dress size, we leap into action. Vanity motivates us where love fails. We waddle to the bookstore or the gym or the local diet center in search of our inner beach body. And even then we don't succeed in losing the weight and keeping it off because overeating is not the cause of obesity, it's a symptom of nutritional deficiency, but no one tells you that because no one makes money from thin, healthy people.

"When you're fifty or sixty or seventy and you start losing your marbles and they start cutting parts out of your body and you have a nightstand covered with little plastic bottles, it's not because your body betrayed you but because you betrayed your body. There's nothing mysterious or hidden about any of this, it's everywhere you look. It's in the autistic kids and the fat adults, and in the sprawling medical complexes in every city, in every bag of groceries you bring home and every form of media you consume, and the main thing preventing you from seeing it clearly is your belief that you already do.

"In my foolishly simplistic opinion, the number of people who die from cancer and heart disease every year should be zero. The number of people who suffer

from dementia and autism should be zero. The number of morbidly obese people should be zero. Maybe that makes me an idiot, but I'm the best kind of idiot because I don't see why anyone should ever be sick. It's unnatural, manmade, and ultimately, self-inflicted. There's no reason for it, it's not supposed to happen. We make it happen just like we make all our childish drama happen, and then we suffer and complain about life in the dungeon when all we ever had to do was get up off our fat asses and leave. I'm not here to drag you out, I'm just pointing at the open door. I understand that the dungeon is also community and family. It's where we participate in the great creative spectacle of humanity, but the price of whatever pleasure and comfort the dungeon provides is that we never discover what we really are, or what lies just beyond the walls.

"Become your own healer, that's the best advice. There's a higher form of navigation available to you, a new and better way of seeing, of understanding yourself in relation to your environment, you just have to learn to access it and trust it. You have to break away from the things of man and develop into your own rightful self. Awake or not awake, integrated or segregated, adult or child, these are binary states. There is no degree of awake, only awake or not. This is a hardline distinction, and everyone is either one or the other.

"I'm sure I'm supposed to say something about how I'm not a doctor, but when it comes to health

and wellness I consider that more of a qualifier than a disqualifier anyway. Of course, if you break a bone or cut yourself or get shot or get banged up in a car wreck, or if you need antibiotics or pain meds, doctors are awesome for that. That's what they're good for, that's their proper sphere of competence. There are many situations that clearly fall within modern medicine's purview, but healthcare isn't one of them, prevention isn't, wellness isn't. Monetizing disease is, curing disease is not.

"What we're really talking about is not the healthcare system, but fear as a vehicle of awakening. Can it work like that? I don't know. It's all more or less theoretical. I think about ways to help people wake up out of the herd, and the glaring gap between health and healthcare seems to suggest itself. If you can't wake up to a system that's trying to convert you and your loved ones into luxury cars and club memberships, what *can* you wake up to? The healthcare system provides us an up-close and personal glimpse of the true nature of ego at herd-level, and maybe the shock and horror of seeing it might act as a call to action. I admit it's a longshot, but it can't hurt to revisit your views on nutrition."

Is Pubasyl Right for You?

Science is the art of creating suitable illusions which the fool believes or argues against, but the wise man enjoys for their beauty or their ingenuity, without being blind to the fact that they are human veils and curtains concealing the abysmal darkness of the unknowable.

Carl Jung

L ET'S SAY YOU'RE HANGING OUT on the couch with your kids watching some family-friendly programming when a commercial comes on. An unimpeachably trustworthy woman – which we know because she's hanging up her the priestly white coat in the immaculate church of the laboratory – is finishing her workday and she informs us that not only is she a fountain of truth, she's also a regular schmo like you and me and as such, she worries about EPI, Embarrassing Pubic Irritation, a condition that if left untreated, she informs us with weighty sincerity,

could lead to brief and infrequent episodes of mild discomfort.

You try to ignore the commercial because you don't suffer from groinal inflammation, but this woman is a loving parent just like you, and she seems genuinely concerned about your crotch. The fact that your nether region doesn't actually itch, she explains, is an early warning sign that you can't afford to ignore.

You do recall that your bathing suit area was a little itchy at the beach last summer. You assumed it was just sand, but now you pay closer attention to the commercial. Doctor Mom is now flying kites with her kids in a sunny meadow as the scene cuts to an animation of a genderless human form with a throbbing red pubis that's causing a sympathetic throb in your own.

Doctor Mom turns back from her laughing children to address you directly: "I don't have time to let EPI sideline me," she says. "That's why I take Pubasyl!"

She then turns to run after her happy, wholesome kids as a voice-over informs us at quadruple-speed that Pubasyl is not safe for pregnant women or nursing mothers or children or the elderly or people who don't enjoy brain aneurysms, should not be taken in conjunction with neuro-lactic re-uptake uninhibitors or where microwave ovens are in use or when commuting by air or while driving or operating machinery heavier than a stapler; may cause anal fissures leading to blurred vision, mild hallucinations and early-onset death; can cause episodes of rage and despair, reproductive

anomalies, and, in rare cases, gender realignment and active-shooter scenarios. Extended use may result in abnormally foul gases, unsightly bloating, painful discharge, uneven weight distribution, hyena-like yipping, projectile diarrhea and, in certain high-risk patients, combustion during sex.

"Sure," you think, "but isn't *all* bloating unsightly?"

Then, the nice lady pauses while buckling her nice kids into her nice minivan and tells you to ask your doctor if Pubasyl is right for you.

So there you are, just watching some cartoons with your kids, but now you're thinking you'd better make an appointment with your doctor to see if Pubasyl is right for you. A minute ago you didn't know you had a problem, and now you're detecting a slight tingling sensation and you're in the market for a solution which your doctor will be happy to provide because, as wonderful as he or she may be, your doctor is just the human user interface of a soulless machine that would much rather you got *all* the symptoms than *any* relief.

And what about *why* you have an itch? Anything about that? Of course not. The Ministry of Health doesn't care about addressing causes, only treating symptoms. It's clearly understood throughout the medical world that healing is not a viable business model. What if the cause was a simple magnesium deficiency? You take some supplements and the symptoms disappear, right? Wrong. That's not allowed in the modern medical environment where curing has

been outlawed as quackery so the death merchants can maintain their stranglehold monopoly. Effective healing modalities have been marginalized because health and healing are in opposition to the Western medical model of disease monetization. Allopathic medicine, we're told, is the only real modality, while holistic models are quackery. If too many people start taking magnesium and stop buying Pubasyl, then dozens of scientific studies highlighting the dangers of magnesium will suddenly come to light, the nightly news anchor will do a hard-hitting exposé of mineral-related overdoses in front of the word magnesium in dripping red letters, and some bought-and-paid-for backwater congressman will introduce legislation to ban the sale of all nutritional supplements. And all the while, brain-swelling, liver-rotting, anus-fissuring Pubasyl is promoted as wholesome and kid-friendly. That's how the high-priesthood of the medical establishment works. Crappy health is their cash cow, no healing allowed, and they maintain market dominance through legislation and message control. The medical establishment – just one wing of the global financial complex – controls media and government because it controls the money, and it controls the money because it knows how to manipulate fear.

In the end, it's not them versus us but us versus ourselves. We create systems which take on lives of their own and turn into monsters that devour their creators. The herd shuffles through a vast and empty

expanse with only itself as a food source, but as bad as the healthcare system is, it's not unique. It's a perfectly natural product of ego, just like every other major system. It makes perfect sense in the context of the herd, but we're not talking about the herd, we're talking about you. The question is not whether Pubasyl is right for you but whether you're right for Pubasyl. Pubasyl is just what the doctor ordered, and who are you to argue with the doctor? Who are you to question government or educators or scientists or clergy? Who are you to argue with all those agencies and organizations and corporations that only have your best interests at heart? Who are you to look for yourself, think for yourself, act in your own best interests? Who are you to do anything but sit quietly and do as you're told? Seriously, just who the hell do you think you are?

Pubasyl: Just shut up and take it.

In the Land of the Slow-Cooked Frog

If one's bowels move, one is happy; and if
they don't move, one is unhappy. That is
all there is to it.

Lin Yutang

T HE KEY TO PERFECT HEALTH isn't having good
insurance, getting regular checkups, and following doctor's orders, it's slipping the bonds of the
healthcare system and reclaiming the effortless perfection that is your stolen birthright. If I had a wife and
she was pregnant, I wouldn't want her anywhere near
a doctor, and if it was legally mandated then I'd go
where it wasn't; no problem since I'd have to get the
kid away from government, garbage food, screens, and
the education/indoctrination system anyway.

How fired up would you have to be to pull up roots, sever connections, burn bridges, and make a new start away from the things of man? How starkly awake would you have to be, how radically independent of thought and spirit, to drag your family to Alaska or New Zealand or some other supposedly remote place to protect yourselves from the toxic effects of the herd? What would it really take to shield your children from pills, needles, soda, screens, and all the corporations and agencies that view kids as consumable commodities? Can it even be done? In days of yore, there were no screens, no traitorous whitecoats, no poisons in everything, and school might have been about reading, writing and reckoning instead of institutionalized daycare, herd indoctrination and forced mediocrity, but what would it take for you to recreate those conditions today?

As a practical matter, you can't. Whatever you do, wherever you go, systemic malignance is going to infect and metastasize throughout your family. You can try to shelter in place, improve your current situation, minimize toxic exposure, but how much can you really do? It will take everything you have, all your time, all your mental, emotional and physical energy, all your money and resources, and it may cost you the affection of those you're trying to save. You can't be independent in the herd and you probably can't get yourself and your loved ones out of it. Small wonder

that everyone just goes along with the program, what else can you do?

The spiritual marketplace, which should operate as a sort of underground railroad helping freedom-seekers make their way to a new reality, seeks instead to make them happier and more comfortable in the reality they're in. In other words, your spiritual solution providers will say the problem isn't that your head is on fire, it's your negativity about it.

We're like fish in a polluted ocean. There's nowhere to run, nowhere to hide. We can always do better, but we can never get clean. Just something simple like having good household water can be a daunting challenge. What about food you can trust, where do you find that? Will you till up your backyard, amend the soil, and grow your own fruits and vegetables? Convert the front yard to an orchard? Dig a root cellar? Go totally off-grid? Amass a homesteader library and become adept in hundreds of new skills? What about electromagnetic radiation? Where can you go to get away from that? What about the toxins off-gassing from all the products in your environment? They're poisoning you whether you're noticeably sensitive to them or not. Are you going to eliminate all synthetic materials from your life? What about all the bad stuff that's already inside you? Just safely removing mercury and aluminum is a major undertaking. And when the schools and state say your kids have to be medicated and vaccinated, do you choose fight or flight? Or do

you just say screw it, everyone else is doing it, and fall into lockstep with the herd?

☀

When reduced to the simplest terms, it seems that many or most health issues result from malnutrition in the form of deficiency and autotoxemia – starvation and self-poisoning – and that the solution is to stop eating crap and give your body, probably for the first time since conception, the nutrients it needs to do its job. Perfect health is your natural birthright, and you have been working every moment of your life to divest yourself of it. Even if you live in a medically enlightened country, which you don't, and eat the best available diet, which you don't, this still applies to you because you're still not getting the nutrients you need. You have to make that happen and it's not easy. More leafy greens and store-bought smoothies won't do it, and even if you woke up tomorrow morning and went full off-grid health-nut whacko, how would you undo the damage that's already been done?

And where is your trusted medical adviser in all this? Why isn't your family physician banging on your door in the middle of the night warning you against drinking city water and eating processed foods? Isn't he your go-to guy for this stuff? Why isn't he screaming from the rooftops about the perils of modern society? Why isn't he selling juicers and blenders in the waiting room next to books and documentaries

detailing the thousands of societal and environmental threats to your family's health and how to shield yourselves against them? Why is he pretending everything is okay? Whose team is your doctor playing for? There are good people out there, true healers, but they're hard to find, probably not covered by insurance, and in some cases, outlawed.

❋

Even as I write this I am alerted to a newly published review of several hundred studies which concludes that supplementing with vitamins and minerals doesn't do much harm, but not much good either. (While at the same time reading another report about how nearly all studies are corrupt, poorly done, and misleading.)

The review says supplements are unnecessary and recommends we eat a government-endorsed diet and consult our doctor before making any changes. It's a very credible-seeming report and probably succeeds in scaring some people away from self-reliance, but it fails to touch upon a few salient points such as the pandemics of obesity, cancer, heart disease, diabetes and other maladies so pervasive that they even clobber our pets, largely attributable to chemicals, preservatives, pesticides and genetic modifications so pervasive that they render our entire food supply unsafe for consumption. Nor does the report mention that doctors receive little or no training in nutrition and are inherently dismissive of the subject because you can't build a massive

profit structure on a foundation of wellness. I didn't read the report too closely, but I don't think it mentioned that your body requires scores of minerals that can't be gotten from diet alone owing to the fact that our growing soil has been long-since depleted of minerals as was read into the U.S. Congressional Record in the 1930s. I think the report also failed to mention that it was authored and funded by a vast medical-financial megaplex that squeezes patients like grapes and crushes opposition like ants. Nor did this report mention the fact that a massive campaign is being waged – of which the report itself is a part – to vilify, criminalize, ostracise, decertify, mock and shame any person or organization that poses a threat to the disease monetization system by promoting actual health and healing. And the report certainly overlooked the fact that authentic healers are commonly subjected to personal, professional and financial persecution and, with curious frequency, untimely death.

Lastly, tellingly absent from the report was any mention of the large and growing number of people who manage to live healthy, vibrant, sunny lives in flagrant disregard of medical orthodoxy and in stark contrast to the far greater number of dying and dehumanized zombies shuffling down the fluorescent-lit corridors of for-profit deathmills. Or maybe that was in the footnotes, I didn't read down that far.

✳

Before making changes to our diet, the report advised, we should consult our physician. During your consultation – them in priestly white coat, you with ass hanging out of paper gown or feet in stirrups – you might ask if tap water, vaccines, electromagnetic radiation, microwave transmissions, rancid oils, preservatives, pesticides, plastics, irradiated and genetically modified foods, junk food, fast food, soda, sugar, gluten, and trans fats are anything to be concerned about and which yo-yo diet fad-of-the-week is best and if Pubasyl is right for you and which TV health guru's new wonderberry is going to reverse a lifetime of abuse and why human bodies are so gosh darn screwy when the rest of the animal kingdom seems to work just fine. And as long as your personal medical expert is in a chatty mood, you might ask if you should be considering vitamins and supplements, smoothies and juices, sunlight and clean water, fasting and cleansing, walking and proper breathing, meditation, vegetarianism, veganism, or any of the many established and emerging health and longevity technologies.

My guess, however, is that you wouldn't get past "Hey doc, as long as I've got you by the finger, lemme ask you something…" before he instructed you to get more exercise and eat more veggies and left you with your ass in the breeze because, while doctors may not know much about health or nutrition, they know a lot about dealing with you in under six minutes because

you're a necessary but annoying step in the insurance billing process, and really, what the hell's the point of a well-insured patient in good health anyway?

Or, you know, maybe I'm wrong. Maybe I'm over-stating it. Maybe it's not really as bad as I make out. All this stuff I'm describing is just what I see when I peel back the cosmetic top layer. If I keep peeling back the layers, it gets so dark so fast that even I, your intrepid Chicken Little, become too horror-fatigued to keep going. It doesn't get worse and worse forever, but it does get worse and worse and, surprisingly, worse.

I don't seek this stuff out, but it has just come to my attention that many children's breakfast foods have now been shown to contain a very popular carcinogenic weed killer, which might very well be the cause of the currently raging and rapidly worsening epidemics of autism and dementia. You'd think that would be enough to wake people up and have the malefactors swinging from lampposts, but we have become so inoculated to such arch-criminality that I was surprised it even made the news. Instead of a call to action, it's just another day in the herd.

❋

As always, the point is not to become an expert on life in the sewer, but to get the hell out. We're not really interested in how corrupted the healthcare system is, we're interested in how corrupted *you* are. You can't change systemic greed and corruption or wake up the

whole world, but you can wake your*self* up. That's all anyone can do, but that's the only thing that matters. Wake yourself up and the crazy-ass world takes a giant step back. You don't need to launch a major revolution, you just need to start tugging on one little thread. Accept the possibility that you might have some wrong-knowing in the area of wellness and go out with soft eyes and take a fresh look. Just by giving your body what it needs to do its job, you will have won a major victory, and unlike your hippy-dippy, woo-woo spiritual beliefs and your tinhat conspiracy theories, your surrounding herdmates will be receptive to a message of wellness because, when it comes to the healthcare system, many people are already near the tipping point. They see what's going on, but their faith is so blind that they haven't processed it yet. Sit virtually anyone down in front of a few decent documentaries and you'll redpill them in a single afternoon. Our healthcare system is pummeling us with physical and financial ruin as a business model, but the same ray of light that can pierce you can pierce others as well. There's nothing to be done for those who cannot see, but when it comes to their health, a great many can see when shown. Glimpsing sunlight through the cracks and tunneling toward it doesn't get any easier than this because a great percentage of your emotional energy will be working with you, not against you. You really *do* want to be healthy and you really *are* afraid of the physical ruin of yourself and your kids, and that

fear can be put to practical use. I mean, I'm kinda guessing, but it sounds right, right?

This is life in the land of the slow-cooked frog. The Orwellian nightmare is not somewhere down the road, it's right on top of us, as anyone who looks will see. We are the lenses through which our reality is projected. Aberrant, sub-evolved people project an aberrant, sub-evolved society. Because the people who make up society have failed to achieve their adult stage of development, so have the systems they create and the world they project. The same ego that traps us in a halfborn state manifests as a halfborn world. Good for drama and spectacle, not so good for you.

Even if you think it's not *that* bad, you have to admit it's bad and getting worse, and even then, my point has nothing to do with healthcare and everything to do with our ability to see what's not and not see what is. Emerging into your adult state isn't spiritual, it's developmental. It's not about becoming something special, only what you were born to be.

DECEPTION: Act IV
The Help Wizard

Bob, Leo and Marion sit in raised director's chairs waiting for the Help Wizard to boot up. An OLD FELLA in gray hair and beard, a well-worn coat and floppy fedora shuffles in.

OLD FELLA

I sing the body electric!

examines his clothing, rubs his hands together, feels his face

I cannot be awake, for nothing looks to me as it did before, or else I am awake for the first time, and all before has been a mean sleep.

DOM

Santy Claus!

MARION

Mon Dieu! L'ange sans ses ailes!

Old Fella

Neither Santa nor angel, merely a man. Walt Whitman, a kosmos, of Manhattan the son. Turbulent, fleshy, sensual, eating, drinking and breeding. No sentimentalist, no stander above men and women or apart from them. No more modest than immodest.

Leo

shaking Walt's hand

Oh, hi Walt. I'm Leo. I like to eat and drink too. I'm not sure about that other stuff.

Bob

Walter is your help system avatar.

Leo

No shit! Say there, Walt, this guy here, uh...

Bob

Bob.

Leo

Yeah, this Bob guy is sayin' that this whole deal – you know, me and Marion bein' movie stars and stuff – he says it's not really *real*, like there's no *meaning* to any of it...

Walt

Have you felt so proud to get at the meaning of poems? Stop this day and night with me and you shall possess the origin of *all* poems.

LEO

Who said anything about poems?

WALT

You shall no longer take things at second or third hand, nor look through the eyes of the dead, nor feed on the spectres in books.

MAL

Spectres?

LEO

Books?

WALT

You shall not look through my eyes either, nor take things from me. You shall listen to all sides and filter them from yourself.

LEO

Say what?

WALT

You shall not look through my eyes...

LEO

No, no, okay, listen bud, we got a situation here. Me and this lady, we're like big Hollywood moviestars. As you can see, we're very attractive and talented and rich, and everyone wants to be just like us, okay?

WALT

This day before dawn I ascended a hill and looked at the crowded heaven, and I said to my spirit, "When we become the enfolders of those orbs, and the pleasure and knowledge of everything in them, shall we be filled and satisfied then?" And my spirit said, "No, we but level that lift to pass and continue beyond."

LEO

Do what?

WALT

Level that lift to pass and continue beyond.

LEO

What the hell does *that* mean? Bob, is this thing even working?

BOB

The help wizard is still in beta.

LEO

Bullshit, this guy is straight outta central casting!

WALT

If you would understand me, go to the heights or water-shore.

LEO

Bob here says you don't even exist.

WALT

I exist as I am, that is enough.

LEO

I'm talkin' about reality, pal. Ever heard of it?

WALT

I accept reality and dare not question it.

MARION

I think it only has certain lines, Leo, like an actor reading a script. You must be asking the right questions!

LEO

Listen, buddy, we're actors too. That's what we do, we play characters, okay?

WALT

There was a child went forth every day, and the first object he looked upon, that object he became. And that object became part of him for the day, or a certain part of the day, or for many years, or stretching cycles of years.

LEO

What the hell are you talkin' about?

MARION

Leo, why does he talk so funny?

LEO

I don't know. Maybe it's like a Shakespeare thing. I played Romeo once, I speak a little Shakespeare.

MARION

You played a halfwit too. Do you speak a little moron?

LEO

You're not helpin' here, doll. I'm tryin' to learn how this guy works.

WALT

Have you learned the lessons only of those who admired you and were tender with you and stood aside for you? Have you not learned great lessons from those who braced themselves against you and disputed passage with you?

MARION

Monsieur, s'il vous plait, we wish only to know what is our situation.

WALT

approaches Marion, takes one of her hands in both of his, speaks tenderly

I could sing such grandeurs and glories about you! You have not known what you are. You have slumbered upon yourself all your life, your eyelids have been the same as closed most of the time. What you have done returns already in mockeries. The mockeries are not you,

underneath them and within them I see you lurk. I pursue you where none else has pursued you.

MARION

But then, am I me or not me? Who am I?

WALT

Whoever you are, I fear you are walking the walk of dreams. I fear these supposed realities are to melt from under your feet and hands.

MARION

Frankly sir, this news comes a little late.

WALT

kisses her hand and gently strokes it
I should have made my way straight to you long ago. None has done justice to you. You have not done justice to yourself. I only find no imperfection in you.

MARION

Mais oui c'est clair! The critics can be so unkind. What must I do?

WALT

Whoever you are, claim your own at any hazard! Undrape!

MARION

Undrape? How can you say such a thing? You say one thing, then you say the opposite!

WALT

Do I contradict myself? Very well, then I contradict myself. I am large, I contain multitudes.

MARION

You are supposed to help, but you talk in riddles!

WALT

I and this mystery, here we stand.

MARION

But I too am here! I am real!

WALT

The powerful play goes on, and you may contribute a verse.

MARION

darkens, pulls her hand back

You are being a little annoying right now. Do you know who I am?

WALT

Whoever you are, motion and reflection are especially for you. The divine ship sails the divine sea for you.

MARION

brightens

Oh, that's *much* better! That sounds nice. Leo, did you hear that? The divine ship sails the

172

divine sea for me!

LEO

What are you listening to this guy for? He's just an actor repeating the same lines over and over.

WALT

I contain multitudes.

LEO

There, see?

MARION

Can no one give me a simple answer?

WALT

You are also asking me questions and I hear you.

MARION

Wonderful! Then please answer. Who am I? Am I a real person?

WALT

I answer that I cannot answer, you must find out for yourself.

MARION

This is not good help. I feel like I'm in a bad dream and cannot wake up!

WALT

Long enough have you dreamed contemptible dreams. Now I wash the gum from your eyes. You must habit yourself to the dazzle of the light and of every moment of your life.

LEO

That's it. I've had about enough of this guy.

WALT

Take warning, I am surely far different from what you suppose.

LEO

I *suppose* you're supposed to be *helping*.

WALT

Do you see no further than this façade? Have you no thought, O dreamer, that it may be all Maya, illusion?

LEO

I don't wanna hear any more of this dream bullshit!

WALT

This is curious, and may not be realized immediately, but it must be realized.

LEO

I have to realize reality's not real? Really? Jesus, I can't tell if this guy's talkin' to us, or just talkin'.

MARION

What, sir? What must we realize?

LEO

If you get a straight answer outta this guy, it'll be a miracle.

WALT

Who makes much of a miracle? I know of nothing else *but* miracles. To me, every hour of the light and dark is a miracle.

LEO

That sounds like a load of crap. All we're gettin' from this guy is more lies!

WALT

There is no lie, or form of lie, and can be none, but grows as inevitably upon itself as the truth does upon itself.

LEO

angry, grabs Walt by the lapels

What are you saying, buddy? That it's *okay* if the whole world is a lie?

WALT

unruffled

I feel in myself that I represent falsehoods equally with the rest, and that the universe does.

MARION

But sir, how can you help us if you don't speak the truth?

WALT

Where has failed a perfect return, indifferent of lies or the truth?

LEO

releases Walt in disgust

Oh boy, here we go.

WALT

Meditating among liars, and retreating sternly into myself, I see that there are really no liars or lies after all, and that nothing fails its perfect return, and that what are called lies are perfect returns, and that each thing exactly represents itself and what has preceded it, and that the truth includes all and is compact, just as much as space is compact, and that there is no flaw or vacuum in the amount of the truth, but that *all* is truth without exception.

MARION

What, Leo? What is he trying to say?

LEO

I think he's saying that *nothing* is real, or maybe it's *all* real in a kind of unreal way, something like that. Like we should just relax and make the best of it and not ask too many questions.

MARION

Mais oui! Yes! That's what I say too! Let's stay here and be happy and not worry about silly truth. Let us not disturb the delicate web of this sparkly, silvery world. I like being a movie star!

LEO

This isn't a very helpful help wizard, Bob.

BOB

There's a scheduled update in the next version. I think they're giving him sunglasses.

LEO

We're not gettin' anywhere with this guy.

BOB

Computer, end program.

Walt gives Bob the finger and shuffles out.

LEO

Listen Marion, I'll tell you a riddle. You're waiting for a train...

MARION

Oh no, Leo! Not again with the fucking train!

Leo opens his jacket exposing bomb vest with a blinking red light. In his hand is a wired device with a red button.

LEO

You're waiting for a train…

MARION

No Leo, please! Shut up about the stupid train!

LEO

…a train that will take you far away.

MARION

I don't want to go anywhere! I want to stay here. I don't care about truth, I want beauty. They are not the same!

LEO

You know where you *hope* this train will take you, but you don't know for sure.

MARION

Fuck truth! I want beauty and happiness and money and stardom! I want to be chic and fabulous and live forever! I don't want to be fat and stupid and live in a tiny house, Leo, *please!*

LEO

How can it not matter where the train takes you?

MARION

No, Leo, please let's stay here. It's so nice here. We're so happy, so rich, so pretty…

LEO

How can it not matter where the train takes
you?

MARION

No, Leo! No, no, no! I do not wish to go!

LEO

How can it not matter where the train takes
you?

MARION

sighs in resignation

Because we'll be together.

LEO

See you in the next life, doll.

Leo presses the button.

Marichelle 6: Go Hack Yourself

Do you know how dumb it is of me to be talking about this? Very dumb. It makes no sense, but I do it, so that's how dumb I am. Pretty dumb, but okay, right?

※

You don't know you're programmed, so saying you're not programmed is a bad way to start. You have to think you're not programmed for the program to work, so that's what emotion does for you. Your emotion makes you not think you're programmed so you can be programmed like crazy.

꙰

So you have this programing that you don't know about. You have to have this secret part and a way to keep it secret, so that's what we want to do is break in there and look at the really secret stuff.

꙰

So I say go hack yourself. That's what we're doing now, breaking into your system, right? You don't think so. You don't believe it, but it's happening right now. That's what this really is. You're hacking yourself, breaking into yourself. You're stealing your own secrets. It's quite an adventure.

꙰

Don't say okay. Of course you don't understand this. If you understood it, it wouldn't be true, right? So try to think more hypothetical.

꙰

I know it looks like people do a lot of thinking, but they don't because real thinking gets you right to point B and how many people are at point B? Pretty much no one.

꙰

You have intelligence to change your programming, but you don't do it, so why not? That's like the secret part, right? How else could there

be this whole thing where you are so happy with everything?

⟐

Stay in coma or get out. It's up to you, or maybe it's not. I don't know. It's not up to me, I'm pretty sure about that.

⟐

The purpose of emotion is to give us stuff to do, okay? It's not bad like maybe it sounds. It has to be there or else nothing happens. If nothing happens then where would be the fun in that?

⟐

I can tell you there is no other world behind the coma world. You wake up and that's it, you're out. There's not like some great prize or something.

⟐

If you want to be happy in coma, I don't know anything about that. That's like nothing to me. Be happy all you want, okay? That's nice, but it's not this. This is not that.

⟐

Take anything apart to see what it's made of, then you can understand whatever you want. You have to take things apart to understand them,

but you can't put them back together, so think about it first.

⁂

Being free or not free only makes sense in coma. Out of coma there's not these conditions. It's just part of coma to think how great not being in coma is.

⁂

What if you learn that right now you are really lying in a bed with your eyes closed for your whole life so far? You have a whole nice world in your head but what if you open your eyes it's all gone? That would be a pretty big deal.

⁂

Obviously, you think I'm wrong about this. If you didn't think I was wrong then I would really be wrong, right? That's the whole point.

⁂

Here's a backward thing you should know. Adding more always makes you less. You have to take away to be more. People mostly go the other way.

⁂

Why nobody sees obvious stuff is not for words to say. I can tell you all day and it's nothing. So

anyway, your little world starts coming apart, that's something to look forward to. I'm using sarcasm there.

⚶

We think we are little monkeys walking around on two feet with other little monkeys. That's how easy to fool we are.

⚶

Anyone doing good thinking will wake up out of coma which no one does, so no one is doing very good thinking. Pretty simple.

⚶

I would say about thinking that it's possible but not encouraged. We are encouraged not to think. Thinking makes a lot of trouble.

⚶

You think reality is obvious because you don't think about it, but as soon as you think about it, it's not so obvious anymore. The more you think about reality, the less obvious it is.

⚶

So how easy was that? Not so easy really because that's just me pointing you in a direction, but you still have to go or else where I point doesn't matter.

185

☖

The question is why are you here with me? Why are you listening to me? That's a pretty good thing to ask yourself because this can get pretty crazy.

☖

If you don't know there's a problem, then there is no problem, right? You don't have to fix a problem if you don't know there is a problem. You are here making problems for yourself, so maybe don't do that.

☖

You think it's crazy to be crazy and not crazy to be not crazy, but the whole thing is crazy so it's really the other way. Did that make any sense?

☖

We are like children who watch a movie full of ghosts or space aliens and think we're watching the news of the world. We believe what we see. How crazy is that? Pretty crazy, I would say.

☖

Someone tells me, hey, you know, enough monkeys with enough typewriters and enough time can write all the Shakespeare plays, and I tell them hey, where have you been? It already happened.

Take me to the volcano!

My father says that almost the whole world
is asleep. Everybody you know. Everybody you
see. Everybody you talk to. He says that only
a few people are awake and they live in a state
of constant total amazement.

Patricia

IT ONLY MAKES SENSE that someone who is awake
would live in a state of constant total amazement.
You'd have to be asleep not to. You'd have to believe
that hands, dogs, a drop of water, planets, order, emotion, ego, plankton – hell, *life* for chrissakes, *life!* – are
all just normal everyday things deserving no special
attention, but the fact is that if you're awake to it, if
you stop taking it for granted and allow yourself to
fully appreciate this phantasmagorical dreamstate
reality for even just a minute or two a day, then the
whole thing explodes in you with such immensity that
you just want to sell the house, sell the car, sell the
kids, and dedicate your life to life itself and never fall
sleep again.

As Jodie Foster's scientist character says in *Contact* in her first experience of unbounded wonder: *"No... no words. No words to describe it. Poetry! They should've sent a poet. So beautiful. So beautiful... I had no idea."* Of course, explorers of consciousness experience similar episodes of clarity without the need for massive engineering projects and alien technology, but as a practical matter you can do it simply by lowering your defenses against it; by merging with your dreamstate experience rather than walling it off with a thousand petty distractions. The source of wonder is always everywhere, it's only our ability to perceive it that's missing.

Who cares what time it is? *Time!* Who cares what the weather is? *Weather!* Who cares who or how or what I am? *I am!* If I wrote ten books about how insanely mindblowing everything is, I couldn't come close to expressing it, and not just everything, *any*-thing, because anything and everything are really the same thing and failure to see that is what it means to be asleep. The universe is holographic in the sense that every part contains the whole. Whatever you behold can, if you let it, act as a gateway into the very heart of creation which lies at the very heart of you. The ocean in a dewdrop, eternity in an hour, the universe in a grain of sand, Brahman in Atman, Atman in you.

I, like anyone, spend most of my time caught up in the minutiae of daily life, but when I wander in the mountains or sit by a fire or walk on the beach, I leave all that behind and allow appreciation and gratitude

to well up and flow through me with such force that I
have to push back so it doesn't blow me apart. And yet,
as mindblowing as it is to trip out on the incompre-
hensible magnificence of mothwings and galaxies and
rusty hubcaps, it's even *more* mindblowing to understand the universe for what it *really* is, which is nothing. No-universe is true universe. Awareness is true
and truth exists. Appearance is untrue and untruth
does not exist. Beholder and beheld are one. Life is but
a dream and the most mindblowing thing of all is that
it's all in your mind.

·⋆·

We can't inquire into the nature of a thing without first proving the thing actually exists, which we
never can. A simple pebble can be so obvious that no
right-minded person would argue against its reality,
but consensus doesn't constitute proof and proceeding
as if it does means that everything we ever learn or
understand about that pebble is built on a foundation
of belief, not fact. Before we can unravel the mystery
of a pebble, we must determine with absolute certainty that there *is* a pebble, which we can't, so we
skip past that little detail and rush forward based on
belief instead of turning back to figure out why we
can't prove the stupid pebble is real.

Just as Descartes did, we must start with a clean
slate by determining what we know for sure. Can
we ever be sure that the pebble actually exists? No,

never, not possible, so what does that tell us about the nature of knowledge? Of reality? Of consciousness? Therein lies the real mystery of the pebble, but we just say yeah, sure, it's just a pebble, it obviously exists, no great mystery, we can't waste time on every little technicality when there's a whole universe to explore. That whole universe, however, was right there in that pebble we just dismissed. Had we learned the real lesson of the pebble we might have moved on to more fertile ground for exploration, but instead we built a world based on the belief that the pebble is real and knowledge is possible. Science is thus reduced to a mere belief system, and since everyone believes, no one cries foul. That's why philosophy can be king, while religion and science can never be more than a couple of jokers.

Carry that pebble in your pocket and whenever you hear philosophers, scientists, religious scholars, spiritual teachers or anyone else talking like they know something, take out the pebble to remind yourself that their authority is built on a foundation of belief and when you strip away their robes and diplomas and worshippers, they're just daffy little kids playing dress-up. The world wants to be deceived so okay, let it be deceived, but what about you? What do you want?

Standing on the shoulders of Descartes, we can make the true statement *sentio, ergo sum*, I am *aware*, therefore I *am*. I Am/Consciousness. Now, armed with a true statement, we are able to divide the universe

into two categories; known and believed. On the known side is awareness, and on the believed side is appearance. The pebble is not a fact, as we'd like to believe; it's just a belief, and that's a fact.

If philosophers were serious people, this would all be Philo 101 and there would be no need for Philo 102 because once you understand that you can't understand anything, you're free to leave the domain of egoic delusion and move on to more interesting realms of cocreative participation where you'll discover your passion, your purpose, your function; the one lock for which you are the one key.

✳

I can never be sure that I'm not alone in my own little dreamstate universe, but obviously, that's not what I believe. I believe I'm a real guy who writes real books for real readers in a real world. If events were to disabuse me of that notion, however, I wouldn't blink. It's a serviceable narrative but I'm not married to it. To take it from me would be like taking a novel out of my hands or turning on the lights when I'm watching a movie. It wouldn't be a big deal because my belief is only lightly suspended. I never forget that this character, this function, this world, are just elements of a gamespace that I can inhabit by relaxing into a comfortable indifference. If I woke up tomorrow inside the universe of Lara Croft or Wile E. Coyote, I would simply adapt and carry on, thinking myself no more a true native there than I think myself here. The

trick for me is not to see *through* the dreamstate, but to see it at all, and as for me, so for you; your disbelief is just a bit more unwillingly suspended than mine.

※

Awakening *from* the dreamstate, enlightenment, is not what anyone really wants and it's probably not on the table anyway, so let's dispense with that. Awakening *in* the dreamstate, adulthood, *is* what everyone really wants and *is* on the table, so let's keep our eye on that prize. Now the question is, do you really have a shot at it?, and the answer is probably not, but maybe. Transition to adulthood is supposed to be a natural process that occurs around the age of sexual maturity, so let's face it, the whole thing is already off the rails. It's much easier to keep a train on the tracks than to put it back on, but that's what we're stuck with. Where does an ersatz adult – a grown-up body with a little kid inside – find the emotional intensity necessary to raise the train out of the swamp and return it to service? As I ponder this question, all roads lead to the Little Bastard. If you want to initiate a change of this magnitude, you have to toss him the keys. He's already gnawing at the bars of his cage – why else would you be reading this? – so you're just awaiting some trigger event that sets him free to do his thing.

Joe provides an interesting glimpse of this process. His feeble workplace outburst expends all his emotional fuel and gets him nowhere, but it does, viewed

correctly, set events in motion by freeing his Little Bastard, just as Prospero in *The Tempest* frees Ariel. Joe, like Prospero, doesn't *become* a sorcerer, he *unleashes* one.

When the crazy rich dude knocked on his door, Joe didn't have any plan, people or purpose, he was just sitting around waiting to die. Hell, *I* could've talked him into jumping into a volcano without incentives, which raises an amusing question: Can I be your Little Bastard? The answer is no, the most I can do is help you rattle his cage and give you a stick to poke him with. You get him riled up and he'll do the rest.

❖

I remember reading about something called the Siberian Dilemma. When you're on a frozen lake or river in an ultra-cold environment and you fall through the ice into frigid waters, you face the dilemma of crawling out of the water and dying quickly like a man, or staying in the water and dying less quickly in a less manly manner. Obviously, the heroic choice is to get out and die fast, but is it? To me, the choice isn't between manly and unmanly but between outward and inward. It's your last act in life and might even be seen as kind of a blessing insofar as you have a little time left, so how do you choose to spend it? Are you going to let ego make your last decision by putting on a show for others? Be a dancing monkey all the way to the end? Waste your last golden moments as a puppet?

Or will you turn your back on your audience, forget about how others see you and use those last remaining minutes to say goodbye to your life and laugh at your fate and rejoice and say thank you? To grant your own absolution and claim your own salvation? To me, the heroic choice looks like fear and the coward's choice looks like liberation That's the real choice we're confronted with, outward or inward, and in that sense we all face the Siberian Dilemma in every moment.

⁕

In Joe's entire journey of awakening, of coming into focus, of rediscovering his courage, he only takes one step that really matters, which is the one from the lip of the volcano into the void; from the last vestige of personhood into the black hole of personal oblivion. The volcano is the black hole within, the gateless gate through which one passes between worlds, and that step into the unknown is the last step in one life and, one dares to hope, the first in another.

In a more realistic depiction of Joe's volcano, it would have been surrounded by a vast bazaar in which thousands of peddlers hawked countless tempting alternatives to the volcano, and in a more realistic depiction of Joe, he would have succumbed to those temptations because, really, who wouldn't prefer the party on the slope of the volcano to the raging inferno within? Who wouldn't prefer a warm-oil deep-tissue chakra-tuning massage to boiling lava? Joe would be

a rare fellow indeed to pass up the garden of spiritual delights and choose the inferno instead.

✳

Escape is a one-way ticket. The archetypal hero can't return to his tribe or flock or herd with an elixir of salvation to bestow, he can only point the way to freedom. True salvation is not a boon to be granted or a potion to be sipped, it's a journey to be undertaken, and no one who escapes from the herd can ever return any more than a chicken can return to the shell or a baby to the womb or the awoken to the dream.

The hero represents a herd-dream of salvation, but the real hero goes and keeps going and is therefore not a hero at all but an escapee. If the hero actually returned with an authentic elixir, his people would thank him by tying him to a stake and setting him on fire. Salvation is devoutly prayed for, but if a savior actually answered the call they'd be branded a heretic and promptly crucified. There's no getting around the death part of the rebirth equation, so any savior would appear to the unawakened as a purveyor of doom and be treated accordingly.

The good news is that you're on your own, no hero is coming to save you. No one who escapes rushes back to save former herdmates any more than you'd rush back to sleep to save people in a dream. Your only savior is yourself and your only hope of awakening is that inner sorcerer I call the Little Bastard. If you want

to find out why I call him that, pick up a pen and open a correspondence with him. Believe me, he's eager to hear from you. When you start this journey, when you start digging toward the light, something greater than yourself kicks in, and like a mother lifting a car off her child, nothing can stop it.

In the dreamstate theater, the heretic-savior is like a blinking exit sign over the backstage door; heresy in breaking the fourth wall of our fictional reality, salvation in offering deliverance from it. After you exit the theater through that door, the first thing you notice is that there is no theater from the outside, it only exists from the inside. That backstage door is a gate from one side and a memory of a dream from the other. Your Little Bastard is the real heretic-savior, an agent provocateur urging you to kick open the backstage door and plunge blindly through. It might seem like going outward, but outward from delusion is always inward toward lucidity. Comic book heroes like God, Allah, Jesus, Buddha, Mohammed and Guru lure us away from the inward journey, but there is no external salvation and the only hero you need has been inside you all along.

The gateless gate is the impassable barrier that distinguishes self from non-self, dream from awake. It has no actual existence, of course, which is why it only appears from the dream side. There is no lock to pick or incantation to speak; impassable means impassable. When you get to this point, you've gone as far as you

can go. You've taken your last step and now your toes are hanging over the edge of eternity. That's what the gateless gate really is; the outer boundary of selfhood and the impossibility of further dreamstate progress. You can't pass through this gate, you can only destroy the reality of which it's a part. Every step has been leading to this point. You can't go back and there's no more road ahead, so where do you go?

Further.

A Long Time on a Crooked Road

I saw the moon when we were out there in
the ocean, shining down on everything.

I've been miserable so long, years of my life
wasted, afraid.

Been a long time coming here to meet you –
a long time, on a crooked road.

Did I ever tell you? The first time I saw you?

Felt like I'd seen you before.

Joe, to Patricia

I MAGINE THAT YOU PLAY THE CELLO and that's all
you're really interested in. Not adulation and fanfare, not dropping a CD or climbing the charts, just being alone with your instrument and exploring your relationship to your music.

Now imagine that every time your doorbell rings, you have to set your cello down and strap yourself into a suit of medieval armor before opening the door, and then, while buying cookies or answering census questions (and making a mental note to replace the welcome mat with a rabid badger) you have to pretend that your ridiculous metal suit is not just a shell but the real you. That's how human interaction looks from the adult perspective; like a pointless intrusion that forces one to impersonate a human being when all they want to do is get back to their music.

Monks take a vow of silence so there's no call to animate their false character. They keep their hoods up and their heads down in an act of self-imposed isolation, otherwise, maintaining inward focus would be impossible and the monastery would turn into a frat house. A mountain hermit doesn't have to take a vow or wear a robe because he's in self-exile and is never called upon to animate a character. He's not reclusive because he hates people, he just hates playing one.

Adults are comfortable with only themselves for company, but the juvenile cannot function in isolation. Like a pyramid scheme that needs a constant infusion of fresh money to keep its fraudulent structure from collapse, the false self needs a constant infusion of external validation. This need to generate self-reinforcing feedback is particularly visible in the world of social media where participants stay safely isolated while projecting an avatar into digital space. The

movie *Surrogates* extrapolates on this theme by depicting a not-too-distant future in which people stay at home and plug into technology that allows them to live vicariously through highly-idealized robotic avatars that go out into the world to work and play. A fat, sweaty old man covered in seeping bedsores might appear in the world as a beautiful young woman. None of the robotic surrogates with whom he/she/it interacts are fooled by the facade, but they're projecting their own fantasies and the social compact states that if we want to be accepted, we must accept.

A world of surrogates might be secretly populated with NPCs, non-player characters, who look and act like player-backed characters but are computer-animated instead of human-animated; silicon-based instead of carbon-based. There are no NPCs in the movie *Surrogates*, but your world might be full of them; the point is, you never know who's real and who's not. NPCs act like they believe they're real, so what does real even mean? How would you confirm the validity of those you interact with, and how would they validate you? Even as I write this, computers can convincingly imitate people in text-based dialog, so your closest online chat buddies might not be real. How can you tell if they're real or not, and if you don't know, what does it really matter if your BFF is an algorithm or your dog is a robot or your spouse is a sexdoll? They're exactly as real as you believe they are, and since you're always wrong about what's real

anyway, why split hairs? Ultimately, no-player is true player, so *all* characters, yourself included, are really non-player characters in a master computer called perfect intelligence, and the impostor you should be concerned with isn't your friend or your dog or your spouse, it's you.

Why would anyone project a false persona instead of venturing out into the world and discovering their authentic self? Maybe they don't believe they have an authentic self, and maybe they're right. In the death-rebirth process, self dies and what is reborn is not another self. Adulthood is not about discovering your true self but leaving the self-construct behind and exploring the relationship between awareness and the interactive, cocreative dreamstate, which cannot be done from within a protective shell or through an avatar. There's no such thing as an adult self. You are not a real person and you never were. You are awareness. You don't awaken to a better self, you leave selfhood behind altogether. We live vicariously through characters, avatars, and surrogates because we don't know that we can integrate with our environment rather than staying in a cramped shell that was only ever meant to protect the young, not to be cultivated into a new species.

You are here because at some level, to some degree, you want to get off the couch and figure out what's real, even though it means the end of the avatar with which you identify. *Surrogates* ends with a mass awakening in

which all the robots simultaneously shut down, and all the pale, flabby, squinty-eyed couch potatoes peak out from their doors and step out into the sunlight, perhaps for the first time in years. That could be you, awakening from the shell of ego into a creative odyssey with the universe as your medium and your emotional intelligence as your unique genius.

✳

Your Little Bastard is not an angry little man trying to get you to blow up your world, it's your healthy but suppressed drive to develop into your fullborn state. If someone wrapped you in tight metal bands at the age of ten and you were still in them today, what would that look like? How would it feel? Those bands would be acting against your natural growth process which would still be struggling to do its job. That's what we see with Human Childhood, but we don't see the victims as hideously disfigured because it's everyone so it's normalized. Adults, however, see it just fine, and it's not a pretty sight.

What is the spiritual quest as we so often see it but a longing to get back to our first, best happy-place; the womb? The lure of heavenly bliss pulls us one way and the impulse to grow and explore pulls us the other way, so we hang suspended in a state of dynamic tension – yearning but unable to go back, drawn but scared to go forward – and that's where we find ourselves both as individuals and as a society, balanced between

regression and progression, devolution and evolution, the death-urge and the life-urge, and dramatically speaking, that's exactly where we should be. In the context of dramatic spectacle, it's perfect. My point is not that the dramatic dreamstate is evil or bad or wrong, but that stagnation isn't compulsory. There's a lot more to this life stuff than is generally supposed, and it's yours for the taking.

I never really lose sight of the fact that my character is just a vehicle and is no more *me* than the old truck I drive or the jeans I wear. I look at people caught in the juvenile state and I am confounded by how in-character they are, how they manage to stay submerged in their roles despite their natural buoyancy, how they can play such outlandish roles without the sheer absurdity of it snapping them into stark lucidity, but then I am reminded every night that dreams have their own reality, that our sleeping selves are completely undiscerning compared to our waking selves, and that a similar discernment gap divides juvenile from adult.

A braincloud might be understood as a mental-emotional occlusion preventing us from seeing what is and causing us to see what's not. Waking up is largely a matter of removing this occlusion, but it's all tangled up in your thoughts and feelings and in your sense of who and what and where you are, so there's no nice way of dealing with it. Your Siberian Dilemma is to live with it and die slow, or tear it out and die fast. Joe

and Patricia figure out that Joe doesn't really have a braincloud because there is no such thing, but they're wrong; there really is such a thing as a braincloud and Joe really did have one. He was mortally occluded at the beginning of the movie and crystal clear at the end. So now, let's take another look at the quote from Joe just before he jumped into the volcano, this time with the understanding that it's not really Patricia he's talking to:

I saw the moon when we were out there in
the ocean, shining down on everything.

I've been miserable so long,
years of my life wasted, afraid.

Been a long time coming here to meet you –
a long time, on a crooked road.

Did I ever tell you? The first time I saw you?

Felt like I'd seen you before.

DECEPTION: Act V
Asshole, Kansas

After Leo detonated his bomb vest, we find two fat slobs slumped on a couch surrounded by crushed beer cans and half-eaten pizzas. They remove their techy headsets and survey their bleak surroundings.

RONNIE

Aw, goddammit, Harley! Why'd you go and do that for?

HARLAN

Had to do it, bro. Gotta keep it real.

RONNIE

We're tryin' to *escape* reality, not get *back* to it!

HARLAN

You were *smokin'* as that actress lady, bro. I was gettin' some thoughts!

RONNIE

Damn, bro, that was sweet! We could have stayed on that level forever. We coulda hooked up and been like Hollywood royalty!

HARLAN

Strap it down, bro. What happens in Limbo, stays in Limbo.

RONNIE

Yeah, but they said it was *all* Limbo, like maybe this *here* is Limbo too!

HARLAN

Don't be a dumbass! How can *this* be Limbo if this is where we got the game?

RONNIE

Damn, I was getting used to that shit! Bein' all fancy and glamorous and whatnot. I think I was Edith Piaf for awhile. *Je ne regrette rien!*

HARLAN

Don't tell me everything, bro. I want to be the French broad next time.

A knock on the door. They pause in silence. Another knock.

RONNIE

yells

We ain't got no money for weed, Herbert.

BOB

Hey, guys! It's me, Bob. Remember? From the press junket? C'mon, open up, I have some good news.

RONNIE

That guy was in the game! How can he be here?

HARLAN

He said he was the game host.

RONNIE

Shit, dude, I told ya! We're into some weird shit here!

HARLAN

How do we get out?

RONNIE

I don't wanna get *out*, I wanna get back to the good parts where it don't smell like stale beer and piss all the time.

HARLAN

Yeah, that French lady smelled nice.

RONNIE

Dude, that was me!

More knocking.

BOB

It's okay, fellas, I'm just delivering your Easter egg. You're going to Westworld where you get to play people who find out they're actually robots who want to become real people. It's a hoot! You get to have a lot of sex and do a lot of killing.

RONNIE

Ooh, I like sex.

HARLAN

How do you know? You ain't never had none.

RONNIE

Well, I like killin'.

HARLAN

Yeah, me too.

RONNIE

Whadda ya say, bro? Stay or go?

HARLAN

Well, it's either piss and beer or sex and killin'.

They get to their feet. There is a louder, more insistent knocking at the door.

HARLAN

Yeah, yeah, okay Bob, we're comin'.

PICARD

yelling from outside the door

Commander Riker, is that you? Thank goodness! Is Counselor Troi with you? You've been drugged and trapped in the holodeck by an alien entity called The Scribe. We're trying to lock onto your signal. Stand by for transport!

RONNIE

Whoa, dude!

HARLAN

Shit, bro, didn't see that one comin'!

RONNIE

What a minute, which of us is which? I wanna be the lady again!

HARLAN

Bro, when you and me are you and me again, we gotta have a long talk. This game is whackin' you out.

RONNIE

takes Harlan by the shoulders

Non, je ne regrette rien! I regret nothing! Not the good things that have happened, nor the bad, it's all the same to me. I don't care about the past! I set fire to my memories. My troubles, my pleasures, I don't need them anymore! I'm starting over, because my life, my joy, today it begins with you!

HARLAN

Aw shit. Enterprise! This is... oh hell, I don't know anymore. Two to beam directly to sickbay!

THE END

Join us next time when the boys return home to find a featureless black monolith in their living room.

Away from the Things of Man

Listen to me. If you have a choice between
killing yourself and doing something you're
scared of doing, why not take the leap and
do the thing you're scared of doing?

Joe

D O YOU KNOW JOE? *Joe Versus the Volcano* is
dismissed by most viewers as a quirky little
romantic comedy, but if I could only recommend one
movie to illustrate the process of awakening, it would
be *Joe*. It's a parable about the transition of a regular
Joe from bondage to freedom, and for a herdbound
humanity, what could be more important than that?

Most viewers seem to think they understand this
simple little movie, including its quaint allegorical
message, but do they? Probably just enough to give it
two and a half stars and forget it, but I've had to invent
terminology to describe the life Joe is escaping and the
one he arrives at, so what is it that all those casually
dismissive viewers think they understand?

Do they understand that they themselves suffer from a braincloud that casts their world in shadow? That the zombie lights are sucking out their life? That they, like Joe, are too chickenshit afraid to live their life so they sold it for three hundred freakin' dollars a week? Sure, everyone understands the cute little story about Tom and Meg falling in love and sailing off into a new life, but no one understands that they themselves are Joe at the beginning of the movie because if they did, they would do anything and everything to become Joe at the end of the movie. It's as obvious as climbing out of a sewer into sunlight, so anyone who doesn't do it clearly doesn't understand where they are compared to where they could be.

Yeah boss, I'm talkin' to you.

We're using *Joe* as a shared map we can look at together as a way of understanding the terrain and where you are in it. I'm not asking you to learn Coptic and move to Cairo to study the Nag Hammadi codices, just that you watch a funny little movie that you're probably already familiar with. It's not perfect, two people wouldn't make the transition in tandem, for instance, so we wink at dramatic license, but what about the events that got Joe out of his apartment and on his way to his own rebirth? According to the movie, he was just sitting around waiting to die when the most unlikely guy in the world knocked on his door

and set events in motion. If we accept the superficial narrative, it means that Joe is just a rich man's flunky and not a participant in his own rebirth, so let's not accept that narrative. Instead, let's see if we can reveal a deeper narrative that restores Joe's missing volition.

We know two things about Joe; he once had courage, and he currently has a mild yearning for a better life. He's not an empowered seeker and he's not burning with hatred of his confinement. The scene where Joe quits his job is where he lights his rocket and burns all his fuel, but his emotional power is only enough to vent some pent-up frustration, scatter some artificial testicles, open an ominous valve to no effect and lose his job. He doesn't have the energy to go further so he ends up sitting in his apartment in his bathrobe waiting for death. Not the stuff of which heroes are made.

That's the surface narrative, but what if we look at Joe's workplace outburst not as a failed launch attempt, but as a successful act of conjuring? As his way of telling the universe, in a way the universe understands, what he really wants? That's a better interpretation because we are cocreative participants in our own journeys, not hapless passengers.

Joe's workplace outburst is the end of one thing and the beginning of another, but he has no idea of what's happening to him. He's so energized by his newfound insights that he's bursting to share them:

> "Who am I? That's the real question, isn't it? Who am I? Who are you? What other questions are

there? What other questions are there, really? You
wanna understand the universe, embrace the
universe, the door to the universe is you!"

That's the kind of gushing mania people exhibit
after first opening their eyes, but after that, for Joe,
nothing. That's as far as his own energy takes him.
His death-rebirth process has been initiated, but only
the dying part is visible. He's wiped out. He shot his
emotional wad and got himself out of the herd, and
now there's nothing to do but die a lonely death. The
good news, though, is that his workplace outburst
wasn't the end of his journey as it seems, but an act of
manifestation that sets his real journey in motion.

We can argue against this interpretation because
Samuel Graynamore's bubaru scheme predates Joe's
outburst, suggesting that Joe is just a puppet hanging from a rich man's strings, but that's a low-level
perspective. This transpersonal stuff is not subject to a
cause-and-effect, arrow-of-time level of understanding.
Miracles occur outside of time. It's our own limitations
that make us think that cause must precede effect and
that time exists independent of the dreamstate. Once
we understand our universe at the structural level, we
see that events obey pattern, pattern obeys mind, and
– beneath the costume and behind the character – you
are mind. Correctly understood, Samuel Graynamore
is a puppet hanging from Joe's strings.

As we know from Joe's south sea fixation, some
part of him yearns for a better life, but given his

circumstances and his state of emotional disrepair, what chance does he really have of rallying to such an all-consuming cause? None. He is reduced to nothing; even his future has been taken from him. He is broken and can't muster the resources or resolve to fix himself. Once your soul is owned by the company store you can never buy it back, so what can you possibly do?

Cry "Havoc!" – and let slip the dog of war.

Your Little Bastard is not just an agitator, fire-bomber and spiritual anarchist, he's a sorcerer. He can do things you can't, things you don't even know are possible. He has a Familiar in the form of a big play-ful puppy with crazy-ass powers, and between them, *anything* is possible. Therein lies the key to your total spiritual victory: You set your Little Bastard free and he'll set you free.

In Shakespeare's *The Tempest*, after being treacher-ously banished from his privileged life, Prospero arrives on an island and, using knowledge gained from his books, frees the imprisoned spirit Ariel who, in return, serves Prospero and summons the tempest. Who is Ariel but Prospero's Little Bastard? What then is this book you're reading but one of Prospero's books showing you how to release your own Ariel? And what then am I but an agent of your Little Bastard, your own Samuel Graynamore slamming a can of none too subtle nuts on the table, speaking not really to you, but to that spark of courage inside you?

Just as your one true healer lies within, so does your one true guru. In both physical wellness and spiritual development, the key is to stop looking outward and turn inward. Everything you're looking outside for has been inside all along. It doesn't matter what you call it – God, perfect intelligence, the universe, Brahman – only that you peel ego's hand off the tiller and allow that higher whatever to right the ship and set a new course for a new world, away from the things of man.

There's not really a crazy spiritual anarchist living in your chest, just the power and intelligence of the universe working in you like it works in everything, and it's only because you've dammed it up for so long that it makes such a big splash when released. Metaphors, allegories and romcoms aside, this is how things really work. You really do have powers beyond imagination, but they're not yours to command, only release. Your Little Bastard is really just an obstructed process seeking its natural expression. The same emotional energy that derailed you in the first place keeps this natural process contained, like the earth's crust over churning magma, but sometimes it violently erupts, destroying your halfborn life and clearing the way to your real one.

It wasn't Joe's exotic lamp and well-worn copy of *Robinson Crusoe* that triggered events, those were just elements of prison decor revealing his inner desire, but desire is a weak and ineffectual motivating force. It's not until he's emboldened by a newfound death-awareness

that Joe exhibits the kind of focused emotional energy that can actually create change. You communicate an authentic desire in a way the universe understands, through action and intent, and suddenly *bam!*, the storm is right on top of you. That's what you're playing at when your own spiritual wanderlust carries you toward your own volcano, which is happening now. Right now you're not in the spiritual carnival, you're in the back alley warming yourself beside a dumpsterfire of the vanities with a guy who's pointing you toward your own dark interior where you're not going to raise your consciousness or open your heart, but get your life smashed to pieces by a personal cataclysm which you'll reckon a tragedy when it happens and the greatest blessing of your life looking back. If you're not up for that, you'll head back toward the pretty lights. If you *are* up for that, welcome to the right book.

As Mark Twain said, the two most important days of your life are the day you're born and the day you find out why. Would Joe, as we see him at the beginning of the movie, have asked for a brain cloud? Would he have asked to be lied to by a doctor and sent to doom by a crazy old rich dude? Would he have asked to be battered by a typhoon and left to go mad from dehydration? Would he have asked to step into an active volcano? None of the above, but looking back he wouldn't have changed a thing because these were the events that delivered him from slavery to freedom. That's the stuff we hide from; all that scary, painful,

non-blissy, death-rebirth stuff. That's why we escape into the Thorazine mist of emotion-based spirituality and live vicariously through our own fictional characters.

And what's Joe's purpose in making the journey to the volcano? What's his intent? He's not going in search of love and rebirth and a new life, he's just going to his death. There's no big payday in his future, no glorious reward, no grandkids bouncing on knees, just a little reclaimed courage and a nasty but honest death. He is in a no-hope situation. Even after his starry-night revelation and marriage to Patricia, he's still going to jump into the volcano because his response to the Siberian Dilemma is not to climb out of the frigid waters or stay in, but the *tertium quid*, the third option, which is to push yourself under and let the current take you.

As Patricia tells Joe before they jump:

Nobody knows anything.

We'll take this leap, and we'll see.

We'll jump, and we'll see.

That's life.

＊

Becoming sane is an insane business. The only way to get out of the herd is to go out of your mind. To the best of my knowledge, thinking and experience,

Spiritual Autolysis is your best hope of setting your own events in motion. Real thinking is a deathmatch and must be externalized. The pen is your sword, the paper is your arena, and you are your own mortal enemy. That's how you can confront your own truth – meaninglessness, impermanence, no-self – and that's how you can unleash your own Little Bastard who can summon your own tempest and take you to your own volcano.

Ego encourages you to be more calm and compassionate, but your Little Bastard is telling you, as Mencken said, to spit on your hands, hoist the black flag and start slitting throats. I'm not inciting you to death and destruction, that's your Little Bastard's job, so if you want to find your real life, find him. Pick up a pen and write to him. Dig your own grave, you'll find him at the bottom. Hear him in the alumni gallery of long-dead youth whispering *carpe diem*. Make a sand mandala and sweep it away to reveal his face. Walk off into the desert, he'll find you there. As always though, be careful what you wish for; the bottle of a wish-granting genie and the plague-filled box of Pandora are one and the same.

*

Joe Versus the Volcano is not about mindless escapism but mindful escape. Not only is it the one movie I'd recommend above all others, I'd recommend it above all the great spiritual and religious teachings which serve only to keep us herdbound and domesticated. For

anyone trapped in the Segregated State, there are not many paths to awakening, there is only one. Forget all the spiritual hype and gimmickry, ultimately there's only you alone on a shoreless sea, looking up into the infinite night, overwhelmed by an inexpressible gratitude:

Dear God,

whose name I do not know,

thank you for my life.

I forgot how big...

Thank you.

Thank you for my life.

That's the first wave of Agapé. That's what comes in when fear goes out, when emotional blockage is released and energetic flow is restored. Sure, when you're trapped in a dungeon, peace and love are grand, but grander by far is getting the fuck out.

Namaste, boss. I bow to the Joe within you.

Wisefool Press

Wisefool Press publishes *Starship Gita: Song of the Borg*, and *Deception: Your Mind is the Scene of the Crime* by Ned McFeely, as well as some books by Jed McKenna.

WWW.WISEFOOLPRESS.COM